Teacher Educatio

Teacher Education Policy:
Some Issues Arising from Research and Practice

Edited by

Rob McBride

RoutledgeFalmer
Taylor & Francis Group

LONDON AND NEW YORK

First published in 1996
By Falmer Press.
Reprinted 2004
By Routledge Falmer,
11 New Fetter Lane, London EC4P 4EE

Transferred to Digital Printing 2004

A catalogue record for this book is available from the British Library

Library of Congress Cataloging-in-Publication Data are available on request

ISBN 0 7507 0487 X cased
ISBN 0 7507 0488 8 paper

Jacket design by Caroline Archer

Typeset in 9.5/11 pt Bembo by
Graphicraft Typesetters Ltd., Hong Kong.

Printed and bound by Antony Rowe Ltd, Eastbourne

Contents

Contents

1 Introduction: The Issues Facing Teacher Education Policy

Rob McBride

For the Annual Conference of the British Education Research Association (BERA) in September 1993 I called for papers on the broad topic of teacher education policy. At that time I was coordinator of a group dealing with this subject. I was overwhelmed by academics wishing to give papers and we ended up with two symposia and in excess of twenty presentations. Most of the papers contained in this volume emerged from these symposia.

The major debating points are covered by the papers contained here but other pertinent questions are raised. In particular, while the main contents refer to the system of education in England and Wales[1], there are two papers which relate to different contexts. Chapter 4 reports on the Scottish system which, while not far away, is still sufficiently different to give a contrast. Chapter 10 is written by Hans Vonk from the Netherlands who has considerable experience of researching the mentoring of beginning teachers (i.e., Newly Qualified Teachers or NQTs) in that country, as well as in several others.

All of the papers emanate from research or research-based practice. Research and researched development could, and should influence educational practice to a far greater degree than they do at present. The chapters in this volume do not just reflect the whims of a few detached people. Researchers, and in this case mostly experienced researchers, have gathered data, processed data, analysed the data, tested their conclusions in other contexts, listened to other researchers, given talks and noted responses and reflected on the relevant literature. That is not to say that anything written here is beyond criticism but research-based evidence should not be rejected casually. Those politicians who seemingly change policy and attempt to influence practice at the drop of a hat really ought to pay more attention to research.

The book is divided into four sections. If teacher education should be a nearly seamless whole from cradle to grave the division of the various chapters of the book into sections is somewhat contrived. Yet writers have tended to focus on a single phase of teacher education and I have grouped the chapters accordingly. Part 1 is broadly concerned with initial or pre-service teacher education; Part 2 deals with the induction of NQTs, covering roughly the first five years of teaching; Part 3 covers in-service education which spans the rest of a teacher's career. The last section includes two chapters which consider central principles and the final chapter is a summary which is built upon the arguments from all of the other chapters.

The central aim of this introductory chapter is to articulate questions and issues which the subsequent chapters have addressed. Some chapters will argue in favour of a particular view and even suggest solutions to problems raised. Others will tend to make the questions they outline more complex and not suggest any changes in policy. I take it as my responsibility as editor to bring together all of the arguments presented and to broadly rough out what a teacher education policy could look like. This is my task for Chapter 20 which will map out the issues contained in the whole book.

In Chapter 2 Chris Husbands provides a history of recent changes in Initial Teacher Education (ITE) policy and goes on to describe the resultant action in one school of education in this context. Policy has dictated, largely through its control of funding for ITE, that schools now play a greater part in the design and delivery of ITE while Higher Education (HE) has a reduced role. We might ask whether the new system is producing better teachers and how the partnership between schools and HE, as demanded by the policy, is working.

Control of funding has been a powerful weapon for the current government in ensuring that policy influences practice. Yet that power will always be limited by the 'slippage' that separates policy and practice. Chapter 3 reports a survey carried out by the MOTE (Modes of Teacher Education) project of teacher training institutions engaged in ITE and concentrates particularly on an area not completely governed by funding, the notion of partnership between schools and HE. This chapter looks at the power relations between HE and schools and asks whether the partnership notion, as defined by the policy, is suited to students or not.

While Chapter 3 gives a broad view of the implementation of the English and Welsh system, Chapter 4, by describing the Scots system, enables us to ask whether the innovations described in the previous chapters are desirable at all. Sally Brown asks whether the Scots, who continue to deliver ITE through an HE-led system, are clinging to an outdated approach or resisting, with a higher moral purpose, the market-led turmoil she sees south of the border. Should the English system have been changed quickly and radically, or should it have evolved from the kinds of partnership which already exist?

Anne Edwards and Jill Collison, in Chapter 5, consider two cases of partnership between HE and schools. In Chapter 2 Husbands was fairly positive about the partnerships he was engaged in but Edwards and Collison do not see major changes or 'metanoia' in the support for the learning of pre-service teachers, as distinct from the changes in organization and management. Are the changes merely organizational? Are we producing better prepared teachers?

But are partnerships between institutions, such as schools and HE, sufficient to bring about better provision? Should we rather work on the partnerships between people who work in them? Chapter 6, the next contribution, from Colin Biott and John Spindler, considers partnerships between established practitioners and pre-service teachers during school placements. Neville Bennett takes looks further into these partnerships in Chapter 7 by focusing on the development of pedagogical reasoning. We can go on to ask if there is enough time during the PGCE (Post Graduate Certificate in Education) year to provide pre-service teachers with the expertise they need to become teachers? Is it enough to consider ITE separately from induction and in-service training? Should we have a longer-term view?

David Clemson ends Part 1 by pursuing a more fundamental issue. Recalling Stenhouse's dictum that good teacher induction issues creatively different individual teachers, Clemson questions whether the broader context of education is dominated by the ideology of a minority group. Are there as many forms of ITE as there are learners? Are radical changes needed? Similar questions will be asked by John Schostak in Chapter 19.

Until 1992 teachers were required to complete a probationary year. Susan Sidgwick opens Part 2 by considering how teachers are inducted without the protection of that measure. Schools now have delegated budgets and the needs of NQTs can be seen as a cost to the school. Are schools ensuring that NQTs have lighter teaching loads? Are they paying for adequate mentoring? If ITE is too short to prepare teachers completely should induction be more, rather than less, important? Who is taking overall responsibility for induction and who should? Will the 'market' take care of induction?

Chapter 10 is written by Hans Vonk of The Free University of Amsterdam. I first met Hans Vonk at the National University of Lesotho where he was conducting a programme in the mentoring of NQTs. He has plainly been researching this area for many years and his chapter provides a broad coverage of the whole field at a time when the notion of mentoring both pre-service teachers and NQTs are major talking points in the English system. Vonk's work prompts many questions such as: Are NQTs developing or merely surviving? Are mentors properly educated? Should the mentor also assess the NQT? These, and others he outlines, are pertinent to the English context.

Still on the topic of induction, Les Tickle asks how can we assist NQTs to become reflective practitioners whose practical judgment has been developed? His research demonstrates that there is a tendency for NQTs to value survival in the classroom rather than reflection. Is the current trend towards policies which value observable technical skills restricting reflective activity to mere technical matters (such as ensuring that equipment is available).

Part 3 opens with a chapter by Eileen Francis which describes her own involvement in Inset since 1981. Her experiences give something of the flavour of the changes that have occurred over that period. In particular she raises a theme which runs through almost this entire section, namely, the centrality of *personal* learning in professional development. Yet Francis observes the difference in approach to Inset between these professional developers, who concentrate on the thought processes of practitioners, and the managers of Inset systems who work with structures. If there are these two groups, and if the latter control funding will they pay for personal learning (as opposed to say, Inset support for delivery of the national curriculum)?

In Chapter 13 Jack Whitehead contrasts raising educational standards through creating a market for schools, to Inset. HE has in mind Inset which raises with teachers educational questions of the form 'How do I improve my practice?' Jack also suggests that institutions of HE are essential to Inset provision. Christine O'Hanlon, in Chapter 14, usefully defines a number of terms in her chapter on action research and professional development. The idea of the involvement of HE in professional development is discussed here. Other issues examined are whether Inset should be lifelong and how personal change relates to institutional change.

Chapter 15, by Chris Day, pursues the same ideas as Jack Whitehead and Christine O'Hanlon with respect to role of HE in Inset; the importance of personal to professional development; and the length of time needed for good teacher education. Yet Chris Day reports on a particular developmental project, giving a considerable number of examples of the materials he has used. He reports too, on the evaluation of the project by teachers. A different project is the topic of Chapter 16 by David Frost. The principles he works by are broadly the same as those used in the previous chapters on Inset but he explores the Inset relationship between HE and schools differently. Like Day, Frost describes a developmental project he is engaged in.

The final chapter in this section discusses my own role as a provider of Inset. If HE is to be a major player in the provision of Inset and if the market remains the means of connecting 'purchasers' and 'providers', how does the practice of Inset appear to staff in HE? Can HE institutions provide good quality educational support, especially Inset, when they are at the 'end of the line', dependent upon the vagaries of school budgets and national policies?

Part 4 contains two chapters which consider broader notions of teacher education as well as my summary of the other chapters. In Chapter 18 David Bridges looks at the weaknesses of school-based teacher education of all types. Is it sufficient to say that it 'works'? Approaches which can be described as pragmatic may not ask the best questions and may not be sufficiently self-critical to find the best solutions. The antidote to pragmatism is critical debate with people from different standpoints which makes problematic what is taken for granted. We might ask where, and with whom, this debate might take place?

John Schostak, in the penultimate chapter, raises the issue of a radical reappraisal of education policy and practice. What are educational ideas and how could they lead to a teacher-education policy? Should we start again with a completely new conception? We might ask whether any government would be prepared to start again with a clean policy sheet. While David Bridges has focused on the need to look outside the body of practitioners, John Schostak contrasts that with the need to look within the practice of teachers. I am sure that both would agree that there is a need for parity of relationship between those who do the work and those who can enrich it through criticism. The reader may ask where the balances are to be struck and how policy might contribute to a way forward.

Note

1 I will occasionally use the term the 'English' system when I mean 'English and Welsh'. This is in the interest of brevity and no disrespect is meant to Welsh readers.

Part 1

Initial Teacher Education

2 Change Management in Initial Teacher Education: National Contexts, Local Circumstance and the Dynamics of Change

Chris Husbands

Solutions must come through the development of *shared meaning*. The interface between individual and collective meaning and action in everyday life is where change stands or falls. (Fullan, 1991, p. 5)

Introduction

Whereas we have a vast literature on the philosophical and pedagogical underpinning of initial teacher education, and on the respective contributions of schools and higher education to the professional learning of new teachers (e.g., Furlong *et al.*, 1988, Booth, Furlong and Wilkin, 1990), we have relatively few accounts of the management of change in initial teacher education. This is a curious lacuna, not least since the last decade has engendered a considerable literature on the management of change and the process of change in the schools to which the 'products' of teacher education proceed. Wilkin observes that 'it is a relatively simple matter to devise and justify theoretical schemes. Putting them into operation is altogether different' (Wilkin, 1991, p. 8); similarly, Fullan argues that 'educational change is technically simple and socially complex' (1991, p. 47). This paper is a contribution to understanding the nature and process of change in teacher education. Its central theme is the development of a school-based model of teacher education in the context of the one-year Secondary Post Graduate Certificate of Education (PGCE) at the University of East Anglia between 1991 and 1994. In describing the background to, assumptions of, and development of, the change process, I draw upon themes relating to the theory of change, notably meanings of change and the attitudes of participants to the nature of change as well as on historical and contextual factors related to the School of Education at UEA and its relationships with East Anglian schools. It is based largely on an analysis of the change process in a single institution, set in and then related to wider policy and theoretical concerns in teacher education. The change process at the centre of the paper was, and remains, complex for a number of interrelated reasons. The first is the location of change at the intersection of political initiatives, educational research perspectives and a period of multiple, discontinuous change all of which called for a range of reactions and assumptions. The second is to do with the multiplicity of actors, personal and institutional perspectives involved in a teacher-education programme involving a complex University School of Education and something in excess of forty secondary comprehensive schools in a large rural area where lines of 'management communication' were of necessity frequently weak. As we shall see, there were different understandings of the central concepts of 'school-based' teacher education and different levels of commitment to, and responsibility for, the process of change. The third complexity derives from the interrelation in the process of change of different financial and educational assumptions in schools, the university and local authorities.

At the centre of the narrative explored in this paper is a political initiative to reshape initial teacher education: the initiative launched by the Conservative Secretary of State for Education, Kenneth Clarke in 1992 (Clarke, 1992, and developed in DFE, 1992). Clarke's agenda was dominated by the proposal to transfer substantial elements of responsibility for initial teacher education from higher education to schools. As we shall see, however, the local dynamics of change in initial teacher education were only *partially* framed by the political and ideological agenda: change management was about far more than the implementation of externally imposed change. There were, we shall see, a number of reasons for this. In the first place, the conceptual roots of school-based training were diverse. Whilst there was a neo-Conservative/New Right agenda for school-based training based on a rhetoric of the superiority of 'practice' to 'theory', there were also alternative roots of the concept and, critically, roots which connected powerfully to the intellectual antecedents of the university and to schools' own views of the nature of professionalism. In addition, several key features of the government's policy initiative — the emphasis of outcome performance indicators, the concept of the 'training school' — were explicitly rejected by those most closely involved in local change management. The rhetoric of school-based training and 'partnership' was developed in ways which reflected internally generated understandings of the purposes and nature of teacher education which those most closely involved in local developments wished to achieve. This account is not, then, one of the implementation of externally imposed policy but of the transformation of policy as it was given different meanings by participants in change management.

The account of change management which is explored here owes a great deal to the work of Michael Fullan (1982, 1991, 1993, 1994). Fullan's arguments about the 'number and dynamics of factors that interact and affect the process of educational change' (1991) were developed in the context of school reform in Canada and North America, but many of the concepts he deploys in his analysis of the 'meanings' of educational change illuminate the process of change in rural East Anglia. Fullan identifies four phases in the change process, described as initiation or adoption, implementation, continuation and outcomes. 'It is during the adoption phase that the direction or content of change is set in motion. Decisions are made about what is to change, at least in terms of goals and sometimes substance. The process of adoption can generate meaning or confusion, commitment or alienation or simply ignorance on the part of participants and others to be affected by the change' (1982, p. 53). Reactions to the process of change at the stage characterized by Fullan as the 'implementation' stage are conditioned not only by participants understandings of the adoption process but also, their own understandings of their role in relation to given change agendas. Hence, a key element in the implementation process is 'the selectivity that occurs as a result of differential access to information' (Fullan, 1991, p. 53); Fullan goes on to explore the critical importance of careful attention to the transition from the 'adoption' to the 'dissemination' phase of change. He observes that 'the more planners are committed to a particular change, the less effective they will be in getting others to implement it if their commitment represents an unyielding and impatient stance in the face of ineluctable problems' (Fullan, 1982, p. 85).

In what follows, I want to explore the nature of the change process in initial teacher education at UEA and its partner schools, largely through the perspective of Fullan's model of change and innovation in education, examining the different, and in some cases contradictory influences on the initiation, adoption and dissemination processes in East Anglia. At each stage, I shall argue that the process and nature of change was susceptible of multiple meanings based on the perceptions of different actors and participants, and that critical to both the understanding of change and the successful dissemination of innovation is the understanding of these multiple agendas.

Initiation: Contexts of Change: National, Political, Conceptual

In January 1992, the Secretary of State for Education, Kenneth Clarke, addressed the North of England Education Conference. Clarke's theme was the education of teachers, based on 'concern about whether new teachers are being adequately trained in the right way for success in the classroom' (Clarke, 1992, para. 15, compare HMI, 1988). Clarke's central proposition was that 'the whole process of teacher training [sic.] needs to be based on a more equal partnership between school teachers and tutors in institutions, with the schools playing a much bigger part'. As we shall see, such a proposition drew on two quite separate sources, one which we shall characterize as 'professional' relating to changes developed *within* teacher education over the previous decade, and one 'ideological' deriving from the activities of, particularly, though not exclusively, New Right pressure groups in the period 1988–91. Clarke developed the proposition into four policy changes, in the first place confined to the preparation of secondary-school teachers. The first was that secondary teacher training should be based on a 'partnership in which the school and its teachers are in the lead in the *whole of the training process from the initial design of a course through to the assessment of the performance of the individual student*'. (Clarke, 1992, para. 22). Secondly, teacher education should be predominantly based in 'those schools in this country which command the greatest confidence in academic and other aspects of measured performance ... such as academic results, staying on rates, truancy rates and the destinations of pupils beyond school' (ibid., para. 32). Thirdly, Clarke proposed extending the amount of time spent by trainee teachers from the then minimum of 50 per cent of their training to four-fifths of the course (ibid., para. 33). Finally, Clarke proposed a change in the assessment framework for new teachers, based on a competency framework which set out the 'specific knowledge, understanding and skills needed by the newly qualified teacher' (ibid. para. 36). In concluding, Clarke acknowledged that such an agenda for teacher education meant that 'for many institutions and for schools significant changes will be involved', not least since 'as more of the responsibility for teacher training moves from the colleges to the schools more of the cost of that training will move with it'. (ibid., para. 39).

We have, then, a political initiative intended to reshape initial teacher education. One commentator described what was proposed as 'the political rape of teacher education'; another argued that there were 'values threatened by the proposal to locate 80 per cent of teacher training in schools . . . what is at stake is not the survival of "irrelevant" or even "ideologically unsound" theory but . . . the spaces which enable student teachers to systematically reflect about the difficult and complex task of educating children (Elliott, *TES*, 7/2/92, p. 18). However, at the level of detail, Clarke's initiative had, as we have suggested, a number of sources. One of these was clearly political. Throughout the 1980s, the Conservative government had pursued a change agenda in teacher education characterized by the deployment and development of a concept of 'relevance' which might be most appropriately delivered by shifting responsibility for teacher education more closely to the classroom. In Circular 3/84, the DES proposed that '[Higher Education] Institutions in co-operation with local education authorities and their advisers should establish links with a number and variety of schools and courses . . . should be developed and run in close working partnership with schools . . . Experienced teachers . . . should be involved in the training of students within the institution' (DES, 1984, para. 3). In 1989, the then Secretary of State for Education paid tribute to already established school-based courses, welcoming 'the increased emphasis on work in schools — not just teaching practice but more formal study too, so that teachers in the schools are more involved in the whole training process' (Baker, 1989, para. 37), and the revisions to Circular 3/84 proposed in DES Circular 24/89 went further not only to suggest that teachers should be involved 'in the planning of initial training courses and their evaluation', but also required institutions to have 'a written policy statement which sets out the roles of tutors, head teachers, other teachers, employers and students in relation to students' school experience' (DES, 1989a). Paralleling such developments was the introduction in 1988 and 1989 of the 'licensed' (DES, 1988) and 'articled' (DES, 1989b) teacher schemes. Such schemes were partly a pragmatic solution to perceived problems of teacher supply and retention, but were premised on the assumption of workplace-based rather than higher education-based training: trainees would learn on the job where they would 'undertake such training as the employer deemed appropriate' (DES, 1988, para. 14). In short, then, the policy initiative towards enhancing the responsibility for schoolteachers in teacher education developed in 1992 was simply an extension of policy initiatives deployed throughout the 1980s; indeed, the figure of four-fifths of trainees time spent in the classroom was derived from the articled teacher scheme.

At the same time, ideological pressure, particularly from the New Right pushed policy development towards workplace-based training for new teachers. Such formulations would expel higher education institutions from the process of teacher education entirely, and meant that much of the debate about school-based training was confused by ideological concerns (Furlong, 1992). New Right authors were critical partly of the practice of teacher education as they described it: 'the fact is that the teacher training system to a great extent embodies the ideas and methods which have made British maintained education the laughing stock of Europe' (Letwin, *Daily Mail*, 23.7.91), and '[new] teachers are not encouraged to develop the style of teaching which time and experience prove best for them' (Lawlor, 1990). In spite of government changes of the 1980s, New Right commentators, admittedly often on the flimsiest of evidence — largely the admissions prospectuses of a handful of university departments of education — argued that teacher education remained overly theoretical. This was not simply a result of the supposed failings of teacher educators, although Lawlor and O'Hear (O'Hear, 1988) in particular were highly critical of many of them, but, in some formulations, a structural failing of higher education-based teacher education: the solution was to abandon notions of 'partnership' (though such partnerships were never analysed) and 'graduates would be sent to the schools to train on the job . . . existing education departments should be disbanded' (Lawlor, 1990, p. 38). It is not clear at the level of detail how far the New Right commentators can be credited with influencing the Clarke speech. Clarke's speech clearly envisaged some coordination role at least for higher education institutions and repeatedly spoke in terms of a 'partnership', albeit one in which schools were clearly the 'lead partner'. For the New Right, such partnerships were both undesirable and unnecessary: Lawlor, for example, insisted that teaching was *sui generis* a 'practical activity' and that schools alone were able to train new teachers (1990, p. 8)

Concepts of school-based training were not confined to Conservative politicians and new Right commentators. As early as 1982 the DES established a research project examining four school-based PGCE courses.

> The motivations behind the political intervention to establish closer partnership between training institutions and schools were clearly very different from those of the profession itself. Indeed it is not totally unreasonable to suggest that government's interest in school-based training may have been in part an attempt to weaken the hold over training by the teacher training profession. Yet. . . . To conclude that the current interest in closer partnership with schools as purely or even primarily the result of directives from the centre would be naive. (Furlong *et al.*, 1988, p. 13)

The development of a far from unproblematic concept of partnership was certainly a characteristic of academic discourse on teacher education throughout the 1970s, and in this sense the 'initiation' phase of school-based teacher education extended some fifteen or twenty years before Conservative policy development. The root of the difficulty to which 'partnership' was a response, for McIntyre, was 'that student teachers frequently find the "educational theorising" they encounter in their courses irrelevant to the practical tasks which confront them in schools . . . that student teachers generally do not learn much, although there is a great deal to be learned, from their observation of the practice of experienced teachers' (McIntyre, 1988, p. 105). As early as 1972, the James Report had suggested that 'schools, and teachers in them . . . asked to undertake new roles in teacher training. . . . Teachers in school . . . be more closely involved in planning and supervising practical work . . . be associated with the selection of students' (DES, 1972, para. 3.47). A decade later, based on its 'first hand knowledge of events and developments in the training institutions' (Wilkin, 1991, p. 17), HMI proposed that 'partnership between schools and initial training institutions should be strengthened at all levels and in all aspects of the student's training' (HMI, 1983, p. 17). Indeed, the rhetoric of 'partnership' between training institutions and schools has been traced by Margaret Wilkin (1991) throughout the 1960s, 1970s and 1980s, both in terms of position papers arguing that 'it is clearly the case that it is in schools that the vast majority of [training in practical skills] must be done, and that primarily under the day to day supervision of school staff' (UCET, 1979, pp. 9–10, quoted in Wilkin, 1991, p. 11) and in terms of individual programme development at universities such as Oxford and Sussex.

It is more difficult to be clear at a national level about the extent to which 'partnership' models of training were clearly embedded in institutional practice. In 1982, the SPITE project reported of PGCE programmes that 'tutors were clearly unwilling to give up their teaching practice responsibilities. . . . [and] disagreed strongly that school staff should take the main responsibility for supervision' (Patrick, Bernbaum and Reid, 1982, p. 197). At Oxford, in 1985, the 'internship' model could still speak of '*new* roles for professionals in the University as much as in schools *new* relationships between the two' (quoted in Pendry, 1990, p. 42, my emphasis). Part of the difficulty was a lack of clarity, again at the level of detail about what 'partnership' or 'school-based' teacher education actually involved. The lack of clarity is apparent in the Cambridge research programme (Furlong *et al.*, 1988). It is clear that in some versions the term was simply deployed to describe initial teacher-education programmes which were *substantially* based in schools — i.e., for more than 50 per cent of their time. In other versions the term and the concept were deployed qualitatively to describe ways in which student experience in schools might be enhanced (Goodfellow, 1992), since as Hirst observed, 'without greater clarity on [the theory–practice relationship] the practice of training is likely to remain as "informal" a practice as much current teaching in schools' (Hirst, 1991, p. 86). Yet a third characterization of the nature of 'school-based training' was one in which 'substantial tasks' in relation to training were delegated to teachers — most commonly the assessment of students' practical competence, and less often shared responsibility for the design of programmes. Closely related to this, but given the exigencies of time, far less common was an understanding that school-based teacher education might allow for a careful definition of the 'different but complementary' roles of tutors and teachers in the task of training (McIntyre, 1990), and it was this direction, it seems that Circular 24/89 was attempting to 'push' teacher education. In short, though, if practice in initial training, with some exceptions, remained resistant to change it was because the opportunity simply did not exist for a thorough-going exploration with all the stakeholders in initial teacher education of the meaning of central concepts in school-based teacher education.

A second relevant feature of developments in ITT in the 1980s was a reconceptualization of the place of theory in initial teacher education. 'Theory', comments Wilkin, was widely perceived as 'a disaster area . . . The failure of theory to provide the answers to the problems of the classroom had forced a reconsideration of its value within the curriculum' (Wilkin, 1991, p. 6). In place of a theory-grounded initial training curriculum defined in terms of the 'disciplines of education' emerged a 'radical' conception of the place of theory.

> Theory was no longer only a body of research-based knowledge to which reference could be made in times of trouble. It was, alternatively and additionally, articulated 'craft knowledge' [which] emphasises theory-as-process. . . . it is the practitioner who is expert since he or she is the owner of a personal theory. (ibid.)

Such a 'radical' model underpins McIntyre's analysis of the conceptual underpinnings of the Oxford internship in the mid-1980s. Central to internship was the notion that 'our long-term influence upon them [i.e., student teachers] can be greatest not so much by trying to persuade them of the merits of various practices but rather by helping them to make their judgements rationally and realistically' (McIntyre, 1988, p. 107). The capacity for 'rational and realistic judgement' was to be developed 'by trying to ensure that each of them has a secure personal relationship with a mentor'. McIntyre explores the nature of the mentor–student relationship in interesting language: the mentor-based curriculum is not for him fundamentally about classroom competence *per se* or about the professional craft knowledge of the teacher, but 'the explicit generation and testing of hypotheses, most typically hypotheses about what can be achieved by acting in given kinds of ways in given types of situation' (McIntyre, 1988, p. 108). Such a process of hypothesis generation has been a characteristic of action-research-based in-service projects with teachers (e.g., Elliott, 1976); its application in and to initial training has been far more narrowly constrained (e.g., Tickle, 1987).

In summary then, the end of the 1980s saw the development of parallel concepts and agendas for change in teacher education, emerging from both an overtly ideological Conservative government and its New Right think tanks, and from teacher educators. For example, McIntyre was able to argue that the government's initiatives in teacher education were largely 'correct' (McIntyre, 1994). At critical points, these agendas overlapped, particularly at the level of diagnosis. There appears to be some common understanding that initial teacher education needed not only to be more intensively school-based but also that the tasks of teacher education needed to be 'shared', certainly by formalizing definitions of responsibility for student experience in school and, in some formulations for collaborative planning not only of student experiences in schools but also of student experiences in higher education. Equally, there was a shifting understanding of the place of 'theory' in initial teacher education, and a clear move from what Wilkin calls 'theory as product' to 'theory as process' (Wilkin, 1991, p. 12).

However, such evidence as exists suggests that with the exceptions of Oxford and Sussex, innovation in school-based teacher education was more circumscribed, and for two reasons. In the first place, the concepts of 'school-based teacher education' were susceptible of multiple meanings. Secondly, responsibility for teacher education and for thinking about teacher education was still largely confined to higher education, and few opportunities were created through funding for a thorough going redefinition of roles in teacher education.

Adoption: The Process of Change in Local Contexts

All of the above suggests that the concepts of school-based teacher education were by no means new in 1992. However, in two important respects, they created novel situations for higher education tutors and for schools. For schools, an implication of the Clarke speech was that for perhaps the first time on a large scale, schools were critically involved in developing responses to policy changes in initial teacher education. In a number of respects, headteachers and teachers found the changes potentially destabilizing. The suggestions in both the Secretary of State's speech and the DES document that schools might be selected for involvement in ITT on the basis of outcome performance indicators was both threatening and, for some schools deeply offensive. One headteacher was insistent that 'there are so many educational changes dividing schools, that we mustn't allow the preparation of the next generation of teachers to become the same'. For another, there was a logical difficulty in the proposal: 'it doesn't make sense; preparing students in so-called "good" schools so that they can go and teach in more challenging ones'. In other respects, too the proposals were destabilizing. East Anglia is an area of small schools. Hargreaves had argued in the educational press that school-based training was unlikely to be cost effective with cohorts of less that ten students in a schools (*TES*, 17/1/92, p. 17). A Cambridge Headteacher complained that Hargreaves' proposals raised the

> issue of the development of a hierarchy of training schools which have the potential to become like teaching hospitals centres of excellence not only for training but for education. Where would small schools fit into the scheme? If fewer than 10 students is uneconomic, is there a role for a school with fewer than 700 pupils? (*TES*, 31/1/92, p. 20)

Some Norfolk and Suffolk headteachers of smaller schools expressed similar views; for one 'it will be sad, but I can see that students will not get this sort of experience. It simply won't be worth anyone's while'. Furthermore, the introduction of changes in teacher education came at a time of rapid, multiple change in schools: the National Curriculum was in the process of implementation; National Curriculum assessment was about to become the subject of teacher industrial action; the local management of schools was still being completed and in many areas — notably Norfolk — schools were considering the possibility of seeking grant-maintained status. One head who subsequently declined to become involved in school-based ITT simply responded 'This is one change we don't need to be involved in'. Another, keen about the concept of school-based ITT observed 'It's simply the wrong time to introduce anything new.' Paradoxically, however, other headteachers recognized that the structural changes in schools since the mid-1980s, apart from any government initiative explicitly concerned with teacher education generated a change agenda in ITT. The change most frequently cited was local management of schools, which had led schools to realize the staff-time cost of student teachers in schools. The need for accurate, realistic costings, subsequently pursued by headteacher associations with some energy, was recognized by headteachers in early discussions.

If there were concerns and apprehensions in schools, there were far more amongst higher education tutors. Secondary teacher education at the University of East Anglia had reflected national trends in the middle and later 1980s and some preparatory work had been done in developing versions of school-based teacher education (Brown, 1985). The most substantial innovation was the university's attachment scheme in which student teachers were, during their second term following an initial short 'teaching practice' in a state school, 'attached' to a second school to explore whole school issues using a 'menu' of activities developed by the university. Responsibility for the assessment of students, though formally remaining exclusively with university tutors, was in practice negotiated between tutors and teachers. Indeed, the stability of particularly, subject staffing in the university meant that the quality of relationships between staff and schools was extremely good. However, in spite of such innovations, there had, in common with many other initial training institutions, been no systematic attempt to explore with schools the nature of school-based teacher education. New staff — including myself and the editor of this volume — in the university were consequently frequently critical of what appeared to be a somewhat static practice. Moreover, the tensions produced by changes such as Local Management of Schools and the National Curriculum in schools were placing what were often seen to be intolerable tensions on the existing course structure. As a result, some preliminary discussions were held with headteachers in the summer and autumn of 1991 on the reshaping of teacher education at the university. These discussions drew on the intellectual threads developed within teacher education, and the consequences of changes in school management but were based throughout on the assumption that teacher education was a higher education responsibility. The situation was fundamentally changed by the Clarke initiative in 1992. If the precise role of higher education was not at all clear, it nonetheless appeared to be the case that much of their role was to be passed to teachers in schools. In the educational press, reaction was angry: 'predictable rhetoric' (Letter, *TES*, 24 January 1992, p. 20). The hostility was frequently encouraged by government ministers. Tim Edgar, Minister of State for Education commented on BBC Radio that he expected as a result of the government policy that 'there will be fewer lecturers and more teachers'. In October 1992, the publication of advice from the Council for the Accreditation of Teacher Education suggested bluntly that 'schools. . . . will be responsible. . . . for training teachers to teach their specialist subjects' (CATE, 1992). For one subject tutor this was particularly difficult:

> I've spent twenty years working to improve the quality of teacher training through the work I have done. Now I'm told that the task can just be handed over to schools. I feel deeply insulted. We should do all we can to resist the changes which are being imposed. (CATE, 1992)

Within the university, the combined effect of such discourse was to entrench opposition to change: the task of reforming teacher education had become confused with the task of implementing government policy and implementing policy which was explicitly described in terms hostile even to the continuation of teacher education in universities.

The dynamics of change, then, were highly complex: we have seen clear evidence of a long period of redefinition of roles in teacher education and the emergence of incoherently defined but widely used concepts of 'partnership' and 'school-based' teacher education. We have also seen that there were tensions within current teacher-education practices as a result of wider educational and policy changes, but that the nature of the political intervention in early 1992 created difficulties and sensitivities in both schools and the university. Within the university, the Clarke initiative weakened the position of those who had opened discussions about reshaping teacher education on a more intensively school-based model the previous year: such individuals were now identified with a political initiative threatening the existence of teacher educators in higher education. The change strategy needed to be located clearly within this framework; the strategy was to identify a series of change agents outside the university to stimulate work within the university. At an open meeting in January 1992, to which all Norfolk and Suffolk headteachers were invited, heads worked in small areas groups to highlight key issues and subsequently to nominate five headteachers — broadly geographically representative — to work with four members of the university staff on the development of a model for teacher education which reflected the imposed political agenda and the perceived tensions within the current structure. This group worked on two main levels. The first was the development of a coherent intellectual rationale for a model of teacher education. Clearly located in some of the assumptions of the Clarke speech was a reductionist apprenticeship model of teaching; the group lost no time in finding such a model inadequate. Instead, agreement was quickly reached on an alternative rationale which headteachers found helpful and which drew centrally on the action–research traditions of the UEA. Learning to teach was seen fundamentally as a process of developing individual responses to classroom situations based on the collection and analysis of observed procedures and practices and the development of personal hypotheses about effective action. For new teachers, the task of the school and of higher education was seen to consist of providing support for this process and of creating situations which reduced the personal risks of failure which followed from early adoption of unhelpful hypotheses. In such a model

> Teacher education . . . is largely a matter of developing a teacher's capacities for situational understandings as a basis for wise judgment and intelligent decisions in complex, ambiguous and dynamic educational situations. (Elliott, 1991, p. 7)

The second level at which the group worked was more detailed and was to do with translating into practical managerial terms both the conceptual action research model of teacher education upon which they had already agreed and the boundaries to such managerial terms imposed by government policy. The latter was far from straightforward. In some respects, the group, after considerable internal debate, rejected the assumptions that outcome performance indicators were an inappropriate tool for the selection of schools and that participation in initial teacher education should be open to all schools which crossed some simple threshold criteria — namely the provision of a broad and balanced curriculum and a willingness to take on board the responsibilities of training in partnership with the university. Again, after considerable debate, and at some later costs, the group was keen that small schools should not be excluded from involvement by the creation of student cohort sizes in schools which made the management of initial training impossible for them. A further complication for the group was that the outlines of policy were shifting throughout the period in which the group was working: for example, the minimum amount of time students were to spend in schools was reduced in Circular 9/92 from 80 per cent to 66 per cent of time.

Discussions in 1992/3 made it clear that any school-based teacher education programme would involve far more individuals in teacher education than a largely higher education located programme. The possibilities for centrifugal tendencies in a programme involving over forty schools were considerable. For this reason, we recognized two central needs. The first was a central coordinating, or managing group seen to be representative of both schools and university and chaired by a headteacher. The second was the need to adopt a very simple structure which was flexible enough to be implemented in a variety of ways in different schools without subverting the overall coherence of the programme. The development of such a structure was far from straightforward. The group recognized the central significance in students' professional identity of their subject specialism, but saw clearly that a programme defined through subject specialisms might easily lack coherence and distract students' and teachers' attention from the real opportunities of a school-based teacher-education programme which was the opportunity to integrate learning through experience in school. In addition, to some extent the most conservative forces in the university were seen to be located in subject-method work. As a result the group adopted a simple structure. In both school and university students would work on a curriculum programme and a professional development programme, in each case published to students and based on common principles, but the professional development element would 'lead' and provide a spine for the course. Throughout the course, subject tutors and teachers would relate their work to the previously published professional development component.

Dissemination: Perceptions of Roles and Understandings of Change

By the autumn of 1992, the group had reached agreement on a framework document setting out the broad structure of a proposed alternative model for teacher education, and the document was launched to other university staff and schools (UEA, 1992). At this point a series of complications immediately appeared. The group had worked exceptionally intensively throughout the spring and summer of 1992. Members had worked bilaterally between meetings; they had prepared briefing papers and read widely; they had visited conferences. A high level of understanding of the issues had been produced and the group, through lively internal debate had a shared vision of a model of teacher education in which roles for schools and the university were clarified and which had, so the group believed, considerable potential for students and for staff. The document was not well received. It was seen as being over-mechanistic and highly formal. University staff, perhaps confronted with the reality of a document which took 'ownership' of key elements of the programme away from them were deeply unhappy. Schools, particularly small schools, were concerned at the level of commitment which they saw being demanded of them: one of the assumptions of the framework document was that any school department involved in the programme would be responsible for training two pairs of students, one in the first half of the year and one in the second. At this stage the working group saw the need, recognized by Fullan to retreat on key elements and a large complex consultation began. The present author spent most of the winter working his way around the schools of East Anglia discussing the document in detail, meeting groups of headteachers and deputy headteachers from different types and groups of schools. A working group adapted the programme to the needs of smaller schools where this was possible. As Fullan suggests, the *personal* contact was essential (1991, p. 65): through delicate negotiations inside and outside the university, consensus was reached on alterations to the framework document. Not all of the original planning group were convinced that the discussions had enhanced the structure of the new programme: 'it has lost something of its cutting edge, its intellectual clarity', but the discussions did mean that by the spring of 1993 a basis had been established for further development of the programme. The real negative consequence of the experience was the extent to which it inculcated a caution on the planning group's part. Anxious lest schools might simply 'walk away' from training, the group thereafter eschewed radical proposals. Whilst there were considerable difficulties in moving from the sharply focused planning work of the development group to wider acceptance of the revised ITE structure in schools and elsewhere in the university, it became rapidly clear that the overall simplicity and clarity of the proposals did allow different schools and different participants to accommodate them within a variety of working practices: in Fullan's terms it was possible for different groups and individuals to give the change process meanings within the context of their own practice.

The widespread acceptance of the revised structure proposals meant that planning could now proceed to the next 'level'. Working groups were set up to develop the programme in detail, again, where possible with a majority of teachers and, where possible, drawing teachers from schools which had not been represented in other groups and discussions. The tasks for these groups were pragmatically defined: they were to work from the agreed structure to levels of detail, reporting back to a now constituted coordinating group on difficulties of the structure for the detail they wished to establish. In fact there were few such references back. The original vision had sufficient clarity, and the structure sufficient robustness. Work was rapid: a working group developed an assessment structure (Barton and Elliott, in press), a separate group developed the model for the professional development strand. In each subject area, groups developed structures for subject programmes which related to the assessment structure and the professional development strand. Another group clarified, within the structure, roles and responsibilities. The structure of the programme has been described in detail elsewhere (Husbands, 1994); the important point here is to emphasize the ways in which the process built concentrically from a core vision to managerial detail drawing throughout on wide consultation, and to note the ways in which the planning structure enabled the elaboration of a dialogue about the purposes and nature of initial teacher education across the school–university divide. At the end of the first year of the new 'partnership' model, two things became clear. One was the extent to which teachers at the review conference spoke of 'our' course, and the other was the extent to which the planning assumptions and programme details had been embedded in the ways teachers thought about the programme. In short, whatever the managerial shortcomings of the process, the key elements of the programme had become accepted in teacher understandings of teacher education. For one teacher, commenting in June 1994, 'I feel at last that I have been involved in a change of which I approve'; for another, 'I was asked at an interview what I'd done in the last couple of years which I had found most professionally rewarding; I said the work I'd done with the University planning and developing the partnership.'

Conclusion: Some Reflections on the Change Process

Viewed from the perspective of 1994/5, the striking element in the foregoing narrative is the extent to which the change agenda dictated by Clarke in the early months of 1992 failed to materialize. In May 1992 the government abandoned its insistence on students spending four-fifths of their time in schools. Neither in East Anglia nor, it seems, in any part of the United Kingdom was initial teacher education located in schools 'selected' on the basis of outcome performance indicators. Whilst subsequent initiatives allowed some schools to develop wholly school-led and school-centred programmes of post-graduate teacher education, by the mid-1990s it remained the case that the 'lead' in the structural management of initial teacher education largely lay with higher education institutions working in 'partnership' with schools along the lines of development already established in the 1980s. What, then, remained of the policy initiative? Two elements, both of them of some significance. The first was that the development of government policy by the Secretary of State at the North of England Conference created what might be called an 'innovation window' in which consideration of the issues of teacher education and the respective roles of higher education and schools *by schools* was essential. In 1993 there were three meetings for headteachers at the University of East Anglia which were attended by the headteachers of all the maintained comprehensive schools in Norfolk, Suffolk and North Essex. It is unlikely that such a level of interest in ITT could have been generated in any other way by the university. However, in key respects the programme for change in initial teacher education generated by the university and the headteacher group which emerged was not simply a matter of 'interpreting' government policy; rather a clear rationale for school-based training was articulated which commanded the support of key stakeholders and provided a basis for development. This was a complex change process with multiple roots. The development of perspectives on school-based teacher education during the 1970s and 1980s was far from straightforward, and the increasingly ideological tone of some of those perspectives generated hostility, confusion and in some cases alienation even from those whose intellectual and personal predilection was towards the enhancement of the role of teachers in the task of training. The adoption and implementation of change was complicated since the 'broader reality' is that educators 'are in the business of contending simultaneously with *multiple innovations* . . . it is only at the individual and small group level that the inevitable demands of overload can be prioritised and integrated' (Fullan, 1991, p. 49). The development of both national policy and local strategy in developing school-based models of teacher education called for precisely the range of reactions anticipated by Fullan partly because of the 'demands of overload' at a time of rapid educational change. Fullan comments that 'what happens at one stage of the change process strongly affects subsequent stages'. Some of those involved in the change process described in this paper saw themselves as responding to an essentially political initiative, which they may have approved of, or been personally opposed to. Others involved saw the task as concerned more generally with the reform of initial teacher education drawing on change initiatives within teacher education (see e.g., Benton, 1990).

Reactions to the process of change at the stage characterized by Fullan as the 'implementation' stage were conditioned not only by participants understandings of the adoption process but also, and particularly for headteachers and teachers in schools, their access to information on the reasons for, and nature of, the enhancement of school-based components of initial teacher education; Fullan, again, suggests that a key element in the implementation process is 'the selectivity that occurs as a result of differential access to information (Fullan, 1991, p. 53). A key factor in the development of school-based teacher education at the University of East Anglia was the creation of a central planning group and subsequently of working groups on key elements of the change package, since 'vision building is crucial . . . [and it is important to] broaden the number of people aware of and committed to the change through communicating about it' (ibid., p. 83). However, whilst such a 'concentric' strategy was a pragmatic and politically sensitive response to the complexity of introducing and managing change across the large number of schools implicated in teacher education in East Anglia, it produced some difficulties at the level of dissemination and continuation. The central planning group established strong internal cohesion and a shared vision of the task of reform in initial teacher education, but found on some key issues that the very cohesion and vision meant that the group had enjoyed opportunities to engage with the conceptual and managerial issues of change in ways which others had not enjoyed, and that, consequently, there was a need to implement partial solutions, accepting, finally 'the possibility that our version of the change may not be the fully correct one' (ibid., p. 106).

Such a consideration prompts a final conclusion about the nature and structure of change initiation and implementation described by Fullan. The experience of change management outlined here certainly suggests that mistakes were made, particularly in dissemination of information and thinking about the planning group's work. However it is also clear that it is difficult to identify clearly the distinctions between change initiation and change implementation in the development of school-based teacher education: this was an educational change which had a complex initiation history over some twenty years, but, critically, a different initiation history for different participants. There were differences in perception of the change process between teachers, headteachers and tutors. As a result the eventual dissemination and [though it is beyond the scope of this paper] embedding of change depended crucially on the ability of those managing the process to address the different perceptions of meaning; and of those involved in change to adopt it within the framework of their own practice.

References

BAKER, K. (1989) Secretary of State's speech to the Society of Education Officers, 27 January 1989.

BARTON, R. and ELLIOTT, J. (in press) 'Developing a competency-based assessment framework in initial teacher education: The example of the University of East Anglia framework'.

BENTON, P. (1990) (Ed) *The Oxford Internship Scheme: Integration and Partnership in Initial Teacher Education*, London, Calouste Gulbenkian Foundation.

BROWN, G. (1985) 'The role of schools and teachers in teacher education', in FRANCIS, H. (Ed) *Psychology in Teacher Training*, Lewes, Falmer Press, pp. 54–65.

CATE (1992) *School-Based Teacher Training: Notes of Guidance for Secondary Schools and Higher Education Institutions*, London, CATE.

CLARKE, K. (1992) Secretary of State's speech to the North of England Education Conference, 4 January 1992.

DES (Department of Education and Science) (1972) *Teacher Education and Training (The James Report)*, London, HMSO.

DES (Department of Education and Science) (1984) *Initial Teaching Training: Approval of Courses (Circular 3/84)*, London, DES.

DES (Department of Education and Science) (1988) *Qualified Teacher Status: Consultation Document*, London, DES.

DES (Department of Education and Science) (1989a) *Initial Teacher Training: Approval of Course (Circular 24/89)*, London, DES.

DES (Department of Education and Science) (1989b) *Articled Teacher Pilot Scheme*, London, DES.

DFE (Department for Education) (1992) *Initial Teaching Training: Approval of Course — Secondary Phase (Circular 9/92)*, London, DES.

ELLIOTT, J. (1976) 'Preparing teachers for classroom accountability', *Education for Teaching*, **100**, pp. 49–71.

ELLIOTT, J. (1991) 'Three perspectives on coherence and continuity in teacher education', Unpublished paper, Universities Council for the Education of Teachers Conference, Oxford.

FULLAN, M. (1982) *The Meaning of Educational Change*, New York, Teachers' College Press.

FULLAN, M. (1993) *What's Worth Fighting For in Your School?*, London, Cassell.

FULLAN, M. (1994) *Change Forces*, London, Falmer Press.

FULLAN, M. and STIEGELBAUER, S. (1991) *The New Meaning of Educational Change*, London, Cassell.

FURLONG, V.J. (1992) 'Reconstructing professionalism: Ideological struggle in initial teacher education', in ARNOT, M. and BARTON, L. (Eds) *Voicing Concerns: Sociological Perspectives on Current Educational Reforms*, London, Triangle.

FURLONG, V.J., POCKLINGTON, P., MILES, S. and HIRST, P. (1988) *Initial Teacher Training and the Role of the School*, Milton Keynes, Open University Press.

FURLONG, V.J., WILKIN, M. and BOOTH, V.J. (1990) *Partnership in Initial Teacher Training*, London, Cassell.

GOODFELLOW, J. (1992) 'Enhancing the quality of school-based work in the PGCE: Warwick University', Unpublished paper at Universities Council for the Education of Teachers conference, Oxford.

HARGREAVES, D. (1992) *Times Educational Supplement*, 17 January 1992 London, *The Times Newspapers Ltd*, p. 18.

HIRST, P. (1991) 'The theory–practice relationship in teacher training', in BOOTH, M.B., FURLONG, V.J. and WILKIN, M. (Eds) *Partnership in Initial Teacher Training*, London, Cassell, pp. 74–86.

HMI (Her Majesty's Inspectorate) (1983) *Teaching in Schools: The Content of Initial Training*, London, DES.

HMI (Her Majesty's Inspectorate) (1988) *The New Teacher in School*, London, DES.

HUSBANDS, C. (1994) 'Integrating theory and practice in initial teacher education: The UEA model of action-research-based teacher education', in FIELD B. and FIELD, T. (Eds) *Teachers as Mentors: A Practical Guide*, London, Falmer Press.

LAWLOR, S. (1990) *Teachers Mistaught: Training in Theories or Education in Subjects?*, London, Centre for Policy Studies.

LETWIN, O. (1991) *Daily Mail*, 23.7.91.

McINTYRE, D. (1988) 'Developing a teacher education curriculum from research and theory on teacher knowledge', in CALDERHEAD, J. (Ed) *Teachers' Professional Learning*, Lewes, Falmer Press.

McINTYRE, D. (1990) 'Ideas and principles guiding the internship scheme', in BENTON, P. (Ed) *The Oxford Internship Scheme: Integration and Partnership in Initial Teacher Education*, London, Calouste Gulbenkian Foundation, pp. 17–34.

McINTYRE, D. (1994) 'Classrooms as learning environments for beginning teachers', in WILKIN, M. and SANKEY, D. (Eds) *Collaboration and Transition in Initial Teacher Training*, London, Kogan Page.

O'HEAR, A. (1988) *Who Teaches the Teachers?*, London, Social Affairs Unit.

PATRICK, H., BERNBAUM, G. and REID, K. (1982) *The Structure and Process of Initial Teacher Education within Universities in England and Wales*, Leicester, University of Leicester.

PENDRY, A. (1990) 'The process of change', in BENTON, P. (Ed) *The Oxford Internship Scheme: Integration and Partnership in Initial Teacher Education*, London, Calouste Gulbenkian Foundation, pp. 35–48.

TES (*Times Educational Supplement*) London, Times Newspapers Ltd, 7 July 1992, 17, 24, 31 January 1992.

TICKLE, L. (1987) *Learning Teaching, Teaching Teaching*, Lewes, Falmer Press.

UCET (Universities Council for the Education of Teachers) (1979) *The PGCE Course and the Training of Specialist Teachers for Secondary Schools*, London, UCET.

UEA (University of East Anglia) (1992) 'Partnership-based teacher education: A framework', Unpublished paper, Norwich, University of East Anglia.

WILKIN, M. (1991) 'The development of partnership in the United Kingdom', in BOOTH, M.B., FURLONG, V.J. and WILKIN, M. (Eds) *Partnership in Initial Teacher Training*, London, Cassell, pp. 3–23.

3   From Integration to Partnership: Changing Structures in Initial Teacher Education[1]

John Furlong, Geoff Whitty, Sheila Miles, Len Barton and *Elizabeth Barrett*

Introduction

The Government expects that partner schools and higher education institutions will exercise a joint responsibility for the planning and management of courses and the selection, training and assessment of students. The balance of responsibilities will vary. Schools will have a leading responsibility for training students to teach their specialist subjects, to assess pupils and to manage classes; and for supervising students and assessing their competence in these respects. Higher education institutions will be responsible for ensuring that courses meet the requirements for academic validation, presenting courses for accreditation, awarding qualifications to successful students and arranging student placements in more than one school. (DFE, 1992, para. 14)

The relationship between higher education institutions and schools has been a central focus of government policy in initial teacher education for more than ten years now (DES, 1984; DES, 1989; DFE, 1992; DFE, 1993a; DFE, 1993b; Wilkin, 1991, 1992). Circulars 3/84 and 24/89 (DES, 1984, 1989) both attempted to reconstruct that relationship by emphasizing the importance of practical teaching competence and insisting on a formal role for teachers in the training process. The central motif of both of these earlier circulars was 'integration'; all initial teacher-education courses had to achieve a close integration between the higher education institutions and school-based elements of their programmes, though the ways in which that integration was to be achieved remained unspecified. What is distinctive about the Government's most recent initiatives in primary and secondary initial teacher education (DFE, 1992, 1993a) is that they specify one particular means of establishing integration; integration is now to be achieved through the development of *partnerships* with schools, where schools exercise 'joint responsibility' for courses. Given the significance of these recent changes, the move towards partnerships between the institution and school-based elements programmes, has necessarily become an issue of central interest in the Modes of Teacher Education (MOTE) study which is monitoring national changes in initial teacher education over a five-year period (1991–5).

Phase one of the MOTE study, conducted in 1991 and 1992, included questionnaire surveys of all initial teacher-education provision and the Licensed Teacher Scheme in England and Wales and case studies of forty-five individual higher education-based courses and five Licensed Teacher schemes. The results of the national surveys, which have been reported elsewhere (Barrett *et al.*, 1992; Whitty *et al.*, 1992; Miles *et al.*, 1993; Barrett and Galvin, 1993) demonstrated that in the academic year 1990–1, there was considerable variation in how far existing higher education-led courses had moved towards a partnership model of integration of the type now being required by the Government (DFE, 1992, 1993). While on 87 per cent of courses, teachers were described as taking joint or primary responsibility for the supervision and assessment of students on school experience, their involvement in other dimensions of training (subject studies, curriculum courses, and educational and professional studies) was significantly less. When it came to involvement in the *planning* of training, even in the field of school experience, it was reported that less than half of all courses gave teachers a significant role.

By 1991 therefore, many higher education-led courses were not operating on a partnership model of training. In this chapter we draw on our evidence from case studies of forty-five courses conducted in 1992, to demonstrate the various ways in which courses, at that time, did attempt to achieve integration.[2] As we will see, the 'partnership' model which has now become mandatory, was at that time only one of several different ways of achieving integration. After describing the ways in which integration was achieved, we go on to explore some of the principled as well as pragmatic reasons why, at that stage, many course leaders had chosen alternative routes to integration.

Strategies for Integration

In developing closer integration between higher education institutions and schools, much recent debate has centred on the role to be assigned to schools and particularly on the work of mentors. However it is vitally important to recognize changes in the institution-based parts of courses as well. Indeed, at the time of our case-study fieldwork (1992), many courses had placed far more emphasis on revising the institution-based parts of their course than the school-based parts. We therefore consider these institution-based changes before looking at changes to school-based practice.

Changes to Higher Education-based Programmes

Compared with the picture of relative insulation from schools that emerged from surveys of initial teacher-education courses undertaken a decade earlier (Patrick *et al.*, 1982; HMI, 1983), it was clear from our case studies that by 1992, courses had been extensively revised in response to Circulars 3/84 and 24/89 with a view to integrating higher education institutions and school-based work. Links with school-based work were achieved in a variety of different ways and included changes to course structure, content, pedagogy, and the more systematic involvement of teachers in different aspects of programmes.

Course Structure and Content

In many courses, new patterns of serial and block practice had been established in order to promote greater integration between the work undertaken in the higher education institutions with that of the school.

For example, one Primary PGCE course tutor in maths explained,

> We prepare them here and then while they are here they go on one day visits and report back. Then we help them prepare schemes of work in the light of their preliminary visits — they go and do it and then they come back and talk about it.

From our national survey it would seem that alternating patterns of serial and block practice were the norm on PGCE courses, both primary and secondary. There were however examples of undergraduate degrees that had developed similar structures too. For example, one four-year primary BEd degree was strongly concurrent; students spent half of each week throughout their whole four years in schools, working in six different schools overall.

We explored the content of higher education courses under a number of common headings — curriculum courses, subject studies and educational and professional studies. In almost all courses there was strong evidence of all areas of work being directly related to the world of schools.

Curriculum courses

The vast majority of curriculum courses in higher education institutions were highly practically oriented. As noted above, a common strategy employed was to exploit serial and block experience in order to integrate higher education and school work. Lecturers frequently used curriculum courses to prepare students for work in school by setting them assignments and by encouraging them to analyse and reflect on their school experience when they returned to college the following week. But even in courses where the pattern of school experience did not include serial visits, there was lots of evidence of the practical nature of curriculum work. For example, the curriculum studies tutor on a design and technology degree, which also had fairly conventional teaching-practice arrangements, explained,

> the whole time one is able to see the student against an imaginary background of the school and try to emphasize the difficulties they will have in coming to terms with the curriculum of design and technology in school, its assessment and with discipline and control.

Subject studies

Subject studies necessarily form a central element in all two-, three- and four-year undergraduate degrees and on two-year conversion PGCE courses. On many such courses, students take their subject studies alongside students studying for other degrees. In these circumstances, as the students on a number of modular degree course commented, the opportunities for integrating subject studies to the work of schools are much more limited. However, even in these circumstances there was some evidence of course designers trying to achieve integration. For example, a tutor in one small college that ran a small programme of 'non-education degrees', explained that other students 'simply have to put up with a slightly "educationally oriented" subject studies'. A large polytechnic, which placed BEd students in a number of different faculties for their subject studies, had adopted a different strategy in an attempt to maintain coherence for students: the polytechnic had agreed a series of 'permeating themes' (race, class and gender) that would be covered in all undergraduate courses.

However, in courses where subject studies teaching was organized directly through education faculties, there were necessarily many more opportunities to link to the work of school. Our case-study courses included a number of examples where subject studies courses had been explicitly constructed so as closely to mirror the National Curriculum. Such developments might well be welcomed by the DFE. However, they raise important questions about the extent to which degree-level studies can and should be directed by vocational concerns as opposed to the specialist interests of students or the subject expertise of the lecturers in post. The development of the new 'six subject BEd' (DFE, 1993a) is likely to sharpen the significance of these questions.

Educational and professional studies

The aspect of course content most thoroughly transformed in recent years has been educational and professional studies (EPS). Evidence from the early 1980s (Patrick *et al.*, 1982; HMI, 1983) shows that at that stage, EPS was still commonly addressed through the teaching of the separate disciplines of education — sociology, psychology, philosophy and history of education. In 1992, the disciplines were noticeably absent from the courses we examined. Instead, EPS was almost universally taught in a highly school-focused manner, usually being constructed explicitly to address the professional issues set out in Circular 24/89. Although there were some examples of specialist teaching, a more common strategy was for a single lecturer to take responsibility for teaching the whole EPS curriculum to their particular group of students.

One striking feature of many EPS courses was that the taught sessions were explicitly designed to meet a range of educational objectives. These included covering cross-curricular themes, providing a link between curriculum courses and school, modelling teaching strategies as well as preparing students directly for school experience. Some courses tried to achieve several of these aims at the same time. Given the range of professional topics to be covered and the complexity of educational aims being pursued, the demands on EPS lecturers were often considerable; several lecturers we interviewed, realized that they could not claim to be experts in everything they were expected to cover and expressed concern at the possible superficiality of some of their work.

As we have already indicated, noticeably absent from the vast majority of EPS courses was any explicit coverage of disciplinary theory. Many EPS tutors were unhappy with this state of affairs. For example, one tutor on a four-year BEd course commented:

> They don't get as much sociology and psychology as they would have had
> a few years ago — they get it indirectly in that when we ask them to

reflect we do make reference to Piaget, Bruner and Vygotsky. But I am unhappy they don't get more of this because they garble it back in essays in an undigested form and I wonder if it would be better not to introduce it at all rather than in the limited way we have to. It concerns me that we have to spend so much time looking at how we should implement the National Curriculum rather than examine how children learn.

Our national survey reported that 72 per cent of course leaders claimed that their courses, like this one, were based on a model of the 'reflective practitioner'. At a general level this model facilitates a link between higher education institutions and school-based work. However, in many courses we visited, the nature of reflective practice was undefined and meant no more than personal reflection. As this tutor notes, without the opportunity to introduce disciplinary theory in a systematic way, encouraging more than personal reflection is difficult to achieve. This raises important questions about the criteria for professional judgments initial teacher-education courses are currently encouraging students to make. The 'flight from theory' may accord with government wishes, but should personal reflection on current practice in school be students' only guide to what is professionally sound? Are we, as Wilkin (1993) has argued, leaving students adrift in a sea of post-modernist relativism? It is certainly true that a number of tutors felt that government reforms had forced their teaching to become more superficial. As a result, it could be that the criticisms of teacher education made by the New Right, have become a self-fulfilling prophecy.

Pedagogy

A further strategy used to link the work undertaken in higher education institutions with that of the school was through the styles of pedagogy used be lecturers. In almost every case, tutors reported that their teaching strategies were carefully chosen. Lecturers, it seemed, seldom lectured; indeed those who did often apologized for doing so. Most tutors though, deliberately employed a wide range of teaching styles that students might come across in school; they deliberately used their sessions as an opportunity to 'model' teaching for students.

The significance of such modelling was clearly exposed in one course where it was missing. In one mathematics, two-year conversion PGCE course, main subject maths was provided by the university's mathematics department. This led to some problems as a mentor noted,

> There are problems with the maths faculty input because they are teaching them in a way which we (in school) encourage them not to use.

In addition to 'modelling', some tutors deliberately put their students in the role of pupils as a way of exploring teaching issues within their subject. For example, the maths tutor on a different two-year secondary maths course explained,

> We don't lecture. We give them problems to work on and they work as a group on these problems — that creates a powerful dynamic of them realizing what they always just accepted in the past . . . it means that they start thinking about it and that raises their awareness of what it means to teach maths in school.

In this course, a carefully chosen and sophisticated pedagogy became possible because main-subject study in mathematics was provided within the education faculty itself.

Involving Teachers

In addition to changes in the structure, content and pedagogy of courses, there were many instances of attempts to achieve integration of institution and school-based work by the involvement of teachers in different aspects of college-based programmes. In many courses, teachers had a role in the process of student selection though a number of course leaders reported increasing difficulties in getting teachers released for this purpose. On a few courses, teams of teachers were involved in 'vetting' the institution-based programmes, but a more common strategy for involving teachers was to include them in the teaching programme in some way. The nature of teachers' contributions to institution-based teaching varied considerably. At one extreme were one-off lectures, where teachers made presentations as part of a programme designed and 'managed' by college lecturers. At the other extreme were instances of joint planning and teaching. For example, one four-year primary BEd course had developed a 'school on site' programme, where local teachers brought their whole class to the college for two weeks. The programme as a whole was jointly planned and supported by the college tutors and the teachers. However, our interviews with students suggested that integration of this sort was not easy to achieve. No matter how careful the planning, the results were not always a coherent training experience as far as the students were concerned.

Changes to School-based Programmes

By 1992 therefore it is clear that nearly all courses had made significant attempts to ensure that their institution-based programmes were closely linked to the world of the school; in order to achieve such integration, course designers and individual lecturers employed a wide range of different strategies. By contrast, when we came to examine the development of school-based work, our case studies confirmed the findings of our national survey which had indicated that fundamental changes to practice at this level were less common. School-based programmes were, we found, still fundamentally 'higher education-led' with teachers taking on the role of 'supervisors' rather than 'mentors'. In this section, we consider such changes as had occurred.

School-based Assignments

One strategy for the structuring of school-based work that was common to most courses was through the use of school-based assignments. Typically these assignments involved investigations of school or classroom practice on some issue, or the development and trialling of materials; school-based assignments played a key role in integrating school and institution-based work. For example, the curriculum tutor on a primary PGCE explained his course's procedures as follows,

> None of the course tutors are long out of the classroom so the work and assignments all have a tendency to be focused on the classroom and they all have an element of preparing materials for use in schools . . . The assignment is an adhesive — it gels the course.

In the majority of courses, as in this one, the selection of topics for investigation was directed by the university or college; students typically chose their assignments from a range suggested by course leaders. There were however a few examples of courses where a more collaborative approach was evident. In one secondary PGCE for example, the idea that the schools should benefit from the course was built into the whole course design, including assignments.

> School-based investigations are not just for the benefit of the student but are intended to contribute to the school. It also gives schools more ownership of the course because assignments are negotiated according to schools' needs and concerns. The fact that the schools must benefit is the *sine qua non* of our partnership scheme.

Assessment

Although teachers typically helped in the development and execution of school-based assignments, at the time of our fieldwork, they rarely had any formal involvement in their assessment. Such a finding is unsurprising given the pressure on teachers' time and the fact that most assignments, however practically based, were normally seen by all concerned — teachers, students and lecturers — as part of the higher education institution's programme. By contrast, when it came to the assessment of student's practical classroom competence, teachers were more frequently systematically involved. In almost all courses, teachers contributed to the formal assessment procedure in some way. While there were examples of courses where assessment of practical teaching competence was seen entirely as the responsibility of the school, it was more common for college tutors to retain a strong role as moderators and mediators.

However, there was evidence that power relations were shifting in a number of courses. As the tutor on another secondary PGCE said 'It's very difficult to pass a student now if the school says they should fail.' The course leader of another scheme explained how she had used the external examiner to make the suggestion that a failing student should be moved to a different school. 'It had to come from the external examiner — the school would not have accepted the college saying it.'

The Role of the Mentor

At the heart of the development of the 'partnership' model of initial teacher education lies the role of the 'mentor', though in 1992, this role was still underdeveloped in the vast majority of courses.

Within our forty-five case-study courses it was possible to identify three rather different approaches to the support of students' school-based learning each of which implied a different vision of the role of the mentor.

The first, and by far the most common pattern of support for students at that time, was the traditional one where lecturers, rather than teachers took formal responsibility for overseeing students' school-based work through their weekly or fortnightly visits. A tutor on a two-year PGCE course expressed an 'ideal' version of this model as follows,

> Integration between school and college work comes about principally from the strength of support we are able to give to students when they go into school — the preparation we go through with them here and the support we give them when they get in. At the moment we are able to spend time talking to students after visiting them in schools and therefore we can bring these issues back into college for general use.

As this tutor makes clear, in this model, 'training' takes place within the college; tutors then support students as they learn to 'apply' that training within the real world of the school; the formal role for the teachers in this process is relatively minor.

A number of case-study courses had, in anticipation of the future transfer of funds to schools, moved to a less frequent pattern of school visits by tutors. As a consequence, in these courses the role of the teacher in supporting students was increased. One BA (QTS) degree called their supervising teachers 'associate tutors'.

> Associate tutors are largely a response to the fact that we are a small department and we have vastly increased numbers — PGCE numbers have quadrupled and undergraduate numbers have doubled and the staff have stayed the same. We cannot cope with the school visits. We have therefore sworn in as deputies twelve associate tutors who are senior teachers who are well known to us and they act as though they were main-subject tutors on their own site. They carry out the support, advice and assessment of the student . . . I just visit them once a term.

What was distinctive about this course, and others like it, was that although the role of the teacher in supporting students was enhanced, the fundamental model of training had not been changed. Students, it seems, were still being 'trained' in the higher education institutions and then 'applying' their learning in school by working under the supervision of a teacher who took on the role of the lecturer. It is significant that in this course and other case-study courses that employed a similar model, very little had been done to support teachers in the execution of their extended role; in each case there was 'the course document' and an annual meeting but little more. What it meant to be an 'associate tutor' was seen as relatively unproblematic.

Both of the above models contrast sharply with those few courses where there had been a sustained attempt to develop the role of the mentor. Such courses, had, to different degrees, begun to reassess their model of training; they were moving from an 'applications' model, where training took place elsewhere, to one where the school was seen as a key training site in itself. In courses following this model of training, teachers, acting as mentors, had significant responsibilities for planning and supporting the development of students' practical teaching competence. As a consequence, mentors had to be fully involved in the planning of students' training, and the flow of information between the schools and the higher education institutions was vital. As a mentor on one such scheme put it;

The tutors support the mentors as well as the students. They usually arrange to see a student, discuss things with them and then come and discuss the student with the mentor . . . The whole thing works because of the goodwill of staff and mentors.

Practising for Partnership?

In 1992 therefore, the dominant approach to integration between higher education institutions and school-based programmes was not one that could be characterized as 'partnership'. Most courses had made a substantial effort to make their institution-based programmes to become practically oriented (some might say at the expense of losing sight of what is distinctive about the contribution of higher education to professional development) but had done little to change traditional patterns of school-based work. While the value of the partnership model has been widely canvassed (Benton *et al.*, 1990; DES, 1991), there has, to our knowledge, been no systematic review of the benefits of other forms of integration in school-based training. Both we, and some of the students with whom we spoke, were impressed by the professional relevance and rigour of some courses that adopted a fairly 'traditional' model of training. Equally, there were some courses which had attempted to move towards a partnership model where students were critical of the quality of particular aspects of their training. Adopting a partnership model is in itself no necessary guarantee of quality in initial teacher education.

Before criticizing those in higher education of resisting partnerships as a way of protecting their own interests (Berrill, 1994), it is therefore important to consider the pragmatic and principled reasons why some courses had not pursued a partnership model. Our evidence points to difficulties some courses will continue to face in developing effective partnerships and raises important questions about the current, single-minded thrust, of government policy in this area.

Practical Constraints on Partnership

Practical Issues

It is important to note that our national survey in 1991 revealed that the most common courses to have developed strong partnership schemes were distinctive in a number of ways. They were more likely to be smaller courses, to be secondary PGCE schemes, and to be located within the then university sector. They were also more likely to be urban rather than rurally based. Fieldwork within our case-study courses suggested that there were important pragmatic reasons underlying this trend.

For example, it was evident from our fieldwork that partnership schemes were highly dependent on close communication and the establishment of routine forms of collaboration between higher education institutions and partnership schools. Close personal relationships of the sort that are more easily achieved within small courses, were seen as vital and developing and maintaining such relationships became a key part of tutors' work in all partnership schemes. As one tutor on an articled teacher scheme put it: 'We drive up and down the motorway and we build relationships'.

Course size is not the only variable in establishing effective communication; distance is important too. Some course leaders asserted there were simply not enough good schools in the local area with which to develop partnerships (a point vividly confirmed by the reports of some students of their experiences on teaching practice!). In other areas, the sheer density of student numbers meant that partner schools had to be physically distant. In these circumstances, developing a partnership scheme became much more problematic. A limited amount was achieved in some cases through good documentation. However, in 1992, we came across no fully developed partnership scheme where there was not regular contact between lecturers and teachers and appropriate in-service support. This raises important questions about the viability of the partnership model in strongly rural settings.

Maintaining close personal contact, even on a small, locally based course, is inevitably expensive in terms of tutor and teacher time. The greater number of secondary partnership schemes points to the continued difficulty (outside the well funded articled teacher scheme) for primary teachers to find the time to take on these responsibilities. In addition, there was evidence that in some courses, pressure on resources meant that it was increasingly difficult for tutors to support the course in the way that was needed. As the tutor on one four-year BEd course that placed heavy reliance on teachers for the support of students complained,

> I think that we used to support teachers a great deal more than we do now because of management pressure. 'I've been here for three years and when I came it was obviously a high priority to promote a relationship between teachers and staff here and we had time to talk . . . That was just to negotiate the partnership. That has been closed down or withdrawn. Everything's grossly reduced.

The end to 'transitional funding' is likely to increase the frequency of this sort of observation.

A further practical difficulty faced by partnership schemes was that of achieving coherence and consistency. The HMI's most recent report on primary initial teacher education (OFSTED, 1993) highlights the fact that not all courses achieve a consistency of approach within different parts of their institution-based programmes. However, if consistency is difficult to achieve within one institution, how much more difficult will it be in the new model of partnership training? Evidence from our study was far from reassuring on this matter. One tutor on a larger partnership scheme freely admitted that 'every student has a different course here'. Questionnaires from a group of students from another course that prided itself on close working relationships with schools, described the very different ways in which their teachers worked with them:

- He was like a safety net — he let me learn by falling over.
- She was a facilitator — she had lists of who I had to see.
- He stayed in the class with me virtually all of the time.
- She decided that I shouldn't have any observation in the first month . . . she simply said I am here if you need me.

This type of variation was typical. Student questionnaires and interviews revealed substantial variations in almost every aspect of school practice in relation to initial teacher education. The challenges for larger courses and those with schools at a great distance are considerable.

Issues of Principle

But practical concerns with resources, communication and coherence were not the only reasons why some course leaders had not adopted a partnership model. Some courses had chosen alternative models of integration for more principled reasons. Once again, the domination of particular types of courses within partnership schemes provided important clues to some of the underlying issues. For example, the frequency of secondary PGCEs having developed partnership schemes highlights the fact that in comparison with the primary BEd, the educational aims of block school experience are often more narrowly focused and perhaps more easily achievable within the secondary PGCE. Other types of course often set a range of aims for school experience over and above learning to teach in a particular school. Some of these aims were not necessarily compatible with conventional partnership arrangements. For example, in one primary PGCE which explicitly intended to develop students as curriculum leaders, serial visits were used to investigate specialist subject teaching in a variety of schools. A primary BEd course made a deliberate attempt to expose students to up to six different types of school over four years including those in rural areas. In many courses, school experience, and particularly serial school experience, was used to achieve educational aims different from those envisaged within a conventional partnership model. While schools and teachers were willing participants in these arrangements, it was more difficult for them to take full responsibility for planning and assessing such experiences. As a consequence, the higher education institutions were necessarily left firmly in control.

Course leaders also identified issues of principle in relation to the development of partnership schemes when working with 'non-traditional' subject areas, such as design and technology and business studies and 'non-traditional' students such as mature entry and access students. Implicit in the partnership model is the assumption that current practice within schools is adequate to form the basis for involvement in initial teacher education. While it is recognized that not all schools are ideal, it is assumed that within any one local area, there will be sufficient schools where good practice prevails. While such an assumption may be justified in the majority of subject areas in secondary schools, tutors on design and technology courses maintained that it was clearly not the case within their subject. In a period of rapid change in the development of a subject, practice within schools may lag behind that within higher education institutions. All of the tutors on design and technology courses that we visited made the same point. As one tutor explained: 'The thing about technology in the National Curriculum is that it is dynamic — it is changing all of the time.'

A group of tutors on a different course elaborated on the consequences,

> In our subject especially there is a very strong contradiction between moving teacher education out of institutions and back into school. I can see the whole development of the subject just grinding to a halt. If you go into the schools the National Curriculum is just not happening. We are constantly trying to get the students not to be too discouraged by what they find in schools.

Similar difficulties, though less severe, emerged in relation to practice within other subject areas such as primary music. Here too, school practice was seen as often inadequate. In both of these cases, tutors maintained that students needed a strong higher education input to their training if they were to develop as effective practitioners. Rather than forming partnerships, tutors saw it as necessary, at least in part, to protect students from the realities of school.

One further issue of principle related to the learning and personal needs of mature students. Partnership schemes place enormous stress on students. Responding to the pressure of two very different institutional cultures is highly demanding. Many of the students we met complained of the difficulties of meeting college deadlines for assignments at the same time as being responsible for teaching a class of children. This pressure was particularly difficult for mature students with heavy family responsibilities and we were aware of otherwise capable students having to leave their courses for this reason alone. Several tutors were sceptical as to whether, in strongly schools-based courses, schools would have the resources or the expertise to support such students in the ways they needed.

But mature students do not simply need a strong higher education institution base to service their emotional needs; tutors maintained that they also had specific educational needs too. These, it was argued, were unlikely to be met through school-based programmes alone. Before they went into school, mature students needed to look again at their subject and 'reconstruct it' in a way that was appropriate for school teaching. As one tutor on a shortened BEd explained,

> It's very difficult because they come in with such tremendously different backgrounds and we are also dealing with people who might come in with quite high-level qualifications but there are areas where they might not have done anything for twenty years. . . . what we do is to reconstruct some of their subject knowledge . . . within six to nine months they have to come to the realization that what they thought they really understood they did not have a clue about. Only then can they start to understand about how they should teach children.

Such opportunities were only available on conversions, PGCEs and shortened BEd courses that had a preponderance of mature entrants. Tutors on other PGCE courses often pointed out that their students had learning needs in their main subjects too. However, the increased time in school meant that there was even less opportunity to address such issues than in the past.

Conclusion

In conclusion, it is important to emphasize that the aim of our chapter has not been to challenge the value of the partnership model of integration. Our research would confirm the arguments put forward by others (Furlong *et al.*, 1988; Benton *et al.*, 1990; Booth *et al.*, 1989; Booth, Furlong and Wilkin, 1991; Furlong and Maynard, 1995) that such a model holds out important opportunities for the development of highly effective forms of initial teacher education. It is also important to recognize that in their efforts to make their institution-based programmes 'relevant', courses pursuing other models may well have lost sight of what the distinctive contribution of higher education should be to professional development. One of the strengths of the partnership model is that it raises in unavoidable terms the question as to who is best placed to contribute what to students' professional development. Lecturers in more mature partnership schemes were reassessing their own role and finding benefits in being released from the unachievable demands of 'doing it all themselves'.

Nevertheless, our research demonstrates the importance of recognizing the existence and value of other forms of integration that in 1992 were being practised within courses in England and Wales. By examining the aims and strengths of these alternative models, as well as some of the potential limitations and difficulties of the partnership model, it is possible to understand more clearly the implications of the Government's current policy in this area. Many courses, may well find considerable difficulties in establishing and maintaining effective partnership schemes, especially in the face of diminishing resources within higher education institutions. It is also apparent that although the educational achievements of the partnership model may be considerable, they are not identical to those of other models of integration. The partnership model, at least as it is currently defined by the Government, represents a particular construction of the process of initial teacher education. It may be well suited to particular groups of students on particular courses; for others it will definitely be less appropriate. The insistence on partnership constitutes a narrowing of the diversity of approaches to initial teacher education that has characterized British provision in the post-war period (Wilkin, 1992); such a narrowing will not necessarily serve all students, or all schools, well. The implications of this narrowing for different models of professionalism are to be the focus of the second phase of the MOTE study.

Notes

1 A fuller version of this chapter appears in *Research Papers in Education*, Vol 9 No 3.
2 The courses we investigated were selected as a stratified random sample on criteria devised as the result of our national survey. Twenty-five courses were 'conventional' initial teacher-education courses (one-year PGCEs, four-year BEd and BA (QTS) degrees); twenty were 'non-conventional' courses (shortened BEd degrees; two-year PGCE conversion courses; articled teacher schemes and part-time courses). Courses within each group were further sampled on a number of other criteria including course size, institutional type, geographical location, degree of 'school-basedness' (calculated as the number of days spent in school), and degree of 'targeting' of student recruitment.

References

BARRETT, E., BARTON, L., FURLONG, V.J., GALVIN, C., MILES, S. and WHITTY, G. (1992) *Initial Teacher Education in England and Wales: A Topography*, Modes of Teacher Education Project, Goldsmith's College, London.

BARRETT, E. and GALVIN, C. (1993) *The Licensed Teacher Scheme: A MOTE Report*, University of London, Institute of Education.

BENTON, P. *et al.* (1990) *The Oxford Internship Scheme: Integration and Partnership in Initial Teacher Education*, London, Calouste Gulbenkian Foundation.

BERRILL, M. (1994) 'Initial teacher education at the Crossroads', *Review of Cambridge Journal of Education* (special edition) 22, 3, *Cambridge Journal of Education*, 24, 1.

BOOTH, M., FURLONG, J., HARGREAVES, D., REISS, M. and RUTHVEN, K. (1989) *Teacher Supply and Teacher Quality: Solving the Coming Crisis*, Cambridge Papers in Education No 1, Department of Education, University of Cambridge.

BOOTH, M., FURLONG, J. and WILKIN, M. (1991) *Partnership in Initial Teacher Training*, London, Cassell.

DEPARTMENT OF EDUCATION AND SCIENCE (DES) (1984) *Initial Teacher Training: Approval of Courses (Circular 3/84)*, London, DES.

DEPARTMENT OF EDUCATION AND SCIENCE (DES) (1989) *Initial Teacher Training: Approval of Courses (Circular 24/89)*, London, DES.

DEPARTMENT OF EDUCATION AND SCIENCE (DES) (1991) *School-based Initial Teacher Training in England and Wales: A Report by HM Inspectorate*, London, HMSO.

DEPARTMENT FOR EDUCATION (DFE) (1992) *Initial Teacher Training (Secondary Phase) (Circular 9/92)*, London, DFE.

DEPARTMENT FOR EDUCATION (DFE) (1993a) *The Initial Training of Primary School Teachers: New Criteria for Course Approval (Circular 14/93)*, London, DFE.

DEPARTMENT FOR EDUCATION (DFE) (1993b) *School Centred Initial Teacher Training (SCITT): Letter of Invitation 5.3.93*, London, DFE.

FURLONG, J. and MAYNARD, P. (1995) *Mentoring Student Teachers: The Growth of Professional Knowledge*, London, Routledge.

FURLONG, J., HIRST, P., POCKLINGTON, K. and MILES, S. (1988) *Initial Teacher Training and the Role of the School*, Milton Keynes, Open University Press.

HMI (1983) *Teaching in Schools: The Content of Initial Training*, London, DES.

MILES, S., BARRETT, E., BARTON, L., FURLONG, J., GALVIN, C. and WHITTY, G. (1993) 'Initial teacher education in England and Wales: A topography', *Research Papers in Education*, **8**, 3.

OFSTED (1993) *The Training of Primary School Teachers*, London, HMSO.

PATRICK, H., BERNBAUM, G. and REID, K. (1982) *The Structure and Process of Initial Teacher Education Within Universities in England and Wales*, Leicester School of Education.

WILKIN, M. (1991) 'The development of partnership in the United Kingdom', in BOOTH, M., FURLONG, J. and WILKIN, M. (Eds) *Partnership in Initial Teacher Training*, London, Cassell.

WILKIN, M. (1992) 'The challenge of diversity', *Cambridge Journal of Education*, **22**, 3, pp. 307–22.

WILKIN, M. (1993) 'Initial training as a case of post modern development: Some implications for mentoring', in MCINTYRE, D., HAGGER, H. and WILKIN, M. (Eds) *Mentoring: Perspectives on School-Based Teacher Education*, London, Kogan Page.

WHITTY, G., BARRETT, E., BARTON, L., FURLONG, J., GALVIN, C. and MILES, S. (1992) 'Initial teacher training in England and Wales: A survey of current practices and concerns', *Cambridge Journal of Education*, **22**, 3, pp. 293–306.

4 School-based Initial Teacher Education in Scotland: Archaic Highlands or High Moral Ground?

Sally Brown

Introduction

Teacher educators in Scotland in 1994 feel themselves to be under great pressure. Looking southward, however, they see colleagues in initial teacher education in England embattled and embittered in ways that have not (so far) crossed the border. Loss of staff, closure of pre-service programmes, students' feelings of neglect, break-up of partnerships with schools and the spectre of 'the wholesale collapse of the teacher training system' (Pyke, *TES*, 3 June 1994) are sources of unease as we watch England's drama unfold, but they are not, as yet, the reality of our system and we have not experienced the acrimony of the south. Complacency is, of course, an inevitable risk, and the Scots are conscious that quite small changes in, for example, the political cast of characters could tip them into very difference circumstances. Scotland is still governed, after all, by a *British* Conservative government from Whitehall, albeit with the intermediary of the Scottish Office Education Department (SOED). Notwithstanding this important caveat, there are, as the Secretary of State for Scotland has said, 'different circumstances and . . . distinctive institutional arrangements' (*Times Educational Supplement Scotland*, 27 May 1994) as well as characteristic cultural and political climates which have a major impact on the ways in which the common aspects of British policy are implemented north and south of the border.

While much of the recent writing about teacher education in England has focused on policies and politics, there is no comparable body of literature in Scotland. Indeed, analysis of educational policy is a minority activity among Scottish teacher educators. The purpose of this chapter, therefore, is to look in an introductory way at the recent changes in policy, which superficially resemble those of the rest of the UK, and to discuss how they are formulated, received and implemented in a more tight-knit Caledonian community. There is a perspective that sees the north as clinging to the past with its heritage of consensus and accuses it of restrictive practices (Scotland has not allowed, for example, the Open University to provide its postgraduate teacher training opportunities north of the border) which reinforce the status quo. The other view is that the high moral ground is occupied by a system that looks for evolutionary rather than revolutionary change, sustains a professional workforce of teacher educators with some measure of continuity and security, eschews tactics to divide and rule, and maintains as far as possible good relationships among higher education, education authorities, schools and central government. Each of these visions is, of course, both misconceived and well-founded, as are most of the stories of the Scottish education myth.

The Political Context for Teacher Education in Scotland

Two areas in which the Scottish systems remained unassimilated to those of England following the Act of Union in 1707 were education and the law. Given the very different party political map of Scotland in comparison with England, it might be expected that there would be stark contrasts in these two areas. Scotland has, for example, only 16 per cent of its constituencies returning Conservative Members of Parliament and the most recent local government elections put the Conservatives fourth after Labour, the Scottish Nationalists and the Liberal Democrats with 14 per cent of the Scottish vote. In practice, however, the overall education policy maps of the non-Conservative north and the Conservative south have similarities. The pattern of British education legislation often takes the form of pairs of Acts; for example, the 1945 Act for Scotland had clear links with the 1944 Act for England, the 1988 Act for England was followed by a 1989 Act for Scotland, and on both sides of the border there is currently a strong move to make teacher education more school-based.

At a crude level, there is little that the dominant opposition parties in Scotland can do to stop Conservative legislation; the multitude of English Tory MPs are wheeled in to vote on Scottish Bills. But things are not clear-cut. Adjacent editorials in the *Times Educational Supplement Scotland* of 27 May 1994, for example, referred in the first case to the Government's defeat of a Labour amendment to the Scottish local government legislation which called for compulsory seatbelts on school transport, and in the second case to a decision by the Secretary of State for Scotland *not* to rush into a package of training measures to match the Government's White Paper for England on 'Competitiveness — Helping Business to Win'. Perhaps the most striking example of north–south differences was in the 1988 and 1989 Acts. The former enacted the National Curriculum and testing in law the latter did not.

Central government traditionally has had considerable influence on Scottish teacher education. Indeed, until the Scottish Higher Education Funding Council (SHEFC) was established in 1992 almost all teacher-education institutions (the then Colleges of Education) were directly funded by the Scottish Office and students successfully completing their courses were automatically registered with the General Teaching Council for Scotland (GTC). Only Stirling University's concurrent degree for the preparation of secondary teachers came under the auspices of the Universities' Grants Committee or Funding Council, and, as a result, its students had to be given 'exceptional registration' with the GTC. Advice from the centre, therefore, has not been a new experience for Scotland and the *Guidelines for Teacher Training Courses* (SOED, 1993) made the point that they 'represent a revision, updating and consolidation of the various sets of guidelines for courses of teacher training issued by the SOED from 1983 onwards'. It appears that this kind of relatively low-key centralized approach will continue; there is (as yet) no sign of the establishment of a body comparable with the Teacher Training Agency and teacher education remains firmly in the SHEFC constituency.

Turning from overarching legislative matters, there are important and distinctive features of the education community in Scotland which impinge in profound ways on teacher education and especially on the ways in which policy is implemented.

The Context for Policy into Practice

A central feature of Scotland's education system is the relatively small size of its population (though not its geography). The strategy for implementation of education policy in the Scottish regions has generally been one of working with the Scottish Office, especially HM Inspectorate. There have been tensions and dramatic confrontations (for example, over national testing), but the general effect has been to create an appearance of consensus, collective responsibility, homogeneity, cooperation and good communication, albeit somewhat tetchy on occasions. This is not the place to present the case which challenges this image (there is plenty of evidence to undermine it); my purpose here is simply to point out that this kind of consensual comfort is what many in Scottish education adhere to as their anchor (real or virtual). Its relatively cooperative pattern has, no doubt, played a major part in enabling HM Inspectorate to retain its size and role more or less unchanged (unlike its counterpart in England), and in encouraging education authorities to continue to behave in responsible ways and avoid 'loony' labels. The stability of the consensus could be destroyed, of course, by individual characters in the play. Scottish teacher educators are aware that although the current Minister for Education, Lord James Douglas-Hamilton MP, appears to welcome rather than deride consensus, the same could not have been said for his predecessor, Michael Forsyth MP.

From the point of view of teacher education, there are two players that, in comparison with the English scene, have particularly important roles: the education authorities and the General Teaching Council for Scotland (GTC). The latter is a statutory body with forty-nine members, thirty of which are elected from primary, secondary, further and teacher education (all are registered teachers); fifteen are appointed by the local authorities, universities and churches and four are nominated by the Secretary of State.

Education authorities continue to be a powerful force in Scottish education. None of these are currently Conservative controlled and the reorganization of local government, planned for 1996, is designed to reduce their power by a change to single-tier, small authorities. The effect of these changes, associated with blatant gerry-mandering of boundaries to create tiny Conservative controlled heartlands, will be to make the resources so small, and the issue of school catchment areas so complex, that education will be more or less unmanageable. This, it is hoped or feared (see headteacher Tony Finn's address to the Scottish Association for Educational Management and Administration, reported in the *Times Educational Supplement Scotland*, 27 May 1994, p. 1), will result in schools having to become self-governing (only one school in Scotland has opted out so far) as the weakened authorities are no longer able to provide the services and safeguards of the past.

As things stand, however, the education authorities still have a major role to play in determining, for example, the patterns of increased time in schools for student teachers. Resistance on the part of the Convention of Scottish Local Authorities (COSLA) to Scottish Office proposals may yet have a powerful impact on the final form of pre-service training. Alongside this, however, there will be a changing scene in the governance of schools. By 1996 mainstream schools (1997 for special schools) will have Devolved School Management (DSM — the Scottish equivalent of Local Management of Schools). It is not inconceivable that opting-out and schools' control of their own budgets could, by the late 1990s, see free market contracting between schools and teacher-education institutions in Scotland in much the same form as currently in England.

Circumstances have certainly changed over the last few years. In September 1989 the GTC's account of a major conference, 'Partnership in Professional Training' reported that

> Concern with the overall quality of teachers led in Scotland to the establishment by the Scottish Education Department of working parties to examine teacher education. These working parties were broadly representative, involving the Scottish Education Department, teachers, the General Teaching Council, the employing authorities and the colleges of education. Partnership between these agencies produced reports establishing national guidelines for the main courses of initial training: the four-year concurrent BEd for primary teachers, the post-graduate certificate course in primary education, and the post-graduate certificate course in secondary education. Partnership between the agencies involved in this initial training — the colleges, the schools and the employing authorities — was also stressed in the reports. (p. 2)

More recently, and in contrast, the growth of central control has seen national guidelines issued directly from the Scottish Office. It has to be acknowledged, however, that HM Inspectorate and civil servants consulted extensively with Scotland's teacher educators (and some south of the border) as they put the guidelines together.

Since the GTC was established more than a quarter of a century ago, its responsibility for maintaining standards in school teaching has included the regular review and accreditation of all initial teacher-education programmes in Scottish institutions. Because the majority of members of the GTC accreditation committee are practising school teachers, teacher educators are kept in contact with their views and what they are looking for, and the teachers become familiar with the justifications for the structure and content of pre-service courses. This, together with the involvement of teachers in the selection of students and the validation of higher education courses, has produced a sense of close collaboration on a national scale; any claim by the Government that higher education institutions are isolated from schools would have low credibility except in the most rural areas.

The Shift Towards more School-based Training

A feature of the recent Scottish developments in teacher education has been a consistency in the avoidance of any notion of the control of teacher education moving into the hands of schools. No mention has ever been made of schools 'taking the lead' in partnerships with higher education institutions, and a press release, *Mentor Teaching Scheme for Teacher Training* (SOED, 12 May 1994), has once again made it clear that

> The higher education training institutions will retain primary responsibility for the preparation of students and the professional and academic validation of their courses. (p. 2)

This contrasts quite markedly with the Conservative Government's approach south of the border where the House of Lords' attempt to secure the link between higher education and teacher training in schools was blocked. *The Times Higher Education Supplement* (27 May 1994) referred to a leaked Tory Manifesto document describing succinctly the Party's position as

> the clear and distinctive view of teacher training — based on the belief that schools themselves should play the principal role in devising and running teacher training courses. (p. 1)

Research by Stark (1993, 1994) has suggested that the retention of the major responsibility in the hands of higher education has strong support from Scottish teachers. In her study of school experience in initial primary teacher education, teachers indicated they were 'not prepared to take on more responsibility in this area than currently is the case' (Stark, 1993, p. 51). Their justification for this arose not just from consideration of their workload, but also from their perceptions of their own lack of appropriate experience and training and their reluctance to divert attention from their priority of the education of children. Leading on from this Stark (1994) also reported concern among the teachers that any further shift of responsibility towards the school could leave student teachers with an inadequate theoretical underpinning to support their practice. There seemed little evidence of unease about any ogre-like theory which might stand in opposition to that practice. None of this is, of course, unique to Scotland; Bolton (1994) for example, has reported very similar reactions from schools in England.

Although, for the time being at least, it appears that responsibility for teacher education will remain in the higher education sector, there has been a clear change in emphasis on the role of schools. The requirements (SOED, 1993, pp. 7–8) for time to be spent on school experience increased from a minimum of eighteen to twenty-two weeks out of thirty-six for PGCE (secondary) programmes, 50 per cent (eighteen) of PGCE (primary), and thirty weeks for four year BEd (primary or secondary). The demands for change are, therefore, rather less than those south of the border. A pilot project was set up by Moray House Institute of Education at the invitation of the Scottish Office to test the feasibility of the new arrangements and to explore the introduction of mentors in support of students in schools. The SOED provided funding for the schools involved (£15,000 for ten students in each school) and commissioned the Scottish Council for Research in Education (SCRE) to undertake an 'external monitoring project' (Powney *et al.*, 1993). It is interesting that this was not called an 'evaluation' and had a rather limited remit:

> to describe some of the advantages and disadvantages of increasing school experience time. In the timescale available, the research will not be expected to evaluate the effectiveness of the course in terms of the eventual quality of teaching, since that would require following up students over several years. (p. 1)

The findings of the monitoring exercise were unexceptional and readily publicized by the SOED. George MacBride of the largest teaching union in Scotland, the Educational Institute for Scotland (EIS), has expressed what seems to be a typical reaction.

> We have only to look south of the Border to see the government's ideal: articled teachers, licensed teachers, the so-called mum's army, each scheme marked by increased hostility to independent thought. As part of its move in this direction the SOED hosted a seminar with the open title National Seminar on Partnerships in Teacher Education last November [1993]. This seminar was notable for the attempt to focus participants' attention off questions of detail in teacher training rather than on matters of principle. It was also notable for its failure to persuade the participants who came from all areas of Scottish education that the government was heading in the right direction. The ostensible occasion was the publication of the evaluation carried out by SCRE ... neither this evaluation nor that produced internally by Moray House argued that the new course produced better teachers ... In general, the students were slightly favourable to the pilot scheme ... felt more comfortable; a number of gains for pilot schools were identified. Although the SOED had made strenuous efforts in planning the seminar to limit discussion only to practical and technical issues, participants made it clear in workshops and in plenary sessions that there is a need for national open debate on the aims of teacher education. (MacBride, 1994)

This kind of reaction reflects a general response to the changes in Scottish teacher education which is unenthusiastic but muted in specific criticism. That muteness may indicate a judgment that the changes are sensible (but few taciturn Scots could bring themselves to tell the Government that), or they are seen as substantially less damaging than those in England and we are 'holding tight to nurse for fear of getting something worse', or they are undesirable but nobody has the energy to put up any substantial resistance. There are two particular concerns, however, which are voiced, especially among members of the GTC: the possibility that a select few schools will become élite teacher training centres, and the future of mentoring schemes which could either produce an élite-group of teachers or be little more than current supervisory roles dressed in new clothes.

Partnership and Mentoring

The articulation of what are seen as the twin dangers of 'training schools' and mentors as 'privileged teachers', reflects something of the culture (shared values and ways of working) of Scottish schools which perceives the teaching tradition as one of equality, autonomy, privacy and professional relationships among teachers that are essentially egalitarian i.e., a 'flat' structure. This is quite unlike some other places in the world such as China; Paine (1990, pp. 149–50), for example, describes how in that country experienced teachers 'bring along the young over a period of three or four years in an hierarchical structure where 'distinctions based on seniority' play a significant part. Mentoring is one of the activities which contributes to the awards of ranks and responsibilities which, in China, underline differentiation and seniority in the workforce.

This leaves Scotland with something of a problem. The experience of the pilot school-based study, indications of work south of the border (e.g., Benton, 1990 on the Oxford Internship Scheme) and the general requirements of school-based experience (if it is going to be of value to the students and contained within the resources available) suggest that student-teachers should be grouped in a subset of schools and not spread thinly across the whole population. There is no reason why the set of schools has to remain unchanged for all time, but the need for some consistency over several years is clear if higher education institutions and schools are to establish a shared understanding of the aims of the school experience, a commitment to joint activity and ways of providing each other with the mutual support required for the 'shared cooperative activity' (Bratman, 1992) of real partnership. Progress towards that could easily be interpreted as setting up 'training schools'. There will have to be a well articulated vision for the future, therefore, if collaboration among higher education, education authorities and schools is not to stumble at that fence.

The implications of the flat culture of Scottish schools for mentoring are also significant. It can be argued that any worthwhile mentoring system would have to provide some kind of recognition and incentive for teachers who take on this role. Not only would they be expected to develop new areas of expertise, in the preparation of their own profession, they would also have to anticipate some kind of reward or satisfaction for pursuing a dual and more demanding agenda in their daily lives. If they are to be rewarded by public acknowledgment for their competence as mentors, however, they would in some sense be set above their colleagues. Leadership roles in guiding professional practice have not been a traditional part of the promotion structure in Scotland; indeed, the introduction of 'senior teachers' in recent years has been, at best, an enigmatic innovation. There may well be suspicions of any moves to offer 'expert' status in the same way that there are suspicions about 'training schools'. If taking on a mentorship role is to open up career opportunities, then it is likely to affect both school organization and the social ethos among teachers in Scotland.

The place and role of mentor teachers in the partnerships and processes of teacher education has only recently come to the fore in government statements for Scotland. A press release (*Mentor Teacher Scheme for Teacher Training*, SOED, 12 May 1994) announced that:

> Under the scheme, to be introduced from August 1995, schools are to be funded to allow the mentor teachers to spend more time with students . . . in such a way as to avoid any disruption of classroom teaching . . . The Scottish Higher Education Funding Council . . . [will] advise on the resource implications for the teacher training institutions of introducing the mentor teacher scheme in the light of resources likely to be available for the funding of initial teacher training . . . It will be for each institution in collaboration with partner education authorities and schools to develop a suitable mentoring system taking account of a set of principles and criteria which the Secretary of State will in due course specify. (pp. 1–2)

There are two important implications of this statement. First, it appears that payment to schools is to have a neutral impact on education funding, that is it will come out of the existing higher education budget and probably heralds free-market contracting with schools of the kind already underway south of the border. The GTC, with its large representation of school teachers, has already voiced its opposition to the use of teacher education funding for the purpose of paying schools. Secondly, there will be no central prescription for what is to count as mentoring, except that it will have to cover 'supervision, training and assessment of students' (SOED, 1994, p. 2).

What 'mentoring' means to Scottish teacher educators is not at all clear. Very little has been written on the subject although several unpublished papers have been commissioned by the SOED (e.g., Brown, McNally and Stronach, 1993; Kleinberg, 1993). Debate about the competing or complementary roles of mentors in staff management, counselling and education (McIntyre, Hagger and Wilkin, 1993, p. 16) or about the distinctions to be made between the traditional supervisory function and the new concept of mentoring (Maynard and Furlong, 1993, p. 71), has either not occurred or has been a feature of within-institution conversation rather than literature in the public domain.

The one example which has provided a public account of mentoring in action in Scotland is the report of the monitoring of the pilot school-based project (Powney *et al.*, 1993). Discussion of this aspect of the project (pp. 6–7, 102–3) suggested an emphasis on the higher education institution making decisions about what mentors should be doing (in line with guidance from SOED) and then providing training, advice and hints on how to set about the practical aspects of the job. The conclusions drawn focused on two issues. The first of these concerned the implications of having 'out-of-subject' mentors, and the residual impact on this of the familiar tradition of 'within-subject' supervisory teachers. The second looked at the concept of 'mentor training' and suggested that the way forward should consider more participative, collaborative development rather than purely higher education-led training.

This last point emphasizes an urgency for Scottish teacher education to consider whether talk about 'training' mentors is appropriate. The logic of the role of mentors sees the teachers' *own* qualities, knowledge and perspectives as central to the activity and, as McIntyre (1992) expressed it 'Where university people are likely to have a major role to play . . . is in support roles for school staff exploring the possibilities and problems of mentoring'. The earlier point, on old supervisory roles, indicates an urgency for those of us in Scotland to conceptualize more fully the mentor's commitment. That commitment has to be quite different, more intimate and focused, from the one which (in caricature) saw a balance to be made between, on the one hand, observation of, and discussion with, the student and, on the other hand, the supervisor's release from class teaching once the student was deemed competent to take over.

A similar priority has to be given to some hard thinking about 'partnership' — a word to which, in contrast with others such as 'contract', many in Scottish education have become addicted. Mutual distrust between higher education and schools is not unknown ('ivory towers', 'backward practitioners') and the sectors' different primary purposes, general unease about funding, paternalism on the part of higher education, issues of where the plans of the partners must mesh and where they can be allowed to differ, inertia in the system and the central importance of students are all factors which have major implications for how partnerships are to be construed and implemented in Scotland's teacher education. The pilot school-based project clearly saw higher education as taking the lead role in the partnership

with schools; no pretence of equal status was apparent. Furthermore, a clear hierarchical model (Powney *et al.*, 1993, p. 94) was evident with the top level of the
partnership being among senior managements in school, education authority and
higher education, a second level among course leader, education authority adviser
and coordinating mentor, and the third level comprising the student — the 'object'
of the partnerships. An alternative conception with the emphasis on students, mentors
and university tutors as the partners would imply a quite different model of practice.
These developments in partnership and mentoring are, as in England and Wales, set
in the context of a competence model for teacher education. It is to that I now turn.

The Competence Model for Scottish Teacher Education

The list of competences to be attained by student teachers before entering their
probationary period as teachers in Scotland (SOED, 1993, pp. 2–6) does not display
an obvious stark contrast with that for England and Wales (e.g., DFE, 1992, Annex
A). There are, however, differences in tone and emphasis. For example, the Scottish
list does not distinguish between 'Subject Knowledge' and 'Subject Application';
instead, it establishes a category of 'Competences Relating to Subject and Content
of Teaching'. The other general categories are: competences relating to the classroom (communication, methodology, class management, assessment), to the school
and to the profession. The language, when compared in similar contexts, implies a
subtle stress in Scotland's document on professional judgment in contrast with
England's managerial accountability. For example:

> 'identify suitable occasions for teaching the class as a whole, in groups, in
> pairs or as individuals' (SOED, 1993, 2.2.2 under 'Methodology') in contrast
> with 'decide when teaching the whole class, groups, pairs or individuals
> is appropriate for particular learning purposes' (DES, 1992, 2.4. 1 under
> 'Class Management') and 'be able to assess the quality of pupils' learning
> against national standards defined for that particular group of pupils' (SOED,
> 1993, 2.2.4 under 'Assessment') in contrast with 'judge how well each
> pupil performs against the standard expected of a child of that age'. (DFE,
> 1992, 2.5.2 under 'Assessment and Recording of Pupil Progress')

Sue Kleinberg (1993) has recognized this distinction in reporting teacher educators' reactions to the Scottish guidelines. Her approval was tempered, however,
with concern about the processes of assessment of student teachers, given the plethora
of individual competences and the potentially artificial divisions made between
interrelated elements which together provide the complexity of this thing we call
teaching.

> Most colleagues are pleased, if not relieved, at the definition of *competence*
> as more than performance. The Guidelines definition implies a concept of
> professional learning and behaviour which recognises the complexity, so-
> phistication and judgement required in teaching. Such a definition is seen
> as mirroring the cultural values of a Nation which has Guidelines for the
> 5–14 curriculum. There are however some concerns about the competences
> — particularly in the divorce of subject knowledge and methodology, the

possible need to aggregate assessments made, and the number of items to be completed on the draft Professional Profile for Prospective Teachers. (p. 3)

At a general level, it could be claimed that the Scottish document maintains its character of 'guidelines' while the English text is that of a 'directive'. Even if that is the case, it is plausible to argue that this is explained by the Government's confidence that the Scots will follow guidelines from the Scottish Office and so directives are unnecessary.

One aspect of the introduction of a competence model that is of importance is the reaction from teachers. There is, as yet, scant evidence on this front and the competences played little part in the evaluators' accounts of teachers' views in the official pilot study of more school-based training. There has been, however, an interesting commentary from George MacBride the Education Convenor of the Educational Institute of Scotland (EIS). The EIS is the largest of four teacher unions in Scotland and claims about 80 per cent of teachers among its membership. MacBride (1994) looked at the model from the perspective of the question about whether Scottish schools need teachers who are

semi-skilled technicians who will manage their classes well while passing on an officially approved curriculum . . . [or] professionals who in addition to teaching effectively remain active thinkers who want the responsibility to determine what best merits the needs of their pupils. (p. 3)

His analysis of the competences suggested that consensus elements of what was expected of teachers had been presented in ways that promoted unquestioning passive stances among newcomers to the profession.

Some of these competences are concerned with the immediate practicalities of teaching such as knowledge of the subject, ability to communicate, and class management. Few would argue with the need for such competences. But these practical competences make clear that it is expected that teachers will accept national policies and national standards and be able to justify (not question) existing provision and policies. So far as competences relating to the school are concerned the focus is on passive knowledge about the system, while the competences related to professionalism use a rhetoric of professionalism but pay little attention to how such professionalism will be fostered among passive unquestioning learner teachers. (MacBride, 1994, p. 3)

The competences have played a central role in the procedures for the 1993 approval of all initial teacher-education programmes by SOED and accreditation by the GTC. Indeed, several such programmes have taken the framework of competences as it stands and used that as their model for teacher education. That strategy runs several risks. First, it encourages the view that anyone (Secretary of State for Education or Mickey Mouse) can sit down in an armchair and prescribe what teacher education should look like; so why bother to have teacher educators? Secondly, it confirms the idea that the Government can impose a model from outside without any requirement to negotiate with teacher educators who might be expected to have clearly articulated ideas about high quality, worthwhile teaching and teacher education. Thirdly, and most importantly it inhibits teacher educators from thinking in creative and constructive ways about what it means to be a teacher, how learning to be a teacher takes place and what particular contribution to teacher education is most appropriately offered by higher education.

There is a general impression, with the implied caveats above, that the HMIs who produced the Scottish list endeavoured to respond to the outcomes of their consultations with teacher educators, despite having to keep within the framework laid down by the politicians. They managed to provide a set of competences within which thoughtful reflection on the part of the beginning teacher is encouraged. They also made it clear that 'professionalism implies more than a mere set of competences. It also implies a set of attitudes which have particular power in that they are communicated to those being taught' (SOED, 1993, p. 6). Those attitudes were identified as a set of teacher commitments to the job, their pupils, their own professional development, the needs of the environment and 'views of fairness and equality of opportunity as expressed in multicultural and other non-discriminatory practices'.

Conclusion

In England the outcomes of policies to make pre-service teacher education more school-based are already visible; in Scotland that is still to come. Will the similarities imposed by the over-arching British political framework ensure that the two systems of teacher education eventually turn out to look pretty much the same? The arguments in this chapter have suggested the more left-wing colour of party politics in Scotland, the consensual education climate, the important roles of agencies like the GTC and education authorities, and the continuing influence of HM Inspectorate combine in a variety of ways to provide a particularly Scottish view of the world. For the time being at least, central government is prepared to temper its innovations in ways that avoid major upsets in a system that has traditionally been more centrally regulated and uniform than that of England. Other aspects of policy, however, especially the reorganization of local government, may change the landscape quite dramatically from 1996. It is these general changes, rather than explicitly teacher education policies, which have the greatest potential for establishing the market-oriented model and bringing Scotland into line with the south.

A free-market model for education does, of course, have to consider its customers. Parents are central to the debates about schooling, but do they have any impact on teacher education? It seems plausible to argue that they may have quite forceful views on their children being taught to a far greater extent than in the past by student teachers. In the market place this may be seen as a situation where the providers (i.e., the schools) have to take action to keep their customers, and that could lead them to withdraw from partnerships with higher education (as is already apparent for a variety of reasons in England). There is some scope for anticipating a rather different set of circumstances in Scotland. Scottish parents seem to exhibit more trust in their education system, have the capacity to band together to influence the Government, are prepared to cooperate with schools and local authorities to achieve common aims and seem disinclined to see their role in purely 'customer' terms. Their behaviour in using school boards to display their confidence in, and support for, their local schools and comprehensive education generally, and in collaborating with teachers and education authorities to oppose successfully government plans for national testing in primary schools, has illustrated the influence they can exert and reminded the Government that its predictions of parental views may be misconceived. How these Scottish parents will react when they realize the nature of the impact of changes in teacher education on their own children remains to be seen.

Where Scotland does seem to be lagging behind is in its thinking about how it will make sense of new conceptions of partnership and mentoring. The Scottish Office has been applauded for running a pilot scheme before insisting on change (Pyke, 1994), but this was not a pilot in the sense of assessing whether the new approach did, in fact, produce better teachers or of testing out alternative ways of construing the innovations. It was essentially a feasibility study of the arrangements (and costs no doubt) which was followed by a statement that the rest of teacher education should follow suit but each institution could do its own thing. Studies which have been undertaken (e.g., Elder and Kwiatkowski, 1993) have looked at how partnership currently operates between higher education and schools, and have offered a list of issues to which we have to attend (shared understandings, resources, agreement on criteria, enabling structures). What they have not done is engage in critical analysis of alternative conceptions of teacher education and their implications for students learning to be teachers.

Crisp conclusions about 'archaic highlands' or 'high moral ground' are, of course, elusive. It is not unreasonable to argue that the softer 'guidelines' approach to innovation in Scottish teacher education is leading to substantially less change than that in the English system. Should we be asking, therefore, whether the northern version is not clinging to an outdated framework in the face of an enlightened market-led model that is sweeping the south? Maybe so, but we also have to ask about the morality of introducing turmoil, distrust and destruction to England's teacher education in the name of a free market. There is no evidence that this has raised standards; the general impression is that they are falling rapidly. The idea that Scotland's system will, in the longer-term, be dragged along the same path to a similar beleaguered state is dreich indeed.

References

BENTON, P. (1990) (Ed) *The Oxford Internship Scheme: Integration and Partnership Initial Teacher Education*, London, Calouste Gulbenkian Foundation.

BOLTON, E. (1994) 'One last push', *The Guardian Education*, 17 May 1992, p. 2.

BRATMAN, M. (1992) 'Shared co-operative activity', *Phil Rev*, 2, 101, pp. 327–41.

BROWN, S., McNALLY, J. and STRONACH, J. (1993) 'Getting It Together: Questions and Answers About Partnership and Mentoring', Report commissioned by SOED, Stirling, University of Stirling.

DFE (Department for Education) (1992) *Circular 9/92 on Initial Teacher Training* (secondary phase), London, DfE.

ELDER, R. and KWIATKOWSKI, H. (1993) *Partnership in Initial Teacher Education*, Dundee, Northern College.

GENERAL TEACHING COUNCIL FOR SCOTLAND (1989) *Partnership in Professional Training*, Conference Report, Edinburgh, GTC.

KLEINBERG, S. (1993) 'Key Ideas and Issues Concerning Mentoring and How They Affect

One B.Ed (Honours) Degree', Report commissioned by SOED, Glasgow, Strathclyde University.

MacBride, G. (1994) 'Professionalism under threat', *Scottish Educational Journal*, February 1994, p. 3.

Maynard, T. and Furlong, J. (1993) 'Learning to teach and models of mentoring', in McIntyre, D., Hagger, H. and Wilkin, M. (Eds) *Mentoring: Perspectives on School-Based Teacher Education*, London, Kogan Page, pp. 69–85.

McIntyre, D. (1992) 'Initial Teacher Education and the Work of Teachers', Stenhouse Memorial Lecture, BERA Annual Conference, University of Stirling, August 1992.

McIntyre, D., Hagger, H. and Wilkin, M. (1993) (Eds) *Mentoring: Perspectives on School-Based Teacher Education*, London, Kogan Page.

Paine, L.W. (1990) 'Chinese teachers' view of time', in Ben-Peretz, M. and Broome, R. *The Nature of Time in Schools: Theoretical Concepts Practitioners' Perceptions*, New York, Teachers' College Press.

Powney, J., Edward, S., Holroyd, C. and Martin, S. (1993) *Monitoring the Pilot: The Moray House Institute PGCE (Secondary)*, Edinburgh, Scottish Council for Research in Education

Pyke, N. (1994) 'In training for Armageddon?', *Times Educational Supplement*, 3 June 1994, p. 12.

Scottish Office Education Department (SOED) (1993) *Guidelines for Teacher Training Courses*, Edinburgh, SOED.

Scottish Office Education Department (SOED) (1994) *Mentor Teacher Scheme for Teacher Training* (Press Release), Edinburgh, SOED.

Stark, R. (1993) *School Experience in Initial Primary School Teacher Training*, Glasgow, University of Strathclyde.

Stark, R. (1994) 'The "giving" can't go on', *Times Educational Supplement Scotland*, 18 February 1994.

TES (*Times Educational Supplement*) Scotland, 'Lang Takes Cautious Stance Over Training White Paper', 27 May 1994, p. 3.

5 Partnerships in School-based Teacher Training: A New Vision?[1]

Anne Edwards and *Jill Collison*

Introduction

School-based training is not just extended teaching practice. It involves a fundamental change to the design, organisation and management of initial training. (CATE, 1992, p. 2)

A thesis might be written on the insertion of 'just' in the first line of this extract from the UK Council for the Accreditation of Teacher Education (CATE) guidelines on the arrangements for secondary school and higher education training partnerships. In the context of these arrangements we shall consider the capacity of 'just' to allow supervisors to see that the future practice of supervision may differ little from that under preceding arrangements. The changes marked as fundamental in the second sentence of the extract are beyond the decision-making remit of most supervising teachers. Consequently teachers are faced with the prospect of a fundamental change which appears to leave them with an extension of their existing function. At the same time school managers face another externally imposed initiative. This is, however, not the limited picture envisaged by McCulloch (1993) in her analysis of the possibilities for a transformation of teacher education in the creation of school–university partnerships. She argues that the quality of initial training can be enhanced by 'challenging the nature and processes of teaching and learning within a social framework which places education as a key experience in the enlightenment of individuals' (p. 302) and cites the University of Reading initial teacher training programme's examples of how this individual enlightenment might be achieved.

However the extract from the CATE guidelines does not appear to be written in order to create the conditions for a reform of teacher education which in McCulloch's terms might enhance the quality of teacher training and may have the potential to transform the participants. The use of 'just' can limit the transformational potential of school-based training and tie partners into existing ways of ordering and categorizing their understanding of teacher training and the schools' roles.

Ways of seeing teacher education will depend upon the categories one uses. Examples of these, gleaned from fieldnote and interview data in secondary and primary schools over the last two years, emerge as a set of distinctions or perceived oppositions on which decisions about teacher training have long been based. Their

(i)	theory	practice
(ii)	supervisor	students
(iii)	pre-service	in-service
(iv)	supervisor–student links	teacher–pupil links
(v)	teacher in department	teachers in other departments
(vi)	teacher in school	teachers in other schools
(vii)	tutor	class or subject teacher
(viii)	university department	schools
(ix)	requirer of placements	providers of placements
(x)	pedagogy	subject/discipline

Figure 5.1: Existing Frameworks for Initial Teacher Training

extensive history in describing initial teacher education may indicate that little radical change will be forthcoming in partnership schemes perceived in this way (see Figure 5.1).

These oppositions impact on practice. Collison and Edwards (in press) have argued that the theory–practice category distinction used by primary-school teachers allows them to function as providers of safe contexts for student trial and error practice. Consequently teachers avoid dialogues that might lead to general explanations that extend beyond the demands of immediate practice. Teachers declared that generalization was 'the responsibility of the College'.

The power of these distinctions as oppositions lie in their ability to limit the possibilities latent in teacher training partnerships. Senge (1990) has argued that ways of seeing in organizations and associated systematic patterns of behaviour are self-perpetuating and persist, because alternatives are not easily apparent. He suggests that organizations can benefit from metanoia or a radical shift of mind. Such a shift enables people to review existing systems and practices and to reframe operational categories to create new possibilities for action which may indeed be transformational. An earlier interpretation of metanoia is repentence or a major turn from the old life to the new.

If teachers are to review and reframe they may take convincing that the effort is worthwhile. Fullan (1993) describes the decision-making practice of North American schools as bedevilled by 'projectitis' or a surfeit of educational initiatives (p. 126) with consequent overload on teachers and fragmentation of planning and experience. The UK experience of one-year-funded initiatives and the imposition of unfeasible practices, which have absorbed teacher energy in debate with central government, have confirmed the majority of teachers in their suspicion that externally imposed initiatives are likely to be transitory and of value only if they provide funds to enable schools to meet their own priorities.

The recent behaviour of staff in university departments has not encouraged teacher review and reframe. Caught in the entrepreneurial thrust of much of higher education, tutors are obliged to promote cost-led models of initial teacher training partnership while relying on in-service fees from schools. Simultaneously the UK Research Assessment Exercise that determines university funding levels has encouraged university staff to separate theory from practice and focus on the former. Goodlad (1990) reporting on a North American study of twenty-nine universities notes:

The rapid expansion of higher education, together with unprecedented changes in academic life, have left professors confused over the mission of higher education and uncertain of their role in it. (pp. 700–1, in Fullan, 1993, p. 106)

One could hazard that this statement would hold true for the majority of UK teacher trainers in higher education. Departments of education are finding it hard to avoid an uncomfortable set of paradoxes as they attempt to define mission and strategic planning.

It appears that both schools and teacher training institutions may be suffering from a lack of control over institutional mission and a vision of teacher education which is limited by the language and frameworks within which it is perceived and operated. Senge (1990) argues that systems need to be levered into change, that they will not change as a simple development of existing practice. If school–university partnerships become increasingly symbiotic any leverage will affect both partners. In this chapter we consider the realities of partnership and pose the possibilities for the transformation of initial teacher training mainly as they relate to schools. We shall do this through an examination of two case studies. The first is a BA (QTS) programme which is preparing infant teachers and the second a PGCE programme for intending secondary school practitioners.

The Two Studies

Background

Since June 1992 researchers at the Unit for Applied Research at Lancaster have tracked the development of school-based training partnerships in a pilot BA (QTS) (early years) scheme. This work was augmented in September 1993 by a similar study of the introduction of partnership into the PGCE (secondary) programme. Both sets of partners aimed to meet the needs of students in school as they developed towards competence. Consequently little difference obtained between the focus of the partnerships and that of previous college-managed teaching practices. The difference lay in the increased responsibility assumed by school partners. In Senge's terms metanoia had not occurred and the categories listed in Figure 5.1 were determining planning.

In the first year of the primary school study data were gathered on the student experience using observations, recorded conversations, interviews and questionnaires. These data are discussed elsewhere (Collison and Edwards, in press). As we became more familiar with the eighteen primary and infant schools involved in the initiative we became intrigued by their institutional responses to involvement in a teacher training partnership with higher education. These observations prompted a further study in the second year of the project in which thirty-four teachers in fourteen primary and infant schools were interviewed. These interviews explored ways in which schools had adapted to accommodate their partnership role together with the potential for staff and school development that teachers perceived after, almost two years involvement in partnership.

The secondary school study was informed by the primary school work. Data were gathered using fieldnotes and group techniques at mentor training sessions and mentor–tutor meetings and in twelve interviews with subject mentors (subject teachers). The interviews were designed to elicit changes in the professional self-perception of mentors where they occurred. Like the more recent primary-school interviews they examined teachers' views of the potential for change for teachers and schools in an enhanced role in teacher training.

Both studies are presented here as case studies of school response to partnership in two programmes. Each case study comprises a number of smaller studies of individual schools. A comparison of the school cases within each programme case study has allowed a set of common themes to emerge in each set of cases. It is these that we shall examine as we discuss the extent and limits of the transformational aspects of school higher education partnerships in initial teacher training.

The Primary School Study

The themes derived from the primary and infant-school interviews corroborated our earlier analysis of fieldnote and interview data from these and other schools (Figure 5.1). Dominant themes were:

(i) Students need to fit into the school. They had to be sympathetic to its philosophy, be a good teacher, realistic in their demands on resources and plan in line with school planning.

(ii) College is where students should find time to reflect. There they should develop their own philosophy or theory and gather new ideas. School is where they try out these ideas in environments safely structured by teachers.

(iii) Funding needs to be adequate. Though in the majority of schools funding was not used entirely to give direct support to students.

Minor themes, not evident in all schools were:

(iv) Staff development was occurring. This tended to focus on the fresh ideas that students brought.

(v) The pupils benefited from additional adults in the classroom. Students freed teachers for high quality time with children.

Some interview questions were derived from observations of the secondary-school experience. We had wondered whether the associate tutors (the specifically trained school-based links with the college) were changing their sense of professional identity through their training and their work with other associate tutors. Clearly this was not happening. Associate tutor meetings were used, 'to check I'm doing things right'.

When probed it became evident that they wanted their professional identities to be located firmly in their own schools.

> We can't afford to change. We still have to talk to our own staff. Our role is to stay in the staff and with the staff.

None saw links between school-based training, induction and inspection. The associate tutors did not appear professionally ambitious and did not see mentorship as a path to promotion in the school system. There was, however, one reference, from a headteacher, that involvement in training might provide a route towards work in higher education.

It appeared that schools were dealing with initial training partnerships as projects rather than partnerships. One headteacher revealed that the memorandum of cooperation remained unread. Suffering from 'projectitis', schools had not developed rationales prior to taking action. Associate tutors reported, for example: 'We had to do it and get on with it.' The majority of schools included school-based training in their school development plans after their first year of involvement in the programme. But we have no evidence that any have made it a priority activity. Rationales for its inclusion in planning related to ensuring that resourcing and staffing could accommodate the responsibility the schools had for training. They were not based on a belief that training partnerships necessitated a reviewing of the function or philosophy of schools.

The Secondary School Study

The themes most evidently important for teachers and captured in the fieldnote and interview data were consistent across all eight subject areas in the programme. They are the following.

(i) Students' subject knowledge is frequently limited. This was interpreted by teachers to be largely a result of the increase in modular and joint honours degrees.

(ii) Subject mentors want their job to be taken seriously by senior management in schools. This was an extension of a concern that the initial training work of teachers in departments should not be seen by their senior managers as a bolt-on activity and accommodated by departments.

(iii) Is it worth it? This sometimes related to the impact of the change on the quality of training. More generally it referred to funding and whether it recompensed schools for the disruption caused.

Their own staff development was not an issue for the majority of mentors. They felt satisfied that they were giving generously to the students. Student evaluations endorsed this view. Links between departments as a result of mentoring were rare. Subject mentors saw their first concern to ensure that the subject was taught well even if that meant increasing student subject knowledge. Consequently subject orientation militated against both the emphasis on pedagogy that McCulloch (1993) identified as the contribution of schools to students' training and the emergence of cross-departmental career development for mentors as staff developers in schools.

Interview data revealed that subject mentors took the job seriously and felt that the partnership arrangements had gone someway to enabling them as they supported students. When pushed to describe differences between pre-1993 supervision and the new partnership mentoring practices this subject mentor's reply contains many of the points made more generally.

If you've been supervising properly all along the new arrangements don't make a great deal of difference except that it is more organized. You have certain times to see the students, things you must cover with them and more responsibility for assessment.

The integration of the training function of schools into school-development planning was a prerequisite of involvement in the programme and a quality control system that recognized this was established. It was serviced by the Quality Assurance Unit of the College which independently provided analyses of evaluation data to school and college staff. We have no evidence to suggest that schools are using these data to inform development planning or indeed that initial training is a priority activity for schools. The relationship between school-management styles and systems and the quality of the experience of students in schools would seem a fruitful area for further exploration.

Shifts in Practice: Shifts in Mind?

An examination of both programme case studies against the oppositional distinctions given in Figure 5.1 will indicate the extent to which some current partnerships in training might be seen to be transforming participants or schools.

(i)   Theory/practice

Data from the primary-school study indicates that a distinction between theory and practice is apparent to teachers. Observational data and recorded mentor–student conversations demonstrate that teacher mentors are unwilling to risk discussion of areas which extend beyond immediate task setting and performance (Collison and Edwards, in press). Teachers valued 'theory' but said they could not provide it. The secondary-school study reveals a different picture. Theory for most subject teachers was first understood as subject theory and not pedagogy. They find that they are dealing with the former as content knowledge sometimes at the expense of the latter as practice: interestingly contradicting the expectations of Circular 9:92 (DFE, 1992) which set out expectations for the roles of school and universities placing content knowledge with the universities and pedagogy as practice in the schools. Meanwhile pedagogy as theory is not so much split from practice but erased from the experience of students.

(ii)   Supervisor/students

We observed little erosion of boundaries between these roles as teachers assumed a mentor function. Detailed observations in the primary-school study revealed no examples of student–teacher co-enquiry (Maynard and Furlong, 1993) or mutual challenge (Collison and Edwards, in press). Rather the most engaged teachers worked energetically and effectively to create contexts in which students could succeed. 'Puzzles' or problematic events which Russell and Munby (1991) argue can be a source of reframing an understanding of practice were not jointly explored, instead teachers supported and guided their students. Similarly the secondary-school data suggest that teachers saw their success in the extent to which they enabled students to perform competently.

(iii)   Pre-service/in-service

Interview data suggested that the programmes were perceived solely as pre-service exercises. Attempts to explore possibilities of tutors, mentors, school-based subject specialists and students working together on for example curriculum-development in-service events elicited responses from teachers indicating that this was either impossible or unnecessary. When probed on the staff-development aspects of partnership one primary head, after stopping the tape recorder, confided 'It happens least to those who need it most'. Only one (head)teacher indicated that he saw how pre-service training may mesh with in-service including induction.

(iv) Supervisor–student links/teacher–pupil links

Schools in both studies clearly saw pupils as their first responsibility. One headteacher explaining the withdrawal of the school from the primary programme explained: 'we are here to teach children . . . not teachers and we cannot do any more for students'.

This anguish was evident throughout interviews with mentors over the two years of the primary-school study. Teachers talked of being 'torn in two' between students and pupils. Several refused to take the free time funded by the college for supervisory work as they wished to remain with their classes. The teacher–pupil link in primary schools prevented most mentors who were also class-teachers from standing back, observing and enabling students contingently as sessions progressed. In the majority of classrooms mentors saw students as valuable adult assistance which lifted some of their pressures and allowed them sustained interactions with small groups of children. Consequently student experience was variable. Teacher support and lack of interest were both reported by students. The strength of the teacher–pupil link was less noticeable in the secondary-school study where both subject teaching and classroom practice rendered this less problematic and satisfaction with teacher support was more widely evident.

(v) Teacher in department/teachers in other departments

(vi) Teacher in school/teachers in other schools

Teachers were constructing their identities as department members in the secondary schools or school staff members in the primary schools rather than as mentors with access to a wider mentor group. A reason given frequently in primary schools for not taking all the time allocated to the role of associate tutor was that they might appear different from other staff. One infant headteacher, sharing her concern about lack of staff cohesion, observed that involvement in mentoring had enabled one teacher to 'develop in ways that have taken her beyond the staff'. These observations suggest that if leverage is to occur it needs to be at school level and not at the level of the subject or class teacher. Goodlad (1990) has already proposed that the focus on training has been too much on the classroom and too little on the school.

(vii) Tutor/class or subject teachers

Both studies indicate that tutors and teachers are assuming new roles. As control of the training process shifts from tutor to teacher, tutors are having to learn to let go. While teachers, frequently surprised by the extent of their control over student experience, are seeking increased guidance. Funding levels make collaboration between tutors and teachers difficult as tutors spend less time in school. Consequently the tutor role is developing into trouble-shooter or encourager. Roles are being reframed but without the financial leverage that might be transformational.

(viii) University department/schools

If tutors are found in schools less frequently, teachers are more often seen in education departments whether for mentor training or programme management meetings. These sessions suggest a one way system with routes from schools to the centre of the programme without equivalent pathways back from higher education to the centre of school planning and management as it relates to the programme. A model of colonization rather than integration into schools persists and corroborates the secondary school mentors' reserve about the extent to which mentorship is being taken seriously by senior managers.

(ix)   Requirer of placements/providers of placements

Funding was a major theme for senior managers in both case studies. Managers tended to see the college as purchaser of school-provided services in a situation where supply might shape the parameters of demand. The relationship was represented more in contractual than flexible partnership terms and finance was central. Conversely mentors felt they were contributing in a distinctive way to a complex training process. In the secondary-school study subject mentors felt that senior managers were not recognizing the complexity and were not giving them necessary support through, for example, more free time. A slippage from partnership which might recognize the complexity at its centre to the sharp oppositional distinctions of a purchaser–provider duality was evident. Our data suggest that partnership was not taking root and that purchaser–provider models are more easily understood and acted upon by senior managers.

(x)   Pedagogy/subject discipline

As we've already indicated in (i) data revealed a difference between the primary and secondary programme case studies around curriculum. When we explore this further some shifts in the supervisory role were observed. The primary teachers were obliged to support students as they tackled the full range of primary curriculum studies. For the first time teachers had to assume a curriculum mentor role and frequently lacked confidence. A counter-shift was evident in the secondary-school study where teachers used material provided by tutors to induct students into basic pedagogical principles and experienced the counter-claims of needing to focus on students' curriculum knowledge. Nevertheless in both cases a broadening of perspective on the supervisory role was achieved.

In the data from the two programme case studies there is little evidence to suggest that partnerships as currently defined are leading to major changes in the experience of initial teacher training. The only metanoia or shift of mind (Senge, 1990) that can be observed is the introduction of a purchaser–provider framework for the organization and management of initial training. Organization and management were two of the areas licensed for 'fundamental change' by the CATE (1992) guidelines.

The general lack of change is unsurprising. New ways of perceiving roles and responsibilities were not licensed by CATE (1992) and were not built into the two case-study programmes. In the final section of the chapter we shall interpret the 'just' in the quotation that prefaced the chapter with optimism and explore possibilities for reviewing and reframing teacher training in ways that might produce a transformation of individual and organization.

Partnerships in Learning?

Both the programmes studied attended to the immediate quality of students' practice and engaged teacher partners in activities aimed at developing student competence.

Both programmes were either following direct guidance from CATE (the secondary programme) or building on previous experience of an enhanced role for teachers in supporting students (the primary programme). It may be, however, that this and other studies of similar programmes will give cause to question too narrow an emphasis on student experience. Starting from the premise that the act of teaching is politically and socially constructed, Goodson (1993) argues against 'the notion that the focus of the teacher as researcher should be mainly upon practice' (p. 223). The focus on practice, he continues, plays into the hands of the New Right by trivializing teaching into a set of routine technical activities. Our evidence would support a similar analysis of student experience where, for example, the major elements of teacher–student conversations have been associated with mundane aspects of task setting. For example teachers describe how to set out paint pots rather than give their reasons for grouping children at a design activity (Collison and Edwards, in press).

Any expectation that an emphasis on student practice might encourage the development of teacher practice has been unfulfilled in the case studies in either observational or interview data. Joint enquiry is not occurring as teachers are not exposing their practice to any scrutiny beyond the provision of model lessons. Discussions of the inadequate knowledge base of teaching (McNamara, 1993) and of teaching and teacher education (Fullan, 1993) provide some explanation for teacher resistance to joint scrutiny. Lichtenstein, McLauglin and Knudsen (1992) in their North American study of teacher empowerment suggest that an improvement in the knowledge base of teachers is an essential prerequisite for an extension of teachers roles. McNamara's (1993) analysis of UK professional authority amongst teachers would suggest that the same might be true in the UK. Teacher vulnerability appears to lead teachers to focus on the support of student practice and to resist opportunities for developing their own practice through collaborative scrutiny. The Reading University programmes, outlined by McCulloch (1993), tackle this issue by ensuring that teachers' and tutors' own learning, through their systematic practitioner research, creates a context for both practitioner and student development.

Systematic engagement of tutors, teachers and students in their own professional development on the Reading initiative testifies to a shift of mind that demands some reframing and reviewing of teacher education. It also moves the leverage point for developing school-based training from student practice to include that of mentors and tutors.

Current quality-assurance systems in higher education, emphasizing substantiated self-assessments, provide a sympathetic context for the 'constructive criticism' and 'open agenda for discussion' (p. 301) that McCulloch argues are features of the initiative she describes. Though there is no evidence from her account that practitioner research is incorporated into quality-assurance systems in the schools and university department.

An institutional focus for leverage is an alternative to the multilevel participant-focused intervention outlined by McCulloch. Institutional leverage does not deny the importance of the quality of the student learning experience. The school-effectiveness literature over the past fifteen years is sufficient witness (Reynolds, 1985; Mortimore, Sammons, Stoll, Lewis and Ecob, 1988). The development of effective learning institutions requires a confident interpenetration of the polarities described in Figure 5.1 as, for example, student and supervisor learn, albeit different things, together; pre-service experiences feed in-service; and teacher collaboration increases.

Aspects of the duality outlined in Figure 5.1, and most particularly, the university–school distinction, appear from our data to be, in part, due to how schools have perceived higher education departments of education. University departments have an 'otherness' that allows no right to apply institutional leverage in schools. The schools' lack of action planning at a senior-management level on the basis of the quality-assurance data they received from higher education in the secondary programme case study is an example of this lack of university power. The attack on Local Education Authorities (LEAs) in the UK has lost the school–university partnership a perhaps vital third element (Edwards, 1991a). The potential of tripartite partnerships is observed by Whitty (1993) in his summary of US Professional Development Schools. The projects are based on a partnership between higher education, schools and school districts. Though Fullan (1993) urges some caution in response to this initiative due to lack of clarity in the Professional Development School concept, current US school climate and 'projectitis'; and the lack of attention by university departments to their own transformation. In a similar vein to Whitty, Turner (1993) writing of educational development sees a team approach as a *sine qua non* of training and development. The gap in partnerships created by the loss of LEA power requires, perhaps, a shift of mind that allows schools and universities to work more closely to the wider benefit of local education provision and to attend to Fullan's caution that higher education should look to its own transformation.

An alternative to a confident interpenetration of the work of schools and university departments is a widening of the gap between them. Our interviews reveal teachers' ambiguity towards partnership in relation to future divisions between schools and higher education. A primary school headteacher's comments give some flavour of this.

> I'm afraid it's the start of a slippery slope. We don't want to run teacher training, but if we cooperate now it might end up like that and schools are doing the most they can do now.

Whitty (1993) surmises that one result of taking the slippery slope towards a wider gap might be the increased detachment of higher education from the realities of teaching. While Whitty was assuming that some university departments might survive the slide and serve a school consultancy function members of the Education Section of the British Psychological Society have predicted pessimistically a future for the 'appliance of science' mode of school consultancy in which, for example, university departments of psychology take on the consultancy role currently undertaken by the university education departments. It is suggested that a consequent loss of the interpenetration of theory and educational practice which currently gives direction to the work of education department staff will ensue (Edwards, 1991b).

Can a Hammer Be a Lever?

Are current partnership arrangements the start of a slippery slope: a hammer to ensure that departments of education join the LEAs in relegation to the archives of educational provision? Or, do they provide the opportunity for leverage which will transform education?

Partnership, like collegiality in the 1980s, can be a weasel word: seductive but disappointing. Collegiality at times became a defensive cosiness that prevented the open discussion necessary for school development. It was a necessary but insufficient element in school development. Structures and procedures were also required (Edwards, 1993). McCulloch's (1993) description of the University of Reading initial training initiative would suggest that partnership too requires such an underpinning.

> All participants contribute distinctively their complementary skills within an agreed definition of roles and with the identification of similarities and differences of perspectives, to be explored between the partners . . . (McCulloch, 1993, pp. 300–1)

Openness, collaboration, joint learning and risk taking 'within the supportive network' (p. 301) are the strategies of the Reading initiative which itself has a base, which unlike the case-study programmes, is theoretical rather than pragmatic.

The Reading reviewing and reframing of initial teacher training into something more than an extended teaching practice was given direction by Adelman's (1989) proposal that it operate through a dynamic, dialectical model 'informed by a process of practitioner research at every level' (p. 178). The programmes were reframed as something other than a simple extension of existing practices however good these might have been in the pre-partnership context.

By applying leverage to individuals at every level: to students, mentors and university staff the transformational potential of school-based training for these groups met the individual enlightenment aim of the initiative. There is, nevertheless, a danger that however supportive the network between levels might be, participants are open to marginalization within their own institutions. It may be that practitioner research, like collegiality, is not enough.

Our data show that although mentors have insights into the complexity of professional preparation and want to address it, their senior managers can see no benefit for the school in recognizing this complexity and are often deemed unsupportive. Leverage, it would seem, may need to be distanced from practice whether that is student, mentor or tutor practice. It needs to move to the organizational development of the institutions in which these practitioners work. A major shift of mind would be to enact developmental interventions at the level of the strategic planning and quality-assurance systems of schools and departments of education.

A developmental intervention at the institutional level might be collaboration in primary schools between curriculum tutors and curriculum coordinators in curriculum-development programmes which engage both the whole school staff and students. In secondary schools a similar collaboration between teachers and tutors might occur in support of a pedagogy-based initiative, for example, flexible learning. At a managerial level a confident interpenetration of the work of schools and universities might be achieved by a tighter meshing of school quality-assurance schemes with those operating in higher education. Within university departments financial distinctions between pre-service and in-service should be eliminated. Peer review in the Research Assessment Exercise may safeguard departmental research funding if evidence of interpenetration of theory and practice becomes a criterion on which research is judged. It appears that a confident erosion of the distinctions outlined in Figure 5.1 which enabled the interdependency of schools and departments of education might have far-reaching beneficial effects for education.

Conversely an enhancing of the differences outlined in Figure 5.1, as our observations of purchaser–provider partnership arrangements indicate, would not. Far from trivializing the experience of becoming a professional into a set of procedures to be mastered, leverage at an institutional level may ensure that the experience is taken seriously by those best placed to both manage the learning contexts and to reveal their complexity in dialogue with policy makers.

There may be a lesson to be learnt from Sir Keith Joseph who, on his first day as Minister for Education, is alleged to have asked the assembled civil servants 'Now tell me gentlemen, what is education all about?' A reassessment before further action might lead partners towards a shared vision. A vision which is premised on institutional collaboration in a mission to enhance the learning of pupils, students, teachers, tutors and organizations. Were this to occur metanoia in education may be interpreted not simply as Senge's (1990) notion of a shift of mind but as its earlier meaning of a major turn from the old life to the new.

Note

1   An earlier version of this chapter was presented as a paper to the Universities' Council for the Education of Teachers Annual Conference in 1992.

References

ADELMAN, C. (1989) 'The practical ethic takes priority over methodology', in CARR, W. (Ed) *Quality in Teaching*, Lewes, Falmer Press, pp. 173–82.

COUNCIL FOR THE ACCREDITATION OF TEACHER EDUCATION (CATE) (1992) *The Accreditation of Initial Teacher Training under Circulars 9/92 (Department for Education) and 35/92 (Welsh Office)*, A Note of Guidance from the Council for the Accreditation of Teacher Education.

COLLISON, J. and EDWARDS, A. (in press) 'How teachers support student learning', in REID, I., CONSTABLE, H. and GRIFFITHS, R. (Eds) *Teacher Education Reform: The Research Evidence*, London, Paul Chapman.

DEPARTMENT FOR EDUCATION (DfE) (1992) *Initial Teacher Training (Secondary Phase) Circular 9/92*, London, DfE.

EDWARDS, A. (1991a) 'Teacher education and Local Authorities: Jointly constructing a future for education', *Local Government Policy Making*, **18**, 1, pp. 33–8.

EDWARDS, A. (1991b) 'The place of psychology in initial teacher training', *BPS Promoting Psychology in Initial Teacher Training Conference*, Morecambe.

EDWARDS, A. (1993) 'Curriculum coordination: A lost opportunity for primary schools?', *School Organisation*, **13**, 1, pp. 51–9.

FULLAN, M. (1993) *Change Forces*, London, Falmer Press.

GOODLAD, J. (1990) 'Studying the education of educators: From conception to findings', *Phi Delta Kappan*, **71**, 9, pp. 698–701.

GOODSON, I. (1993) 'Forms of knowledge and teacher education', in GILROY, P. and SMITH, M. (Eds) *International Analyses of Teacher Education*, Abingdon, Carfax, pp. 217–29.

LICHTENSTEIN, G., McLAUGLIN, M. and KNUDSEN, J. (1992) 'Teacher empowerment and professional knowledge', in LIEBERMAN, A. (Ed) *The Changing Contexts of Teaching*, Chicago, University of Chicago Press, pp. 37–58.

McCULLOCH, M. (1993) 'The democratisation of teacher education: New forms of partnership for school based initial teacher education', in GILROY, P. and SMITH, M. (Eds) *International Analyses of Teacher Education*, Abingdon, Carfax, pp. 293–303.

MAYNARD, T. and FURLONG, J. (1993) 'Learning to teach and models of mentoring', in McINTYRE, D., HAGGER, H. and WILKIN, M. (Eds) *Mentoring*, London, Kogan Page, pp. 69–85.

McNAMARA, D. (1993) 'Towards re-establishing the professional authority and expertise of teacher educators and teachers', in GILROY, P. and SMITH, M. (Eds) *International Analyses of Teacher Education*, Abingdon, Carfax, pp. 277–91.

MORTIMORE, P., SAMMONS, P., STOLL, L., LEWIS, D. and ECOB, R. (1988) *School Matters*, Wells, Open Books.

REYNOLDS, D. (Ed) (1985) *Studying School Effectiveness*, London, Falmer Press.

RUSSELL, T. and MUNBY, H. (1991) 'Reframing: The role of experience in developing teachers' professional knowledge', in SCHON, D. (Ed) *The Reflective Turn*, New York, Teachers College Press, pp. 164–87.

SENGE, P. (1990) *The Fifth Discipline*, New York, Doubleday.

TURNER, J. (1993) 'Teacher preparation and educational development', in GILROY, P. and SMITH, M. (Eds) *International Analysis of Teacher Education*, Abingdon, Carfax, pp. 311–21.

WHITTY, G. (1993) 'Education reform and teacher education in England in the 1990's', in GILROY, P. and SMITH, M. (Eds) *International Analyses of Teacher Education*, Abingdon, Carfax, pp. 263–75.

6 Learning about Primary Schools as Workplaces: Aspects of Active Staff Membership during Placements

Colin Biott and *John Spindler*

Introduction

This chapter is about opportunities students in initial training have for learning about whole schools as workplaces. It explores how, and what they might learn about active staff membership during placements. It is an issue which has been neglected in much of what has been written about school-based teacher education. So far, most attention has been concentrated, quite rightly, upon how students learn to teach in classrooms and upon approaches to mentoring and assessment. As a consequence, much has been done to improve relationships between students and individual, experienced teachers who have been designated to support and assess them. Less has been thought about the wider role of a whole-school staff in supporting students. We need to know more about what students learn informally about adult relationships and school life in the everyday events and processes of ordinary working days.

There are some key questions for both host schools and their higher education partners. What are the challenges to a school staff of having a student teacher on placement? What kinds of school cultures provide favourable conditions for students to learn about, and to take on, the wider roles of teachers? In relation to the latter point, Little (1982) has suggested that schools 'can be distinguished from one another by the interactions that are encouraged, discouraged or met with indifference' (p. 331). Those of us who are engaged in teacher education might ask what kinds of interactions and relationships amongst established teachers in placement schools are most educative for students? McCulloch and Lock (1992) have considered the managerial implications of a whole-school approach to training and have suggested that if students are to be active, critical learners, they will learn best in, 'a school ethos in which challenge and change, risk and evaluation are central to the teaching task' (p. 71). In a similar vein, Wooldridge and Yeomans (1994) have advocated a school culture which is socially cohesive and professionally diverse, as one which will educate students, rather than merely acculturate them into local customs and habits. We shall return to this question following our summary of our own studies of how two cohorts of final year BEd students experienced and conceptualized temporary staff membership during their final placements in primary schools. First we shall outline our underlying rationale for focusing upon adult relationships in schools and for seeking to understand more about how students learn to be staff-members.

Why Should Student Teachers Learn about Adult Relationships in Schools?

Active staff membership has become an increasingly important part of a teacher's work. At one time, teachers were able to carry out most, if not all of their work, in the confines of their own classrooms. Some even took pride in claiming that they didn't bother anybody and, in turn, they were unlikely to be bothered by others. Recently, however, and especially since the 1988 Education Reform Act there has been a rapid increase in teachers' obligations to work together. Since active membership is given such emphasis, it is important that students have opportunities to experience it and to learn about it.

There are at least two dimensions of active membership. First, it involves a sense of belonging; of participating in, and accepting, the norms, symbols and rituals associated with a staff group. Second, it involves contributing. Contribution can be thought of in terms of the skills and knowledge that an individual can offer to a group. However, it also refers to ways in which individuals, through daily and complex interactions, shape the group's norms, symbols and rituals. Active membership involves adapting to the ways of a group, but it also requires that individuals negotiate their own roles and participate in ways which preserve their sense of self. It means that beliefs and values are open to debate and change, rather than being taken for granted and fixed. In this sense full, active membership would be particularly challenging for student teachers. It is unrealistic to expect all students to achieve a complete sense of membership, but, as our data from students show, some feelings of belonging and contributing are possible. As a starting point we suggest that students should at least learn about how established teachers enact their membership roles.

Learning about active staff-membership of primary schools is likely to require some knowledge of staff relationships, and a number of recent studies have stressed its importance. Nias (1989), for instance, has shown, from extensive interviews with primary teachers, that even in schools where teachers operate with the maximum of autonomy and minimum of interaction, their own classroom teaching is affected by what other adults do and say in the school. She has argued that:

> many of the frustrations which primary teachers suffer arise from the perpetuation of the false expectation that the job of teaching involves a relationship with children alone. They are not generally prepared by their training or by the conventional wisdom of the profession for the fact that participation in the life of the school is inseparable from teaching itself. (Nias, 1989, pp. 112–13)

There are, at least, three interrelated reasons why membership of a school staff may be important to teachers, both for themselves and for the sake of the school. First, staff membership may bring a sense of belonging, and the kinds of mutual support and encouragement which help to share and reduce the stresses and strains of the job. Second, there is a need to be prepared for the increasing demands of formal teamwork to complete tasks, produce various policies and write an annual School Development Plan. Third, by working and learning together informally members create and develop a collective vision which helps to shape what a school becomes.

Taking the first of these reasons, it is important both for easing stresses of the job and for the retention of new recruits to the profession, that newly qualified teachers are made to feel that they belong and can contribute from the outset of their careers. Acker (1991), for example, found evidence that teachers are getting together to interpret the demands of government policies, to help each other to cope creatively and to help each other find sensible ways to do what is expected of them. This is worthy of increasing attention in view of concerns about the emotional as well as technical demands of constant external change. An emotional dimension is an intrinsic and critical part of practical teaching.

In his research with newly qualified teachers, Tickle (1991) has provided recent evidence of the significance of the emotions of learning to teach:

> Excitement and elation as well as anxiety and anger, satisfaction and success as well as fear of failure, were aroused by the experiences of classroom events, staffroom relationships, and contacts with parents or LEA person-nel. Feelings fluctuated erratically; contrasting ones sometimes co-existed; at times they were controllable and controlled; at other times they seemed unstable and explosive. Making sense of this element of the learning equa-tion was at least as important for each teacher as understanding how best to 'teach' . . . the emotional aspects of their learning had a direct relation-ship to technical and clinical competences. (Tickle, 1991, p. 322)

From his analysis of the reflections of beginning teachers, Tickle (1991) has claimed that the understanding of the self and the management of emotions is an essential aspect of teaching competence and because of this it should be an explicit part of initial training. He suggests that this would help to alleviate the surprise experienced by new teachers when they realize how important it is to learn how to manage their own emotions in teaching. He goes on to suggest that 'the equation of the establishment of competence with suffering would at least have been a shared professional problem' (p. 328).

Yeomans (1992) has also advocated that learning about the self, and about adult relationships and staff membership should be an explicit and continuous part of initial training. He says that students need time for reflection and analysis with fellow students so that they may develop analytical frameworks to make sense of the significance of the self and their relationships with others and how this has shaped their experiences and interpretations of the norms, symbols and rituals which form the schools cultures they have encountered.

Our second reason for emphasizing knowledge of schools as workplaces and for understanding active staff membership is because students will be expected to meet future obligations to participate in formal activities and tasks as part of a staff team. For example, the National Curriculum Council's document on initial teacher edu-cation (NCC, 1991) suggests that students should have opportunities to 'observe and take part in school-based INSET which involves whole-school or team curriculum planning and review related to the National Curriculum'. It should not be assumed, however, that participating in formal planning and policy-making is straightforward, even for established teachers. Debates have shifted recently from how the isolated, individualistic nature of teaching has hampered teamwork, towards disquiet about the negative effects of enforced or imposed arrangements for working together (Biott, 1992). In some circumstances, it may give rise to what Hargreaves (1991) has aptly called 'contrived collegiality'; a form of working relationships which are more controlling than enabling. Whilst students need to be prepared to play a part in formal teamwork, they also need to be able to interpret circumstances critically and not come to expect that teamwork invariably means little more than going through the motions to fulfil a sense of duty.

The third reason for advocating that we make active staff membership one of our concerns in initial teacher education is to emphasize, the less obvious, but more important part which teachers play in whole-school development through working and learning informally with their colleagues. Processes of whole-school development are more than just step by step target setting, action planning and policy-making. It is informal patterns of staff interaction which bring policies into action, test them, modify them and infuse them with meaning. Nias *et al.* (1992) have shown how it is the processes of creating 'likemindedness' and not achievement which is the key to building a whole school, and Staessens and Vandenberghe (1994) have pointed to how making shared meanings and understandings or creating 'vision' is a core component in a school culture. Nias *et al.* point to ways that individuals come to internalize key beliefs by learning 'what' and learning 'how' from each other using the events and structures of ordinary, working days. Similarly, Staessens and Vandenberghe refer to the degree of consensus which grows amongst members about the value of daily activities, decisions and goals. They emphasize 'cathetic goals' which embody a school's primary values and give meaning to teachers' work, rather than 'cognitive goals' which are formally drawn up and which tend to function as control mechanisms.

For these reasons then, we have set out to seek more understanding of what and how student teachers might learn about influential processes which are embedded and integrated into daily life of teachers in their placement schools. We anticipate that opportunities for this kind of learning will vary depending upon the nature of the schools in which the students are placed, and we shall return to this point. To begin with we wanted to know how students experienced temporary staff membership.

The Projects

Two investigations were carried out, in 1992 and 1994, as an integral part of an enquiry-based course unit on staff relationships in the final year of the primary BEd degree. Summary reports of their responses to questionnaires were given to the students to inform their group discussions about the concept of active membership. This activity was followed by seminars on staff relationships and whole-school development, and on the effects of educational reform on how staff work and learn together. We were not trying to produce predictive, generalizable knowledge but to enhance students' learning through systematic enquiry in which they were centrally involved.

As a step towards understanding what students had learned about working in whole schools, we set out to explore how they had experienced and conceptualized staff membership during placements. In November 1992 a questionnaire was completed by eighty-seven students one week after they had finished their final placement of six weeks in primary schools. The questionnaire mainly requested open responses, and the students were invited to write about the things that made them feel, or not feel, like staff members, and what they had observed which they thought had contributed negatively or positively to staff membership amongst permanent teachers in the school. Other sections covered the extent to which they thought that they had been helpful to other teachers and asked for descriptions of those teachers (without naming them) that they had admired and learned from.

In 1994 a similar approach was used to explore ninety-three students' experiences of membership in their final year. This time we included questions about the degree of explicitness or implicitness of values, how discernible they were both from individual teachers and the staff as a whole, and whether the students had expressed their own values and beliefs in different contexts in the school.

A Sense of Belonging and Contributing

The majority (72 per cent in 1992 and 73 per cent in 1994) reported that they had felt like staff members most or all of the time. Only five of the 1992 students and one 1994 student had not felt like staff members at all during their six weeks of school placement in their final year.

When asked to list factors which had, or had not, made them feel like staff members, most students indicated both negative and positive experiences. Students referred mainly to their general sense of inclusion or exclusion and the extent to which they were able to contribute and take on a wider role in the school.

Different students had felt varying degrees of exclusion and exclusion in general staffroom activity, in opportunities for social contact with staff groups out of school, in informal discussions with a range of teachers and in various events and activities to which they felt they might have contributed. Many students reported being welcomed into staffrooms, making comments such as 'they knew how I liked my coffee' and 'by the end of my block the teachers acted as though I was one of them, and didn't keep any staffroom talk from me'. Some also mentioned being invited to social events outside school, such as going to the pub on a Friday lunchtime, and joining in the staff nights out.

Whenever students were given encouragement or support by teachers other than their classteachers this also increased their feelings of belonging in the school. They appreciated approachable people with whom they could discuss things and they also said they appreciated informal visits from teachers and heads who just 'popped in' to see how they were getting on. In contrast, some students had felt excluded from, or unwelcome in staffrooms throughout the placement. Some continued to go there but remained uncomfortable because of social awkwardness over such things as coffee arrangements or because conversations stopped or changed when they entered the room. Some had used the staff room very little or not at all. One student wrote: 'I wasn't taken to the staffroom and so I never had the opportunity to go there. This was because my teacher never went to the staffroom herself.'

Students were sensitive to atmosphere and appreciative of friendliness. 'Basic manners and politeness can make a big difference' and 'it is a great advantage if the teachers actually like each other'. Whilst some students had noted negative aspects of general staffroom atmosphere, they were also often aware of its causes, 'There were obvious conflicts in the staffroom. Certain staff never entered the staffroom and staff talked about each other. There was bad cohesion of staff, due to pressures of assessment.' In some cases, the students had felt that their 'student status' had been constantly emphasized and that this had created a barrier to their sense of belonging — 'other staff members audibly referring to me as "the student" ', 'head introducing us to the parents and the children as students', 'constant talk of when you leave', 'the class being referred to in assembly as the permanent teacher's class, and me sitting there with them'. Their own sense of 'low status' was sometimes reinforced by tutors' visits and by the actions of other adults in the school — 'the school secretary refused to pass on any messages to me or ask me for any information which concerned my class'. One student referred simply to 'bad mannered staff who made no effort to communicate — [it was as though they thought] — she's not important, she'll be gone in a couple of weeks, we'll just ignore her'.

In contrast, many others had been treated as colleagues and called by their proper names, rather than 'the student', both in casual conversations and on more formal occasions. Whilst some students had felt undermined, overridden and patronized, others reported having been respected, trusted, confided in and made to feel equal with other adults in the school. They mentioned numerous examples:

- hearing other teachers' problems;
- small talk with other teachers in corridors;
- being on good terms with office staff and domestic staff;
- auxiliary staff asked me for instructions;
- other teachers asked my opinions about which books to buy;
- the headteacher asked for my comments on a new child before he had consultation with the parents;
- they treated me like a teacher, asked my advice and permission. We also discussed weekly plans; and
- discussed ideas, good points, problems etc. with several teachers not just my class teacher and they would ask my opinions as a teacher.

As well as describing their own feelings the students were asked to list what they had observed that they thought had contributed positively or negatively to existing features of staff membership in their placement schools. Three themes emerged from their observations: social relationships between teachers; teachers' informal working relationships; and the ways in which headteachers related to the school staff.

It was apparent from this list that students were observing some of the difficulties as well as some of supportive aspects of relationships at work. Sometimes they described incidents which conveyed graphically the meaning they were making of everyday occurrences and illustrating awareness of interpersonal and micropolitical dimensions of membership:

- one teacher kept picking on children from another class for minor matters, knowing it's deliberately against the policy of that class teacher; and
- there was some fighting about who should put the kettle on. It went on for six weeks.

Some descriptions caught the tensions of staff relationships:

> During the time of the 'block' the school was rehearsing for a Christmas play. The rehearsals depended on staff availability and hall availability. As a result, very short or no notice was given about the rehearsals, and schedules had to be changed. A comment was made by a permanent member of staff whose class was involved, but she was personally not, that the first they knew of the rehearsals was when a child was knocking on the door to inform them that they were waiting for her class in the hall.

Overall, students' experiences were mixed. Some were in schools in which all of the staff used the staffroom regularly, and others were in schools where some staff avoided contact with each other as far as possible. Some referred to caring relationships between teachers, rather like what Nias *et al.* (1992) have called 'being watchful of each other', whilst others heard constant gossiping and witnessed persistent disputes about staffroom 'house keeping'.

Students had observed staff working together with various degrees of formality and informality: having discussions in places like corridors, corners of the staffroom or each other's classrooms; talking about plans, expenditure, timetables, resources and topics; having small semi-formal meetings to arrange teaching links and working together on special events, clubs and assemblies. Some negative observations included some teachers' possessiveness over resources, some keeping ideas to themselves and not sharing, competitiveness over display, and tensions arising from different views about standards of discipline in the school.

There were also references to both positive and negative influences of headteachers upon staff membership. Dominance, lack of interest in staff and unwillingness to spend time in classrooms were contrasted with enthusiasm, intelligence and encouragement. For example, one headteacher was seen as a good staff member himself because of the ways in which he mixed with the staff, joined in informal conversations and was aware of what was going on in the school. This was like the principals in Staessens and Vandenberghe (1994) high-vision schools who were seen to use 'dailyness' as a strategy to increase the perception of vision' (p. 199), and Manassee's (1986) observation that 'leadership involves the infusion of routine activities with meaning and vision'.

Being Responsible and Having a Wider Role

Students seemed to want to play a full, active role in whole-school activities. This even included having a share of chores such as 'doing yard duty' and meeting implicit obligations such as 'helping with school parties and fund raising'. A number mentioned being involved in special events and daily routines like assemblies, as well as being asked to deal with incidents like arguments between children or looking after sick children. Some had sole charge of their own class and some had covered for other teachers by taking responsibility for different classes in the school; they had filled in record books, marked registers, sat with classes in assemblies, been included in staff photographs and had access to pooled resources.

Some students, however, were denied opportunities for experiencing general responsibilities. They recalled things such as:

- having to mark the register in pencil or not at all;
- not hearing children read because the teacher wanted to continue her own system which was quite complicated; and
- being constantly monitored by the head or classteacher and never being allowed to have the class to myself.

Some incidents made them feel merely temporary and unimportant:

- the class teacher always took the children out at the end of the day to meet their parents;
- being told to do my own thing for a topic and not follow the planned topics of the school;
- not being informed about children in my class being in trouble; and
- not being given information about what was happening in the school which was given to other teachers.

Another factor frequently mentioned was the extent of the students' involvement with parents. Whenever students referred to meeting parents they affirmed its positive effect on their professional identity:

- I was introduced at the parents' evening as a teacher and not as a student;
- parents asked me about their children and were very friendly;
- parents addressed letters to me as the classteacher; and
- I liked being involved in the parents evening in the classroom when parents came to see the teacher and I was asked for my opinion.

However, during the same period, some students had felt excluded from formal parents' meetings.

There were a number of ways in which students felt they had contributed to the schools. Some students mentioned specific new ideas, materials and worksheets they had brought to the schools and left behind. Some helped with displays and demonstrated their approaches to classroom organization. Some referred to being able to contribute special skills, such as playing the piano, helping with computers and being the only art specialist. One confessed to volunteering for 'anything and everything' to get some 'brownie points'. Others reacted differently through lack of confidence or shyness. Some reported purposely holding back rather than appearing too knowledgeable or overconfident, and some isolated themselves to cope with their own heavy workload and/or to concentrate on getting a high grade in their formal assessment.

Clearly, students orientations to, and the nature of, their placement contexts had varied. This was not apparent until after the placement was completed. Prior to placements they had been engrossed in preparations for class teaching, collecting materials and planning schemes of work. It was only after their stints of practice were over that they appreciated the luck of the draw in terms of the whole school, rather than the classroom, in which they were placed . . . As well as their sense of belonging and contributing being enhanced or limited by their relationships with staff, it was also affected by physical arrangements and circumstances, such as 'teaching in a mobile which isolated me from the main school', the size of schools, school rotas which prevented contact with subject coordinators, staff absences, and some teachers simply being too pressured and too busy to talk.

Participation in Formal Teamwork

In the same way that doing chores and duties and sharing common suffering with established teachers had enhanced their sense of belonging and contributing, time spent on formal and semi-formal meetings was also seen positively by most students. Some students had been involved in small semi-formal meetings such as planning sessions with year-group teachers, and in discussions about individual children with a headteacher, a special-educational-needs support teacher and a classteacher. These kinds of opportunities made them feel better during their placements and they saw them as providing useful preparation for the future.

Even so, few students had been able to take part in formal teamwork. It was a source of regret for some students that they had felt excluded from formal staff meetings. Overall, 76 per cent of the 1992 students had not been invited to attend any staff meetings at all, and 87 per cent of these students had been aware of meetings taking place during their time in school. It was especially difficult when they felt barred from the staffroom during meetings 'especially when I had to creep in during one to collect my coat'. Those who had attended staff meetings said that it gave them a strong sense of membership, especially if they were asked to comment or give opinions. This tended to reduce the discomfiting aspects of student status by confirming trust and colleagueship. Of the meetings attended, two-thirds were about curriculum policies, planning and review and the other third were about forthcoming events such as carol services, Christmas productions, parents' evenings, fund raising and school outings.

Beliefs and Values

The 1994 cohort of ninety-three students was asked specifically whether the beliefs and values of the whole staff of their placement schools were clear or unclear to them and, if clear, whether they were consensual or diverse. Seventy-nine students had thought that they were clear, nine had found them unclear and five did not respond to the question. Those who were uncertain said they had not heard much talk about beliefs and values. Some thought that talk did go on in staff meetings to which they were not invited. In one school there had been a lot of worrying about inspection and policies were being written, but there was little talk about their content whilst the student was there.

Our approach to interpreting these data has been cautious, tentative and exploratory, partly because of concern about the data itself, and partly because of difficulties of disentangling relationships between consensus and diversity, especially in cases where they were thought to coexist. Our main purpose was to explore the meaning of this distinction with the students themselves. We have said, earlier, that Wooldridge and Yeomans have suggested that a social cohesiveness and professionally diverse staff would offer a favourable context for student learning, and Nias *et al.* have shown how, in a unified, 'whole-school', active staff membership involves willingness to confront professional differences as well as to support colleagues. For this reason we wanted to avoid crude polarizations in the analysis. In all, forty-three of the ninety-three students had categorized their placement schools as both socially cohesive and professionally diverse. Broadly this seemed to have been interpreted to mean, that there was some sharing of ideas through teamwork and that individuals could voice their own varied opinions and to apply things in their own ways.

One clue to understanding how consensus and diversity of beliefs and values might coexist was revealed in the number of students who had found consensus and commonality about moral values, particularly about ways to treat children, and, at the same, had also witnessed some diversity over teaching styles. In this sense the 1994 students' perceptions of common beliefs and values in action closely resembled the 1992 students' descriptions of qualities they had admired in teachers they had observed. There was an emphasis upon how 'admirable' teachers related well to children and how they also got on well with other adults in the school. Even references to admired teachers' classroom abilities were framed in terms of caring about and motivating children and about creating good environments for them, rather than technical skills, such as questioning or explaining, which were listed on the schedules against which the students themselves were being partly assessed. Respect for children, placing their interests first and working on the development of their social skills and self-discipline were a source of shared views and a focus for consistent action in many schools. 'In a Church of England Aided First School there was great commitment to teaching/showing children how to live a socially accept-able life. Consideration to others was actively encouraged.' The distinctions that students made tended to be between innovative and progressive as opposed to traditional teachers. Overall, they seemed to see progressive or innovative teachers as those who encouraged children to take responsibility for their own work.

Whilst neither cohort of students mentioned any specific aspects of teaching or learning curriculum subjects, some of the 1994 group did refer generally to 'proper' or 'correct implementation of the National Curriculum' both as a source of dispute and debate between staff in some schools and as an unifying factor in others. Headteachers were often seen as key figures in statements about consensus and diversity, either because they articulated and demonstrated what was common, because they were a focus for what the rest of the staff resented or because they embodied a source of division between factions 'a lot of internal politics based on school management v. the teaching staff'. As one student said 'The headteacher and my classteacher had the same values and beliefs which they were trying to get the rest of the staff to follow — unsuccessfully.'

Some students referred to consensus within, and diversity between, different groupings and different parts of schools: between infant and junior teachers; be-tween key stage one and key stage two teachers and between different year-group teachers. Others mentioned older and younger staff having different beliefs and values. 'The school was debating the merits and otherwise of streaming and mixed-ability grouping. There were diverse views from key stage one and key stage two teachers and between long-experienced and newly qualified teachers.'

Students' responses indicated that there were differences in how diversity was handled in the placement schools. In some cases the students had thought that staff took entrenched positions and in others it seemed that differences were aired in open debate and discussion — 'all the staff had quite strong beliefs and values — they listened to each other, but still went their own way'. Sometimes, it seemed that one teacher might be seen as the 'odd one out' and this was talked about when she

	A lot	To some extent	Not at all
(a) I talked about my beliefs and values with my class teacher	29	60	4
(b) I talked about my beliefs and values with other individual teachers	6	70	17
(c) I talked about my beliefs and values informally with small groups of teachers	3	51	38
(d) I expressed my own beliefs and values in formal staff meetings	1	11	77
(e) Generally I felt comfortable about expressing my beliefs and values	13	67	11

Figure 6.1: The extent to which, and to whom, students expressed beliefs and values

was not present 'one teacher had an alternative teaching style to the others and this was occasionally discussed by certain staff'. Some students who referred to diversity in their schools, did not make it clear whether it was apparent to them through open discussion, through hearing separate conversations or through entrenched position taking.

One clue to disentangling the extent to which the school context supported openness was whether the students themselves had felt able to express their own beliefs and values, whilst they were in the schools. Figure 6.1 shows the numbers of students who said that they had talked about their beliefs and values to their classteacher, to other teachers, either as individuals or groups, and in formal meetings. It also shows the extent to which students felt generally comfortable about expressing their own beliefs and values during the placements.

Of the twenty-nine students who had talked a lot about their own beliefs and values to their classteachers, twenty had been in schools which they categorized as socially cohesive and professionally diverse. More students had expressed their beliefs and values when talking with individuals than they had to groups, with even fewer expressing them in formal meetings. This relates partly to them having less opportunities to be involved in group discussion than informal talk with their classteacher and other individuals.

Implications

Overall, most of the students had been able to experience active membership during their placement; most felt a sense of belonging and contributing, and most had observed a range of positive and negative aspects of adult relationships. Opportunities to talk about beliefs and values had been variable and were more likely to have arisen in informal rather than in formal contexts. Students tended to have expressed their own beliefs and values to individuals, particularly their own classteachers. All students were able to respond to questions about beliefs and values in their placement schools. It seems that, whatever the circumstances in the schools, students had interpreted aspects of adult relationships and staff membership. However, as much of this learning is *ad hoc* and from unanticipated sources, and as much of it is spasmodic, ambiguous and sometimes contradictory, it is important for teachers and tutors to consider how they can support the students as they learn to be active members of primary schools. Ambiguities and contradictions are endemic in school life, and we are not suggesting that tensions and difficulties of staff relationships should be hidden from students. It is, after all, important that students learn about schools as workplaces as they really are. Placements offer students opportunities to see schools with an insider's eye and to appreciate how ordinary yet complex aspects of school cultures influence both teachers' and children's learning. There is a need for teacher educators in schools and higher education to work out ways for students to manage their participation in daily school life in ways which enhance their learning opportunities.

We will conclude this chapter by drawing out some implications for host schools, for higher education tutors and for partnerships of emphasizing active staff membership during placements. We shall also highlight some areas for further research and development.

There are at least three implications for host schools. First, it would be useful for all involved in supporting students, and especially those in host schools, to consider what they think about the status and role of students in relation to that of qualified teachers. It seems to us, from what students have said, that it is educative and practically helpful if they have opportunities to take on the full role of teacher. It enhances their sense of belonging and self-esteem, it challenges them to contribute to school life by, for instance, helping with school plays, being included in conversations about planning and talking with parents. The dilemmas for the placements schools is to offer opportunities for full participation without overburdening or exploiting students, and to balance the demands of classroom teaching with those arising from wider aspects of a teacher's role. Whilst schools may seek to protect students from what they see as unnecessary burdens, students may view such protection as an indicator of their lack of competence, inability to contribute and general low status in the school. Placement schools will need to give opportunities for wider responsibilities which offer challenges that are practicable, legitimate and fit into patterns of students' overall workload.

Second, having a student in school involves the whole staff. It would not be helpful for the mentor or classteacher to be seen as the only person with responsibility for a student's professional training. Some of the students in our study admired, and learned from teachers other than their designated classteacher. Many appreciated opportunities to talk with other teachers and groups about their beliefs and values, they liked being included in informal discussions and social activities, and they wanted to contribute to the school as a whole in areas where they felt they had some expertise. Opportunities seem to depend mainly upon students being able to negotiate a place within the existing informal patterns of interaction between teachers. Attempts to make it a formal requirement for every student in every school, might be to deny what this form of active membership really means in practice.

Third, part of learning to participate constructively in a school culture involves being able to interpret and work within its norms, symbols and rituals. This requires students to reflect critically on their experiences of working with other adults in schools. If schools are to encourage such reflection, it is likely that they will need to be open to discussion of aspects of staff membership as experienced by students and teachers in host schools. It will be unrealistic to assume that students' needs can be met by what senior staff tell them in briefings, or be covered by documents about school arrangements and organization. Analysis and discussion of adult relationships within a school has the potential to lead to unhelpful tensions and conflict. Schools may need to find ways in which aspects of membership can be discussed with students, without damaging relationships or disrupting the running of schools.

Implications for higher education arise from the need to prepare students for their placements, to help them to find ways of negotiating their roles in schools and to help them make sense of their learning when placements are completed. There are two main ways in which support might be given. First, through assisting the students to develop conceptual frameworks that will enable them to analyse their experiences of working with adults in schools in terms of relationships between the self, groups and cultures. Tutors may need to pay more attention to the ways in which students experience staff membership during their placements. More knowledge of temporary membership is likely to be needed.

Second, rather than acting as advocates for students within their placement schools, tutors might help students to negotiate for themselves. They might spend some time helping each student to recognize the significance of daily interactions with other adults in the school, assisting them to act in ways which enhance their sense of belonging and maximize their opportunities for contributing. Further research is needed to illuminate how this might be achieved.

Faced with a need to respond rapidly to changes in requirements for school-based teacher education and to formalize partnership arrangements between schools and higher education, it may be tempting to think in terms of defined and separate responsibilities enshrined in carefully worded contracts. If students are to learn about schools as workplaces through everyday events and interactions, the support given by the whole school staff and higher education tutors will need to be flexible and tailored to the many and varied contexts in which students are placed. Rather than merely build elaborate systems we need partnerships which embrace discretionary choice, experimentation and shared enquiry into what happens. It is people, not systems, who make learning partnerships. When it comes to learning about schools as workplaces and about active membership, it is the judgments of those doing the work that should determine how the partnerships grow.

Action research offers one fruitful way for groups of local participants to investigate how students make meaning of their experiences in particular placement schools and for teachers and tutors to develop approaches to supporting them. In more general terms, we need more research projects to help us learn cumulatively about the characteristics of school cultures which provide favourable contexts for students to learn about active membership. McCulloch and Lock's (1992) citing of 'challenge and change, risk and evaluation' and Wooldridge and Yeomans' (1994) reference to 'social cohesion and professional diversity' need to be tested through further systematic enquiry. Other conceptual frameworks which do not refer specifically to student teachers, but which could be helpful, include McLaughlin and Yee's (1988) characteristics of schools that make them educative contexts in which teachers can develop individualized careers, Nias *et al.*'s (1992) factors and processes which are important in the development of whole schools and Straessens and Vandenberghe's (1994) high, as compared to low-vision schools. The latter is particularly promising because of its reference to the strength of its socially constructed consensus about goals; 'communication, shared experiences, conflicts, practical planning, ongoing evaluations and other activities are part of a process that supports teachers and principals in their daily efforts to construct a vision' (p. 198). In such schools it seems more likely the students will become aware of processes of active membership.

Whatever the frameworks that provide the starting points, one challenge is to learn how students reconstruct the interactions and processes of active membership that create both common ground and diversity amongst teachers in a placement school. The second challenge is to identify the features of the schools themselves which enable this to be done most effectively in the short time available to students.

References

ACKER, S. (1991) 'Teacher relationships and educational reform in England and Wales', *The Curriculum Journal*, **2**, 3, pp. 301–16.

BIOTT, C. (1992) 'Imposed support for teachers learning: Implementation or development partnerships', in BIOTT, C. and NIAS, J. (Eds) *Working and Learning Together for Change*, Buckingham, Open University Press.

HARGREAVES, A. (1991) 'Curriculum reform and the teacher', *The Curriculum Journal*, **2**, 3, pp. 249–58.

LITTLE, J.W. (1982) 'Norms of collegiality and experimentation: Workplace conditions for school success', *American Educational Research Journal*, **19**, 3, pp. 325–40.

MANASSEE, A.C. (1986) 'Vision and leadership', *Peabody Journal of Education*, **63**, 1, pp. 150–73.

McCULLOCH, M. and LOCK, N. (1992) 'Student teachers' School experience: The managerial implications for schools', *Cambridge Journal of Education*, **22**, 1, pp. 69–78.

McLAUGHLIN, M.W. and YEE, S.M. (1988) 'School as a place to have a career', in LIEBERMAN, A. (Ed) *Building a Professional Culture in Schools*, New York, Teachers' College Press.

NCC (1991) *The National Curriculum and the Initial Training of Student, Articled and Licensed Teachers*, York, National Curriculum Council.

NIAS, J. (1989) *Primary Teachers Talking: A Study of Teaching at Work*, London, Routledge.

NIAS, J., SOUTHWORTH, G. and CAMPBELL, P. (1992) *Whole School Curriculum Development in the Primary School*, London, Falmer Press.

STAESSENS, K. and VANDENBERGHE, R. (1994) 'Vision as a core component in school culture', *Journal of Curriculum Studies*, **26**, 2, pp. 187–200.

TICKLE, L. (1991) 'New Teachers and the emotions of learning teaching', *Cambridge Journal of Education*, **21**, 3, pp. 277–85.

WOOLDRIDGE, I. and YEOMANS, R. (1994) 'Induction, acculturation and education in school-based initial teacher education', in YEOMANS, R. and SAMPSON, J. (Eds) *Mentorship in the Primary School*, Falmer Press.

YEOMANS, R. (1992) 'Preparing for school staff membership: Students in primary teacher education', in BIOTT, C. and NIAS, J. (Eds) *Working and Learning together for Change*, Buckingham Open University Press.

7   Learning to Teach: The Development of Pedagogical Reasoning

Neville Bennett

Introduction

The nature and quality of teacher education is the subject of much concern in many countries around the world. Confidence has been lost, it would appear, in the ability of current courses to provide teachers with the appropriate knowledge and skills for high-quality teaching. In Britain, for example, Her Majesty's Inspectorate has constantly criticized teacher training institutions for failing to provide adequate study of subject knowledge, and for curriculum courses which fail to cover such crucial professional skills as planning, assessment, and differentiation. Teachers with inadequate levels of knowledge, they argue, do not understand the progressive development of pupils' knowledge, skills and attitudes, and lack the detailed and rigorous conceptual framework needed to examine the purposes, methods and uses of assessment. In surveys of beginning teachers they claim that these same weaknesses persist.

Similar concerns have been expressed in the United States. Teacher-education programmes have been characterized as brief, technologically impoverished, and lacking in conceptual clarity and programmatic consistency. Goodlad (1991), for example, stated that 'The research we conducted points rather painfully to incoherent programmes not tied to a mission, with no basic principles of curriculum guiding them, no organising themes or elements . . . Teacher education . . . requires reconstruction.'

It would thus seem that all is not well with teacher education. But how true is this characterization? What independent research evidence is available on the nature and acquisition of teaching skills and competences, or on what is taught and learned in teacher-education courses? Sadly, very little. There is yet inadequate understanding of the domains of knowledge on which student teachers should draw, or of the relationships between knowledge bases and teaching performances. Significant insights have been provided in case studies of secondary student teachers by Shulman and his colleagues at Stanford, and at the National Centre for Research on Teacher Learning at Michigan State, but their generalizability to the training of elementary school teachers outside of the United States is at best unclear. What was needed, we felt, was a careful examination of the extent to which, and how, knowledge bases for teaching develop through training, and the relationship of these knowledge bases to student-teaching performances and competences. Our approach combined what Zeichner (1992), has called the 'academic' and 'social efficiency'

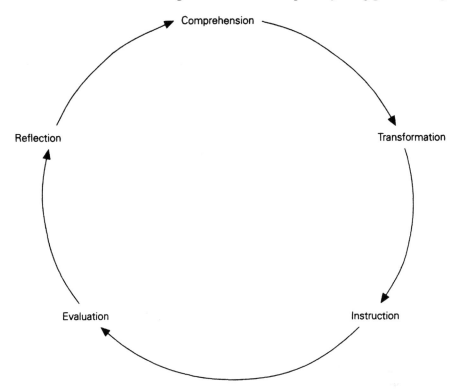

Figure 7.1: A model of pedagogical reasoning

research traditions. This allowed us to integrate models based on our own research on teaching–learning processes in elementary classrooms, with those developed for teacher education, notably Shulman's ideas on pedagogical reasoning and action. The resultant model is shown in Figure 7.1.

The model presents as a cycle of planning, in which the content to be taught is conceptualized in relation to intentions and purposes:

- task design, where content is transformed into representations appropriate to the diversity of learners in the class;
- instruction, where decisions are made concerning modes of presentation and classroom organization;
- evaluation, in which pupils work is assessed, both formatively and summatively; and
- reflection, where the teacher utilizes pupil assessments and reflections on his or her own performance to inform the next round of planning.

This model thus locates reflection within a process of conceptualization and classroom action.

In order to answer the questions posed we followed four cohorts of students training to be elementary teachers through their one-year postgraduate training course. They were recruited into four semi-specialisms, maths, science, music and early years, and were expected to have academic qualifications in the subject, at degree, or subsidiary degree, level (although this was not always, or indeed generally, the case). These four courses were common except that additional time was devoted to the curriculum study of their specialist subject.

On entry to the programme each student was assessed on their knowledge of the core curriculum subjects of the British National Curriculum i.e., English, maths and science, together with music, to level six — that level which an able 11-year-old (or an average 14-year-old) should be capable of achieving. In addition their attitudes and beliefs about teaching and wider educational issues were ascertained. These assessments were repeated at the end of the course.

In order to investigate course processes the tutors were interviewed about aims and content, and about the supervision of teaching practices. The students agreed to keep diaries of their reactions to every lecture attended, and a separate diary relating to their experiences in, and reflections on, their school-based work. Finally, in order to ascertain the relationships between knowledge-for-teaching and teaching performance, a sample of students were observed, audio-recorded and interviewed teaching their specialist, and non-specialist subjects.

Knowledge for Teaching

The first questions we asked of these data were 'did these graduates have the knowledge of maths, science and English that they would be obliged to teach when they qualified?', and 'to what extent did their knowledge change as a consequence of the course?'

In science, their responses indicated that many had limited substantive and syntactic knowledge, and that many of their understandings of fundamental science concepts differed from consensus views. Indeed many of their misconceptions were similar to those found in primary-school children. For example, only 30 per cent were able to correctly wire up a circuit containing a switch, a battery and a lamp, and only a quarter appeared to know the principles of photosynthesis. Little improvement occurred as a consequence of the course, which is not perhaps surprising given that postgraduate courses are designed, on government criteria, to stress curriculum and pedagogy. It is interesting to note however that where specific improvements did occur they were related to practical work carried out on the course, e.g., on electric circuits and investigations.

The pattern in maths was similar. Most students showed only a basic understanding of the topics they would have to teach in primary school. Less than one in seven could answer questions on tesselation, or on relationships between sets of shapes. Here too there was little improvement in substantive knowledge through the course, although there was some positive changes in pedagogical applications. In English, their responses did not suggest extensive knowledge about language, particularly knowledge about grammatical forms and rules. Only 30 per cent were able to identify adverbs in a sentence, and 23 per cent pronouns, although they were somewhat stronger in sections dealing with cultural variation and literary devices. The course appeared to have a more marked impact in this area. More was known about functional aspects such as the use of language in differing contexts, and about the literary uses of language. However there was little improvement in knowledge of the structure of language, especially grammar. Overall, therefore, the students' knowledge of subjects was somewhat insecure, and their understandings of the structure, and ways of knowing the disciplines, even that which they had recently graduated in, was poor. Improvements in knowledge were slight and usually occurred in relation to pedagogical or practical aspects of the course.

Changes in attitudes to subjects were more visible. In their attitude to the nature of science there was a tendency to see it less as a fixed and rigid set of facts and laws, and more as tentative inquiry influenced by social and personal attitudes. This was aligned to a changing perception of science teaching as being more a problem-solving approach based on constructivist principles. In maths there was a shift toward less absolutist, and more open, flexible views, and a greater feeling of liking and confidence about the subject. In English, they left the course thinking more of language as a process — a learning tool rather than a set of skills to be acquired — and a more holistic view of literacy learning.

Changes in beliefs and attitudes to teaching and wider educational issues were slight. They were well formed on entry but were not, as American studies so often suggest, antithetic to the aims of the course. The changes that did occur were in relation to the realities and constraints of classroom life, reflecting a move from idealism to pragmatism, and a greater understanding of how beliefs relate to practice.

The manner in which changes in knowledge, skills and beliefs related to aspects of the course were evident through the analysis of student diaries, interviews and observations of their teaching. Their reflections, and evaluations, of their curriculum courses provided extensive evidence of perceived learning about curriculum and pedagogy. Here they developed interpretations of classroom life based on constructivist principles, and their study of such issues as teaching skills, children's responses, grouping strategies and task design gave them a vocabulary to describe and explain classroom action, and provided a vision of the pedagogically possible.

Student reflections and evaluations of their teaching practices supported the increasing body of evidence on the overriding influence of the cooperating class teacher. Where the teacher was helpful and generally supportive the student gained in confidence and enjoyment; where help and support were lacking it led to feelings of resentment and abandonment. The majority of the teachers in this study were supportive, but it was apparent that they had no agreed common mission, and no appropriate training for their role. This was equally true of the university supervisors, whose interest and expertise varied widely, as did their conception of their role in the absence of an institutionally agreed set of purposes.

In the absence of an institutionally agreed set of criteria relating to teaching competences, neither teacher nor supervisor could satisfactorily consider the development of students over successive teaching practices, and students themselves had no coherent or consistent basis for self-reflection.

Knowledge and Teaching Performance

We had hypothesized, on the basis of previous case-study research, that there would be a relationship between subject knowledge and teaching performance. And within the limits of our sample this was shown to be the case. Extensive cycles of data collection in line with the model of teaching outlined earlier i.e., i) pre-lesson interviews, ii) observation and audio-recordings of students teaching their specialist

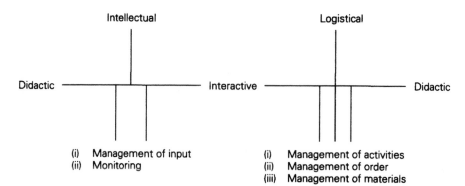

Figure 7.2: Categorization of student–teacher talk

and non-specialist subjects, and iii) post-lesson evaluations and reflections, provided a rich database from which to examine this complicated relationship.

The audio–recordings were transcribed, and analysed using a classification system developed from our underlying model, each category containing four levels of development (see Figure 7.2). Quantitative analyses of these data, supported by contrastive case studies of individual students, demonstrated the role of subject knowledge in how lessons are conceived and implemented. They showed, for example, how knowledge-for-teaching was related to all aspects of pedagogical reasoning, from the framing of intentions, through task design and representation, to evaluation and reflection.

Representation, for example, shows itself in both task planning and in the ability of student teachers to spontaneously develop coherent explanations 'on the hoof'. One student in our study was sufficiently competent in his subject knowledge to provide spontaneously the following representation explaining the rotation of the earth and its effect on night and day. 'Has anyone ever been on a merry-go-round at the fair? If you have a friend watching you, you can imagine your friend is the sun, because he stays still. And this merry-go-round is the earth spinning around and around. When you can't see your friend on the ground, then you can imagine that it is night time. As you go round and round to you the whole fairground seems to be moving doesn't it? But it isn't really. It is still — you are the one who is moving. And all of us on this earth are moving around as if we are on a merry-go-round at the fair, and the sun is standing still in the sky'. Contrast this with a student who did not know the difference between density and heaviness. After discussing with children why different objects immersed to different depths in liquids of different density—such as cooking oil and syrup—she ended her explanation as follows 'Do you remember what density means? No? It means heaviness. Right?'

In general the data highlighted how lack of knowledge crippled students' ability to develop or elaborate a theme. This was particularly apparent in attempts to model the cooperating teacher. These frequently turned out to be disastrous for both students and pupils alike, as, for example, when the student failed to comprehend the impact of the tasks on the children, and his or her own role in that process. As McDiarmid has argued, providing beginning teachers with ready-made repertoires will not ensure that they can effectively connect their pupils with subject matter.

Teachers must be able to appraise the pedagogical content of an available representation and determine how well it fits the context. This is not to deny a useful role for modelling incidentally, particularly when it is combined with structured attempts at reflection and evaluation. Nevertheless its success would seem to be related to the student's understanding of the appropriate knowledge base.

The relationship between knowledge and performance is not, however, unproblematic. Appropriate knowledge would appear to be a necessary, but not sufficient, basis for competent teaching performances. Teachers cannot teach what they do not know, as Mary Kennedy has pointed out, but neither can they teach well what they do know without the other knowledge bases for teaching. Effective teaching in these terms involves the orchestration of knowledge bases appropriate to the requirements of particular groups of learners in particular learning contexts.

The relationship of knowledge bases and action is mediated by several contextual factors, one powerful mediating variable being the context in which student teachers teach. The cooperating teachers were variable in the support that they offered, often imposing their own organizational framework on the student, irrespective of whether or not it conformed to the student's, or the training institution's, conceptions of an acceptable system. In these circumstances the student was caught between the incompatible demands of the cooperating teacher and the supervisor.

Learning to Teach

These findings generally support or extend those of studies elsewhere. But where do they lead us in terms of the development of theory? In reflecting on the utility and validity of the models underpinning our study it became clear that they were inadequate to explain the processes of development of learning to teach, not least because they are based on the pedagogical actions of experienced teachers. The only indication of how student-teachers can develop in the model is learning from experience via reflection. However, current thinking about the role of reflection in the early stages of learning to teach is casting doubts on its appropriateness in this regard. What experience of classrooms do students have to reflect on, for example? Most have had little or no experience of primary classrooms for a decade or more, and then only from the perspective of learner. They thus have little experience or knowledge to bring to bear on their reflections, and as a consequence they have difficulty zeroing in on what is instructionally important for reflection because of the lack of developed schemata for organizing information about classroom experiences.

McIntyre (1993) has recently argued that reflection is a much more central means for learning for experienced teachers than it can, or need, be for beginners. He believes that student-teachers' first steps in teaching need conscious deliberation and planning. Competence is thus achieved through conscious control; they do not need to reflect in order to be conscious of what they have been trying to do and know. He proposes three levels of reflection: the technical, the practical and the critical. In the early days of student teaching reflection is at the technical level; their major task being the attainment of given goals e.g., goals related to basic competences of teaching, such as achieving and maintaining classroom order or gaining pupils' attention. Practical reflection occurs later, where the emphasis is on articulating their own criteria, and evaluating and developing their own practice. Critical reflection concerns wider ethical, social and political issues, and is, according to McIntyre, rarely practised even among experienced teachers.

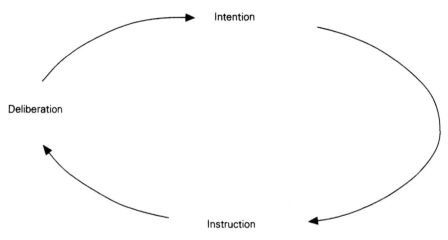

Figure 7.3: A model of early pedagogical reasoning

These notions of reflection indicate a limited role for reflection in initial training as a means to learning, even though learning to reflect must be an important goal in training; and this conception generally accords with student experiences in our study. It is clear from their diaries, and the case studies of their teaching, that their early attempts at teaching were characterized by modelling, or imitating, activities suggested either by the cooperating teacher, their course tutors or those personally experienced on the course itself. In these circumstances there were no attempts at transformation of content. They usually had a good idea of what they wished to achieve, but these intentions did not necessarily involve a comprehension of the content to be taught. As such these lessons often tended to flop. Nevertheless they usually deliberated, or technically reflected, on their intentions and goals, and the extent to which the lesson worked or not.

A model of pedagogical reasoning and action based on these early teaching experiences will not therefore be well elaborated, as shown in Figure 7.3, which contains only three elements — intentions, instruction (where tasks are modelled) and deliberation (technical reflection).

Modelling can have unforeseen, and sometimes unfortunate, outcomes as our case studies show. Nevertheless it does appear to have value in stimulating reflection, and in building up a repertoire of teaching activities and actions. Modelling of routines underpins Schon's (1987) notion of the reflective practicum and might, as others argue, be an essential stage in the process of becoming a reflective teacher (Calderhead, 1991; Maynard and Furlong, 1993). Modelling, and the associated notion of apprenticeship, are also congruent with recent work in the field of situated cognition. The underlying premise of this work is that thinking is inextricably interwoven with the content of the problem to be solved and draws on Vygotsky's model of cognitive development through social interaction. From this perspective, cognitive development is an apprenticeship occurring through guided participation in activity.

The use of modelling, although having theoretical validity, is but a stepping stone to more informed and independent practice. This requires more experience,

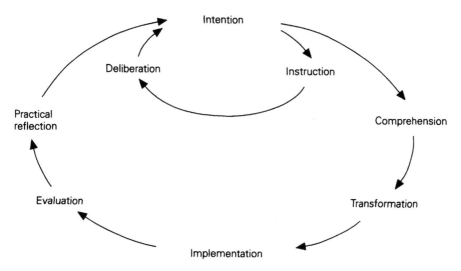

Figure 7.4: A model of the second stage of learning to teach

more confidence and a shift, in McIntyre's terms, from technical to practical reflection. A model of the second stage of learning to teach is thus much more elaborated than the first, as Figure 7.4 indicates.

All the core elements are now in place; each element requiring particular combinations of knowledge bases. Comprehension, and transformation, for example, demand in Shulman's terms, subject-matter knowledge for teaching, pedagogical content knowledge, knowledge of curriculum and of learners. The implementation element, on the other hand, relies more on general pedagogical knowledge.

The third stage of the model would be characterized by developing teaching competences in each element through improving knowledge bases and skills, together with a move toward critical reflection. This stage of development is likely to be characterized by the kind of personal theorizing we, and others, have recorded as beginning teachers progress through their first year of teaching, leading to more coherent and cohesive personal belief structures about teaching and its wider purposes.

Implications

Several major implications flow from this analysis. Of these the most important appear to be the training environment, the content of training and the role of competences. The role of reflection is writ large both in student-teacher accounts, and in the wider research literature. Reflection is, unfortunately, a much overused and abused term, and here the terminology of cognitive science is useful where, as one theorist succinctly put it, reflection 'provides declarative access to procedural knowledge' (von Wright, 1992). The critical question for training is what kind of process underpins the development of reflection, and how can it be best achieved?

Some believe that self-reflection is more a skill than a capacity: it can be learned and trained through the development of metacognitive skills and knowledge (von Wright, 1992). It is these skills that regulate and modify the progress of cognitive activity. It is argued that social interaction should be emphasized in such training, on the grounds that social contexts elevate thinking to an observable status (Glaser, 1991). The reflective processes of participants then become apparent, providing the opportunities for understanding and shaping them. Focusing on context also directs attention to the fact that knowledge is always 'situated'. One implication of this is that training environments should be as similar as possible to the environment in which the knowledge and skills are to be used. This in turn appears to argue for a substantial proportion of training to be classroom-based, initially, at least, within an apprenticeship model.

However there is a fundamental dilemma here since our data, and other research evidence, indicates that although this is likely to lead to improvements in some aspects of teaching, it will seriously neglect others — most noticeably the development of subject knowledge for teaching. As it is, understandings of subject matter rarely figure prominently in teacher preparation. 'Constrained by limits of time, teacher educators tend to take prospective teachers' subject matter knowledge for granted, focussing instead on pedagogical knowledge and skills' (McDiarmid *et al.*, 1989). Indeed this is written into the national accreditation criteria in Britain for the one-year postgraduate courses, where student-teacher knowledge of subjects is taken for granted. However, if subject knowledge were to be incorporated into these courses, which are already widely regarded as being too short, what aspects of curriculum and pedagogy would be dropped or postponed? Kennedy (1992) perceives this to be an enduring dilemma and concludes that there is a need to shift our conceptions from teacher knowledge as a problem to be solved, to a dilemma that must be managed. One way out of this dilemma is, she believes, to assume teacher learning as a continuous process, and to search for ways of facilitating that development.

Her Majesty's Inspectorate in Britain are singing a similar song, arguing that 'it would be unreasonable to suppose that initial training could prepare all teachers for all aspects of their professional work and for schools to expect that they will receive fully-fledged practitioners.' Strong arguments are thus being put forward that initial training should be a preparation for the early years of teaching, and a foundation on which subsequent training and development can build. So, for teacher training to become more effective, 'there must be a clearly understood division of labour between the initial, induction and inset (in-service) stages, and a formal obligation laid on those responsible for each to deliver their part of the training process' (Alexander *et al.*, 1992). This would seem to be a critical obligation. We found, as have the Inspectorate, that the quality of induction for teachers in their first year of teaching was generally poor and variable.

However the notion of continuous teacher learning requires a baseline from which to work, and towards which to aim. Such thinking requires a model of broad-based core, teaching competences much along the lines adopted in our study. This would provide each teacher with a competence profile achieved on exit from the initial training programme, and on which further training would be based. Such a system could also fruitfully integrate continuing teacher development and modes of teacher appraisal. A competence system is also necessary to delineate which aspects are to be targeted at each phase of training. However laudable, these proposals do not address the problems of the lack of subject knowledge of beginning teachers in the short term. There is no doubt that teacher educators must now overtly address this issue and implement more flexible programmes to allow, for example, self-diagnosis and evaluation of subject knowledge, and independent learning units addressing the knowledge required for teaching different levels and areas of the curriculum.

Work will also need to continue on developing an acceptable set of core teaching competences both for the purposes outlined above, and as crucially, for informing the design and implementation of training courses. Our data show very clearly that an agreed set of competences and levels bind student, teacher and supervisor to a common, understood, mission. It is equally clear that any form of apprenticeship requires adequate training of the cooperating teacher/mentor, and the supervisor alike. Little is yet known about what characterizes effective mentoring, and some commonsense assumptions, for example, that good teachers make good mentors, have been disputed. Studies in this area thus need to address what models of mentoring exist, their conceptual underpinnings, their effectiveness in practice, and their impact on those involved.

The paucity of models of learning to teach, and lack of systematic data on such central issues as teaching competences and mentoring, highlight the lack of a sound empirical base from which to develop teacher education. The resultant conceptual void has thus, in recent proposals for reform, in Britain at least, been filled by political polemic in the absence of empirical evidence. As teacher educators we must take some responsibility for this, and learn by the experience. In future we must be as reflective of our own practice as we expect teachers to be of theirs.

References

ALEXANDER, R., ROSE, J. and WOODHEAD, C. (1992) *Curriculum Organisation and Classroom Practice in Primary Schools*, London, HMSO.

BENNETT, N. and CARRE, C. (1993) *Learning to Teach*, London, Routledge.

CALDERHEAD, J. (1991) 'The nature and growth of knowledge in student teaching', *Teacher and Teacher Education*, **7**, pp. 531–6.

GLASER, R. (1991) 'The maturing of the relationship between the science of learning and cognition and educational practice', *Learning and Instruction*, **1**, pp. 129–44.

GOODLAD, J.I. (1991) 'Why we need a complete re-design of teacher education', *Educational Leadership*, **49**, pp. 4–6.

KENNEDY, M. (1992) 'Merging subject and students into teaching knowledge', in KENNEDY, M. (Ed) *Teaching Academic Subjects to Diverse Learners*, New York, Teachers College Press.

MAYNARD, T. and FURLONG, J. (1993) 'Learning to teach and models of mentoring', in McINTYRE, D., HAGGER, H. and WILKIN, M. (Eds) *Mentoring*, London, Kogan Page, pp. 69–85.

McDIARMID, G.W., BALL, D.L. and ANDERSON, C.W. (1989) 'Why staying one chapter ahead doesn't really work: Subject specific pedagogy', in REYNOLDS, M.C. (Ed) *Knowledge Base for the Beginning Teacher*, New York, Pergamon.

McINTYRE, D. (1993) 'Theory, theorising and reflection in initial teacher education', in CALDERHEAD, J. (Ed) *Conceptualising Reflection in Teacher Development*, London, Falmer Press.

SCHON, D.A. (1987) *Educating the Reflective Practitioner*, San Fransisco, Jossey-Bass.

VON WRIGHT, J. (1992) 'Reflections on reflection', *Learning and Instruction*, **2**, pp. 59–68.

ZEICHNER, K.M. (1992) 'Conceptions of reflective practice in teaching and teacher education', in HARVARD, G. and DUNNE, R. (Eds) *Action and Reflection in Teacher Education*, New York, Ablex.

8 Initial Teacher Education Policy and Cultural Transmission

David Clemson

Introduction

In this chapter I am concerned with the political control of initial teacher education in England and Wales now, and the dangers that I see in any ideologically homogeneous group taking control of the 'Initial Teacher Education' curriculum. To explain my concerns it is necessary to explore some of the features of initial teacher education and a range of topics which should impinge upon any discussion of 'Initial Teacher Education' curricula. These include such wide-ranging issues as the meaning of 'culture' today, the use of ideological models in education, and some important tenets of British democracy. I am also mindful of what we have come to know, over many years, about teaching and learning, and the beliefs which may be embedded in initial teacher education traditions. In presenting this web of issues and ideas I am conscious of the breadth of related topics and the difficulties that this presents in terms of constructing 'a model'. However, such a difficulty is entirely consistent with my thesis which can be summarized by the following assertions:

> Teacher education (including ITE) must not be, made to fit a unified theory, or used for narrow ideological purposes, but, rather, it should be dynamic and organic, and should concentrate on supporting the *education* of a variety of teachers in respect of their values as well as their knowledge.

Culture

'Culture' is a word with many different meanings and connotations. Williams (1976) suggests that the term 'culture' is complicated and elusive due to the different ways in which it is used and the fact that usage changes over time. In a later work (Williams, 1981) he distinguishes between culture as a noun of *process* in which it can be seen as cultivation of, for example, the human mind, and as a noun of *configuration* or *generalization* where the concern is with . . . 'the "spirit" which informed the "whole way of life" of a distinct people' (p. 10) . . . This latter usage leads us to an acceptance of pluralism of cultures and of traditional patterns of life and thought from which can be drawn distinct features. These features characterize the future of groups as well as defining their commonalities now. Williams goes on to identify a range of meanings which draw together some of these ideas.

(i) a developed state of mind — as in 'a person of culture', 'a cultured person' to (ii) the processes of this development — as in 'cultural interests', 'cultural activities' to (iii) the means of the processes — as in culture as 'the arts' and 'humane intellectual works'. (Williams, 1981, p. 11)

He suggests that the last of these is the most common usage now. Evidence for such a suggestion is readily available. For example, in January 1993 the BBC broadcast a programme entitled 'Cultivating the Nation'.[1] In this broadcast a number of individuals expressed their views. David Pascall, then Chair of the National Curriculum Council.

> . . . . We have always, over the centuries, welcomed into our midst those from different cultures. They, in turn, have influenced the society we are today. But that doesn't mean to say that there isn't broadly a dominant culture. It is a culture which draws its roots, which draws its authority from the past. It has shaped and informed our society. That means our children in school as well as participating actively do need to be introduced to great works of literature; they do need to be introduced to texts of central importance to our literary heritage; they do need to hear the music which, through the centuries, has made up society today, the works of art. . . .

There are some clear tensions in the beliefs expressed in this statement. Whilst there is clear acknowledgment of the value of a pluralist society there is an over-riding view that we have to inculcate all of our children into a common core of knowledge and experience drawn from the important aspects of predominantly western European culture. There is also an assumption that culture = heritage. However, it is clear to many educationalists that the 'culture' of young children in the UK is not circumscribed by such traditional boundaries and expectations. Teachers know of the importance of peers and family, and the impact of the media on children's learning and priorities. Lawton (1983), for example, sees the curriculum as a selection from a society's culture but asserts that this is not synonymous with 'high culture' but rather the curriculum should embrace what is important *now*. However, it is within the context of an élitist view of knowledge linked to a concern for control over the curriculum, in schools and teacher-education departments, that initial teacher education is having to operate — this in itself creates tensions, of course, as the colleges and university departments have an inheritance of their own. Such tensions can be made self-evident through the writings of Stenhouse (1975) where he confidently states:

> Education enhances the freedom of man by inducting him into the knowledge of his cultures as a thinking system. The most important characteristic of the knowledge mode is that one can think with it. This is in the nature of knowledge — as distinct from information — that it is a structure to sustain creative thought and provide frameworks for judgement. *Education as induction into knowledge is successful to the extent that it makes the behavioural outcomes of the students unpredictable.* (Stenhouse, 1975)

In the present climate the final sentence would clearly be seen as anathema and as antagonistic to an ideology which embraces certainty, prescription, objectivity and testing against predetermined outcomes. It is necessary, then, to reflect upon our definitions of 'culture' in the context of ideologically set imperatives.

Ideology

The modelling and categorization of ideologies have been within the concern of many academics for some time. Of these Williams (1961) distinguished three ideological groups (the industrial trainers, the old humanists and the public educators), which have been widely referred to since their publication. The initial development of teacher training was authoritarian-utilitarian (industrial trainer) in nature. The intention was to produce elementary teachers who would instruct pupils in a prescribed and narrow curriculum for the purpose of equipping them for particular roles in society. These roles were fundamentally prescribed by a belief in ability being fixed and inherited. This utilitarian approach is most starkly to be seen in the first National Curriculum — that of the Revised Code of 1862 — where a commitment to the 'basics' is clear and total. Associated with such a curriculum was the payment of teachers by results as measured through external tests and inspections. The influence of the old humanists then began to affect the view of what might be an 'educated teacher' and the curriculum in the early training colleges gradually became broader as did that of the schools. By the beginning of this century there was a concern that:

> each teacher shall think for himself, and work out for himself such methods of teaching as may use his powers to the best advantage and be best suited to the particular needs and conditions of the school. (Board of Education, 1905)

At the time that the curriculum was becoming more 'liberal' there was a growing conviction that all children should have the opportunity of schooling. This brought about a growth in the numbers of teachers in training and, though there continued to be many unqualified teachers, there was a steady growth in the positive valuing of ITE. The public educators of the twentieth century eventually prevailed and universal schooling became the norm as did, in comparatively recent times, the need for a well-educated and fully qualified teaching profession.

Presently we are experiencing a resurgence of the influence of the industrial trainer with the associated emphasis on 'basics', hierarchy, and a view of the child as being a receptacle for knowledge. Associated with this is a questioning of the need for ITE at all; a knowledge of the subject being seen as the only necessary prerequisite. Ernest (1991) tabulates the characteristics of Williams' three ideological groups with additional categories which he terms the 'Technological pragmatist', and the 'Progressive educator'. Antipathy to progressivism with its concern for child-centred education, liberal views, and teacher-led assessment is a central part of current policy. The industrial trainer and/or technological pragmatist views emphasize child as 'empty vessel' (and 'fallen angel'), radicalism (the New Right), meritocracy, and external testing, certification and skills profiling. In this climate both the teacher and the teacher educator can be pilloried as 'progressive' and culpable for low standards in schools.

We are also witnessing the tensions inherent in government driven by a particular ideology. As Williams (1961) acknowledged, ideological aims are never pure, there are always compromises, and objectives may be shared with other ideologies than the one which is at the heart of broad-policy statements. This means that it is possible to castigate teachers (and parents) and then enact policy which gives teachers the major responsibility for teacher training, and parents the 'power' of choice. The nesting of issues and the selectivity embedded in such nesting has, of course, major implications for our democratic processes.

Democracy

An important part of the checks and balances of a democracy is keeping open the possibility of views which may be at variance with one another and allowing these views to be operationally trialled and tested. In the historical development of ITE intellectual and vocational divergences emerged, as the numbers of teachers in training grew. Whilst these divergences might be seen as unhelpful to an 'efficient' national system they do have the virtue of offering platforms for different voices. However, once a state education system is instated and universal schooling is established it is inevitable that diversity and choice will be reduced. Given the undoubted emphasis on 'market forces' in currently prevailing political ideology this assertion might seem perverse. But it is clear that state intervention and control must limit diversity especially in respect of deviation from overarching ideological and/or the state imperatives. It is also the case that the democratic system in the UK is dependent on a 'checks and balances' approach which, in its evolution and enaction, favours moderate decisions through compromise — fanaticism and extremism have not been part of our history. But, over the last decade and a half there has been a significant shift in the way in which the checks and balances necessary for the functioning of our unwritten constitution have been adjusted. And these have major implications for the future of the teaching profession, our schools, and our newly qualified teachers.

Duverger (1972) distinguishes, in a discussion of democracy, between 'negotiation' and 'arbitration'. By the former he means the accomplishment of policy initiatives through argument, collective bargaining, and, by implication, compromise. In the latter the process is characterized by the State acting as arbiter (after consultation) and as autocrat. I believe that the experience of teacher educators, and others, would incline us to believe that the second of these is currently seen as being our version of democracy, though this runs counter to British traditions which have not adopted a 'presidential' style of governance. Duverger also indicates that our political systems need to take account of culture when he states that:

> By contrast with 'techniques' and 'institutions', the term 'culture' refers to the beliefs, ideologies, and myths, that is, the collective images and ideas of a community, which are in a way its spiritual and psychological elements; technology and institutions constitute a community's material aspects.

But in the current climate there would seem to be a concentration on the material aspects and an avoidance of the spiritual and psychological dimensions of communities. Thus some of the traditionally important aspects of the contributions of our educational establishments seem to be being ignored or swept aside.

Reynolds and Skilbeck (1976) pointed out that:

> The school may be thought of as an institution engaged in complex trans-actions within its environment, which involves exchanges of ideas, re-sources, and people through an elaborate, criss-crossing network of communications systems. That is, the school has a culture and schooling itself is one of the key cultural processes in modern society.

I would wish to extend this to all of our formally constituted education estab-lishments and emphasize that an important vehicle of our cultural processes is democracy. In operating without a written constitution it has been vital that free-dom of thought and expression have been safeguarded and that academic communities, particularly the universities, have been required to offer a critique of the way in which our society functions. In moving to a culture of democracy by state arbitra-tion we are in danger of rendering ineffective the necessary checks and balances which have been the characteristic of our democratic system for so long. Whilst it is inevitable, given the political nature of a formal, state-run education system, that different groups exert varying influences at different times we must, at this time, be conscious of the dangers in controlling what teachers think and what they are required to 'deliver'.

These issues, and what they have to say about the developments we are witnessing in ITE in England and Wales raise a number of concerns which centre on the dangers of control of ITE and the transmission of selected aspects of our 'culture'.

Initial Teacher Education

The 'Initial Teacher Education' curriculum has now been subject to close control for more than a decade with the setting up of the Council for the Accreditation of Teacher Education in 1983. Despite this fact there continue to be attacks on the teacher education community based upon assertions about the ITE curriculum! As Bernler and McClelland (1989) state:

> For the teacher educator, the 'ivory tower' of the college of education is less a safe haven than an often dangerous parapet from which to participate in the ideological battle between academe and community, a battle in which the teacher educator may become the object of a fusillade from either or both seemingly opposing forces.

Whilst it is true that there has always been scrutiny of, and active political interest in, initial teacher education (ITE) historically this was mainly in respect of teacher numbers, level and appropriateness of award, and the process of establishing qualified-teacher status. The ITE curriculum was traditionally defined and devel-oped by those with particular educational experiences, values and beliefs. Much of the growth in ITE came about through the pioneering work of individuals often linked to the aims, commitment and endeavours of a range of interest groups.

The ambitions of a number of the early teacher educators in the UK was to improve the opportunities offered to pupils in the elementary school through the advancement of well-trained and professionally qualified teachers. These ambitions came to override the narrow perspectives of, for example, Lancaster and Bell and broadened the perceptions and expectations of the Church and, later, the Government. In this century the concerns of such educators as Montessori and Froebel and the work of researchers such as Piaget led to movements which transcended the local and became core to the thoughts and activities of many teacher educators — certainly those concerned with the education of young children. The important lesson that we might draw from this aspect of the history of ITE is the growth in understanding of the importance of individuality in learning and the primacy of the learner in schooling provision.

It is in this century that we see the growth of interest in 'education' in our traditional universities. This interest was, however, generally with the education of teachers for the secondary school and manifested itself in the establishment of a postgraduate certificate year. Indeed some universities rejected the notion that teacher *training* could form part of the higher education sector at all except in respect of the validation of certificate courses in teacher training colleges. This attitude reinforced status issues surrounding primary and secondary teachers, which still pervade our education system, and may have allowed a distinction to be made between ITE and the continuing professional development of the teacher workforce. I will return to this later. At this juncture the main point is that the affirmation of education as an academic study, linked to a professional, vocational outcome, is symptomatic of the development of a national system. And, by virtue of the traditions of higher education such a system was able to accommodate different perspectives on effective teacher education. The importance of diversity within a national framework accords with Wilson's cautionary views (1979):

> . . . we have to avoid the idea that there is some *one* method of defending teachers against the wrong sort of attitude: that they will learn, for instance, only by being prodded into moral virtues by sermons, or only by habituating themselves into certain 'social skills', or only by absorbing psychological or sociological theory. (Wilson, 1979)

Wilson identifies three models of ITE which he summarizes as 'Saints and Heroes', 'Drivers and Potters', and 'Doctors and Engineers'. In the first teachers are born, not made, and there is, therefore, no role for ITE. In the second we rely upon apprenticeship and practice with an experienced 'driver' sitting next to you. It is essentially practical and instrumental. Finally there is the 'dose of theory' and 'dose of practice' model which, until recent times was perhaps the common experience. More recently, of course, we would seem to be moving to the 'Drivers and Potters' model with a particular set of assumptions about the role of teachers, the value of 'practice', and the role of higher education. The characteristics of current policy outcomes have been well rehearsed elsewhere (see for example Elliott, 1993) and it is not my intention to explore such characteristics here. However, there are two underlying features which support my concern for the danger inherent to any state system which, wittingly or unwittingly, contrives to prescribe selections from culture, and to control professional discourse and diversity of view — these are 'common-sense', and professional language.

Hargreaves (1993) argues that we need to take a 'common-sense' view of ITE seeing the professional development of teachers as involving the acquisition of professional common-sense knowledge through school-based teacher education using mentors on the basis of which teachers are better placed to 'research, discuss and deliberate in a highly sophisticated way'. The first part of this view chimes well with that of many politicians and others who often seem to have a distrust of the professions, and a mistrust of 'theory'. The problem about taking 'common-sense' views is the question as to what this precisely means. If it means that we educate prospective teachers 'sensibly' as seen by 'sensible' people how does this contrast with educating teachers to 'transmit' ideas which we are invited to agree as being sensible? In other words are we considering the professional common-sense know-ledge of Hargreaves or the common-sense of those who would reject the need for a sophisticated analysis of teaching and learning matters? It is difficult to answer such questions, and it is certainly so without also considering the language available for any such analysis.

Bruner (1974) in the context of a discussion of pedagogy, including teacher training suggests that:

> one of the most crucial ways in which a culture provides aid in intellectual growth is through a dialogue between the more experienced and the less experienced, providing a means for the internalization of dialogue in thought. The courtesy of conversation may be the major ingredient in the courtesy of teaching. (Bruner, 1974)

This would seem to support the views of Hargreaves and others. However, crucial to Bruner's statement is the need for dynamic language within conversation. Language and thought are linked (Vygotsky, 1962). It is not unreasonable to suggest, therefore, that professional language and thoughts about professional concerns are also linked. In other words the key conversations between mentors, tutors and student teachers will be dependent on the language used. Yet, within the current climate the very language we use has increasingly been prescribed by policy makers. It is sufficient, in making this point, to identify a few items of vocabulary. 'Delivery', 'key stage', 'programme of study', 'mentor' 'customer' and 'common-sense' will suffice.

Conclusion

Rooted in the development of ITE provision there are a number of central tenets upon which teacher education has traditionally been based and, until recently na-tionally affirmed. These are that:

- teaching and learning need to be contiguous with what we know of how people learn;
- the education of teachers should be over a professional life and not confined to ITE;
- ITE and continuing professional development can be viewed as mutually supportive and part of a seamless opportunity;
- diversity in curriculum development is healthy; and
- there is no single teaching style or method of 'training' teachers.

These tenets are now at the centre of a debate which is ideologically driven and which is, at best, ambiguous about the value of teacher education. Current policies seem to be undermining the beliefs and values of many teacher educators and appear to be ignoring what we know about learning, teaching and curriculum design. Reynolds and Skilbeck (ibid.) make the point, in a consideration of revolutionary mainland China during the chairmanship of Mao Tse-tung, that '. . . it would be a mistake to condemn education elsewhere for being "ideological" whilst failing to recognize the ideological character of our own schooling'. They wrote this at a time when it was accurate to identify the curriculum as being rooted in a liberal ideology. This ideology has now been superseded and we operate within constraints which are not designed with flexibility and alternative patterns of thought, language and beliefs in mind. We are in danger of having our future teaching force being trained to transmit selections from our culture based upon a minority, monocultural and élitist view. This we must resist, though the pattern of logical resistance is hard to delineate — partly because the sentiments behind this chapter inevitably embrace ambivalent views. There is no intention here, then, to answer the questions that I have raised. Rather this chapter should be seen as an attempt to deconstruct the situation in which ITE would seem to find itself. Tentative conclusions would lead me to advocate the rather unexciting 'middle way'.

Our democratic processes essentially depend upon such an approach. In order to pursue such a path there are a number of dimensions to educational enquiry and provision which we might seek to address. These include the nature and purpose of educational research, the relationship that ITE should have with higher education, and the need to recognize that we are genuinely part of a changing multicultural society. It is no good, for example, to promote 'teachers as researchers' if that means we encourage teachers to better teach what they are told to teach. It is unacceptable to see ITE as separate from higher education and divorce continuing professional education from ITE and induction of the newly qualified teacher. It is dangerous to adopt a common, provided, language with which to attempt to offer a healthy critique of educational policy and practice. In the short term perhaps we need to re-examine the possibilities for local and regional differences in provision. As Turner (1990) indicates:

> The area training organisations were devised for distancing the academic control of teacher education from the direct influence of government. In this they succeeded admirably, largely because the government also believed that academic independence was an important route to the development of high quality teacher education. The combining of initial and in-service education was also an important feature of the ATOs which was several decades ahead of its time. (Turner, 1990)

Whether such an approach would wrought the changes that I perceive necessary to avoid the dangers of cultural transmission through state control of ITE is, importantly, a debatable point. I am certain, though, that we are at a stage where all those concerned with the quality of education and the promotion of the 'educated teacher' must voice their opinions and do so in a climate of freedom of speech, thought and opportunity.

Note

1   BBC Radio 4 'Analysis: Cultivating the Nation' 28 January 1993 (repeated 31 January 1993).

David Clemson

References

BERNLER, N.R. and McCLELLAND, A.E. 'The social context of professional development', in HOLLY, M.L. and McLOUGHLIN, C.S. (1989) *Perspectives on Teacher Professional Development*, London, Falmer Press.

BOARD OF EDUCATION (1905) *Handbook of Suggestions for the Consideration of Teachers and Others Concerned in the Work of Public Elementary Schools*.

BRUNER, J.S. (1974) *The Relevance of Education*, Harmondsworth, Penguin Books.

DUVERGER, M. (1972) *Party Politics and Pressure Groups: A Comparative Introduction* (translated from French by Wagoner, R.), London, Nelson.

ELLIOTT, J. (1993) *Reconstructing Teacher Education: Teacher Development*, London, Falmer Press.

ERNEST, P. (1991) *The Philosophy of Mathematics Education*, London, Falmer Press.

HARGREAVES, D.H. (1993) 'A common-sense model of the professional development of teachers', in ELLIOTT, J. *Reconstructing Teacher Education: Teacher Development*, London, Falmer Press.

LAWTON, D. (1983) 'Unit 3: Culture and the Curriculum', in Open University Course E204 *Purpose and Planning in the Curriculum*, Milton Keynes, Open University Press.

REYNOLDS, J. and SKILBECK, M. (1976) *Culture and the Classroom*, London, Open Books.

STENHOUSE, L. (1975) *An Introduction to Curriculum Research and Development*, London, Heinemann.

TURNER, J.D. (1990) 'The area training organisations', in THOMAS, J.B. (Ed) *British Universities and Teacher Education*, London, Falmer Press.

VYGOTSKY, L.S. (1962) *Thought and Language*, The Massachusetts Institute of Technology.

WILLIAMS, R. (1961) *The Long Revolution*, Harmondsworth, Penguin.

WILLIAMS, R. (1976) *Keywords*, London, Fontana.

WILLIAMS, R. (1981) *Culture*, London, Fontana.

WILSON, J. (1979) *Fantasy and Common Sense in Education*, Oxford, Martin Robertson.

Part 2

The Induction of Newly Qualified Teachers

9 Government Policy and the Induction of New Teachers[1]

Susan Sidgwick

Introduction

The structures through which new teachers enter the profession are changing as a result of government policy for initial teacher education (ITE), the induction of newly qualified teachers (NQTs) in their first teaching post and for the funding and management of schools. In this chapter I will focus on the post-ITE, induction phase of entry into the profession and, on the basis of interviews with educators with responsibility for new teachers, identify some of the major issues which have been generated by these policy changes. I will then argue that many of these issues can be understood as instances of the tensions and problems which have emerged in other sectors of the welfare state as a consequence of government attempts to introduce market principles into the provision of public services.

In 1992 the Government rescinded the formal, mandatory requirements relating to a probationary period for all new teachers (DES, 1990) and replaced them with less detailed and non-mandatory guidance (DES, 1992b). Its stated reasons (DES, 1991) were that induction is best improved through extending schools' role in initial teacher education (ITE) and through improving the transition from ITE to induction by developing the use of profiles of competence and by encouraging the tailoring of provision to individual needs. Dismissal under normal employment law would be sufficient to deal with those few cases where new teachers do not reach a satisfactory level. At the same time local management of schools (LMS) and opting out (or its possibility) have diminished the ability of local education authorities (LEAs) to provide services or direct resources and policy. As a consequence, services which many LEAs used to perform for NQTs (e.g., visits by advisors or inspectors, the running of subject or general sessions, providing extra support for failing NQTs and handling cases of failure) are increasingly being either withdrawn, or offered as a service which schools can buy into if they choose. It is becoming more common for a school to be in the position of being able to choose to buy into an LEA service, to purchase services from some other provider, to make its own provision from within its own resources, or to make no provision at all. In the absence of any external requirement in this area schools are increasingly in the position of determining their own priorities and criteria of cost efficiency or 'value for money' in relation to the school's perceived interests. A further dimension is provided by developments in ITE, where, for example, in the London area schools which have partnership arrangements with HEIs in ITE may wish to extend these into their provision for induction, particularly if the costs of the latter are reduced as an incentive to engage in the former arrangements.

In common with other HEIs Goldsmiths College is involved in a number of initiatives in the education of beginning teachers, including developing partnerships with schools in ITE and with schools and LEAs in the induction of NQTs. Along with colleagues, I have written elsewhere (Sidgwick, Mahony and Hextall, 1993) about the tensions and opportunities we have experienced in attempting to manage the interaction of principles and practice in the context of current government policy. It was partly in an attempt to gain a better understanding of that context that we undertook research into the impact of government policy on the arrangements that schools and LEAs were making for their NQTs.

The research consisted of interviews with senior teachers or deputy heads with responsibility for induction, LEA Inspectors, representatives of professional associations, researchers based in higher education and research institutes, and members of departments of education in HEIs. Twenty people were selected to be interviewed on the basis of their involvement in the development of good practice in induction, whether this be in the formulation of policy, the management or the delivery of provision. Interviews were carried out on the basis of non-attributability, but were tape recorded and transcribed. Although the respondents included people based in Scotland and Wales and other regions of England, there was a bias towards London and the secondary phase in our selection of people to interview, partly because of the limited funds available, and partly because of the origins of the research in our involvement with partnerships in ITE and the provision of induction, all of which are at the secondary level.

For the purposes of this chapter I do not intend to explore the components of what is regarded as good practice in the induction of newly qualified teachers (NQTs). There are now several accounts which delineate these at the level of school and LEA (Bolam, 1987; Earley, 1992; Earley and Kinder, 1994; DES, 1992a; OFSTED, 1993; Calderhead and Lambert, 1992; Goddard, 1993). My interest here is to identify respondents' perceptions of the effects of government policies on good practice and their concerns regarding the provision of induction, now and in the future.

Concerns and Dilemmas

As might be expected, underlying specific concerns was a sense of lack of direction or structure following the dismantling of the former framework for organizing provision. This was often expressed in terms of a sense of uncertainty concerning accountability and responsibility, which was manifested in a number of related areas.

Employment Rights and Contracts

The abolition of probation and the transfer of responsibilities and powers from LEAs to schools and governing bodies has created considerable uncertainty concerning support for, or dismissal of, struggling or failing NQTs, the allocation of responsibilities and the procedures which need to be followed in order to be able to move to dismissal, if this should be necessary, without the school incurring financial or legal penalties. Few of the teachers were familiar with employment law, or with the details or implications of the situation with respect to employment rights before and after two years in post. More of them, however, were aware of the potential for using one-year temporary contracts as a means of avoiding problems of dismissal, although opinions here differed sharply. One school regarded the use of temporary contracts as a straightforwardly sensible measure, and another had adopted from private-sector consultants a model contract for all staff which incorporated a probationary period before contracts were confirmed permanently. Other senior managers were worried about the defensiveness which could be engendered by what would amount to a one year's extended interview and thought that the potential for the use of NQTs as a flexible element in the school's labour force would be counterproductive in terms of creating a supportive context for professional development. While acknowledging certain benefits for the school, these managers were concerned about the losses in terms of wider professional considerations.

Obviously the professional associations have a large stake here. An example of how employee rights could be protected is offered by the ATL's proposals (Thompson, 1993) for a six-month probationary period, during which NQTs would have intensified support and rights, which can be seen as a consolidation and extension of the guarantees formerly provided by probation. As Thompson (op cit.) has pointed out, these are even more necessary in the light of HMI's judgments (DES, 1988) that 40 per cent of schools have excessively high expectations of new teachers. These pressures can be expected to intensify as resource considerations become more salient.

To a certain extent there is a coincidence of interests between school and NQT in relation to providing mechanisms for support and clear procedures to follow in the assessment of new teachers in their first year. However, there comes a juncture at which these interests diverge. The point at which it is no longer in the school's interest to continue putting resources into an NQT may well not coincide with the point at which it is in the NQT's interest to withdraw from teaching. The divergence between these points is likely to increase in a context where school budgets are under increasing pressure and the workload of NQTs is also increasing. Again this raises dilemmas for some senior teachers over reconciling the claims of school and a wider sense of professional responsibility. How much support is reasonable? Who decides? An industrial tribunal? Who or what can take on the responsibility previously exercised by the LEA of exploring other channels of career development for individuals, for example by moving them to another school where they may be successful? The loss of this possibility in the current circumstances was felt by many to constitute a real diminution in NQTs' conditions of service.

Induction, Recruitment and Retention

Induction can be considered in terms of a calculation of its costs and benefits in relation to the costs of recruitment and a high staff turnover. Most of the senior teachers valued good induction provision as a means of building stability and commitment among the staff, although not all were confident that their colleagues in senior management or governing bodies shared these perceptions. Fewer still felt able to cite evidence to support their beliefs, or to produce the kinds of financial data with which to calculate the relative costs.

The LEA Inspectors who were interviewed tended to be very aware of these issues and much better informed of the financial aspects. In one case, where the LEA suffered from a 23 per cent turnover of young teachers, an extensive induction programme, linked to partnership with ITE institutions, was being implemented with the specific intention of addressing longstanding problems of low teacher expectations and pupil underachievement in the borough.

Another inspector was able to identify with precision the various costs of advertising, screening and interviewing candidates and providing an induction programme, and was convinced of the value to schools of investing in induction (particularly since they can use their greater scope for flexibility in deciding pay scales to reduce costs by starting NQTs on a low increment). For him, 'any school that ignores induction does so at its peril'. Both of these respondents were anticipating the disappearance of LEAs in the near future and, for them, the ability of schools to take on these issues was a matter of great concern.

A more sceptical note has been struck by Bolam (1994) who has argued that induction provision moves up and down the policy agenda according to the intensity of recruitment and retention problems and, ultimately, patterns of graduate unemployment. Certainly, an inspector based in a region which he described as having experienced few recruitment problems proved the most sceptical about the willingness of schools to invest in induction. One outcome may well be differential provision for new teachers across the country, matching regional differences in patterns of recruitment and retention.

Induction and School Effectiveness

Given the basis on which our respondents were selected for interview, it is not surprising that most of them were convinced of the value of good induction provision in raising the quality of teaching, the school's delivery of the curriculum and, ultimately, pupils' achievements. In part, this is a matter of investing in the professional development of the NQTs themselves. But of equal importance is the value of induction as an element in a whole-school structure and culture of professional development. Respondents mentioned several ways in which school-induction arrangements can contribute to this. Experience of a regular programme of observation, feedback, target setting and action planning can help to create a climate where continuous reflection and improvement becomes part of the culture. There are potential links with the involvement of schools in partnership arrangements in ITE and the development of profiles for assessing student teachers, and these in turn may link to the development of professional portfolios and the potential of appraisal to support professional development. Induction and work with student teachers can develop the mentoring skills of heads of department (HoDs) and other middle managers, skills which are directly transferable to classroom management and so to raising the quality of classroom practice (Shaw, 1992). Several of the schools placed considerable value on the participation of experienced teachers in running sessions for NQTs, seeing this as a means of engaging them in reflection upon their own expertise.

However, while the potential benefits are exciting, the practice can be somewhat different. Several senior managers commented on the variability of the quality of mentoring of the HoDs, the difficulties of gaining access to, or the complexities of developing good mentor training programmes, and the difficulties of finding the time to share good practice within the school. The costs of providing a good induction programme are high. On the other hand, the value to the school is not readily calculable in a form which can be used to convince colleagues. As a representative of a professional association commented

> A key issue will be the extent to which heads can convince governing bodies that investment in professional development and the induction of NQTs is worthwhile when the budget is tight.

Many staff, including senior management, hold what one respondent termed a 'deficiency model' of induction, seeing a programme of observation, feedback and support as appropriate for NQTs who are struggling, but not for those who are 'coping well'. The study by Draper and her colleagues in Scotland (Draper *et al.*, 1991) similarly found a widespread perception of the Scottish two-year probationary system as a 'time of trial' in which probationers 'proved' their fitness to teach, rather than as the first steps in a career's long process of continuous self-development.

Given these perceptions, it is not surprising if colleagues and governors are sceptical of the value of investing scarce resources into induction, except where it is geared to clearly perceived school interests. Provision organized on this basis might prioritize the following as aims: monitoring all NQTs sufficiently to identify those who are 'not coping'; managing the problem of failing NQTs; providing the information necessary to 'ease' new recruits into the school (e.g., through documentation or a programme of sessions focusing on school procedures and practices); ensuring that the school has met its legal obligations in the case of dismissal. In contrast to the vision of the 'learning organization', one inspector offered a rather more limited expectation for the future:

> Perhaps what can reasonably be expected is for schools to provide something for the NQTs to work with in the first few weeks; to watch them early on to make sure they are coping; after that, if they've got any spare energy to maybe have a systematic way of discussing things with them. But they're not picking up the NQTs' own personal development in terms of observation and feedback.

Another inspector suggested the following 'tiered' provision as the emergent pattern:

> Schools would buy into a programme of two one-day conferences per term, for about £40, plus subject specific days. The better schools would then provide school-based support, and the even better ones would provide that and some half days off where NQTs could have a rest or go to other schools. The ideal model would be half a day a week for the whole year.

Individual, School, Profession

Most respondents made reference to professional responsibilities over and above those related to their schools or NQTs. Even, or perhaps especially, in schools where the senior manager felt a sense of professional responsibility for providing high-quality induction, a distinction was drawn between the needs and interests of the school and those of the NQT. Thus in one school, where the LEA has devolved all funds for induction to the school, the senior manager negotiates with the HoD and NQT an individual programme of experiences (including observations, visits within and outside the school, attendance at advertised INSET, conferences etc.), seeing her role as being, in part,

> to balance the HoD's perception of needs, which tend to be related to departmental and school requirements, with a perception related to the profession more generally.

There are clear benefits from the school's new system whereby NQTs identify their needs, negotiate the subsequent INSET and are involved in calculating the budget. However needs can become very self-defined — 'No one is saying you don't know it, but you do need this.' This same senior manager was concerned that, with the demise of the LEA's programme, NQTs do not have the opportunity to get out of school on a regular basis 'when they can just flop'. Although the school's system is carefully structured and efficiently targeted it leaves no unstructured spaces for the 'human relations' of the former system. Bolam's reminder (op cit., 1987) that NQTs' prime need is for timetabled release indicates the complexities of balancing individual needs against other requirements.

Another senior manager described one of her major responsibilities as being to help the NQT to become aware of the school as a whole, what processes are important, why particular policies are in place and how these are related to the whole-school development plan. The individual NQT then is helped to see both how the school's INSET resources can be used to help her move forward with the school plan, and where her individual needs diverge from the school's priorities.

The needs of the school with regards to induction are not necessarily congruent with the needs of individual NQTs nor with the profession as a whole. As one respondent pointed out, there are two gaps in current methods of allocating professional development money: (a) no one takes responsibility for the long-term future of the whole profession; the only national view is that of the Government's which is mainly concerned with implementing its own reforms; (b) there are no means of meeting those individual needs of teachers which do not happen to match the priorities identified in the school-development plans.

Former arrangements for induction involving LEAs and statutory guidance from the DFE, albeit often functioning inadequately, at least provided a putative structure of responsibilities and accountabilities which extended beyond the individual school. For many respondents a critical issue was the question of what (if anything) in the future would move schools towards providing high-quality induction. An optimistic answer is provided by those respondents who saw the mechanism as being schools' self-interest.

> In a context of open enrolment, where funding largely depends on pupil intake, then it is in the school's interest that it has a reputation for high quality. There is a general consensus within the profession that, to do this, staff will have to be continuing to learn and hence management within schools will see this as an important priority.

The influence of management initiatives such as 'Investors In People', which focus on improving practice and organizational efficiency through processes of evaluation and the encouragement of a 'developmental culture', will help to create the conditions for a good induction provision. It will come about as a result of schools acting in their own interests.

Others were more pessimistic and believed that, without some kind of external mechanism guaranteeing provision, induction would move down the agenda despite otherwise potentially favourable developments in schools. In the words of one respondent, speculating about future developments,

> If schools were to organize systematically for staff development and needs identification, then they would begin to look at delivery of the National Curriculum in terms of what goes on in the classroom. As schools became good at this then there would be a need for them to include classroom practice in their planning and reviewing. This could be an aspect of management responsibility and therefore training. It could be a continuous 'seamless garment' of staff-development process, underpinned by competences . . . (However), while there are lots of nice strands which could be knitted together, in practice, I suspect, there (will be) nothing to drive the knitting.

Professional Structures

The absence of an external structure, through which the requirements and values of the 'profession as a whole' in respect of new teachers might be implemented, was at the root of many of our respondents' concerns. Induction conceived of as the next step (after initial training) in a lifelong professional career, as the entry point into a highly skilled and complex profession requiring many years in which to reach full competence, makes challenging demands on those responsible for supporting new teachers in this initial stage. It is also costly.

One way of specifying adequate provision for induction conceived of in this light is to treat it as a continuation of ITE. It would make sense for initial training and the induction year to be treated as a whole, particularly given the increased demands on teachers and the opening up of diverse routes into qualified teacher status. The ATL's proposals (Thompson, op cit.) for a six-month probationary period, drawing on Calderhead's discussion (Calderhead and Lambert, op cit.) of the isolation of teaching as an activity, are based on a notion of induction as a continuation of initial training. The ATL's model envisages all new teachers engaging in an initial period of intensive team teaching necessary for professional skills to be developed.

> New entrants (should) experience a constant but manageable challenge to their work, learning from their experience with the support of an experienced professional colleague. A negotiated, supportive and intensive structured induction programme should replace the present professional isolation of new entrants. (Thompson, op cit., p. 13)

A precedent for a model of induction as a continuation of ITE exists in the UK. Professional associations and HEIs in Scotland have argued (General Teaching

Council for Scotland, 1992) that primary teachers cannot adequately be prepared within the confines of a one year's postgraduate certificate of education (PGCE) and that all new primary teachers should be guaranteed an induction programme, organized by the regions (i.e., the Scottish equivalent of LEAs), covering a specified range of expertise, which has been drawn up by a central body, representative of the professional association, HEIs, the regions and the Government, and defined in relation to the content of the PGCE programme. The acceptance by the Scottish Education Office of these proposals stands in sharp contrast to the policies of the DFE. A critical feature of this model of induction is that it is an entitlement for all, in contrast to recommendations such as those of the School Teachers Review Body (House of Commons, 1993) that induction provision should be conditional on the needs of the individual NQT.

A different (although not necessarily opposing) model for a professional structure beyond the school is that embodied in the concept of a General Teaching Council (e.g., GTC (England and Wales), 1992; Sayer, 1993; Hextall *et al.*, 1991) which, within its functions as a professional association, would include those of defining the competences expected of new teachers, prescribing the required provision and monitoring the quality of its delivery. It was a sense of the need for a body carrying out these kinds of functions that lay behind the concerns of the deputy head who commented that

> There are no quality checks on the people who are acting as mentors and teacher tutors. There should be some kind of accreditation (and) recognition from the DFE so that one is identified as a properly qualified school-based tutor, who has met certain criteria. Otherwise how is there going to be any kind of quality control over developing the profession and moving it forward?

Again, it is worth noting that there is the beginning of such a professional association in Scotland, where the GTC for Scotland, representing the profession as a whole, controls entry into qualified teaching status and has a substantial influence on the content of ITE and induction. (Although it falls short of being a full professional body in that it does not control professional development after the probationary period.)

If the system found in some other professions were to be adopted in teaching, one might envisage a structure whereby a professional body defines a framework of desired training outcomes and competences, and supports and liaises with individual schools, HEIs and other institutions providing courses or training experiences, monitors the quality and certificates the outcomes. The potential components of such a system exist in such current developments in education as profiles of competences, in-school mentoring, professional portfolios, accreditation of school-based professional development, diversification of HEI courses, NVQs. Out of these could emerge a structure, organized by a professional body, which would provide a clear direction and entitlement to the development of new teachers in their first few years. In such a scenario the content and structure of the competences would be of crucial significance, since it would be through them that the nature of the profession would be defined (Sidgwick, Mahony and Hextall, op cit., Mahony and Whitty, forthcoming).

Management of the Teaching Force

Teaching is the largest occupational category in the economy (School Teachers Review Body, 1994), with 470,000 teachers in 26,500 schools in England and Wales and with a pay bill of £11 billion. State schools are the largest single employer of graduate manpower in the UK. It has been pointed out (Keep, 1993) that in comparable sectors of the economy, e.g., the health service, or large multinationals, there are structures for managing these human resources.

> Human resource management, linking recruitment, staff development, reward systems and career structures, is an integral part of successful management in large-scale modern enterprises. (Keep, op cit., p. 53)

Keep argues that in education these functions were formerly dealt with (however imperfectly) at three levels: schools, LEA and nationally. As a consequence of government policy, LEAs are decreasingly able to carry out many of their former functions (e.g., redeploying teachers, providing INSET, supplying personnel advice and support services) and schools have gained greater control over the management of staffing. These changes have occasioned considerable tensions (as well as benefits) for schools. Several of the senior managers expressed a sense of unease that responsibilities previously undertaken by the LEA were being dropped, or unevenly transferred to schools which often are not in a position to discharge them. These problems are compounded by a lack of a strategic role at the national level. The DFE is undoubtedly exercising much greater control in certain areas, for example, over the curriculum, the direction of INSET and the conditions within which ITE operates. However,

> The range and importance of these activities arguably serves to disguise a fundamental problem. The DFE has no single personnel management department or unit with overall responsibility for personnel issues affecting the teaching work force . . . Moreover, the DFE's structures often appear geared up to undertake routine aspects of personnel *administration* as distinct from personnel *management*.
> The education system's lack of any central national focus for strategic personnel management is distinctive within the public sector and is particularly noticeable given the size of the work force involved. (Keep, op cit., p. 56)

The Government appears to believe that the education service would become more efficient if it adopted management practices from the private sector. But, again, Keep has made the point (1992) that the lessons from the private sector concerning the management of human resources are ambiguous, in that there is no single private-sector model, rather a number of different models, deriving from differences in companies' different structures and strategic purposes. Are schools to be seen as 26,500 autonomous small businesses, competing for pupils and responsible for their own recruitment, retention and staff-development policies? The record of small businesses in the UK with respect to strategic planning, training and development does not give grounds for optimism. Or is the education system as a whole to be regarded as one large firm and the relevant model ICI, where a central HQ formulates strategic policies? If it is the latter then one would expect a national framework of policies for education addressing such matters as: teacher supply, recruitment and training numbers; a framework of criteria for staffing matched against audits of actual staffing resources (at both local, regional and national level); career structures; design of national INSET programmes to support nationally driven policies; dissemination of good personnel practice throughout education; a structure for managing training, retraining and career development which meets the needs both of the system and of individual teachers.

If the teaching force were managed in this way, induction would constitute a stage in a system for professional development which offered long-term career development and the maximization of individual potential necessary for teaching to compete with other employers of high-quality graduates. As one of our respondents put it:

> Good practice in personnel management is to see it holistically: initial training, induction, reward structures appraisal are not seen as separate elements but as inextricably linked . . . If schools were operating as big companies do, someone would be looking at new recruits with potential, for example as heads of department, to plan what suite of experiences they need to go through in order to build them up into potential senior managers. They would be asking: what do we need to plan for them — what sorts of job rotation, responsibilities, training? Instead, it is left to the individual teacher's whim and initiative to work out their own salvation and plan their own career. Unless this kind of planning happens, efficient use is not going to be made of a scarce resource.

At present the structures do not exist for staff development to be planned in relation to the needs of the system, the school and the longer-term needs of the individual. Whether they should exist is, in part, a question about the relative merits of planning and the market as mechanisms for the effective provision of a service such as the education and development of teachers.

Markets, Schools and the Induction of New Teachers

> There is a paradox (in that) the Government, which in some respects is centralizing and taking an active role in determining the characteristics of teachers, is in other respects withdrawing and handing over the process of shaping teachers to a number of decentralized sites. (Respondent in interview)

> Who will drive development, keep an overview and make sense of what needs to be developed and how? (Respondent in interview)

Many of our respondents' concerns and dilemmas can be understood as expressions of the tensions consequent on the introduction of market relations into areas of welfare provision such as education. 'The market' and 'planning' constitute the two major principles for coordinating wants and needs with the delivery of the goods and services to meet them. Markets exist when the transactions of buyers and sellers are coordinated by a price mechanism which indicates how much purchasers are prepared to pay and producers willing to sell of various goods and services. The present Government has made no secret of its belief in the virtues of the market over local and national state planning as means of organizing behaviour and has sought to extend the areas of economic activity which are subject to market forces. Le Grand and Bartlett (1993) have argued that government reforms of the welfare state, beginning in 1988/89, have created a series of 'quasi-markets' in public services such as education, housing, health and community care in an attempt to restructure provision to make it conform to market criteria. Such quasi-markets are characterized by a decentralization of decision-making, a reduction or elimination of the role of the State in providing services directly, the creation of competition between a number of independent providers in internal markets and/or for public contracts, and the representation of consumers by agents or a single purchasing agency.

A growing body of work has engaged with the nature and effects of this project in education (e.g., Bowe, Ball and Gold, 1992; Ball, 1993; Jones, 1989; Hatcher, 1994). With colleagues I have argued elsewhere (Sidgwick, Mahony and Hextall, forthcoming) that it is also appropriate to think of an emerging market in initial teacher education. In terms of the issues raised earlier in this chapter, as shift towards market relations can be seen in the following developments: LMS and formula funding has decentralized decision-making to schools and diminished LEAs' powers to exercise administrative discretion (Levacic, 1992); LEAs' role as direct providers of services is being reduced and the ability of schools to choose amongst different providers is being increased; LMS has introduced a price mechanism into schools' decision-making:

> (LMS) is an organisational form which changes the way resources are allocated, the incentives and sanctions facing decision makers and the information to which they respond. With LMS more of the information to which schools respond is expressed in monetary terms and this changes incentives and decisions. (Levacic, op cit., p. 16)

The virtues of 'the market' have been proclaimed with almost religious zeal by the Conservative Right. In its view, LEAs and teacher-training departments constitute prime examples of the evils of 'provider capture' (i.e., the use of monopolistic positions to organize provision in line with producers', rather than consumers', needs and interests) and of the waste of resources consequent on the separation of control of resources from the discipline of the market. Elimination of the ideological domination supposedly exercised by the 'educational establishment' provides a further motive for weakening its institutional basis in LEAs and HEIs and decentralizing control of resources for teacher education into 26,500 small businesses.

However, one does not have to embrace the New Right's project, nor its idealized representations of the benefits of competition, to acknowledge that there is a growing debate, which includes positions from across the political spectrum, concerning the relevance of the market as an organizing principle in the public sector. Drawing on experience in education, health, housing and community care, commentators have proposed a less ideologically committed adjudication between the benefits of market and planning forms of organization for reconciling the claims of efficiency, equity, choice and responsiveness in welfare provision (Barr and Whynes, 1993; Le Grand and Bartlett, op cit., Glennerster, 1992). In particular, there has been considerable debate concerning the criteria and conditions under which markets may or may not be successful in these sectors of the economy. Along with colleagues (Sidgwick, Mahony and Hextall, op cit.) I have summarized some of this debate as it pertains to ITE. In the remainder of this chapter I will discuss those conditions and qualifications which throw light on the concerns expressed by our respondents about provision for new teachers.

Discussions of markets in other public sectors give a critical role to information. It is crucial that users or purchasers have access to the information which will enable them to make choices on rational grounds. Decisions about investment in induction may be affected and distorted by absence of relevant information. Amongst the concerns of our respondents, there were several which indicated problems of this kind: obtaining independent information about the range and quality of provision on offer in a situation of competition between different providers; doubts about the ability of many schools to identify accurately the real costs of the different elements in provision for induction; difficulties in evaluating the outcomes and long-term impact of investment in induction on school effectiveness; concerns about convincing colleagues and governing bodies of its value. All of these indicate potential points at which the dominance of market criteria in provision for this aspect (or indeed any other) of staff development may fail to deliver desired and appropriate outcomes.

Where the structure of the market is such that there is a distinction between purchasers and users, there are issues concerning the motivation of the purchasers, whose actions must be derived from a concern for the needs and wants of the users if the market is to be effective in delivering provision. This is more likely to be the case the closer purchasers are to users. The example of GP fund holders is a case in point. If the NQT is to be regarded as the 'user' of induction and the school-induction coordinator as the purchaser, then there are questions about how 'needs' become constructed and defined. The issue is highlighted by the proposals for a voucher or ear-marked funds for induction, put forward by the ATL (Thompson, op cit.) and by the School Teachers Review Body (1994), to come with the individual NQT to be used by the school on her or his behalf. An alternative would be for control of the voucher to lie with the NQT. This would eliminate problems to do with whether the school would use the funds in the interests of the NQT, but return us to the information problems discussed before. Would NQTs be in a position to obtain the information which would enable them to make rational choices? Are they in a position to be able to grasp the relationship between their short-term needs and those arising from a longer-term perspective on their long-term professional and career development?

These issues concerning purchasers and users lead us into a further set of questions concerning the purpose of induction or, in market terms, the nature of the 'goods' being traded. One of the fundamental qualifications made in welfare economics lies in the distinction between private and public goods and the ensuing possibility that some goods and services cannot be distributed efficiently by the market, thus leading to market failure. Private goods are those which can be bought and consumed or owned by an individual (person or institution) and as a consequence are no longer available. Public goods are goods which, by their nature, are diffuse and indivisible and hence difficult to own.

> Once produced, they enter the public realm. Indeed, one definition of a
> public good is a good that, once produced for any member of a group,
> automatically is available for any other member of that group . . . The

beneficial effect of a technical improvement on economic growth, the existence of a well-tended public park, the public educational system, national disease control, and an effective deterrence system are all examples of the nondiscriminating quality of public goods. (Begg, Fischer and Dornbusch, 1991, p. 93)

This indivisibility generates issues concerning private and social costs and benefits. The system as a whole may benefit, for example from the training of a teacher, but the costs may be borne wholly or partly by the individual institution. Conversely, 'free riders' derive benefits from the activities of others without themselves having to bear any of the costs. These problems make it difficult if not impossible for such goods to be produced and distributed through the market.

At a macroeconomic level the difficulty is that private costs and benefits cannot be linked to social costs and benefits. As with externalities, this distorts resource allocation and leads to an undersupply of public goods. (Begg, Fischer and Dornbusch, 1991; p. 94)

This is an instance of wider source of market failure arising from the possibility of externalities — i.e., where people benefit from, or suffer from, the effects of transactions conducted by others and to which they were not party. In consequence there may be no market mechanism for signalling the true demand.

The provision of support and further training for NQTs can be seen as sharing some of the characteristics of this kind of market failure. It would be possible to regard the support which a school defines its new teacher as needing, or the skills which it wishes to foster in its new recruits, as possessing some of the characteristics of private goods, in that there would be identifiable benefits to the institution which it could include within calculations when allocating its resources. However, as previously discussed, there is a distinction to be drawn between the training required by an individual school or NQT and that required in order to produce a highly trained teaching force. The collective body of knowledge and expertise which sustains the work of individual teachers and schools is better seen as a public good which benefits all schools, and ultimately the nation as a whole. The implications for education are suggestive. Can or should individual schools be expected to bear the costs of activities which benefit all? Can the costs be accurately identified and a system of reimbursement implemented? What of schools which derive benefits, for example by appointing teachers with three or four years experience who have been trained and inducted by other schools, without sharing costs (e.g., by not participating in ITE or providing a high-quality induction themselves)? These questions return us to considerations of the purposes of induction, its intended beneficiaries and appropriate lines of accountability and responsibility.

Ultimately what is at issue, not only in education but in other sectors of welfare provision, is the split between micro and macro in considerations of welfare needs. For the Right, the archetype of social relationships is the voluntary exchange based on the assumption that each person or individual institution knows best what he or she wants. Human life is ultimately a matter of maximizing private satisfactions in the context of resource constraints and it is the market which can deliver this with the optimum combination of efficiency, responsiveness and choice. In opposition to this is the position that individual choices, aggregated together, are unlikely to meet broader patterns of socially defined needs and that macro-economic coordination is needed to overcome the weaknesses of fragmented market systems.

Conclusion

In this chapter I have attempted to indicate points at which problems arising out of the effects of government policy on the context for induction provision can be related to more general problems concerning the applicability of market principles to welfare provision. My purpose in doing so is to suggest where educational debates might begin to be illuminated by the experiences of those working in different but comparable sectors of the economy which are further down this particular policy line and where there is a growing body of work offering a framework for identifying the conditions under which these quasi-markets do or do not provide an effective means of coordinating needs and provision.

Many of our respondents believed that an external structure was necessary in order to guarantee an effective provision for induction, whether this be statutory requirements, vouchers or guaranteed funding, the extension of ITE or some other mechanism. There is considerable support within education for some kind of supra-school body which could undertake the strategic management and professional functions discussed earlier, and which would provide a context for induction provision. Many educators favour a model based on the concept of a professional body which would define and represent the interests of the profession.

However, it is unlikely that the present Government would be sympathetic to such a development. Insofar as it moves to put in place structures for coordinating the 'training' of beginning teachers, one would expect it to turn to models derived from market theories and its experience of introducing reforms into other parts of the Welfare State, such as the super-purchasing bodies in health and community care or the use of 'Next Step' agencies to marketize the activities of government bodies. A further such model is provided by the Training and Enterprise Councils (TECs), which represent an attempt to implement a market-led structure for organizing and providing training (Bailey, 1993; Peck, 1991). In this context, it is salutary to note the criticisms which have been levelled at the TECs (e.g., Peck, op cit.) for promoting short term, low-quality training. These initiatives may well hold lessons for educators concerning possible directions of policy for the education of teachers. In this respect the terms of reference and conditions of operation of the new Teacher Training Agency will repay careful scrutiny.

Note

1 This chapter is based on research undertaken in 1993 by the author and Ian Hextall. I am greatly indebted to Ian for his collaboration on the research and for the many discussions from which this chapter has grown.

References

BAILEY, T. (1993) 'The missions of the TECs and private sector involvement in training: Lessons from private Industry councils', in *Oxford Studies in Comparative Education*, 3, 1, pp. 7–26.

BALL, S. (1993) 'Education markets, choice and social class: The market as a class strategy in the UK and the USA', *British Journal of Sociology of Education*, **14**, 1, pp. 3–19.

BARR, N. and WHYNES, D. (Eds) (1993) *Current Issues in the Economics of Welfare*, London, MacMillan.

BEGG, D., FISCHER, S. and DORNBUSCH, R. (1991) *Economics*, McGraw Hill.

BOLAM, R. (1987) 'Induction of beginning teachers', in DUNKIN, M.T. (Ed) *The International Encyclopedia of Teaching and Teachers in Education*, Oxford, Pergamon Press.

BOLAM, R. (1994) 'Teacher recruitment and induction,' in HUSEN, T. and POSTLETHWAITE, T.N. (Eds) *The International Encyclopedia of Education*, Oxford, Pergamon Press.

BOWE, R., BALL, S. and GOLD, A. (1992) *Reforming Education and Changing Schools*, London, Routledge.

CALDERHEAD, J. and LAMBERT, J. (1992) *The Induction of Newly Appointed Teachers*, London, General Teaching Council Initiative for England and Wales.

DEPARTMENT OF EDUCATION AND SCIENCE (DES) HER MAJESTY'S INSPECTORATE (HMI) (1988) *The New Teacher in School: A Survey by HM Inspectors in England And Wales*, London, HMSO.

DEPARTMENT OF EDUCATION AND SCIENCE (DES) (1990) *The Treatment and Assessment of Probationary Teachers*, Administrative Memorandum 1/90, London, DES.

DEPARTMENT OF EDUCATION AND SCIENCE (DES) (1991) *Consultation Letter, 17/9/1991*, London, DES.

DEPARTMENT OF EDUCATION AND SCIENCE (DES) HER MAJESTY'S INSPECTORATE (HMI) (1992a) *The Induction and Probation of New Teachers, 1988–1991* (HMI Report 62/92), London, DES.

DEPARTMENT OF EDUCATION AND SCIENCE (DES) (1992b) *Induction of Newly Qualified Teachers*, Administrative Memorandum 2/92, London, DES.

DRAPER, J., FRASER, H., SMITH, D. and TAYLOR, W. (1991) *A Study of Probationers*, Edinburgh, Heriot-Watt University, Moray House Institute of Education.

EARLEY, P. (1992) *Beyond Initial Teacher Training: Induction and the Role of the LEA*, Slough, National Foundation for Educational Research.

EARLEY, P. and KINDER, K. (1994) *Initiation Rites: Effective Induction practices for New Teachers*, Slough, National Foundation for Educational Research.

GENERAL TEACHING COUNCIL FOR SCOTLAND (1992) *Primary Postgraduate Review: Final Report of the Working Group on the Implementation of a Scheme of Enrichment Training for PGCE (Primary) Probationers*, Edinburgh, GTC for Scotland.

GENERAL TEACHING COUNCIL FOR ENGLAND AND WALES (1992) *Proposals for a Statutory General Teaching Council for England and Wales: A Report from GTC (England and Wales, July 1992)*, GTC (England and Wales).

GLENNERSTER, H. (1992) *Paying for Welfare: Issues for the 1990's*, London, Harvester Wheatsheaf.

GODDARD, D. (1993) 'The role of the LEA in Induction', *Journal of Inservice Education*, pp. 46–54.

HATCHER, R. (1994) 'Market relationships and the management of teachers', BRITISH JOURNAL OF SOCIOLOGY OF EDUCATION, **15**, 1, pp. 41–61.

HEXTALL, I., LAWN, M., MENTER, I., SIDGWICK, S. and WALKER, S. (1991) 'Imaginative projects: Arguments for a new teacher education', in GRACE, G. and LAWN, M. (Eds) *Teacher Supply and Teacher Quality*, Clevedon, Multilingual Matters.

HOUSE OF COMMONS (1993) *School Teachers Review Body: 2nd Report 1993* (Cm 2151), London, HMSO.

HOUSE OF COMMONS (1994) *School Teachers Review Body: 3rd Report 1994* (Cm 2466), London, HMSO.

JONES, K. (1989) *Right Turn: The Conservative Revolution in Education*, London, Hutchinson.

KEEP, E. (1992) 'Schools in the market place? Some problems with private sector models', in WALLACE, G. (Ed) *Local Management of Schools: Research and Experience, BERA Dialogues No. 7*, Clevedon, Multilingual Matters.

KEEP, E. (1993) 'The need for a revised management system for the teaching profession', *Education Economics*, **1**, 1.

LE GRAND, J. and BARTLETT, W. (Eds) (1993) *Quasi-markets and Social Policy*, London, MacMillan.

LEVACIC, R. (1992) 'Local management of schools: Aims, scope and impact', in *Educational Management and Administration*, **20**, 1.

MAHONY, P. and WHITTY, G. (forthcoming) 'Teacher education and teacher competences', in TOMLINSON, S. (Ed) *Alternative Education Policies*, Rivers Oram Press.

OFFICE OF STANDARDS IN EDUCATION (OFSTED) (1993) *The New Teacher in School: A Survey by HM Inspectors in England and Wales 1992*, London, HMSO.

PECK, J. (1991) 'Letting the market decide (with public money): Training and enterprise councils and the future of labour market programmes', *Critical Social Policy*, Issue 31, **11**, 1, pp. 4–17.

SAYER, J. (1993) *The Future Governance of Education*, Cassell.

SAYER, J. (1993) The General Teaching Council and Teacher Supply, in *The Recruitment and Retention of Teachers*, Longman.

SHAW, R. (1992) *Teacher Training in Secondary Schools*, Kogan Page.

SIDGWICK, S., MAHONY, P. and HEXTALL, I. (1993) 'Policy and practice in the professional development of teachers', *International Studies in the Sociology of Education*, **13**, 1, pp. 91–108.

SIDGWICK, S., MAHONY, P. and HEXTALL, I. (forthcoming) 'A gap in the market? A consideration of market relations in teacher education', *British Journal of Sociology of Education; Special Issue: 'Teacher Education: Past, Present and Future*.

School Teachers Review Body (1994), London, HMSO.

THOMPSON, M. (1993) 'The weakest link: ATL's proposals', *British Journal of In-service Education*, **19**, 1, pp. 12–15.

10 A Knowledge Base for Mentors of Beginning Teachers: Results of a Dutch Experience

J.H.C. Vonk

Abstract

This contribution examines the practical and theoretical knowledge base for mentoring during teacher induction and has its basis in a longitudinal and close-to-practice research programme called The Professional Development of Beginning Teachers in Secondary Education which has been conducted since 1979. The programme concerns a study into the process of professional development of beginning teachers during their first five years of service. In addition, data was collected from a large number of in-service courses for beginning teachers, and from in-service courses for mentors of beginning teachers — i.e., senior teachers who are responsible for mentoring their beginning colleagues. This chapter describes the practical and theoretical knowledge base which is basic for good mentoring practice and which has been developed over the years. It suggests that there are three essential elements of a mentor's knowledge base: first, the various facets in beginning teachers professional development; second, a framework for analysing their classroom performance; and third, a model for understanding the process of learning from experiences.

Introduction

Nearly everywhere in the world beginning teachers (BTs) experience their first year of teaching as problematic. They feel inadequately prepared for their jobs as teachers. In most schools, beginners have, from the first day on, exactly the same responsibility as their colleagues with many years of experience, and pupils, parents, colleagues and management often expect them to act as full professionals. Many beginners fail to meet these expectations, and the drop-out rate during the first three years of service can sometimes reach up to 60 per cent.[1] In many schools induction is not part of the culture and reconstructed induction programmes are required.

The growing emphasis on the quality of teaching in recent years has not only led to experiments with other models of teacher education but also to greater attention to staff policies, staff development and supervision of instruction and curriculum in schools.[2] In this context we consider mentoring of BTs as part of the 'Supervision of Instruction', i.e., an element in the supervisory services of schools.[3]

Supervisory leadership functions are aimed at stimulating the enhancement of the quality of the individual teacher's performance as well as that of the organization of the school as a whole.[4] These functions are not strictly bound to school management, but are viewed as a function of the school as a whole, i.e., all teachers are co-responsible and can be involved in one way or another. The mentoring model discussed in this contribution assumes teachers develop into self-directing professionals, and therefore the formalized mentor–*protégé* relationship is adopted as the starting point, and the individual teacher's professional development as organizing principle for the induction of teachers into the profession[5] (Andrews, 1986).

However, only a minority of schools offer a well-balanced induction programme.[6] Effective induction of teachers in schools depends heavily on the extent to which the instructional and curricular leadership functions in those schools are implemented (Vonk, 1992). This is the more true because most teachers still spend the major part of their time isolated from their peers, and, as a consequence, BTs most often do not receive, as is natural in other professions, ongoing direction and assistance from more experienced colleagues (Huling-Austin, 1990).

The motives for this research programme were threefold. First, the everlasting but not very solution-oriented discussions in the late 1970s about the theory–practice gap BTs experienced during induction regardless of the quality of their initial training; second, the lack of theorizing about teacher development during induction and in relation to that the lack of real insight into the problems of BTs; and finally, the absence of a knowledge and skills base as well as a structure in schools for good mentoring practice. In our research we have tried to tackle those problems in that order.

Research Background and Methodology

In this section we will give an introduction to the research programme which provided the context for our study into the knowledge and skills base for mentors of BTs.

Conceptual Framework

The process of becoming a teacher is developmental in nature and concerns the first three phases in a teacher's professional development. If we look upon teachers' careers as a coherent whole, from initial education and training to retirement, it will be obvious that throughout their careers, based on their personal life experiences and their formal and informal professional experiences, a continuous and coherent set of changes is taking place in their ideas about the profession and in their professional way of thinking and acting. These changes are both qualitative and quantitative in nature.

Although the term development connotes internally guided rather than externally imposed changes, professional development is considered to be the result of a learning process which is directed at acquiring a coherent whole of the (practical and theoretical) knowledge, insights, attitudes and repertory that a teacher needs for everyday practice in the profession (Vonk, 1991). Such a development, however, is not a simple, spontaneous process, but the outcome of a complex interaction between the individuals and the various environments in which they are participating (Lacey, 1977; Zeichner and Gore, 1990; Hargreaves, 1992).

Vonk (1991) contends that teachers' professional development is a function of that interaction between person-related[7] and environmental[8] factors. This learning process, which cannot be envisaged separately from its environmental context, has the following characteristics:

- Professional learning is based on continuous reflection on one's everyday experiences in a certain context. The frame of reference for that reflection consists of teachers' practical and theoretical knowledge (McIntyre, 1993).
- Professional learning is a lifelong process. Teachers are continuously confronted with new situations and challenges that give them opportunities to learn (Vonk, 1994).
- Professional learning does not take place in isolation, but in the context of a particular school. Professional development and school development are inextricably linked. This means that teacher development does not only depend on individuals, but also on teachers and administrators with whom they work (Fullan, 1991, p. 315).

In this context we define 'teacher induction' as the transition from student-teacher to self-directing professional. It concerns the first two stages in the process after initial training of teacher professional development: the 'threshold phase' and the 'phase of growing into the profession' (Vonk, 1991, p. 65). Teacher induction can be best understood as part of the continuum of the process of teacher professional development which can be described as follows (Figure 10.1).

Initial Training ---------> Induction ---------> Self-directed Professional Development

Figure 10.1:   Continuum of the process of teacher professional development

Initial teacher training (pre-professional phase) is aimed at developing teachers' starting competences — i.e., mastery of the basic classroom-teaching skills; induction (threshold phase and phase of growing into the profession) is aimed at helping novices develop a professional identity and an appropriate repertoire of actions and finally to structure their self-directed professional development.

The importance of teacher induction both for beginners and schools is that it contributes to avoiding unnecessary tension and future malfunctioning. In addition, a good start definitely influences a teacher's abilities and willingness to develop in a positive direction. It is known from studies on teacher professional development that teachers who have been left to fend for themselves in their first years of teaching tend to develop a strongly 'survival-oriented' repertoire of actions, sometimes called a 'survival kit'.[9] This results from a trial-and-error approach, influenced by immediate circumstantial pressure and is most often inflexible in nature. With the inevitable constraint of time BTs are hardly able to reflect, and if they do, they do not know what to reflect on: they lack a solid 'orientation base'.[10] As a consequence, such a repertoire offers very few points of contact for expansion and further development. Changes in that repertoire demand great effort on the part of those teachers because it could again lead to class-control problems, which is something they wish to avoid anyway (Vonk and Schras, 1987). However, during induction many BTs do not receive much help from mentors or from the school management, and if they do find support, it is mostly inadequate. Adequate mentoring can aid novice teachers to tackle effectively the problems they meet and hence to cope with the reality-shock they experience. Eventually, we may expect this to lead to the development of a more flexible repertoire of actions and a more open-minded attitude to change.

The second concept which is of importance is the concept of mentoring. Mentoring is not just the transfer of existing craft knowledge and skills to a novice (Brown and McIntyre, 1988). It is helping a BT develop his or her own flexible repertory of teaching and classroom-management skills, to develop a proper insight into pupils' learning processes and a perspective on himself or herself as a teacher. These four elements are vital in the process of a BT's professional development. As a consequence, the mentoring model we have developed can be seen as an example of the formalized mentor–*protégé* model with BTs' professional development as its organizing principle.

We consider mentoring to be a dynamic, reciprocal relationship in a work environment between an advanced career incumbent and a beginner aimed at promoting the career development of both (Healy and Welchert, 1990). The beginner's interest in the relation is the help received from an expert in acquiring a professional identity, i.e., growth from novice to self-directing professional. The mentor's interest in this relationship is that, in order to be able to help other teachers effectively, he has to reflect continuously on his own professional knowledge and repertoire of actions.[11] This nearly always results in improvement of that repertoire. For older teachers, the mentoring relationship means practicing 'generativity'.[12] Essential in this definition, however, is the reciprocity. The mentoring relationship contributes to the professional development of both participants, i.e., it boosts the quality of the professional practice of both participants.

Overview of the Research Activities in the Programme

The development of the knowledge base we offer mentors in our training programme followed a series of longitudinal and close-to-practice studies (1979 and onwards) on the process of professional development of BTs (first five years of service). These studies include:

- (1979–84) A series of qualitative case studies aimed at the close-to-practice analysis of problems of BTs during the threshold period (first year of service) in their career (Vonk, 1982, 1984);
- (1984–6) A study (a series of half-open retrospective interviews) on BTs' professional development during the phase of growing into the profession (second to fifth years of service) (Vonk and Schras, 1987).
- (1986–8) A study on the causes of BTs problems (an experimental in-service training programme with data collection through interviews and classroom observations) and the description of some heuristics to help BTs to tackle the problematic situations they envisage (Vonk, 1989);
- (1988–92) A study (experimental course with systematic feedback interviews with mentors and *protégés*) on mentoring BTs (Vonk, 1992).

Next to gaining insight into, and understanding of, the process of becoming a teacher, the outcomes of these studies resulted in the identification of a knowledge and skills base needed for the effective mentoring of BTs. Particularly in the last study we were able to bring together various elements of our previous work and so develop a coherent and practice-oriented training programme for the mentors of BTs.

Methodology

As our interest is in insight, discovery and interpretation, rather than hypothesis testing, we chose a phenomenological position with respect to our research activities from the start of the project. During the act of teaching, teachers use themselves as instruments. Consequently, we do not consider the world of teaching as an objectively measurable unit, but as a function of personal interaction and perception (Merriam, 1991, p. 17). Our major interest was what BTs actually experienced in their classrooms, what meaning they gave to those experiences, how their problems evolved over time, and how to help BTs to tackle those problems effectively. This approach includes description and interpretation, the latter leading BTs to more general insight into problems and into associated strategies. Although our approach used primarily qualitative data-collection instruments — such as, in-depth interviews, logbooks, learner reports, and self-evaluations — we also used, where appropriate, more quantitative research-oriented instruments — such as pupil questionnaires, checklists and classroom-observation instruments.

Our research began with a qualitative case-study approach (Vonk, 1984, p. 16), in which every BT or mentor was considered as a case and data was collected from each of them (thick description approach). As mentors we were participant researchers investigating the process of the professional development of BTs. In addition, we trained mentors, and after a certain period of time we collected data on the adequacy of the knowledge and skills base provided by means of retrospective interviews in which the mentors reflected on their experiences as mentors and BTs on theirs as *protégés*. To arrive at generalized conclusions the methodology of the continuous comparison of cases (Glaser and Strauss, 1967; Miles and Huberman, 1984) was applied. Generalizations in this context are 'hypotheses' to be carried on from one case to the next, rather than general laws to be applied across a population (Brown and McIntyre, 1988). The conclusions were constantly verified and/or adjusted in a series of discussions/interviews with the participants of in-service courses for BTs (annually three groups of twenty BTs) and training courses for mentors (annually twenty to thirty participants). On the basis of the outcomes of these investigations provisional programmes were adjusted.

As we strongly believe that valuable knowledge in the educational arena can be gained from a permanent interaction between practice and theory, we continually tried to connect our findings (practical theory) with 'academic theory' (explanatory function).[13] In so doing we developed step by step practice-based knowledge of, and insight into, the process of becoming a teacher, i.e., in the nature, the history and the causes of BTs problems and in effective strategies to help them tackle their problems. Simultaneously we gained knowledge of, and insight into, the process of mentoring BTs which led to the development of a practice-based mentor training programme.

Mentors' Knowledge Base

In the formalized mentor–*protégé* model which is basic to our research, apart from being a qualified teacher with excellent classroom-management skills and an expert in the subject and its methodology, a good mentor must have the following personal qualities: open-mindedness, reflectiveness, flexibility, listening skills, empathy, creativity and a helping attitude.[14] Mentors should also meet some prerequisites. The first is a knowledge base. Mentors need to understand the nature of the process of the professional development of BTs, the nature and the causes of the problems beginners experience and how these problems evolve. Above all, they must have insight into the essentials of the teacher's professional learning process. The second is a skills base. In the mentor–*protégé* relationship a mentor has to play a variety of roles including, observer, provider of feedback, instructor, and evaluator.[15] The setting of the relationship is like counselling in that mentors can be considered 'skilled helpers' (Egan, 1986). To act effectively a mentor must have mastered a wide range of types of interpersonal behaviour, know how these types of behaviour affect their *protégés*, and be able to match behaviour to situations. It will be clear that mentors have to be selected carefully as not all teachers meet the prerequisites mentioned above or the abilities to develop them. After selection they will still need substantial training to be able to act effectively as mentors.

With respect to subject expertise and methodology, a mentor's basic knowledge base has three elements. First, insight into, and understanding of, the process of the professional development of BTs, second, knowledge of guidance and support strategies to support BTs as they tackle their problems, and finally, insight into, and understanding of, the process of learning from experience. In the following sections these issues will be discussed.

Issues in the Professional Development of BTs

Before we start defining the concept of professional development as it relates to the teaching profession, we need to raise the following question: 'What makes the teaching profession so special?' If we look closely at the act of teaching, it is easy to observe that when teaching, a teacher uses himself or herself as an instrument. As a consequence, the act of teaching is more than a simple technical activity and the teacher as a person is strongly involved in this act. Consequently, there is no set of teacher-proof teaching skills. Although research on teaching may offer a considerable amount of knowledge about effective teaching skills, these never can be more than valuable suggestions for practice (McIntyre, 1993). In essence, teacher development is self-directed development, i.e., teachers have to develop their own individual style of teaching.

In a number of studies (Burke, 1987; Levine, 1989; Vonk, 1989; Burden, 1990; Fessler and Christensen, 1992; Huberman, 1992) the different phases in teacher professional development have been investigated. We distinguish the following phases in a teacher's career[16]:

- the pre-professional phase, the period of initial education and training;
- the threshold phase, the first year of teaching;

- the phase of growing into the profession, generally the period between the second and seventh year of service;
- the first professional phase;
- the phase of reorientation towards oneself and the professions, sometimes indicated as the mid-career crisis;
- the second professional phase;
- the phase of winding down, the period before retirement.

In the context of this document, only the characteristics of the pre-professional phase and threshold phase will be described.

1 Pre-professional Phase

The pre-professional phase of a teacher's career encompasses that period of training typically associated with the initial college or university preparation for a teaching certificate. It may also include retraining a practising teacher for a new role or assignment (Christensen, 1992). The training of teachers for their formal role actually begins long before they enroll in a teacher training programme. Prospective teachers have been watching their own teachers for at least sixteen years (Lacey, 1977; Vonk, 1984; Zeichner and Gore, 1990). One might expect that in doing so, they already have developed strong perceptions of the nature of both classroom teaching and a teacher's role. Whether these perceptions can be changed or not during initial teacher education is still questionable. Research on the effectiveness of initial teacher education does not give firm answers.[17] Initial teacher education trains for a starting competency, aiming to give novices the opportunity to continue to develop and has to be followed up by a guided teacher-induction programme.

2 Threshold Phase

The threshold phase is the first year of teaching or probationary period, when teachers are confronted with all the responsibilities of a teacher for the first time and have to learn how to cope with the associated problems. This phase is often called the 'survival' period. BTs focus mainly on the day-to-day mastery of their new job (Vonk, 1984; Veenman, 1984; Ryan, 1986; Letvin, 1992) and strive for acceptance by students, colleagues and school management. In his study on similarities in beginning primary-school teachers' experiences, Veenman described the first year of teaching as a 'reality shock'. He identified and ranked eight problem areas experienced most frequently by BTs: classroom discipline, motivating students, dealing with individual differences, assessing students' work, contacts with parents, classroom management, inadequate teaching materials and supplies and the problems of individual students. Vonk (1984), from his research on problems of BTs in secondary education, identified a similar set of problem areas but also investigated the origins of those problems. He came to the following conclusions: first, many problems originate from the fact that beginners have too little pedagogical content knowledge;[18] second, the lack of 'overview' makes classroom teaching so complex[19] for most beginners that problems with classroom discipline, classroom management are inevitable;[20] third, during initial training, most BTs do learn how to cope with discipline problems;[21] fourth, most beginners have a perspective on their role as a teacher which is too optimistic, and are not prepared for meeting and dealing with unmotivated pupils.

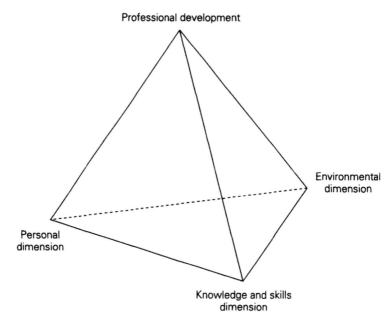

Figure 10.2: *Dimensions in BTs professional development*

Experienced teachers face similar problems when they change school, move from primary to secondary education, or are confronted with radical innovations (Burke *et al.*, 1984). But by relying on their experience, they will master these problems more quickly.

Dimensions in BTs' Professional Development

For mentors it is important to understand both the origin and the nature of BTs' problems. In order to help mentors analyse those problems we distinguish three dimensions in the complex process of teacher induction: the personal dimension, the environmental dimension, and finally the professional knowledge and skills dimension. Experiences in all three dimensions interact and form the basis of the professional development of BTs (Figure 10.2).

The Personal Dimension

An essential characteristic of being a teacher is that in teaching–learning situations the teacher uses himself as an instrument. Therefore, in education the teacher as a person is always at issue. Many beginners experience this as frightening and stressful. As the majority of the beginners are still in the transition stage from adolescence to adulthood, becoming a teacher, for many of them, means growing to maturity under high pressure. They have to develop a new perspective on themselves, 'I as a teacher', and to learn to develop professionally. In the beginning, many young teachers do not have the slightest idea, for example, how they will behave under environmental pressure or in situations of great stress. They are so self-concerned i.e., survival-oriented that they can barely distinguish between problems that originate from their personal transition and those that originate from their classroom practice. They lack experience in this regard and therefore have to develop new behaviour to cope with these situations and sometimes have to adjust their self-image. Mentoring in this context is particularly concerned with helping novices develop a clear perspective on themselves and their situation.

The Environmental Dimension

The situation of the BT in school is characterized by a confrontation with:

- new responsibilities: from the first day and the first lesson on, beginners have exactly the same responsibility for the classes they teach as those teachers who have been teaching for twenty years.
- a school environment in which various teaching cultures exist: each school and each department has its own set of written and unwritten rules (Hargreaves, 1992). Most often novices discover the rules concerned with some surprise. They are so obvious for the existing teachers that nobody explains them in advance.
- expectations concerning the way in which one functions, i.e., colleagues, school management, pupils or students and parents. Novices are supposed to meet these expectations; however, they do not precisely know what the expectations are and if they discover them, they do not know how to cope.

Their confrontations compel beginners to *reorient* themselves with regard to their own ideas about 'I as a teacher' and to their newly acquired knowledge and skills. What worked well during initial training, will not always work in the new school environment. Additionally, many novices have to make the change from identifying themselves with the pupil role to that of the teacher role. This process of reorientation is often accompanied by feelings of uncertainty and stress. Furthermore, the organization and physical resources of a school, and perhaps more significantly the beliefs that are not only held and valued within the institution (written rule pattern) but have become embedded within its many taken-for-granted practices (unwritten rules), inevitably exert a powerful influence upon the novice teacher (Calderhead, 1988). Especially in situations where beginners do not receive any support, they experience the first months of their induction rather as a rite of passage than a valuable learning experience (Vonk, 1984). Although the process of adaptation to the new school environment is interactive in nature, our research indicates that there are three major adaptation strategies. First, those teachers who feel familiar with the existing school culture simply *adopt* that culture. The second group of teachers *adapt* strategically to the culture of the school, because they feel they first have to show their colleagues and pupils that they are able to function in the existing school culture before changing their teaching approach. The last group does not agree with the existing culture and the teachers decide to *follow their own pace*. The members of the last group only survive if they have considerable frustration tolerance. From their studies on teacher socialization Lacey (1977) and Zeichner and Tabachnick (1985), reported similar adaptation strategies.

Professional Knowledge and Skills Dimension

The professional knowledge and skills a BT has to develop have three subdimensions: pedagogical content knowledge, classroom-management skills and teaching skills.

1 Pedagogical content knowledge

In general, novices have an elaborate academic background and do not expect to meet problems with subject matter. Quite soon, however, they realize that they did not master their subjects at school level. They have major problems in translating academic knowledge into school knowledge and have to reframe their subject knowledge base.[22] If we take a closer look at BTs' professional knowledge, we see that BTs draw on sources of knowledge which can be identified as knowledge of subject content, pedagogical content, aims and purposes, learners, and, educational contexts, settings and governance. Shulman (1986) suggests that it is these sources of understanding which make the process of pedagogical reasoning and action possible. For BTs, pedagogical content knowledge is the most important element.

Pedagogical content knowledge has three origins: (i) The discipline perspective, which is based on the breadth and depth of content knowledge, i.e., understanding of the organization of concepts and principles in the discipline and the strategies the discipline uses to discover new knowledge as well as the development of strategies and materials to enable learners to understand those concepts and processes. (ii) The pupil perspective, which concerns a rich factual knowledge base with many inter-connections, such as, the knowledge of analogies, similes, examples and metaphors by which to explain the subject matter to the pupils. This perspective also includes knowledge of pupils' preconceptions, experiences in everyday life, and the difficulties they commonly experience. All of these help teachers to communicate effectively with their pupils. (iii) The general methodology perspective, which concerns the knowledge of the different ways topics can be taught and the pros and cons of each approach is also an essential part of teachers' pedagogical content knowledge. It is this pedagogical content knowledge that distinguishes the veteran teacher from the novice.

All in all, pedagogical content knowledge represents a much more thorough understanding of the subject matter than BTs have normally achieved during their initial training. Mentor activities aimed at improving the quality of teaching, i.e., the development of beginning teachers' professional knowledge base, should focus on the widening of BTs' pedagogical content knowledge. This means the presentation of content and methodology from all three perspectives mentioned above, simultaneously.

2 Classroom management skills

Most BTs have poor classroom-management skills, i.e., they are not able to organize their lessons in such a way that an on-task working climate emerges and can be maintained effectively (see model of Figure 10.4). They have problems with reacting adequately to unrest and discipline problems because they have no overview of what is happening. They lack an adequate set of classroom rules and, if they have established such a set, they do not know how to maintain it. Finally, they do not know how to deal effectively with those who break those rules.

One of the major origins of the problems of BTs is that they are not familiar with the complexity of the classroom in which they have to work.[23] Classroom teaching is one of the most difficult modes of teaching in that one teacher is brought

For the beginners the 'learning' environment is characterized by:

- multi-dimensionality — during teaching a teacher has to do many things: teaching, monitoring, helping, maintaining discipline, etc.;
- simultaneity — most of the above have to be done simultaneously;
- immediacy — a teacher has to react immediately to pupils' actions, in particular to those that tend to disturb the working climate in the class;
- unpredictability — many things that happen in class are unpredictable, as a consequence teachers have to improvise constantly;
- publicness — teachers act in public, i.e., their actions are subject to discussion in various groups: pupils, colleagues, parents, community etc.; and
- history — every class or group has its own history and because a teacher sees that class only for a limited number of periods a week, he or she has only few opportunities to influence its behaviour.

Figure 10.3: Characteristics of the ecology of the classroom
Source: Doyle, 1979, 1986

together with twenty-five to thirty pupils in one space, and that group is expected to be engaged in activities that lead to externally defined objectives as they are laid down in the curriculum. The characteristics of the environment which co-define teachers' actions and are directed at maintaining desired pupil activities, i.e., on-task behaviour, are listed in Figure 10.3.

The main question for BTs is how to manage a group in such a complex environment. A mentor has to consider in what way he or she can help, support and advise a beginner to function properly under these stressful conditions.

3 Teaching skills

At the start of the threshold phase BTs experience numerous problems with ordinary classroom teaching. Although they have learned a number of teaching strategies, both in theory and school practice, they still seem to lack effective classroom-teaching skills, such as: the skills to structure the teaching–learning environment in order to tackle the time-on-task problem; to vary learning activities which last a limited amount of time; to monitor the individual pupil's progress and so on. An even more difficult problem is to adapt their teaching to individual differences between their pupils. During their first months of teaching many BTs do not even see individual pupils in their classes. Rather classes are seen as unstructured noisy groups with some nasty pupils who permanently attract their attention.

The whole situation in which the BT operates can be characterized as a 'difficult control situation'. For BTs who have a number of different classes it is even more problematic to act adequately under those circumstances. At the same time, it appears that the concept of the teacher's role, which was developed during initial teacher education, barely offers a basis to tackle the difficult control situation (Vonk, 1984, pp. 11–14, p. 109).

How to Assist BTs to Improve

Elsewhere (Vonk, 1994) I have defined the different mentor roles: observer, provider of feedback, instructor, and finally evaluator. The first mentor task is to help his or her BT to master the basic classroom-teaching skills. In order to be able to do so, a mentor needs to have insight into those basic skills and into the process of how BTs acquire those skills, i.e., learn from their experiences.

Mastering the Basic Skills of Classroom Teaching

Most BTs start their career in a rather traditional school environment where classroom teaching is the usual mode of teaching. Most of our findings with respect to BTs' professional development corresponded closely with those of Brown and McIntyre (1988) from their investigation of the professional craft knowledge of teachers. From our studies of BTs' problems and from our experiences with inservice courses, we discern the most crucial problems for beginners as:

- the planning, organization and management of teaching and pupils' learning activities (maintaining continuity in 'pupils' activities' and maintaining 'progress in pupils' learning');
- adapting the subject content to pupils' abilities (for most BTs, however, this particular issue did not become a problem until they had ended the threshold phase, i.e., crossed the threshold in the second half of their first year of service).

Experienced teachers' actions are mainly directed at maintaining a desirable state of pupil activity and at making appropriate progress. Starting from a permanent evaluation of the situation in terms of the state of pupils' activities and of making progress, they take appropriate action. The nature of those actions are based on teachers' professional knowledge and skills, their personal dispositions and the estimation of environmental constraints.

As many of the problems BTs experience originate from mismanagement of pupil activities and progress, we have placed these issues in a central position in our mentor activities. With respect to these issues our help is based on the principle:

A good lesson is a lesson during which all pupils are engaged all the time in one activity or another, and which is aimed at making progress (i.e., contribute to achieving the objectives set for that particular lesson). (Vonk, 1989)

This principle is supported by, amongst others, the research from Matthijssen (1984) and from Brown and McIntyre (1988). Matthijssen was interested in the extent of pupils' 'off-task' or 'escape' activities during different patterns of classroom teaching. He observed a great number of lessons and afterwards interviewed both teachers and pupils. He concluded that in a highly teacher-centred pattern, in which the teacher acts in a directive way (strict control and little pupil initiative), few escape activities occur. In these lessons all activities were task-oriented and the course of the lessons was strictly functional. In more open or decentralized lesson patterns, where pupils were able to use their initiative, the extent of off-task activities was much higher. It strongly depended on the teacher's management skills whether he or she was able to keep pupils' activities within acceptable limits or not. Lack of those skills often led to disruption of the working climate in the class.

Brown and McIntyre (1988) observed lessons of 'excellent' teachers, selected

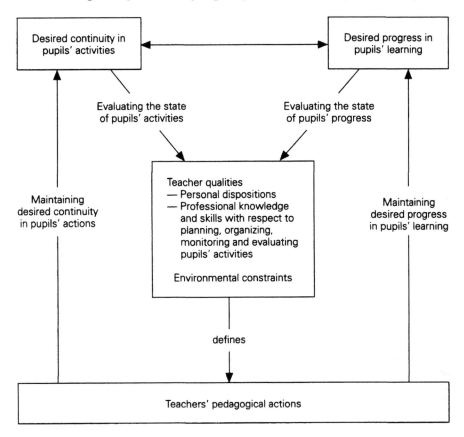

Figure 10.4: Classroom teaching: concepts and relationships
Source: Variant on the scheme of Brown and McIntyre (1988)

on the basis of interviews with pupils, staff and management, and interviewed them afterwards. They came to the conclusion that these 'teachers evaluated their lessons in terms of maintaining particular normal desirable states of pupil activity'; i.e., they evaluated a lesson as satisfactory as long as pupils continued to act in those ways which were seen as routinely desirable (p. 43). These teachers' second criterion was that the activities should result in progress. Depending on the contextual factors teachers directed their actions at maintaining pupils on-task activities and on maintaining progress.

Starting from our own findings of the problems BTs experienced in classroom teaching, and using a variation of the model developed by Brown and McIntyre (1988), we developed a model of classroom teaching in which the continuity in pupils' activities and making progress are the central topics (see Figure 10.4). We added permanent evaluation, i.e., the 'observation' and 'interpretation' stage in Figure 10.5, and the element of 'teacher qualities'. On the basis of this classroom-management oriented model the nature and origins of problems experienced by BTs in the classroom can be illustrated.

This management-directed approach is an effective strategy for BTs to create a workable working climate in their classes. The more so, because during the first couple of months most BTs do not have sufficient 'classroom knowledge' of their classes, so that more open-classroom management is nearly impossible.[24] Essential in this approach is that BTs plan, organize and manage pupil activities instead of planning and organizing only their own teaching activities. For many BTs this means a fundamental shift in thinking about their teaching. Mentors' most important task is to help their *protégés* develop proper classroom knowledge during their first months of service. A second task is to help their *protégés* develop a more directive, task-oriented way of planning, organizing and managing their pupils' learning activities.

Planning and organizing pupils' learning activities is, however, not sufficient for learning to be meaningful to pupils. Teaching is more than simply transferring academic knowledge or forcing pupils to learn by rote. Here we come to the second issue in which mentors can play a crucial role at helping their *protégés*: BTs have to reframe their subject-knowledge base. Teachers are expected to be experts in translating academic knowledge into school knowledge that can be understood by their pupils. In this context professional teachers may see teaching as open-ended exploration in which they express their pedagogical knowledge in action; i.e., the view of teaching as an inquiry informed by a self-consciously held body of principles in which these principles are put to the acid test of practice. We share Stones' view of teachers 'as inquirers attempting to solve pedagogical problems' (Stones, 1992, p. 14). Pedagogical problems, however, are mainly concerned with the conceptual structure of the subject to be taught and the most effective method of teaching aims at meaningful learning. In this context, Kirkham (1992) argues that 'with the help of a mentor, the student-teacher/novice could make a systematic attempt to match the structure and the coherence of the subject matter to the cognitive and effective development of a particular group of children in a specific context' (p. 68). Through assistance with the preparation of lessons, the analysis of the subject content, and the selection of methods that lead to meaningful learning, a mentor can be of great help to the BT. Pupils as well as BTs will profit from this approach.

Learning from Experiences: Meaningful Learning

Teacher development includes a lifelong learning process — a process of professional growth — which is related to the needs of teachers in the various phases of their careers. Developmental processes are change processes. Besides, teachers are adult learners. This implies that the general principles of adult learning prevail for in-service activities. In terms of teacher development, these principles are:

1 Teachers wish to have a decisive say in the content and the process of their learning.
2 Professional learning only takes place when teachers feel a need for change and are convinced of the practicability of the intended change.
3 Assimilation of new knowledge and skills only takes place when teachers are able to relate it to their existing knowledge and repertoire.
4 Changes in teachers' practical knowledge base takes place through reflection. That reflection has to deal with their knowledge (subject knowledge

and pedagogical content knowledge), methodology (knowledge and skills), as well as their beliefs about 'good practice'.

5   Before teachers are prepared to implement a change they weigh up the investment and profit balance.

Although these principles are true for all teacher learning, a distinction has to be made between the learning processes of novice and veteran teachers. The novice teacher, for example, lacks an extended professional knowledge base and has to learn to refer to theory for insights into a particular situation both in the planning of lessons for pupil activities and in examining the consequences in terms of normal desirable pupil activities and progress (Kirkham, 1992).

Their capacity for reflection is rather limited, and is always connected with their practical experiences. They see the function of both reflection and theory as a means to gain new ideas: i.e., suggestions for improving their practice. At first, however, many beginners tend to think that their 'theoretical luggage' is of little use for tackling the problems they meet in practice. Obviously they will not refer to theory in order to develop that insight and understanding. Only when theory can be directly connected with their practical experiences — most often dealing with problematic situations for which they are trying to find a solution — and can provide an explanation for, and/or a perspective on, a solution, will it be accepted by the novice teacher. A mentor can help a BT examine problematic situations and try to help him or her reflect on that situation.[25] This examination, however, requires a well-developed insight into how professionals learn from their experiences from a mentor, and especially, how these experiences have to be processed in order to lead to new flexible behaviour, i.e., to result in meaningful learning.

Figure 10.5 illustrates the 'learning from experience' model. In that process we distinguish the following steps. When teaching, a teacher participates in a teaching–learning environment, in which he has to deal with a series of pedagogical problems. He observes what happens in relation to those actions which are aimed at solving those problems, and gives meaning to those observations in terms of desired–undesired pupil activities. So far he only *experiences*. Subsequently, he stores the observations and classifies them together with the meaning given to them in his cognitive system; now they have become part of his classroom knowledge — he can verbalize them. At this point we can speak of an 'experience'. This experience is accompanied by either positive (success) or negative (failure) feelings. If he does not reflect on his experiences, the teacher can only try to repeat the experiences of success and to avoid those of failure. A repertoire developed in this way is based on 'trial and error' learning. The result of this mode of learning is mostly a 'survival kit', and such a repertoire is inflexible.

To develop a flexible repertoire of actions, however, one has to reflect on both the experience of success — why it went well, and in what other situations is it usable — and of failure — why it went wrong and how one might act more appropriately in comparable situations. The latter will lead to a process of problematizing — translating a (negative) experience into a problem which can be solved — and problem-solving. In answering the 'why' question one has to confront or relate the experience to existing, more general, research-based knowledge of teachers' actions and other educational theory (explanatory function). Processing experiences in this way a BT will develop a flexible repertoire of actions which will lead to pupils' meaningful learning and a solid professional knowledge base.[26]

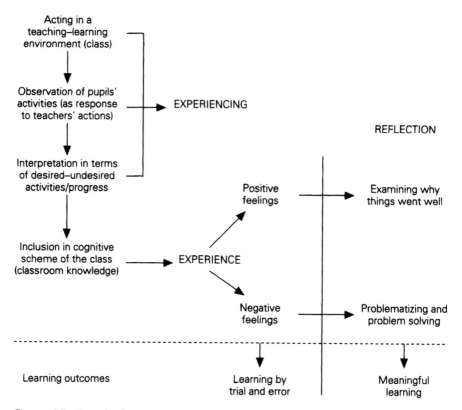

Figure 10.5: Learning from experience

Much of experienced teachers' practice is automated or intuitive, dependent on understandings that are not always articulated. For them learning is bringing to consciousness and examining the assumptions and considerations which make sense of their actions as teachers. Teachers cannot change their practice in a controlled and deliberate way without reflection. Furthermore, experienced teachers have a rich professional knowledge base which contains extensive repertoires of past experiences on which they can draw in order to analyse current problems; and when they use the possibilities of constructing new frames by modifying and combining old ones, they have very rich, even though bounded capacities for thinking creatively through reflection in, and on, their experience (McIntyre, 1993, p. 41). Traditionally, however, the knowledge base of teachers is rather particularistic and not profession-focused. This is emphasized even more because many teachers work or prefer to work in isolation. Based on his study on teacher development, Lortie (1975) concludes:

> The conceptions voiced by . . . teachers are not those of colleagues who see themselves as sharing a viable, generalizable body of knowledge and practice. Such a view point presumes that there are identifiable principles and solutions which are possessed by all those within the colleague group. The image projected is more individualistic; teachers are portrayed as an aggregate

of persons each assembling practices consistent with his experience and particular personality. It is not what 'we, the colleagues' know and share which is paramount, but rather what *I* have learned through experience. From this perspective, socialization into teaching is largely self-socialization; one's own predispositions are not only relevant but, in fact, stand at the core of becoming a teacher. (Lortie, 1975, p. 79)

This is, however, one of the weaker points of the teaching profession. Even today, individualized professional development is common practice, i.e., most (beginning) teachers still have to develop their own knowledge and skills base without systematic communication with relevant others about it. In our view however, professional development should be viewed as individual development in a school context and not a purely individual enterprise.

Conclusion

I have discussed issues in the professional development of BTs during their first year of service and plotted connections with the knowledge base mentors require in order to be able to act effectively. I have also emphasized that mentoring of BTs can only be fruitful when it is embedded in a school's staff policies.

Proper induction is based on a plan for the mentoring of BTs, which every school should establish. The mentor activities should be set out in a written document — maybe a contract — in which the rights, obligations and responsibilities of both parties — BT and school — are clearly defined. In order to create an open relationship between mentor and *protégé* the school should ensure that at least the mentors involved are independent, i.e., not concerned with the final assessment of the beginner. Mentor activities are intended for the beginners in the first place, although the school will certainly profit from successful mentoring.

To each beginner who applies, the existence of a mentor programme in the school and the associated rights and obligations are pointed out. If the beginner is appointed he is given a mentor for the first year of teaching. The school, in the person of the mentor, as well as the BT are obliged to participate constructively in the mentor programme. Beginners who react otherwise often appear to have difficulties with reflecting on their own performance, which I usually associate with inflexible behaviour.

An argument on the part of the school for this obligation is that every BT still has to learn the tricks of the trade during which there will be unrest in certain classes, and possibly a lowering of pupils' examination scores. Schools have to avoid this and mentor programmes have proved to be helpful. Schools are also obliged to organize mentor programmes for the benefit of beginners and should select the most able teachers to carry out the task. By no means all teachers are suitable. Only those teachers who have an extended experience of teaching, i.e., considerable practical and theoretical knowledge, who have a reflective attitude, are open-minded, empathic, communication-oriented and flexible, are suitable for the function of mentor. Such teachers should be given sufficient time to carry out their tasks.

In general the school-management team which believes that it should be responsible for the BT programme underestimates the differences between a beginner's position and that of the more experienced teacher. Practice demonstrates that the roles of mentor and assessor are difficult to combine. In such a situation it is not unthinkable that a beginner might not be given tenure at the end of his first year of teaching because he or she discussed too many problems with the mentor who also happened to be the director or head. It is preferable to ensure a strict division between persons who are responsible for mentoring and those who are responsible for the final assessment of the BT concerned. Assessors have other instruments at their disposal to gain information for assessment of the BT. In addition, school managers should consider whether they have the knowledge and skills to act effectively as mentors. Managers who are no longer teaching tend to lose sight of the nitty gritty of everyday classroom teaching.

In our model of teacher induction which is based on the idea of the teacher as a self-directing professional, we see the mentoring of BTs as a contribution of the profession to the supervisory function of the school as a whole. However, to perform their tasks effectively, mentors need additional training. Mentors of BTs should be attributed with a status in the school similar to that of a 'confidential person', i.e., the code of silence applies to them. The school has to assure the BT that mentoring and assessment are two entirely separate issues. All matters discussed with the mentor are 'confidential' and may not be used in an assessment.

In this chapter we have outlined some elements of the knowledge base for mentors. Although it is written from a Dutch perspective, it should be regarded as a contribution to the improvement of the 'Supervision of Instruction' with respect to BTs in schools elsewhere.

Notes

1 Based on the study of Ooms (1991). She reported on BT drop-out in the Netherlands during the period 1980–1990.
2 E.g., the Licence Teacher Training model in the UK, while in the Netherlands the sandwich-model of teacher training with greater emphasis on teaching practice, i.e., a 50–50 theory–practice division in the professional preparation of teachers, and with models comparable to the Oxford Internship scheme are winning ground.
3 Glickman (1990) defines supervision of instruction as: 'The comprehensive set of services provided and processes used to help teachers facilitate their own professional development, so that the goals of the school might be better attained. It is the function in schools that draw together the discrete elements of instructional effectiveness into whole school action under a common purpose' (p. 4).
4 See Glatthorn (1990).
5 See for the principles of individualized professional development Christensen and McDonnell (1993).
6 A recent report of the Dutch inspectorate for primary education (1994) concludes that only 5 per cent of all primary schools have an 'induction plan' in writing. According to our own experience in secondary education the number of schools that have an elaborate induction plan is also low. And of 70 per cent of the schools which report to more or less support BTs during their first year of teaching, that support is mainly administrative in nature, instead of offering support to tackle the real problems and to help BTs to learn from their experiences.
7 The set of person-related factors is defined as those factors in personal life that influence one's professional functioning, such as individual disposition, life stage, crisis, family, leisure activities and participation in non-professional organizations.
8 The professional environment consists of several groups of persons with whom one is

confronted while practising the profession. These are colleagues, students, school administration, school board, local authorities and parents. Each group has its own expectations concerning the teacher's professional behaviour and each will try to influence the development.

9   'Action' is defined as a purposive change in the world of objects with which an individual is confronted.

10 'Orientation base' is defined as a conceptual framework related to a repertoire of actions and which is based on an integrated whole of theoretical knowledge and practical experiences.

11 'Reflection' includes analysing one's own professional knowledge and repertoire, i.e., putting it in a wider context and relating it to existing knowledge and research. See Schön (1987) and Calderhead (1988) for a more detailed analysis.

12 Levine (1989), p. 62, quotes Erikson: 'Generativity is primarily the interest in establishing and guiding the next generation or whatever in a given case may become the absorbing object of a parental kind of responsibility.'

13 Here we strongly agree with Stones (1992) as he argues: 'Theory and practice can be best conceived as two sides of the same medal' (p. 13).

14 See Vonk (1992) *Begeleiding van Beginnende Docenten* (Elements of this model are described in English in Vonk (1993)).

15 For a detailed description of these roles see Vonk (1994).

16 'Phase' is a rounded period in someone's career which is identifiable by characteristics specific to that period. The use of the term 'phase' evokes the notion of some general 'developmental sequence' that all teachers may go through. Attractive as this notion may be, also for purposes of planning in-service education and training (Huberman, 1993), career cycles of 'real' teachers do not follow easily predictable paths. Individual idiosyncrasies and environmental influences play an important role in shaping individual careers.

17 See Doyle (1990).

18 This concept was introduced by Shulman (1986). It refers to how a teacher's understanding of subject matter is transformed to make it 'teachable' (see in this chapter 'Professional Knowledge and Skills Dimension' for an analysis of this concept in more detail).

19 See 'classroom management skills' in this chapter.

20 For a detailed overview of the problems of first year teachers see Vonk 1984, pp. 64–118.

21 Vonk (1989) argues that teaching practice during initial training is very often too protective, i.e., it does not always offer the opportunity to gain crucial experiences and to learn from them, such as working under stress, confrontation with discipline problems, and losing grip on a situation.

22 For a detailed overview of problems on this issue as reported by novices, see Vonk (1984), pp. 110–12.

23 Doyle (1979; 1986), describes the characteristics of the 'ecology of the classroom': Multi-dimensionality, simultaneity, immediacy, unpredictability, publicness, and history (see Figure 10.3). To be able to act effectively in such an environment 'classroom knowledge' is essential. This type of knowledge is basic for having 'overview'.

24 We borrowed this concept from Doyle (1986). 'Classroom knowledge' represents the cognitive scheme a teacher has from a certain class. It contains information about pupils' behaviour, learning results, background information, like and/or dislike of certain pupils, expectations a teacher has for individual pupils and from the class as a whole, etc., and the experiences the teacher has in dealing with that class as a group. Classroom knowledge is the basis for teachers' acting in that class.

25 In fact, theory and practice are best conceived of as two aspects of the same process. In that context, Stones (1992) proposes as a working definition of 'theory': 'bodies of principles that have explanatory power and the potential of guiding teacher action' (p. 13).

26 Gilroy (1989), discusses the concept of 'Professional knowledge'.

References

ANDREWS, I.H. (1986) 'An Investigation of the Academic Paradigms Underlying Induction Programmes in Five Countries', Paper presented at the Annual Meeting of the AERA, San Francisco.

ASHTON, P.T. (1990) 'Editorial', in *Journal of Teacher Education*, **41**, 2, p. 2.

BROWN, S. and MCINTYRE, D. (1988) 'The Professional Craft Knowledge of Teachers', in *Scottish Educational Review*, Special issue: The Quality of Teaching, Edinburgh (Scottish Academic Press), pp. 39–48.

BURDEN, P.R. (1990) 'Teacher development', in HOUSTON, W.R., HABERMAN, M. and SIKULA, J. (Eds) *Handbook of Research on Teacher Education*, New York, MacMillan, pp. 311–29.

BURKE, J.P. (1987) *Teacher Development*, New York, Falmer Press.

BURKE, J.P., FESSLER, R. and CHRISTENSEN, J.C. (1984) *Teacher Career Stages: Implications for Staff Development*, Bloomington, ID, Phi Delta Kappa.

CALDERHEAD, J. (1988) 'The development of knowledge structures in learning to teach', in CALDERHEAD, J. *Teacher's Professional Learning*, London, Falmer Press, pp. 51–65.

CALDERHEAD, J. (1993) 'The professional development of teachers in a changing Europe', in LEINO, A., HELGREN, P. and HÄMÄLÄINEN, K. (Eds) *Integration of Technology and Reflection in Teaching: A Challenge for European Teacher Education*, Proceedings of the 17th Annual Conference of Association for Teacher Education in Europe, Lahti, Finland, 1992, University of Helsinki, pp. 16–30.

CHRISTENSEN, J.C. (1992) 'Pre-service education', in FESSLER, R. and CHRISTENSEN, J.C. *The Teacher Career Cycle*, Boston, Allyn and Bacon, pp. 45–59.

CHRISTENSEN, J.C. and MCDONNELL, J.H. (1993) 'The career lattice: A structure for planning professional development', in KREMER-HAYON, L., VONK, J.H.C. and FESSLER, R. (Eds) *Teacher Professional Development: A Multiple Perspective Approach*, Amsterdam, Swets and Zeitlinger, pp. 295–315.

DOYLE, W. (1979) 'Making managerial decisions in classrooms', in DUKE, D.L. (Ed) *Classroom Management* (78th Yearbook of the National Society for Studies in Education), Chicago, University of Chicago Press, pp. 42–72.

DOYLE, W. (1986) 'Classroom management and organization', in WITTROCK, M.C. (Ed) *Handbook of Research on Teaching*, New York, MacMillan, pp. 392–432.

DOYLE, W. (1990) 'Themes in teacher education research', in HOUSTON, W.R., HABERMAN, M. and SIKULA, J. (Eds) *Handbook of Research on Teacher Education*, New York, MacMillan, pp. 3–25.

EGAN, G. (1986) *The Skilled Helper: A Systematic Approach to Effective Helping*, Belmont, California, 3rd ed, Wadsworth, Inc.

FESSLER, R. and CHRISTENSEN, J.C. (1992) *The Teacher Career Cycle*, Boston, Allyn and Bacon.

FULLAN, M.G. (1991) *The New Meaning of Educational Change*, New York, Teachers College Press.

GILROY, P. (1989) 'Professional knowledge and the BT', in CARR, W. (Ed) *Quality in Teaching*, London, Falmer Press, pp. 101–15.

GLASER, B.G. and STRAUSS, A.L. (1967) *The Discovery of Grounded Theory: Strategies for Qualitative Research*, Chicago, Aldine.

GLATTHORN, A.A. (1990) *Supervisory Leadership: An Introduction to Instructional Supervision*, Glenview, Illinois, Scott, Foresman and Co.

GLICKMAN, C.D. (1990) *Supervision of Instruction: A Developmental Approach*, Boston, Allyn and Bacon.

HARGREAVES, A. (1992) 'Cultures of teaching: A focus for change', in HARGREAVES, A. and FULLAN, M. *Understanding Teacher Development*, New York, Teacher College Press, pp. 216–41.

HEALY, C.C. and WELCHERT, A.J. (1990) 'Mentoring relations: A definition to advance research and practice', in *Educational Researcher*, **19**, 9, pp. 17–22.

HUBERMAN, M. (1992) 'Teacher development and instructional mastery', in HARGREAVES, A.

and FULLAN, M. *Understanding Teacher Development*, New York, Teacher College Press, pp. 122–42.

HUBERMAN, M. (1993) 'Steps towards a developmental model of the teaching career', in KREMER-HAYON, L., VONK, J.H.C. and FESSLER, R. (Eds) *Teacher Professional Development: A Multiple Perspective Approach*, Amsterdam, Swets and Zeitlinger, pp. 93–118.

HULING-AUSTIN, L. (1990) 'Teacher induction programmes and internships', in HOUSTON, R.W. (Ed) *Handbook of Research on Teacher Education*, New York, MacMillan, pp. 535–49.

INSPECTIE VAN HET ONDERWIJS (Dutch Inspectorate for Primary Education) (1994) *Een goede Start*, De Meern, Inspectierapport, nr 1994–7.

KIRKHAM, D. (1992) 'The nature and conditions of good mentoring practice', in EILKIN, M. (Ed) *Mentoring in Schools*, London, Kogan Page, pp. 66–74.

LACEY, C. (1977) *The Socialization of Teachers*, London, Methuen.

LEVINE, S.L. (1989) *Promoting Adult Growth in Schools: The Promise of Professional Development*, Boston, Allyn and Bacon.

LETVIN, E. (1992) 'Induction', in FESSLER, R. and CHRISTENSEN, J.C. (1992) *The Teacher Career Cycle*, Boston, Allyn and Bacon, pp. 59–87.

LORTIE, D.C. (1975) *Schoolteacher: A Sociological Study*, Chicago, The University of Chicago Press.

MATTHIJSSEN, M.A.J.M. (1984) 'Ontsnappingsverschijnnselen bij Oudere Leerlingen' (Escape symptoms amongst older pupils), in *Pedagogisch Tijdschrift*, **9**, 1, pp. 2–11.

MCINTYRE, D. (1993) 'Theory, theorizing and reflection in initial teacher education', in CALDERHEAD, J. and GATES, P. (Eds) *Conceptualizing Reflection in Teacher Development*, London, Falmer Press, pp. 39–53.

MERRIAM, S.B. (1991) *Case Study Research in Education: A Qualitative Approach*, San Francisco, Jossey-Bass.

MILES, M.B. and HUBERMAN, A.M. (1984) *Qualitative Data Analysis: A Source Book of New Methods*, Beverly Hills, California, Sage.

OOMS, C. (1991) 'Dropout of BTs', in VOORBACH, J.T., VONK, J.H.C. and PRICK, L.G.M. (Eds) *Teacher Education 7: Research and Developments on Teacher Education in the Nether-lands*, Amsterdam/Lisse, Swets and Zeitlinger, pp. 131–45.

RYAN, K. (1986) *Induction of Teachers*, Bloomington, Phi Delta Kappan Educational Foundation.

SCHON, D.A. (1987) *Educating the Reflective Practitioner: Toward a New Design for Teaching and Learning in the Professions*, London, Jossey-Bass.

SHULMAN, L.S. (1986) 'Those who understand knowledge growth in teaching', in *Educational Researcher*, **15**, 2, pp. 38–44.

STONES, E. (1992) *Quality Teaching: A Sample of Cases*, London, Routledge.

VEENMAN, S.A.M. (1984) 'Perceived Problems of BTs', in *Review of Educational Research*, **54**, 2, pp. 143–78.

VONK, J.H.C. (1982) *Opleiding en Praktijk*, Amsterdam, VU-Uitgeverij, Abridged version in English: VONK, J.H.C. (1984) *Teacher Education and Teacher Practice*, Amsterdam, Free University Press.

VONK, J.H.C. (1989) *Beginnend Leraarschap*, Amsterdam, Free University Press.

VONK, J.H.C. (1991) 'Becoming a teacher, brace yourself', in HO W.K. and WONG, R.J.L. (Eds) *Improving the Quality of the Teaching Profession: An International Perspective*, Singapore, Institute of Education, pp. 63–82.

VONK, J.H.C. (1992) *Begeleiding van Beginnende Docenten* (Mentoring BTs), Amsterdam, Free University Press.

VONK, J.H.C. (1993) 'Mentoring beginning teachers: Mentor knowledge and skills', in *Mentoring*, **I**, 1, pp. 31–41.

VONK, J.H.C. (1994) 'Teacher induction: The great omission in education', in GALTON, M. and MOON, B. (Eds) *Handbook of Teacher Education in Europe*, London, David Fulton Publishers/Council of Europe.

VONK, J.H.C. and SCHRAS, G.A. (1987) 'From beginning to experienced teacher: A study of the professional development of teachers during their first four years of service', in *European Journal of Teacher Education*, **10**, 1, pp. 95–110.

ZEICHNER, K.M. and GORE, J.M. (1990) 'Teacher socialization', in HOUSTON, W.R., HABERMAN, M. and SIKULA, J. (Eds) *Handbook of Research on Teacher Education*, New York, MacMillan, pp. 329–49.

ZEICHNER, K.M. and TABACHNICK, B.R. (1985) 'The development of teacher perspectives: Social strategies and institutional control in the socialization of BTs', in *Journal of Education for Teaching*, 11, pp. 1–25.

11 Reflective Teaching: Embrace or Elusion?

Les Tickle

Reflective Teaching: Embrace or Elusion?

The pursuit of reflective educational practitioners, and the prozelytization of action research, hotted up during the 1980s and has continued into the 1990s, at least among teacher educators. The development of reflective practice as an aim attached itself to initial (pre-service) teacher education (see MOTE Report, 1991), in Britain, mainland Europe, North America and Australia. In programmes of continuing professional development for experienced teachers the labels of action research, teacher research, or research-based teaching have tended to displace 'reflective practice', though such distinctions are not clear-cut in the rhetoric of teacher education. These terms have become often used, sometimes interchangeably, as watchwords in relation to both stages of professional development (Elliott, 1991; McKernan, 1988, 1991; Tickle, 1994; Winter, 1989; Zeichner and Tabachnick, 1991).

Recently my attention has been drawn to the loose use of 'research-based teaching' (Tickle, 1987), and towards discerning variants and inflections in such 'readily employed generic conceptions' as reflective practice (Zeichner and Tabachnick, 1991). My focus has also shifted from research with pre-service and experienced teachers to researching the place and nature of, and the possibilities for developing, reflective educational practice among teachers in their first year of full-time teaching, and the immediately subsequent years. Within the field of teacher education I see this latter application as new territory to be both explored and developed.

The practical basis of the shift in focus was twofold. In my participation in the design and implementation of an induction project for first-year teachers I sought to establish and achieve a single major aim: to promote the development of classroom practice and the capacity for reflective thinking about that practice. In the design and introduction of a BPhil (Teaching) degree at the University of East Anglia, based on principles of research-based teaching, for teachers who have recently completed their first year of teaching, the central aim was the development of the application of professional judgment in practice.

The pursuit of reflective educational practice took two routes simultaneously. In the anthropological sense I wanted to see if it already existed among new teachers, and if so in what form(s). In the missionizing sense I sought to ensure that if it didn't exist already then it certainly would, so far as I could determine it; and if it did, I would seek to extend its assumed potentials for professional development and the enhancement of teaching quality.

The first route was followed especially with a research group of five teachers who were not part of the induction project, nor of the new degree, and with whom I met regularly throughout their first year. The second was pursued within the induction project itself, especially with six teachers with whom I worked in their schools, and in the introduction of the BPhil (Teaching) degree at UEA. Research with the five teachers provides the background to the present chapter. More extensive aspects of that research, the work with the induction project teachers, and in the BPhil degree can be found reported in Tickle, 1989, 1991, 1992a, b, c, d; 1994.

Newly Qualified Teachers and Reflective Practice

The view I held of the first year of teaching was one of a period of frenetic activity in which practical experience is built rapidly, as the demands of teaching are met in full for the first time. The problematic nature of teaching, confronted in its most extensive and acute form at this stage, characterized for me a particular kind of potential for the educational experiences of new teachers. Those experiences, I believed, could be established on the basis of constructive acknowledgment that teaching is perpetually problematic, and hence the source and basis of reflective practice.

I adopted the view that new teachers represent a particular example of Schon's (1983, 1987) reflective practitioner, particular because they have only a limited repertoire of experiences to draw upon in unfamiliar situations, and because most situations are, at least initially, unfamiliar. Schon's view suggested to me that new teachers would be extensively engaged in research as he defined it.

Schon argued that the relationship between practice and research in the professions centres on reflection in- and reflection on-action. His theory is based on the idea that when a person reflects in- or on-action he or she becomes a researcher in a specific and particular practical situation. Because situations are complex and uncertain, and always unique because of the combination of variables which come together, practice problems are difficult to identify. They are also difficult to act upon since judgment and action need to be taken to fit the particular characteristics of each case — 'selectively managing complex and extensive information'. He points out that the purpose of the action in an activity like teaching is to change the situation from what it is to a desired state, so that once action has been taken further management of the situation is required to judge the effects of action and assess the newly created situation. According to Schon this constant activity of appreciation, action, reappreciation, further action, leads to the development of a repertoire of experiences of unique cases, which are then available to draw upon in unfamiliar situations. That repertoire, he claims, is used in the recombination of elements of those other experiences, rather than as 'recipe knowledge', so that each new situation is dealt with through reflection, further enriching the repertoire of practice and enabling the quality of judgments made in practical situations to be improved. In this view the process of reflection in the construction of professional practice involves experiment and enquiry which is different from methods of controlled experiment, because the practitioner attempts to make an hypothesis come true, in situations where he or she does not have control of all the factors involved. Unstable situations and relatively unpredictable outcomes both pertain.

This seemed to me to be not only a plausible view of professional practice, but an attractive model of practice to encourage among new teachers, since it was my view that the quality of teaching and learning depends substantially on the quality of teachers' judgments and actions, based on sound assessments of situations, events, and people. I regarded the pursuit of quality in professional action in terms of the development of the application of professional judgment in practice; the quality of such judgment being based on the capacity to perceive problems, elicit information, analyse and synthesize evidence, determine appropriate action, and monitor its consequences and effects. In short, in Schon's terms I believed that in attempting to become effective first-year teachers would need first and foremost to become effective researchers, capable of enquiry from which problems could be framed adequately; capable of constructing hypotheses as a basis for experiment; capable of taking appropriate action to effect their aims; and capable of monitoring action and its consequences.

In my role within the development project and the BPhil (Teaching) degree programme I held an idealized view (consistent with Schon's model I believe) of the flexible and creative teacher, constantly in search of understanding and practice which might be developed within specific contexts through further and unending research questions. Although this model is perhaps less focused, selective, and systematic than modes of enquiry implied by action research, they too carry the same implied idealized view: an aspiration to be realized rather than a description of what already is. Or to use my earlier analogy, a missionary rather than anthropological view. Schon's claims are purportedly of that which *is* among experienced professionals, though with a concern for what ought to be among *all* professionals (Schon, 1983), and what *will be* among novices given the right kind of education (Schon, 1987). My work with the research group was of the anthropological intention, to identify and understand the nature of the processes and the foci of attention of their thinking. It was that understanding which would hopefully allow for more sophisticated practices on my part in the induction projects and degree programme.

I was cautious of this image of reflective practice as research. It had been associated closely with models of action research in which procedures of data gathering, recording, interpretation, analysis, and action are attached to carefully selected cases. In so many unfamiliar situations, being confronted simultaneously, actions, and hence repertoire building, I imagined, might depend upon the rapid processing of 'data', conducted in the face of essential yet inaccessible information. The worlds of new teachers seemed to be complex and fragile informational and decision-making places. There was a need to research the nature of experience, and particularly reflective thought and action among the teachers, and to take account of that research alongside 'models' of reflective practice and action research which might otherwise be inappropriately implanted into the programmes.

I believe that I have shown in other recent reports (Tickle, op cit.) how the teachers recognized and demonstrated the practice of reflection in- and on-action, in a search for professional know-how. Situations of a practical, problem-posing kind, and of considerable variety, were reported by the teachers. Some aspects of the search for know-how could be equated with the classifications of teacher knowledge made by Elbaz (1983) and Wilson *et al.* (1987) — self, subject matter, students, school curriculum, and strategies for instruction. Others formed a host of events and matters for consideration not so readily classified — relating to parents, the social behaviour of colleagues, the conduct of headteachers, salary and conditions of employment, provision of support services for students and for teachers, and so on.

Within these, unsurprisingly I suppose, teaching strategies and specific incidents within the classroom held centre stage in the theatres of their minds. In their accounts of reflections in- and on-practice the teachers provided extensive evidence of their thoughtful deliberations on the detailed tasks, actions, incidents, reviews, predictions, feelings, images, and responses which were part and parcel of their first experience of being teachers. The range of specific phenomena which came in for reflective attention was extensive and the intensity of focus considerable.

I do not propose to reiterate these, or the processes of thinking which I have reported in those other accounts. The interested reader is referred to Tickle op cit. What I do want to do is explore a specific aspect of their thinking: the relationship between their thoughts on 'technical' performance in teaching, 'clinical' judgment-making, and consideration of the aims and values which underlay their practice. In particular I will consider the relationship between their deliberations in- and on-practice; their coming to take things for granted; and aspects of teaching which may have been taken for granted in the first place.

Teacher Competences

The particular ways in which I used the notion of 'competence' in the analysis of data from the teachers (and correspondingly in the development projects) stems from the work of Zimpher and Howey (1987). In their analysis of forms of teaching practice supervision Zimpher and Howey identified different 'orientations' (or what may be regarded as different ideologies) in the kinds of practices which were expected and encouraged among novice teachers. They drew distinctions between four kinds of teaching competence, which, they argued, could be detected in the central aims associated with the different orientations of supervisors and supervisory programmes and practices. The competences, set out briefly, were as follows:

- **Technical competence** refers to the effective use of day-to-day teaching skills employed in classroom management and instruction and the employment of craft knowledge in teaching strategies.
- **Clinical competence** includes the ability to make judgments about problematic situations, and to solve problems, through reflective action and inquiry.
- **Personal competence** is the achievement of 'self-actualization' especially in terms of a willingness and capacity to develop values through 'self-confrontation' as well as through dialogue with others.
- **Critical competence** is the capacity to engage in the critique of social situations, social structures, and the norms and values which operate within them.

I will argue that among the research group of teachers with whom I worked many of the detailed technicalities of teaching performance became encapsulated as routine practice, and hence removed from the realms of reflectiveness. Their reflections were focused on the problem-solving, clinical judgment-making aspects of classroom and school events, though even here they themselves recognized a tendency towards the unreflective.

Ironically it appeared that the notion of personal competence in their circumstances meant 'self-actualization' in terms of the acquisition and employment of technical craft knowledge, and the development of solutions to problems in the form of recipe strategies which 'worked', rather than the capacity to develop values through self-confrontation and dialogue. Aims and values underlying practice barely entered the realms of reflective consciousness, let alone becoming subject to scrutiny and critique. Engagement in critique of social and institutional situations, of broader aspects of social structures which affect educational practice and experiences, and of norms and values which operate within them, were not much evident in the teachers' deliberations. This is not to say that the capacity to engage in such critique was necessarily missing; rather that the field of view which gained attention was the field of personal responsibilities and performance.

In the sense that to embrace can mean to perceive or understand, and to elude can mean to escape discovery and understanding, it appeared that elusion prevailed in much of these teachers' thinking about their work. This is not to suggest that the teachers were not thoughtful, self-critical, troubled by events, concerned in striving for perfection, and filled their time with reflective actions. It is, rather, to try to distinguish kinds of reflectiveness and the aspects of teaching subjected to such reflection. It is also to suggest that in their strivings for their version of personal excellence some of those other kinds of competence may appear to have been precluded by the very conditions which personal and critical competence might have sought to address. Along with the extensive and intensive deliberations of the teachers there came a point when they themselves began to ask just how considerable was their reflectiveness? Their thoughts about their own rigour in reflectiveness came to challenge my and their optimism about 'opening up' the potential for their educational experiences to be developed constructively, and in ways which acknowledged teaching as perpetually problematic, as value-laden, and as socially situated. They and I came to ask if they were adopting a research stance towards their practice, in which they would maintain and develop a sense of open-minded inquiry, and if so towards which aspects of practice? An antipathetic question was whether there was some other driving force, purpose, and interest behind their deliberations? Several illustrative accounts of these phenomena, and aspects of answers to these questions, emerged from the discussions with the teachers.

I considered the data in relation to Zimpher and Howey's notions of competence; Schon's (1983) cycle of appreciation of a situation, action, reappreciation of the newly created situation, and further action eventually accumulating in an enriched repertoire of practical experience; and distinctions in action research between *reflective* and *reflexive* practice (Carr and Kemmis, 1986; Elliott, 1991; Winter, 1989). The latter asserts a difference between the day-to-day *ad hoc* reflectiveness which may attach to most practical situations and events, and a deeper, introspective scrutiny of an individual's educational aims and the personal values which underly them.

Extracts of data illustrating these fluctuations and variations, as the teachers reported them, are provided in the following details from a conversation with the teachers. They have been left to provide their account of the processes of thinking about the problematics of teaching and the retreat from reflective practice which occurred.

Les But there are other things about your teaching which would not show through in achievements of the pupils — the way you speak, the way you ask questions, the way you discipline the children, and whether it is effective or not.

Kathy The sort of things you were always told about by your tutor on teaching practice.

Liz It seems so long ago, doesn't it.

Kathy Your . . . control is coming along nicely, dear. [laughs]

Les Are those sorts of things irrelevant now?

Liz I think they almost are because I've not really thought about that. Seeing the poor student in our school and seeing the worries that she's got, it seems so long ago that I had the same worries. I mean, I can go into other years now and talk to them, talking in the corridors . . .

Kathy I tell you one thing I do notice about myself, is that I often say to myself, 'you really must listen when the children talk to you' because it is so easy when you've got about twenty children asking you a question all at the same time, to just say 'yes, no, no you can't, yes, you can' — to really listen. I often hear myself saying 'Miss . . . , yesterday I did so and so' — 'did you, dear' and you sound really like Joyce Grenfell and you think, I don't know, it's so awful, I often think I must be just like Joyce Grenfell because I always try and sound so interested but half the time your mind is totally somewhere else, and it's very rarely that you actually sit down and talk to a child properly, and I really wish I did that more often, but I'm not very good at that.

Liz It's suddenly something that has got so much easier because it is not a worry any more, I just accept, I know I've improved, I know I've progressed. When I think back to the teaching practice and my first term at this school, the children's work I can see does need improvement — I'm sure really if you'd come in you'd say, 'well, you should have moved around the classroom more', or whatever improvement, but that's not a major worry or concern any more.

Les Or is it even, you're implying earlier, it isn't even a consideration.

Liz No, it probably isn't because that's the first time I've thought about it since you mentioned it.

Kathy I do think about some things that we've done. Like I often think, where shall I sit? Because if I'm sitting with a group, the tutor always used to tell me it's obviously stupid to sit with your back to the rest of the class, because they'll just run riot and you won't notice, so I consciously seat myself somewhere where even if I'm right at the other end of the class-room I can see everybody, and I consciously . . .

Liz Don't you think you do that because you're tutor told you when you were a student, or — I mean, that's the sort of thing as an experienced teacher I would do.

Kathy Yes, but I still think about it, I don't just do it automatically, and I consciously make myself look around the room a lot because that was one thing I was very bad about on teaching practice, and I still don't do it naturally. I have to make myself do that (17 May).

Liz One thing that I'm definitely learning, that I've appreciated lately is that I'm definitely feeling part of the school now, more established as a teacher, I don't feel nervous going into other people's classrooms and I can train the netball team and arrange away matches and things like that and I can organize school trips, just all those countless things that on teaching practice, if ever you thought about it, they just seemed really impossible, but they seem so easy now, or so matter-of-fact, and so much part of your job, and you don't really think twice about them. But when you stop and think you realize just how far you have come, that you can help supply teachers or the students in the school quite positively.

Les It's that 'countless things' that you refer to — which is of interest . . .

Liz To actually pick something out because, as Kathy says, there's so many things that you are learning all the time. Taking over different classrooms when the teachers are away — having to do spur of the moment lessons. The netball team was a quite important learning experience, 'cos that was something which I did feel very worried about last summer — that I had been given the responsibility for the third-year netball team.

Les The teaching of it and the organizing of it?

Liz The organizing of it and the training of it — actually selecting them at the beginning of the year, actually selecting fourteen girls to be chosen, to organizing them, arranging matches, getting involved with the middle-school league, and all that kind of stuff.

Kathy Do you think it's because you've stopped panicking about it?

Liz Yes, I'm sure.

Kathy If you just sort of calm down and think, well, I can ask people's advice . . .

Liz And also other people accepting your role as well, like parents accepting that you're a teacher and children in school accepting you're a teacher, really helps such a lot, whereas I'd probably always seen myself just as a student or a student-teacher, never quite accepted that I was a real teacher, and that does help because it gives you confidence and makes you realize that you are taken seriously.

Les Those examples are very similar to Debbie's one about the computer in that, it's new things which cause the apprehension, things which you've not done before.

?? Like parents' evening.

Deb I was just thinking of the school trip. I've organized one for the whole 4th year. First of all last term I organized doing a questionnaire, and going into town and organizing the whole thing . . . with a couple of parent helpers, organizing the parent helpers and briefing them, and then recently I've organized trips up to Strangers Hall, for the whole 4th year and the daunting thing was the fact that I was going last, the other two teachers were taking groups before I was taking mine. So it was sort of, not just if I'd bungled it, bungled it just for me and my class, if I'd bungled it for the whole of the 4th year, I wouldn't know until I'd got there because they were going first. So, I was a bit apprehensive until a colleague came back, first trip, and said it was fine — interesting.

Liz . . . assemblies, having to do class assembly, like you said, but also having to do, every third week, you take your year group, so there's three second-year classes, so I'll take all the second years for class assembly, and I never would have thought I could have thought of different assemblies and stories to read to these 100 children, but, you know, I've coped with it and quite enjoyed it, don't feel nervous any more. Whereas the first time I was very — practised it for ages and planned it.

Dave One thing that came up, I suppose you'd call it teaching of the teachers, this training course for . . . scientists, I had done this forensic science course several times, . . . setting everything out and sort of talking to these . . . teachers about this part of this course, I don't know how I felt actually, it was a weird feeling, but actually having that acceptance that you were competent enough to say, 'well, this is the way I've done it, and these are the reasons why'.

Liz Yes, all the things that took so long to work out in the first half term and yet I couldn't begin to put into words to Susannah (a student-teacher) to help her, they are just things she is going to have to go through and find out for herself.

Les Things that you now take for granted?

Liz Yes.

Les Like where things are located (exactly) how many classrooms there are, and where they are.

Liz Where you go if you want an extension lead. What happens on the morning before you break up for Christmas, all these silly little things that — the way you sit your class in assembly. There are so many — hundreds of things that I've learnt that I just take for granted now — do them so naturally now, and yet were really problems last year.

Les All of those things are specific to the institution that you are working in, not things which you can bring with you to a job.

Liz Nobody can teach you them, or help you out on a PGCE course.

Deb And the same applies when you are going to a new school, however long you've been teaching.

Liz But I'm sure you take it much more in your stride.

Dave But you have the confidence of having been through it once, you know that you can manage — that's always an advantage.

Liz At least you know you can get on all right in your classroom because you have taught a class before, even if you don't know where the books are you can — whereas a new teacher has that worry as well.

Deb Yes, it was interesting I must say doing the talk last week to the postgrad students. *C'est moi*, yes. It was me. Really I only brought out all the things that we've talked about, parents' evenings, reports, I must be more confident because school things are taking up less time outside of school. I don't know what that says about anything really, but things aren't taking as long and therefore I have actually got more time for myself, or I am making more time for myself, or I am not allowing it to take longer, and I am getting now a social life and I am getting involved in other things, non-school things, which I think is important.

Les Is that true for you, Liz?

Liz Yes, definitely. I don't feel that quality is suffering either, which of course is important. I am preparing it just as much as working out ideas, but I don't spend hours and hours working it out and writing out notes for them.

Deb And you do it in your head, you know, you find yourself mulling over ideas for a long time, and mulling over the way that it is then going to be put into action, so a lot more is done up here rather than writing copious notes of everything and how things are going to be done.

Liz When I look back to my first week at school, it had every minute mapped out, from 8.55–9.10 we will do this, and from 9.10 — I mean, I don't need to worry about that now. I know basically in the first part of the morning we will do, you know . . .

Les Tell me how that works, how has that come about?

Liz What?

Les That you can plan in your head.

Liz It's called laziness, well, I spend just as long sorting it out — all I need to do now is jot down notes in my diary, perhaps a word, and I will know enough, probably what it is is that — if I were to get my diary for the first week it would have every single little thing written down. It would have — everything is written down, all the people I've got to talk to, when I've got to take the register back, what we are doing in the library, where they put the library tickets, first thing I've got to tell Sarah something, all little notes for, every little detail is written down. Now I don't need to write down that they've got to put the library ticket back in the book before they take out another one — I don't need to write things like that now. So, all the little details that used to — I used to have so many things going on in my head that I had to do before I could get through a lesson, I don't need that now — most things are in control or ticking over or working to a routine, so now all I have to concentrate on is the lesson. All I need if I've thought about it a lot, like . . . mull things over in my head, all you need in is the one word, you know, sliding experiments, and that sends it back to me, oh yes, that's the particular experiment that we are doing and the way that we are going to set it out when we start it up to get the equipment, that's all I need now, I don't need a whole page of equipment to get out.

Deb And it has to be thought out. I find myself thinking over things at odd times in the middle of the night, driving somewhere, when I'm doing other things, and just thoughts come into my head about something that I may well be doing later on in the week, or the following week, or tomorrow, whenever it may be, and thinking, oh yes, what have I got to do during the day — I've got that lesson now, I'm doing that so that needs to be . . . and I'll think about it, or if there's a lesson that I've got to really start thinking about how I'm going to approach that — a lot of thinking, it's almost subconscious in one sense because you are not concentrating on a thing, these ideas are just mulling around and ticking around and you are doing lots of other things. And then when it comes to actually then formally thinking, right, what's happening, all these things have already been mulled over and so it's very quick just to make either a mental note . . . or just a quick jot down somewhere.

Les So, it's mental designing?

Deb Unless, of course, it's a subject I know absolutely nothing about and I need to actually do some background reading myself to actually feel confident with the subject before, then I can ask the children to go and research it because when they ask me something and I know nothing about it, it doesn't make me feel very confident.

Liz The other thing is I think I'm teaching much more real lessons now, on teaching practice at the beginning they were very much one-off lessons; they might even have been following the scheme but even so, I'd done a particular introduction, a particular middle bit and a particular end for each lesson, whereas now I know what I did last week and I know the natural development from last week's lesson to this week's. It's much more realistic than thinking Week 2 of this particular scheme is so and so, now I've got to go and teach so and so. I might well be teaching it, but I'll be teaching it in a much more natural way, I think, so much follows on . . . (5 July).

Reviewing Reflective Teaching

Set alongside this and other extensive data from these new teachers Schon's model of reflective practice appeared to fit their case. Action research and particularly reflexive practice, on the other hand, did not appear to fit the kind of thinking which they conveyed. Certainly it did not insofar as the teachers' reflectiveness was conducted in recognition of the pace of events of classroom life, the need to seek so much evidence at once, much of it elusive, to elicit what they could by pragmatic methods, and to handle it rapidly in the formation of judgments towards the provision of practical solutions. These were problems encountered in situations where there was no opportunity for the niceties of agreeing research procedures, recording data by a variety of means, adopting principles and criteria for establishing rigour in their handling and interpretation of evidence.

In this informational anarchy there was, again unsurprisingly I would suggest, a search for order. Attempts to deproblematize teaching, to 'know' that life can be secure in proven actions, seemed to be a major impetus underlying at least some of the teachers' thinking. So one question which arose for me was whether they were to fall in among the many teachers who are characterized by the notion of technical expert, who find no occasion for reflection, but who are

> skilful at techniques of selective in-attention, junk categories and situational control, techniques which they use to preserve the constancy of their knowledge-in-practice. For them uncertainty is a threat; its admission a sign of weakness. (Schon, 1983, p. 68)

The teachers acknowledged their search for situational control. They acknowledged that as they proceeded through the year they engaged in selective inattention. How else could they manage the pace of events and the demands of the tasks before them and have a life outside school? Being skilled implied being skilful at techniques of selective inattention, the sense of coming to act quickly, intuitively, and without conscious thought in the multitude of situations faced. As the year progressed they reported increasingly how in the technical aspects of teaching they came to take some of their practices for granted and conduct some actions without conscious thought. They identified elements of their practice which they came to perform unthinkingly, which became routinized.

They also reported that in the clinical aspects of judgment-making they judged 'what worked' (or what didn't) and established particular instructional strategies or amended practices by way of 'honing' or 'fine-tuning' towards sharper or more skilful performance, judged by the 'what works' criterion. In some circumstances attention was regained when evidence emerged of misjudgment, or when evidence which had previously been hidden from view suddenly or unexpectedly presented itself — surprising evidence which drew them back from complacency. Such surprises occasioned reflection on the actions they had taken, might have taken, or would in future take, and why. Shifts of this kind, between unconscious action and conscious reflection, were indicated throughout the discussions.

On the other hand there was still a good deal which remained problematic. So while there was not yet a 'constancy of their knowledge-in-practice' to preserve, there was an apparent search for it, as a substantial intention in wanting proven, practical proficiency in classroom management and instruction.

There were also, on occasions, deliberate and self-conscious challenges to the barricades of inattention — decisions to break out from 'boring' and routine teaching, as individual teachers willingly engaged in uncertain and risky practices in the search for the 'best' teaching strategies, a search for new ideas, for sound judgments in the implementation of teaching plans. There were, too, perpetual conditions in the circumstances of teaching which affected the realization of some of their aspirations, and which thus occasioned comment about those conditions and their effects on teaching.

The routinization of administrative and managerial techniques, including specific instructional strategies such as the use of language, the adoption of physical presence, ways of asking questions, marking of pupils' work, and those 'hundreds of other things' which constitute the tasks and skills of instruction — those things which had been the teachers' concern in pre-service courses and now forgotten about, or which were problems at the start of the year and now routinized — can be seen to have an effect on the quality of teaching and learning. These prerequisites to quality (as I called them in Tickle, 1987) are not, in my view, simply candidates for the unreflective storerooms of teachers' minds. Yet these aspects of technical competence were candidates for storage. There is a tension here between the idea of developing intuitive, skilful performance and consolidating inattention.

Assessments that particular instructional strategies (in the clinical realm of problem-solving) 'worked' might lead to lack of reflection in future on these aspects too, and further deproblematization of teaching. There were indications that this was likely, as the notion of making 'adjustments' to practice was seen as a refining process, or as honing, rather than to sustain reflection. The teachers' experimenting was purposeful action aimed at achieving a desired state. The process of assessing the experimentation was governed by concern to discover 'what works best'.

The paradox is that making the discovery is, potentially at least, also a process of deproblematizing teaching. This could be seen as a search for the kind of recipe knowledge which Schon himself disparaged. Schon explicitly argues that his notion of reflective practice would potentially overcome the tendency towards selective inattention and habituated practice. Yet while I could not doubt that these teachers were being reflective, and believed I had revealed substantial data on the substance and modes of their reflections, I was also witnessing the emergence of non-reflective practice as the teachers became embedded in the 'experience' of 'what worked'. The same tension arises, then, in relation to clinical, problem-solving competence.

The selective management of complex information allowed for such deproblematization — or so seductively it seemed in the teachers' search for security. But a further element of the paradox was that such deproblematization was hardly possible, given their lack of access to information, its undependability, and the unpredictability of situations. At best they seemed only able to engage in semi-appreciation of situations, to act largely speculatively but in good faith that they knew enough to make adequate judgments. When information was unmanageable and uncontrollable the constancy of unpredictability pertained. In discussing those circumstances there was a sense that the turbulence created was unwelcome. The predictable was pursued. So 'security' in knowing what worked was both an interest and an illusion.

A Stance towards Reflective Practice

Perhaps most important of all for me was my recognition that throughout the discussions the teachers' deliberations appeared to be contained within the realm of technical and clinical competences (or Schon's technical problem-solving) rather than the ends to which practice was directed. The educational aims and the realization of values which underlay them were mostly implicit in their discussions. They did not 'surface' aims and values and consider them as candidates for development. There was little articulation of aims and values, and even less concern shown for the elaboration of them. Discussion focused on pedagogical knowledge in the sense of ways of teaching, rather than reasons for doing so, or for doing so in particular ways. Zimpher and Howey's notion of personal competence, and the mode of action research which involves reflexive thinking, were not in evidence. Nor was there that sense of critical thinking about circumstances, beyond considerations of how to cope with them in the search for personal efficacy as teachers.

These interpretations of the discussions led me to consider more carefully how these paradoxes might apply in my own pursuit of the development of reflective practice, as set out in the aims of the programmes for which I was responsible. Perhaps I had been seduced by Schon, and by loosely held conceptions of action research? Perhaps I needed to scrutinize those ideas, which I had adopted in the form of values and beliefs, for pitfalls and inconsistencies, or for lack of understanding. One of those pitfalls appears to lie in assumptions not only about just what the nature of professional practice is in a case like teaching, where technical know-how might be, or become, in many respects justifiably, a predominant focus of attention in attempts to secure deproblematization and inattention. The pitfall also lies in assumptions about reflection in- and on-, and reflexivity about- such practice.

The kinds of knowledge such as aims and values might be hidden by inattention in the first place, not by default on the part of the individual teacher, but as a cultural norm. That applies to the aims and values of teacher education — in this instance reflective practice — as much as to those held by teachers for the education of children.

But the most crucial question for me became that of whether it is possible, and ethically reasonable, to pursue the development of personal competence and reflexive practice, in the Zimpher and Howey sense, at the same time as new teachers are in pursuit of realizing their (albeit implicit or tacit) aims in practice, and if so by what means? The subsequent and more serious question may be whether the aims, conduct and modes of assessment of teacher education and training can bring those aspects of competence out of the shadows and on to centre stage. If the predominant assumptions in teacher education systems, as well as among individual teachers, are about the need to achieve efficient performance in observable, 'workable' technical and clinical skills, then it may that Schon's notion of reflective practice will remain limited to thoughts about procedural matters and the means of effective teaching. Or it may be used simply, as an implicit or tacit aim. The more fundamental and educationally necessary focus on the purposes and values of education, including those of teacher education, may continue to elude not just these teachers but the teaching community in general.

References

CARR, W. and KEMMIS, S. (1986) *Becoming Critical: Knowing Through Action Research*, Lewes, Falmer Press.

ELBAZ, F. (1983) *Teacher Thinking: A Study of Practical Knowledge*, London, Croom Helm.

ELLIOTT, J. (1991) *Action Research For Educational Change*, Milton Keynes, Open University Press.

McKERNAN, J. (1988) 'The countenance of curriculum action research: Traditional, collaborative, and emancipatory-critical', in *Journal of Curriculum and Supervision*, **3**, 3, pp. 173–200.

McKERNAN, J. (1991) *Curriculum Action Research*, London, Kogan Page.

MOTE (Modes of Teacher Education) Report (1991) (see also Ch. 3 in this volume).

SCHON, D. (1983) *The Reflective Practitioner*, New York, Basic Books.

SCHON, D. (1987) *Educating The Reflective Practitioner*, London, Jossey Bass.

TICKLE, L. (1987) *Learning Teaching, Teaching Teaching*, Lewes, Falmer Press.

TICKLE, L. (1989b) 'On probation: Preparation for professionalism', in *Cambridge Journal of Education*, **19**, 3, pp. 277–85.

TICKLE, L. (1991) 'New teachers and the emotions of learning teaching', in *Cambridge Journal of Education*, **21**, 3, pp. 319–29.

TICKLE, L. (1992a) 'Capital T teaching', in ELLIOTT, J. (Ed) *Reconstructing Teacher Education*, London, Falmer Press.

TICKLE, L. (1992b) 'The first year of teaching as a learning experience', in BRIDGES, D. and KERRY, T. (Eds) *Delivering In-service Teacher Education*, London, Routledge.

TICKLE, L. (1992c) 'The wish of Odysseus: New teachers' receptiveness to mentoring', in WILKIN, M. (Ed) *Issues in Mentoring*, London, Kogan Page.

TICKLE, L. (1992d) 'The Education of New Entrants to Teaching', Thesis submitted for PhD Degree, School of Education, University of East Anglia.

TICKLE, L. (1994) *The Induction of New Teachers: Reflective Professional Practice*, London, Cassell.

WILSON, S.M., SHULMAN, L.S. and RICHERT, A.E. (1987) '150 Ways of knowing: Representations of knowledge in teaching', in CALDERHEAD, J. (Ed) *Exploring Teachers' Thinking*, London, Cassell.

WINTER, R. (1989) *Learning From Experience*, Basingstoke, Falmer Press.

ZEICHNER, K. and TABACHNICK, B.R. (1991) 'Reflections on reflective teaching', in TABACHNICK, B.R. and ZEICHNER, K.M. (Eds) *Issues and Practices in Inquiry-oriented Teacher Education*, London, Falmer Press.

ZIMPHER, N. and HOWEY, K. (1987) 'Adapting supervisory practices to different orientations in teaching competence', in *Journal of Curriculum and Supervision*, **2**, 2, pp. 101–27.

Part 3

In-service Education

12 Embedding Living Methodologies into the System: The Introspective Practitioner

Eileen Francis

Introduction

This research review is derived from three periods of in-service work in Scottish education during the twelve years between 1981 and 1993. Project One on discussion development focused inwards seeking to influence an educational community coping with curriculum development in schools. It represented a concern for communication across the curriculum, a growing awareness of the difference between process- and content-orientated approaches in secondary schools and a recognition of the need for teachers to relate differently to students through participative methods. Project Two built on innovations in personal and social development programmes in schools to define the notion of the enterprising person in the context of the world of work. Project coordinators faced outwards building new systems to discuss ideas and action plans with colleagues and representatives from commerce and industry. Project Three examined the gains and losses from these two periods of development to ask questions about schools' ethos, values in teaching and learning, social and personal values in a climate of educational change.

Evidence from the three projects conducted at Moray House Institute, Edinburgh is used to raise issues about action-research methodology in the in-service context and implications for policy development. Project One — the Discussion Development Project — involved eighty-three teachers in an in-service training programme based on action-research principles. The project was funded by the Scottish Office Education Department (1986–6). Project Two — the Process Innovation Network (1989–91) developed as a project group within the Scottish Enterprise Consortium, an organization consisting of representatives of ten educational institutions funded by the Department of Employment. Project Three — the ROVE project (1991–3), funded by the Gordon Cook Foundation, involved forty+ teachers, administrators and members of other academic disciplines in research on values education.

The review reflects on segments of verbal report data which have provided the basis for descriptions of the action research in previous reports (Francis, 1982; Francis and Davidson, 1987; Francis *et al.*, 1989; Francis, 1992a, 1992b, 1993) and subjects them to further scrutiny. The aim is to highlight the connections between the projects. The focus on this occasion will be the supra-segmental features of the research. These larger units of connected data will provide an insight into the significance of introspection and dialogue in the management of change. The analysis will show the lack of synchrony in integrating policies for the professional development of teachers with the management of changes in the structures and systems of education.

Improving the Reporting of Action Research

Replicability is one of the criteria by which funding bodies judge an effective research method. The difficulty with data management in action research is that the thin descriptions contained in research reports often bear little relationship to the thick descriptions shared between the participants. The assertion that 'learning is unique' in experiential learning programmes appears to contradict evidence which demonstrates the reliability of the methodology for managing change.

There is rarely enough time, particularly on externally funded projects, to analyse and evaluate the data fully. The expectations of the funding body and the assumptions of the researcher will have an effect on the selection of data for evaluation and the type of data which will represent the argument of the final report. Action researchers need to become more effective in reporting the complexities of their approach. They have tended to assume that educational research colleagues would understand the nature of their 'living methodology' and would be aware that results cannot be achieved by surface structure activities alone. Print on paper constructed in a linear fashion interferes with conveying the dynamic of the research process. Research reports appear to describe conscious processes without adequately describing that the boundary between conscious and unconscious processes has changed as a result of research intervention.

Action research is a complex undertaking. At an overt level there is the research task to be considered, the authority of the research partners and a variety of research roles matched to the different phases of research. At the covert level there is management in the mind, the boundary system around task, authority and role and the difficulty of staying with immediate experience.

The criticism which is often levelled at action researchers is that they are engaged in 'development' rather than research. This fails to take account of the nature of the task which is being managed. The person who initiates the research, the principal researcher or the grant-holder, has the responsibility of holding the boundaries of a triple task-a triangulation of dynamics which occurs between the researcher, the practitioner and the body of knowledge underpins the research study.

There is always an 'I' who is researching, a 'we' negotiating the action steps and an 'it', a body of knowledge which informs each research phase. The vocabulary of 'containment' (Bion, 1970) *is* crucial to understanding the dynamics of this triangulation. The triangulation is observed on three levels and in two dimensions. Both surface and deep-structure observations are contained within the triangulation. For example, when systematic reflection is focused on the research group created by a research consultant and classroom teachers — the group learning level — evidence will be acquired on the elements of task management, the generation of ideas and problem-solving. The collection of further evidence can shift the focus to the interpersonal level — the relationships between the research partners in institution and classroom, their attitudes and abilities in relation to the task. The evidence from the different levels of the task needs to be considered prior to undertaking the next action step.

At the levels of group research/learning and interpersonal research/learning it is possible to confine observations on the surface of the triangulation, noting cognitive and behavioural features of the action. The research will be enriched if attention is subsequently focused on unconscious processes — 'What is being managed in the minds of the research partners at the different stages of the research process?' This question shifts the focus from the overt to the covert aspects of the research study and focuses attention at a third level, on the intrapersonal dynamics of the triangulation.

Action researchers have the potential to be process innovators. Process innovators in educational institutions have a vision and a commitment to a style of educational change which is not shared by the majority of their colleagues. That is the purpose of action research — to operate on the periphery of an organization, aware of the boundary system, to attempt to expand the boundaries and to expose the leading edge of change to view. Exposition may lead to interest in the research process at the centre of the organization and incorporation may take place, the nub of the action research findings being adopted, internalized and articulated as policy. The task of the researcher is to move on to new research questions, different visions.

The research question which is constant within action research, concerns the success or failure of dissemination. Making research descriptions explicit is an intrinsic feature of action research. Researchers who focus on the fit between 'learning' and 'change' will have greater success in transferring the benefits of the learning from action research to the policy-making process.

Emphasizing Introspection and Dialogue

The term 'living methodology' refers to an open-system approach in which the dynamics of learning groups and intergroup processes within educational systems are the focus of research. The action researcher believes that such systems are best understood when they are seen in actual operation. Research based on this model is explorative and interpretative.

While educational researchers generally have become more interested in process thinking during the last decade, attention appears to be focused on conscious rather than unconscious processes in action research. Research questions are based on what I can describe, what I think I might do, the kinds of evidence I might collect to help me and how I might check that my judgments are fair and accurate. Schon's concept of the 'reflective practitioner' has become popular and the research process is articulated as a reflective enquiry with an emphasis on 'becoming critical'. One of the effects of this discipline of systematic reflection is to focus the researcher/practitioner on the concept of ideal practice. Observations are based on comparing and contrasting actual behaviour with ideals which emanate from the values, expectations and assumptions of those involved.

The living methodology described here has components of this type of enquiry but in addition focuses attention on the intrapersonal subtext of the research study. Unconscious processes, the nature of immediate experience, the unique aspects of personal learning, are the constituents of this subtext. The purpose of this style of action research is the development of process-thinking skills which lift the experiences of educationalists from covert feeling and thinking to manifest description. It is a research methodology based on introspection through dialogue and the objective is to understand the rhetoric of self in order to manage the reality of a task from the evidence of verbal reports.

Teachers who achieve this transition commented:

> A new perspective for me was concerned with the meaning of 'process'; that it should apply to what goes on inside your head not what you do or say. I suppose until the (research) group I had completely ignored that aspect, to me process was just what people were doing and saying.

> I feel I have developed an awareness of what is going on (in discussion) in terms of the underlying factors rather than in terms of what people say.

> I had no real notion of how unconscious ideas affected people (in a group).

> I think the course has made me much more aware of how complex the whole activity is.

Verbal reports such as these focus on the process of negotiating the meaning of the specific vocabulary used within the research group; attending to the development of awareness and insight as a primary task; understanding the dynamics of the research task at a deep-structure level as well as at a surface level; providing a support system so that teachers can progress from the development of insight to the development of understanding and skill; seeking out contexts conducive to the application and dissemination of research findings.

CHANGING 'I': Project One (Francis 1982, 1985; Francis and Davidson 1987; Francis 1988, 1990)

Introspection and dialogue were key concepts in the discussion development programme for secondary teachers introduced in 1981. Project One aimed to change the traditional relationship between teachers and tutors. It was anticipated that modelling this process in a learning group would have an effect on teachers' relationships with groups of students and colleagues.

The project was informed by general experience during the 1970s and 1980s with college-based INSET as a context for the professional development of teachers. The aim of the college-based programmes was to empower participants on in-service courses so that they could return to their schools to embed research findings into the system. Evidence was available from post-course evaluations that these objectives could be achieved, although it was also observed that many teachers experienced a sense of being de-powered by subsequent educational events which distorted and disabled their intentions. The methodologies they had developed on in-service courses were sometimes ignored, sometimes opposed. It was observed that new skills tended to atrophy under the conditions the teachers encountered when they returned to school.

The role of the lecturers responsible for these courses was that of map maker and guide. Observing this as a novice member of the lecturing team it seemed to me that the role of 'tutor as expert' was inappropriate. My own work with practising teachers encouraged the development of a different approach which had intellectual and experiential roots in speech and language therapy (clinical linguistics), group analysis (psychology/psychoanalysis) and educational research (action research/new paradigm research). The new approach we developed together was designed to offer teachers a more authoritative role in their own learning process.

There was a climate of innovation and change in Scottish Education during this period. Standard grade developments for 14–16 year olds were underway. It was apparent that the insights gained in developing in-service training programmes were relevant to professional development in the Standard Grade context. There was concern that a 'package approach' to innovation and dissemination was being assembled and that the emphasis of teacher involvement would be focused on establishing new systems and structures for curriculum development. The difficulties of transferring innovations developed by one group of teachers to other groups was being encountered. Those responsible for the development of the new curriculum were becoming aware that the embedding of process innovations was different from that of content innovations. The insight that a 3–5 year period of development may be required for the dissemination of process innovations was a daunting prospect for those seeking to accelerate change.

Project One, supported by the Standard Grade development programme, aimed to address the problem of process innovation. It focused on changing 'I', the teacher, with the objective of achieving teacher commitment to the ongoing study of classroom discussion. The role of the researcher/consultant was defined by the task. The person who changes 'I' is oneself. While the research group worked on 'I' the teacher, the researcher sought to model the patterns of effective listening, responding and enabling relevant to the task of discussion management — the researcher as servant of the research group, rather than its leader. Seven teachers piloted the model which is described in Discussion Development Group (DDG) reports and which was used subsequently with seventy-five others. The pilot group, selected by the Scottish Office Education Department, recorded on videotape and in a report (1982) their perception that change had occurred. They emphasized that the 'change' was difficult to describe and that their colleagues expressed little interest in their personal/professional development.

The research team responded to this concern by conducting an enquiry with new groups of participants (three groups: seventeen teachers). Pre-course and post-course interview data was collected and compared. What were the teachers' expectations of the potential of this learning experience? An analysis of the transcripts showed a reluctance to define their expectations other than to express the view that they approached the course with an open mind, with optimism and with a degree of caution. Changing 'I' was greeted by some with scepticism and apprehension. The nature of the learning — change continuum needed to be negotiated during the pre-course interviews. There was general agreement that the primary objective was to gain confidence in managing student discussion. The transcripts contain comments which were tempered with realism. The teachers recognized the constraints of the current content-orientated curriculum which did not lend itself to process-orientated approaches. The post-course interviews were more optimistic in tone. The teachers indicated that the intended learning about self and the deep structure of discussion had been achieved. There was evidence of growth in awareness and insight about the nature of conscious and unconscious group processes. The development of process thinking was remarked on as a significant achievement for future work in the classroom. The teachers were motivated to develop discussion programmes of specific relevance to their own contexts.

Members of the newly formed Discussion Development Group (DDG) were successful in applying the learning from their own group experience to the classroom. In the early 1980s they were concerned that their ideas would not become embedded into the system. They thought of themselves as isolated process innovators within a system somewhat resistant to change. A resource centre to support the teachers was established to moderate the feelings of isolation. Ten years later schools in Lothian region are still using discussion skills programmes developed by DDG members. Several teachers have moved to different schools and are applying the programme in their new schools while colleagues maintain the existing programmes in the original school. Several teachers produced publications reporting the results of their action research (e.g., Johnson, 1985). Three teachers were prime movers in the development of the Lothian Teacher Researcher Group, the first group to be affiliated to the Scottish Educational Research Association. Members of the DDG now hold posts in the Scottish Examination Board, the Scottish Consultative Council on the Curriculum, Lothian Region Advisory service and as deputy and assistant headteachers. They are now in a position to influence change.

The catalytic effect of the DDG programme is expressed by an English teacher:

> I remember it was very, very unsettling. That was the first experience I'd ever had of actually having to develop my own model. I found that very difficult and I think everybody else did too. It was the first time I'd actually had to work and think for a long, long time. I'd never really taken on board before the sort of feelings it can create — just feeling unsure of yourself when you think you should be able to do it . . . it helped to justify the idea that innovation should be an ongoing thing and you don't just stop when you've got a package and never do anything else for the rest of your career.

CHANGING WE: Project Two (Francis et al., 1989; Francis, 1991, 1992)

The introspective approach used by the DDG was a novel and powerful experience for the secondary teachers involved. Central and local-government officials, however regarded the primary task of training as empowering the system rather than the individual teacher. They were interested in the products of the DDG rather than its processes.

In the 1980s and early 1990s arrangements for school-based in-service training were enhanced and regional support systems such as the employment of curriculum development officers increased. During this period there have been attempts to embed 'living methodologies' into the system. In-service work on aspects of group work, personal and social education, on investigation, problem-solving and enterprise have been developed with marginal reference to the introspective model proposed by the DDG. Recently the attention of in-service planners has shifted from process innovation within the curriculum to whole-school issues such as bullying, differentiation and equal opportunities. Local education authorities now have the added pressure of implementing the new 5–14 curriculum proposals in Scotland.

Project Two was in harmony with this shift of attention from personal/professional development to the management of change within systems. It occurred within the framework of the Enterprise in Higher Education programme sponsored by the Department of Employment 1990–2 and involved ten higher education institutions in Scotland. The Scottish Enterprise Consortium (Francis, 1992a) was designed as an innovative system to stimulate higher education in Scotland to be increasingly flexible, function-related and responsive to change. The system had a flat organizational structure without hierarchies. It was a system which was perceived by its participants to be open in that any member of staff with the time, interest or commitment could become involved in a variety of enterprising projects. The consortium established successful working relationships with representatives of government agencies, industry and commerce. The Scottish Enterprise Consortium committed itself to a fellowship model rather than a leadership model and the developing system was intended to contrast with existing systems which were perceived as closed and hierarchical.

Enterprise development brought together individuals with similar experience of managing process innovations such as the Discussion Development Group. They regarded themselves as change agents within their own institutional settings and the Scottish Enterprise Consortium provided them with an opportunity to work on a cross-institutional basis. Project Two: the Process Innovation Network (PIN) represented the potential of the Consortium model in action — a small group of colleagues from different higher education institutions sharing their experience of teaching and learning.

The first meeting of PIN was held in June 1990 following a seminar which disseminated the ideas contained in a research project conducted at Moray House on perceptions of enterprise in educational contexts (Francis *et al.*, 1989). Representatives of seven of the ten institutions involved in the consortium contract participated in the network and all institutions received regular reports of PIN activities at management group meetings. PIN was intended to be a vehicle for expressing consortium commitment to improving the quality of student learning. Its role was as a catalyst, a supportive reference group within the consortium for those advocating innovations in teaching and learning. Members of PIN agreed to research and disseminate examples of effective practice in learning and teaching.

The concept of 'network' was discussed in detailed terms by the group. It was recognized that consortium funding was insufficient for regular meetings of the project group. As an alternative, one member acted as coordinator collating the work and initiating contact when it was necessary for a decision to be made on the next action step. When the network did function as a group the purpose was introspection. The group reflected on the intergroup dynamics of the consortium, the role of members in the group and relationships within their institutions. Five projects based on an explorative–interpretative methodology were initiated by members of the group with institutional colleagues. The outcomes of these projects are reported in a publication which was disseminated on completion of the consortium contract (Francis, 1992b).

Six consultations were held with researchers working on similar projects on teaching and learning in the United Kingdom and with a visiting research fellow from Canada. Members of PIN were invited to share their expertise on staff development with members of other institutions and promoted the idea of cross-consortium collaboration between the Eastern Region Teacher Education Consortium (ERTEC) and the Scottish Enterprise Consortium at two conferences on process innovation in teaching and learning.

The PIN initiative operated on the basis of 'added value', a monetary concept which encouraged the use of small sums of development funding allocated by the consortium to enhance the ongoing activities of members of the project team in their roles as researchers, development consultants or as holders of cross-college posts associated with staff development and enterprise. The SEC benefited from the relationships to which the PIN Group had access. Previous work with the Discussion Development group had shown that networks need 3–5 years to develop as active systems. It was therefore of great benefit to a system which would receive funding over a period of eighteen months to have a base on which to build.

Three institutions who were less concerned about teaching and learning innovation had neither the networks, the time allocation nor the capacity to adopt the 'value-added' approach which would have encouraged their participation in the PIN project. There was also an unwillingness to engage in introspection. These factors affected full engagement with the values and commitments of the consortium influencing the institutions to select other projects to fulfil their contractual obligations.

DEVELOPING 'IT' — Project Three 'ROVE' (Francis, 1992)

The SEC Project showed the disadvantages of attempting to accelerate change in institutions by pump-priming new systems and explicitly promoting a variety of different relationships between change agents who do not share similar values and commitments about institutional development. The issues which were raised by the SEC project have been documented elsewhere (Francis, 1989, 1991, 1992b). The members of PIN continue their enterprise activities within their own institutions and maintain an informal network. It became evident that there were a number of values issues underpinning enterprise developments which were not being addressed. Conflict was created in institutions concerning the increase of vocationalism in education, competition versus cooperation, the management of planned change i.e., change described in the corporate plan and unplanned change, developments which resulted from changes promoted by central and local government. The project-centred approach adopted by government departments enlivened the work of individuals but challenged values relating to leadership style within the educational community and respect among colleagues. It could no longer be assumed that staff and students shared a common set of values. The study of philosophical and ethical questions, after a lean period during the 1980s, once more appeared on the educational agenda.

Project Three, funded by the Gordon Cook Foundation, provided the opportunity to research on 'values education' (ROVE). What was it? How might it become a central element in the curriculum? What were its underlying philosophical and methodological principles? ROVE would show that if personal communication in education was the issue of the 1970s and organizational communication the issue of the 1980s, that communication about values would be the priority of the 1990s.

The experience gained from previous projects was embedded into the research methodology. Dialogue between individuals was explicitly organized. The researcher selected the individuals involved on the basis of their willingness to engage in introspection about values in education. There was an expectation following the development of the DDG and PIN that a dialogical community on values education could be created. The dialogical community would be coordinated as a network. Written evaluation — the notion of the dialogue journal — would be a feature of the research design. The report would be produced in the form of a staff-development programme and documented on video.

The initial aim of the project was to present subject matter from the moral arena on survival and being, transcendence, cooperation and personhood which concerned a small group of sixteen interviewees to a wider group (forty) of teacher educators, educational administrators and representatives of other academic disciplines. Responses were collected in writing and analysed from a behavioural-linguistic, cognitive and psychodynamic perspective (Francis, 1992a).

The reactions to DDG and PIN research had shown the resistance there is among educational researchers to the subjectivity of research evidence gained through introspection and dialogue. In common with Brown (1980), ROVE maintained that the notion of operant subjectivity deserved exploration: 'what is interesting is not predicting what people will say, but getting them to say it in the first place, in the hope that we may be able to discover something about what they mean when they say it'.

The findings of the project indicate that a range of views exist among educationalists in relation to the philosophical triad of objectivism, subjectivism and relativism. Educationalists have difficulty in sharing their philosophy of education and finding the language which expresses a shared value system. The axis between psychological and philosophical understanding seems to be crucial. Perceptions about the nature of self affected interpretations of the working papers. Some informants considered the subject matter of 'values education' as a construct of the super-ego, the idealized self, rather than associated with ego development and were consequently wary of it. They perceived values educators as promoting conscience, shame and guilt to prolong the influence of parents and others in society. Values educators were regarded as making premature demands, desiring that their judgments and prohibitions should be internalized by children, before the child was able to question them.

Several respondents made the point that values education must locate itself in ego development rather than through a process of inculcation which may cause 'splitting' (the notion of the compromised ego and true and false selves was being discussed here). There was agreement with Taylor (1989) that we need to examine 'the lack of fit between what people officially and consciously believe, even pride themselves on believing and what they need to make sense of their moral reactions'. These philosophical issues are currently being debated in schools and colleges. It seems there is no easy consensus. Values statements from different areas of the curriculum show, for example, that a robust description of the self can become a thinner description of the self by the addition of phrases such as 'learn to cope', 'come to terms with', 'accept limitations', 'be responsive to people and events', 'accept the consequences of decisions', 'be responsive'. Do such phrases intentionally convey the impression that conformism is more highly valued than diversity and are these opinions on 'self' being debated by curriculum developers? Teachers contacted during the ROVE project agree that education is no longer concerned solely with 'teaching subjects'. They perceive their role to include the personal and social development of young people in its widest sense. The pedagogical descriptions used in personal and social-development courses, however, indicate considerable differences in perspective. An analysis of PSD courses shows little consistency in the values statements which accompany the programmes. PSD programmes can be based on differentiation, competency, information-based or socialization models, or a combination of models. It appears that more attention is directed towards the development of the systems and structures which will deliver these curricula and that there is little appraisal of the sense of self which they convey.

The final series of action steps which was undertaken by ROVE was to take the dialogue on these issues to eight schools to investigate the depth of the debate in day-to-day practice. Data was collected to describe the curriculum and the systems which the schools interpreted as 'values education'. One school engaged in an ongoing dialogue which assessed progress of their school-development plan alongside the findings of the dialogical community developed by ROVE. Another school matched activities to develop a student record of achievement with the issues raised by ROVE on the nature of the self. Two other schools developed specific action-research projects on the development of values education. The first 'DOVE' group was conducted with a group of sixth-year students as an extra-curricular activity. The second, involving a group of fifth-year students, was part of a PSD programme which examined the media as a context for learning about values.

Case studies and a videorecording intended for use in staff development are contained in the report 'Making Values Explicit' (1993) which describes the different phases of the study from dialogical community to action research in schools.

The dialogical community has the title 'VECTOR' (an acronym which reminds us of our focus on the direction of values education, consultancy, training and organizational research). Designed as a support system similar to that of the Discussion Development Group, VECTOR currently provides: evaluation services to the Gordon Cook Foundation; research services to teacher researchers in secondary schools; consultancy support for local and international professional development projects. The VECTOR fellowship which meets three times a year for policy discussions is described as a 'fellowship of leaders' from a range of institutions representative of all sectors of education.

Change through Introspection and Dialogue

The primary focus of the research methodology used in the three projects was introspection on the patterns of language use, interpretation, rules of speaking and attitudes integral to the projects. The aim was to understand the dynamics of process thinking by studying introspective verbal reports derived from the project activities. The required action steps were identified through the progression of language use from the 'ideal' to the 'real'. The titles of the research reports during the period emphasize the reality of 'verbal report' as a means of identifying the development of process thinking by the use of the gerund in titles such as 'Learning to discuss', 'Working together on discussion'. The titles convey the nature of the ongoing work — learning in which there is always the potential for further analysis and understanding. In 'Making the Rhetoric Real' it was explicitly suggested that verbal reports emanating from senior management in education could be perceived as rhetoric by other members of staff and that the lack of shared understanding about the meaning of the enterprise vocabulary interfered with the change process. The starting point of each project was an explicit investigation of the key word — discussion, enterprise, values education — framed in the research proposal.

One of the purposes of process thinking is to avoid 'splitting the object'. Teacher-researchers might compare research findings on 'affective education' with programmes on 'thinking skills' and decide that the latter will be more effective. Bion (1970) warns 'but if the idea is subjected to splitting it may split again repeatedly, each split growing and having to be split again. Thus one gets not division but division and multiplication — cancerous not qualitative increase'.

Process thinking encourages the teacher to adopt a holistic approach. During each project there were phases in which the image of the 'container' and the 'contained' needed to be made explicit. It was necessary to ask 'What do the words mean?', 'What meanings are contained in the words?', establishing the nature of the link in an attempt to heal the splits. Exploring the link between the description 'discussion skills' and 'discussion process' in Project One, for example, provided a framework for understanding cognitive, behavioural and psychodynamic levels of the task.

It was often difficult to demonstrate process thinking to a funding body more concerned with action than pedagogical description. Using 'discussion skills' synonymously with 'discussion process' or 'entrepreneurialism' with 'enterprise' is evidence of a fundamental communication difficulty which the research group was sometimes unable to resolve. The ROVE project was affected by values education being interpreted in the active mode by the sponsors. A definition of values education was issued during the first year of the project: 'Values education is an activity during which . . .' and the research question redefined: 'How do you do values education with 14+.' The recent report 'Making Values Explicit' (1993) reflects on the effect this had on the research process.

This is work which requires patience. Teachers who can cope with uncertainty and doubt are more able to be stimulated by the process than those who have a preference for working with fact and reason. While there is no denial of the validity of fact and reason in the research process it is recognized that understanding the notion of containment is often difficult and that the capacity for verbal expression frequently disintegrates — 'it's as if'. The primary task is to hold to the belief that significant learning will emerge from this process. Taylor (1989) aptly refers to the process as the 'ethics of inarticulacy'.

Each project followed a similar learning path. During phase One the research partners selected themselves for the task. Those who accepted the uncertainty principle, the immediacy of here and now, elected to work in the project team, those who did not — one or two on each occasion — opted out. Those who opted to participate in the research probed the boundaries of conscious and unconscious level of the task. While all the participants demonstrated evidence of learning, some would be more successful than others. They would be the research partners who would show the extent to which we underestimate our capacity for making thought processes conscious.

A pattern emerged in the research questions as confidence grew in the validity of the approach. What is the primary task of the research? Is it being interfered with by secondary tasks? How are we perceiving the boundary systems of the task? Which boundaries are implicit, which explicit? How are issues relating to authority, role and influence affecting management of self and task? Is the project team developing a language appropriate to the task which will allow one verbal report to be compared with another?

Introspection based on verbal report produces three types of evidence (Cohen,

1987). 'Self-report' provides descriptions of what researchers do. 'Self-observation' inspects specific aspects of behaviour governed by short-term memory which is accessed introspectively during an event or retrospectively after an event. The third type of evidence — 'self-revelation' — is neither a description of general behaviour nor based on inspection of specific behaviour, it externalizes the content of the mind through a stream of consciousness disclosure of thought processes.

Evidence of Self-revelation

A practical example which illustrates an improvement in the quality of verbal reports is contained in the DDG research. The researchers reflected that if the course had been successful in achieving its objectives there would be a qualitative difference in the language used in pre- and post-course interviews. Anecdotal evidence indicated that the teachers were more reflective about 'I' the teacher in discussion and talked less about the constraints of school and pupils as the research progressed. 160 pre-course comments and 159 post-course comments were collated and analysed. The methodology used was similar to that of Q methodology (Brown, 1980).

A comparison of the data showed a shift from school-centred comments to person-centred comments in pre- to post-course interviews (School 87 per cent to 23 per cent, Person 13 per cent to 77 per cent). To validate the selection of person-centred comments as an accurate representation of the views of teachers about the course, a group evaluation was conducted with six teachers in which they rank-ordered sets of comments for significance in terms of their own learning. The two comments which referred to the notion of how unconscious ideas affected individuals in the group received the highest ranking.

Research Activity as a Metaphor

It is not the result of this activity which is significant. The researchers recognized the limitations of quantitative methods and the difficulty of small samples. What was being defined during the evaluation exercise was the value of the introspective data. The teachers had engaged in a group-learning experience in which they had initiated the talk with the support of one of the researchers. The thoughts and feelings experienced by the group were reviewed by the teachers with the second researcher in individual unstructured interviews which enabled them to conceptualize their learning. The researchers were able to demonstrate through the sorting procedure that the group experience had achieved a valuable learning outcome. Their unique personal experience was regarded as equally valuable by other members of the research team. In comparing the statements that each teacher had produced they were able to make the framework of the learning experience explicit as evidence of their discussion ability.

The different phases of group activity experienced at a cognitive/psychodynamic level were made explicit at a behavioural level by the consultant through the pre- and post-course activities. The pre-course interviews represented the significance of personal history, expectations and assumptions in forming the group. The post-course interviews validated the unique nature of personal experience, the similarities and the differences as the group began to work on the primary task and the ability to maintain the momentum of the experience. The group evaluation marked the ending of this phase of group development asserting learner autonomy. It defined the role of the teachers as critical friends ready to pursue the application of their group experience in their own contexts in the knowledge that they had created a viable support system.

A Different Gaze: Holding the Task

During Project One the researchers asked themselves if their philosophy of educational development differed significantly from that of their colleagues. They constructed two statements about the 'ideal teacher', the first emphasizing the teacher as content innovator, stressing professionalism based on competency, the other emphasizing the teacher's role as a process innovator stressing consulting and enabling skills. The statements distinguished between 'having skills' and 'being' a teacher. Twenty-nine teacher educators and forty-three graduate students considered the statements. The participants were unaware of the origin of the statements.

In 1985 fourteen lecturers and twenty graduate PGCE students perceived themselves as Teacher One. Seven lecturers and twenty-three students selected Teacher Two. Eight lecturers did not wish to discriminate between the descriptions regarding both as applicable. A teacher commented: 'I was trained to be Teacher One but I see myself now as Teacher Two.' In 1987 a section of the report on the DDG described features of failure in dissemination. The researchers described the ambivalence that had been observed in the educational community in relation to the living methodologies which produce process innovations. It commented on the lack of readiness in the educational community to make use of the research findings interpreting it as conscious and unconscious resistance.

The teacher-researchers reported on the difficulty of sustaining the impetus of the innovative mode within school surroundings where the physical spaces were unsuitable, where the behaviour of students created difficulties and where colleagues were apathetic. Commitment to a whole-school policy on discussion was an idealized vision when compared with the priorities within the management group. Even the schools which allowed teacher-researchers to be seconded to the study placed content innovation higher on the agenda than process innovation. One teacher reported that he had found it 'impossible' to move his management group in the direction of a whole-school policy.

Ten years later the situation has changed. A new senior-management team is in place and process innovation has become a priority. The ideas advocated by the teacher-researcher are articulated in the current development plan but are owned by a different voice. Productive pairings within the senior-management group are now possible. Has the patience and persistence of this teacher-researcher been rewarded or has his energy and enterprise been eroded by this lack of fit between his learning experience and the embedding process? He has held to his task but he no longer has ownership of the innovation. These are factors in the management of change which discourage process innovators.

Evidence was also collected from students who experienced the differing attitudes of teachers to innovations in teaching and learning. The enthusiasm of the students captured on videorecordings during the research project was later tempered by cynicism. They observed a lack of commitment to embedding changes in discussion practice as they progressed through the school. One group of verbal reports obtained three years after innovative work was undertaken shows that students valued a discussion innovation because it made them feel more confident and helped their understanding of subjects. They were disappointed, however, that at a later stage in their education their newly acquired skills had been allowed to atrophy because of a lack of commitment within the school to a methodology which they felt they understood better than their teachers.

Conclusion: Self-revelation Made Public

In 1993 three statements were constructed for the ROVE project describing different educational value systems: education as transmission; as social change; as personal development. The ROVE network, which involves former members of the DDG and PIN, selected the personal-development metaphor as their preferred description of their value system, however each member could identify colleagues who perceived education differently.

While this group became increasingly familiar with interpreting the self-revelatory aspects of verbal reports an equal number experienced disequilibrium. Disturbance of equilibrium may have been caused by explicit description of the I–We–It triangulation. If the project is perceived to concern 'I' it may be disconcerting to uncover the 'We' and the 'It' in the 'I', or the 'I' and the 'It' in 'We'. For some educationalists even the 'I' and the 'We' in schooling continues to be contentious. This appeared particularly true in the case of the Scottish Enterprise Consortium. The executive group and representatives of the Department of Employment assumed that introspection on the dynamics of the consortium would be a task undertaken by the evaluation group, although this was not expressed explicitly in the language of the contract. Several institutions were unwilling to accept this implicit commitment. They perceived the consortium solely as a funding body dispensing project finance to their institution and were not interested in cross-institutional dynamics.

The self-revelation strategy requires practitioners to explore and interpret their own vulnerability as learners. Both researchers involved with the DDG had undertaken analytical group work and believed that a willingness to explore vulnerability under controlled conditions was a sign of strength rather than weakness in personal and professional life. There is a risk involved in making elements of such explorations public. Confidentiality issues are constantly on the research agenda. Reports may disconcert readers and in certain circumstances be interpreted as politically naive. Evidence was collected which indicated that the nature of the task of introspection can be misperceived. The researchers concern is with truth, with the real rather than the idealized overview and not with the political processes of education.

The evidence of the verbal reports shows the different levels of involvement in the introspective work of the three projects. In Project One all the participants were actively engaged in introspection of a self-revelatory type. In Project Two, members of the Process Innovation network were actively introspective while other members of the Scottish Enterprise Consortium were not. Project Three shows active introspection being promoted as a crucial element of values education through the formation of the VECTOR fellowship.

This twelve-year period of research illustrates some of the issues which need to be considered in assessing the validity of educational research results based on an introspective methodology. Educational managers may be more knowledgeable than they were about interpreting evidence from self-reports and self-observation, but they continue to have difficulty in identifying and validating evidence of the third type of verbal report, self-revelation. Furthermore, the three research projects described here show that evidence derived from self-revelation will be resisted. Educationalists draw personal/professional boundaries differently. It is evident that many regard the disclosure of thought processes as personal and private rather than professional and public. Some educationalists distrust the evidence derived from introspection. They function on the assumption that learning which takes place at an unconscious level is not accessible to mental probing and that there is no pro-fessional requirement to explore personal processes. In policy terms this has had the effect of compartmentalizing the insights of staff who contribute to the professional development of teachers and those involved in the management of new structures and systems in education.

References

BION, W. (1970) *Attention and Interpretation*, London, Tavistock.

BROWN, R.S. (1980) *Political Subjectivity: Application of Q Methodology*, Harvard, Harvard University Press.

COHEN, A.D. (1987) 'Using verbal reports on research on language learning', in FAERCH, C. and KASPAR, G. (Eds) *Introspection in Second Language Research*, Philadelphia, Multilingual Matters.

FRANCIS, E. (1982) 'Learning to Discuss', Report to Scottish Education Department, in FRANCIS, E. and DAVIDSON, J. (1987) *Working Together on Discussion: A Study of Process Innovation and Dissemination*, Report to Scottish Education Department.

FRANCIS, E., JARVIE, M., SINCLAIR, A. and SMITH, C. (1989) 'Making the Rhetoric Real: Perceptions of Enterprise in Educational Contexts', Report to Standing Committee on Research, Scotland.

FRANCIS, E. (1992a) 'The Scottish Enterprise Consortium: Evaluation Report to Department of Employment', Sheffield.

FRANCIS, E. (Ed) (1992b) 'Negotiating teaching and learning: Process innovation network', Stirling, Scottish Enterprise Consortium.

FRANCIS, E. (1993) 'Making Values Explicit at 14+', A report to the Gordon Cook Foun-dation, Aberdeen.

JOHNSON, T. (1985) 'Learning to discuss: A teaching approach', in BROWN, S. and MUNN, P. (Eds) *The Changing Face of Education 14–16*, Slough, NFER-Nelson.

TAYLOR, C. (1989) *Sources of the Self*, Cambridge, Cambridge University Press.

13 Reconceptualizing Policy on In-service Teacher Education

Jack Whitehead

Introduction

My arguments for a reconceptualization of in-service teacher education policy are based on my experiences as an educational researcher and provider of in-service programmes for teachers from the School of Education of the University of Bath. These programmes have developed over the past twenty years in my work with teachers on their in-service education in Somerset, Avon, Wiltshire and Gloucestershire. My arguments are also based on my experience of examining Diploma, MEd, MPhil and PhD programmes on teachers' professional development in a range of colleges of higher education, polytechnics and universities.

My central point is simple. Rather than trying to derive policy from existing conceptual forms of social or educational theory, I am suggesting a policy which would support the creation of living forms of educational theory. I will be showing where these living forms are embodied in the in-service professional development of teachers as they explore the implications of answering questions of the form, 'How do I improve my practice?', in the context of developing a good social order which supports the power of truth against the truth of power. However, the practical implications of my argument for policy formation and implementation are complex. This is because of the value-laden nature of teacher education and the political, intellectual and economic context which influences educational policy. These contexts have been influenced directly, since 1979, by Conservative Governments and their legislation. The central principle in much of this legislation is the belief that educational standards will be improved by enabling the market forces of free competition to operate between schools. These forces operate as the money which accompanies individual pupils goes to those schools chosen by parents or the pupils.

The Context

With the delegation of budgets from local education authorities to schools, the schools are free to buy programmes of professional development from the providers. The traditional providers of in-service programmes have been the local authority advisers, advisory teachers and higher education institutions. Because of the impact of market-driven legislation, some advisory services in counties such as Gloucestershire are now reorganizing themselves as business units. Their expertise may be brought in by schools to support the professional development of teachers. Whether such business units will survive from services purchased by schools is not clear. However, what is clear from the fact that a majority of the new school-inspection teams have been formed by advisers, is that this expertise, whilst inspecting, will be lost to in-service teacher education. One local-authority service in the South West of England which, only three years ago, could offer support to its schools from over sixty full-time members of staff is now cut back to less than thirty. In this authority, policy documents have been sent to schools on the professional development of teachers. They consist of delightful rhetoric but are out of date almost as soon as they are received in terms of the resources needed to deliver them. Further public-expenditure cuts have been made for 1994–5 and the provision of local-authority services is being further undermined by market-driven legislation. Given these conditions it is difficult to see how a comprehensive policy of in-service teacher education programmes can be based on a service provided within the present organizations of local-authority advisers.

Are the university schools of education in a better position to offer clear policies with a realistic possibility that they could be delivered? Evidence from the in-service teacher-education publicity of university schools of education, shows that many are similar to those of Bath and Nottingham in offering modular programmes for advanced qualifications. Whilst the numbers of local-authority-funded, full-time secondments, have fallen dramatically over the past four years, some universities have responded flexibly with their modular programmes offered at outstations in twilight sessions. These reduce a school's need to provide supply cover. In the absence of a consensus about the nature of an educational theory of professional development there is a tension between seeing professional development as a matter of aggregating a number of modules which can be studied independently, and the idea that 'development' involves more than an aggregate of skills and knowledge.

Reconceptualizing

My argument for reconceptualizing in-service teacher education rests upon two assumptions. The first is that teacher education involves a process of development which goes beyond adding 'modules' of skills and knowledge to one's understanding. I am thinking of education as a process in which valued learning involves a developmental process which is not just additive but also transforms the ways in which one understands and acts. The second is that the curriculum of in-service teacher education should be justified in relation to educational theory. The second assumption places a responsibility on teachers and other educational researchers to clarify and to seek a consensus about what counts as educational theory. I would go as far as to say that the creation and testing of educational theory is, along with gathering educational information, the primary responsibility of a community of educational researchers.

In seeking to establish a new policy for in-service teacher education I will draw together ideas about educational development and educational theory in a stipulative definition of educational theory. I claim that educational theory is being constituted by the descriptions and explanations of their own educational development which individual learners are producing as they explore the implications of asking questions of the kind, 'How do I improve my practice?'. Whilst I stipulate this definition with no further justification, I can offer the empirical evidence to persuade you of the value of such descriptions and explanations in a collection of case studies which have, since 1982, been accredited for PhD, MPhil, and MEd, degrees and Advanced Diploma and Advanced Certificates in Professional Development by the University of Bath (Reason, 1993).

These studies constitute the 'Action Research and Educational Theory Case Study Collection' in the School of Education. I first outlined the action–reflection cycle which has since been used in these studies in a paper to the British Education Research Association (BERA), 1977. This cycle involved the experience of problems when values were negated, the design of an action plan, acting and gathering evidence which could be used to make a judgment on the effectiveness of the actions, evaluation and, modification of the problems, ideas and actions in the light of the evaluation. The 1977 paper was followed by a paper on the 'Observation of a Living Contradiction' delivered at BERA in 1980. I explained how videotapes of one's own practice could reveal one's existence as a living contradiction in the sense of recognizing that whilst holding particular values, one could be seen to be denying those values in practice. I termed the experience of this tension, a living contradiction.

I pointed out that the existence of 'I' as a living contradiction in questions of the kind, 'How do I improve this process or education here?', or, 'How do I improve my practice?', could form the basis for the creation of a new form of educational theory. I also speculated on the possibility that the claims of individual teachers to know their own educational development could be accredited for higher degrees and suggested the procedures through which this legitimation could be achieved. The results of a sustained commitment to test the validity of this idea in practice can now be seen over ten years later, in the above collection.

The idea that in-service teacher education is a developmental process, is based on a relationship between values and extending understanding. Additions to the cognitive range and concerns of teachers, which can be assessed through their increased understanding of the contents of 'modules', are located within a process in which the teachers are exploring how to live values more fully in their practice. It is a combination of the process of attempting to live educational values more fully and of extending cognitive range, concern and skills which in my view constitutes professional development. I recognize that my focus on the role of teachers' values in constituting their programme of professional development has implications for a modularized curriculum which has a prespecified content of what is to be learnt. I will try to justify my insistence on the necessity of integrating teachers' values in their programme of professional development in terms of what constitutes educational knowledge.

Educational Knowledge within the Academy

The curriculum of a university has traditionally embodied what counts as the highest form of educational knowledge. Different forms of knowledge, which are distinguished by their conceptual frameworks and methods of validation, constitute the major part of the curriculum of a university. Since my first paper to BERA in 1977 I have explored the implications of reconstructing educational theory and educational knowledge. I now want to suggest the possibility of creating a new form of educational knowledge which could be legitimated within the academy. What I have in mind is a form of knowledge which can be created by educational researchers in the form of autobiographies as they explore questions of the kind, 'How do I improve my practice?', in the context of supporting the power of truth against the truth of power in their workplace and society.

I recognize that this will require a transformation in the form of thinking of many academic, educational researchers who now represent their contributions to educational knowledge in abstract and conceptual language. The transformation I have in mind will require these academics to ascend from the abstract to the concrete in seeing the significance of dialogical representations (Eames, 1993b; Ghaye and Wakefield, 1993) of educative relationships, educational theory, educational knowledge and educational development.

I will begin my case for this transformation from propositional to dialogical forms of representation with significant omissions from the Index of the presentations to the 1993 Annual Conference of the American Educational Research Association, the largest annual gathering of educational researchers in the world. The index contains no references to educational knowledge or educational theory or educative relationships and only one to educational development. On looking up the latter the title does not contain the concept, educational development! I am pleased to say that these omissions were rectified in the 1994 programme in New Orleans.

My second point is that in-service teacher education is essentially about the *Education* of teachers. I find myself echoing a point made by Brian Simon in 1977 that educational researchers should focus directly on education itself. This was my first experience of a BERA conference and I wondered what educational researchers had been focusing on if not education itself. In arguing a case for the reconceptualization of policy on in-service teacher education I am suggesting that we focus directly on education itself as it is expressed in the educative relationships of teachers and experienced in the quality of students' and pupils' educational development. I am suggesting that professional educational knowledge exists as a relationship between the educational knowledge which teachers embody in their competent practice and the traditional forms of educational knowledge which exist in the conceptual structures and methods of validation of the forms of knowledge in the curricula of our universities. I have also suggested that the most fundamental purpose of educational research is the creation and testing of educational theory.

I am making at least three assumptions. I am assuming that the vast majority of our teachers are professionally competent, that they embody educational knowledge in his or her competent practice and that it will be possible to develop a research-based policy on in-service teacher education from their practical questions of the kind, 'How do I help my pupils' to improve the quality of their learning?', 'How do I live my values more fully in my practice?' and 'How do I know that I am contributing to my pupils' educational development?' In other words my case rests on a positive view of teachers' professionalism. I also include full-time academics as having responsibilities in both teaching and research.

I am a university academic with a responsibility for examining teachers' claims to know their own educational development. One criterion for accrediting a teacher's claim to know his or her own educational development, for an advanced professional qualification, is that the claim should be related to the wider field of knowledge. This criterion ensures a relationship between the educational knowledge embodied in the teachers' professional practice and the forms of knowledge stored in the academy. As the teacher constructs a case study of an educational enquiry of the kind, 'How do I help my pupils to improve the quality of their learning?', a relationship is formed between the educational knowledge embodied in their living practice and the conceptual forms of understanding stored in the academy. I am suggesting that the key to implementing this new policy on in-service teacher education is the form of professional support which can assist teachers to explore such educational enquiries and to offer them for accreditation to the academy.

Between 1977–83 three papers were published in the British Journal of In-Service Education, which explained my intention to develop this form of in-service support for teachers from the University of Bath, School of Education. The papers were entitled,

1977 Improving Learning in Schools — An In-service Problem
1980 In-Service Education: The Knowledge Base of Education
1983 The Use of Personal Educational Theories in In-Service Education

In 1993 I want to base my case for a reconceptualization of in-service teacher education policy, on a practical example, rather than an intention. The practical example has been provided by Kevin Eames (1993a, 1993b), the head of English at Wootton Bassett School in Wiltshire. In 1985 Eames presented a paper to BERA on his classroom research, as he explored the implications of asking a question of the kind, 'How do I help my pupils to improve the quality of their learning?' In a series of publications, he has outlined his attempts to improve the quality of his pupils' learning and to enhance the professional development of his colleagues through forming and sustaining a partnership between lecturers in the Action Research Group in the University of Bath, School of Education, and teachers at Wootton Bassett School. He has recently linked this work to the professional development of teachers and the work of The Education Council (Eames, 1993b, 1994).

The classroom research of colleagues which included, Daniela De Cet, Paul Siebert, Deanna Harper and Paul Hayward (now head of technology at Christopher Whitehead School in Worcester) has been accredited by the University of Bath for MPhil and MEd degrees, and Advanced Diploma and Advanced Certificates in Professional development (Reason, 1993). The enquiries all included a question of the kind, 'How do I help to improve the quality of my pupils' learning?' and their forms of representation were dialogical and dialectical rather than propositional. I do not want to underestimate the significance of this later point. Munby and Russell (1994) have pointed out how difficult it is to communicate an epistemology of practice from within a propositional form such as this paper. I want to emphasize that the propositional content of my arguments rests upon the dialogical content of the case studies I am drawing your attention to.

Erica Holley and Andy Larter of Greendown School in Swindon, have also been carrying out school-based action research and presenting their accounts in a dialogical form. Holley (1991, 1992, 1993) has focused on improving and under-standing the quality of her educative relationships with pupils and colleagues. In three papers she documents and analyses her educative relationships with a pupil, a class and a colleague as they work together on appraisal. She goes further than accepting the increasing emphasis in educational research, particularly in Canada and America, on enabling teachers to speak with their own voice (Russell, 1993; Richert,

1992; Clandinin and Connelly 1993; Craig, 1993). Holley shows the meaning, grounded in her experience and educative relationships, of enabling pupils to speak with their own voices.

Since his report to BERA '85 Larter (1985) has been awarded his MPhil (Larter, 1987) for his analyses of his work in improving the quality of learning with his pupils. Elliot Eisner's (1993) Presidential Address to the American Educational Research Association, with his call for educational researchers to extend the range of their forms of representing educational experiences and meanings, served to emphasize Larter's achievement and emphasis on dialogical and dialectical forms of representation. His present research on a PhD programme is focused on understanding the problems of establishing a school-based research group in partnership with a university school of education. He locates some of these problems within the power relations which sustain traditional views of educational knowledge within the university.

Policy Making — Formation and Implementation

I have suggested a way of reconceptualizing policy on in-service teacher education, which is based on policy makers exploring the implications of asking themselves questions of the kind: How do I support autonomous professionals who are exploring action enquiries of the kind, 'How do I help my pupils to improve the quality of their learning?', and 'How can I ensure that my management practices and processes contribute to the professional development of my colleagues and to improvements in the quality of pupils' learning?' This reconceptualization is not to argue for the abandonment of conceptual thinking in policy making. Rather, it is an attempt to place the personal commitment of the teacher and researcher as policy maker into the formation and implementation of policy on in-service teacher education.

I think it is a characteristic of conceptual thinkers to develop frameworks and structures which they impose on whatever they are analysing. This was clearly the case in the 1960s and 1970s when philosophers of education at the London Institute of Education explained how their conceptual view of education, imposed a structure on practical decisions, imposed integration on a collection of disparate entities and imposed its stamp on the curriculum (Hirst and Peters, 1970).

In contrast to policies which impose a structure I have two examples of policy makers who have found ways of enabling teachers to speak with their own voices within 'dialogical' research communities. Professor Pamela Lomax, at Kingston University and Dr Tony Ghaye at Worcester College of Higher Education have implemented such policies on in-service teacher education through their advanced course programmes. This has led to the accreditation of case studies by teacher researchers of their enquiries of the kind, 'How do I improve the quality of my pupils' learning?' and 'How do I improve the quality of my management practices in a way which can contribute to the professional development of teachers and the quality of pupils' learning?'

Lomax (1986) was the first academic to publicly recognize the significance of the ideas presented to BERA '85 by members of the action research group in the School of Education of Bath University. Lomax (1989, 1990, 1991) is one of the few academics within higher education to show what it means to establish a partnership with teacher researchers within which teachers speak for themselves. She has recently explicated the standards of judgment (Lomax, 1994a) for testing the validity of action-research accounts of teachers' professional development. Similarly, Jean Clandinin's (Clandinin and Connelly, 1993) support for teachers, within a Canadian context, is also outstanding.

Let me raise two contentious possibilities concerning research and educational-policy formation and implementation. The first is that researchers on the political right, such as some in the Centre for Policy Studies, have accepted a much too limited set of parameters for formulating policy on teacher education. Their acceptance of the centrality of market forces and competition for improving educational standards, rather than the values of education itself, has led to a lack of emphasis on the central values of education concerning truth, knowledge, care, justice and freedom, and a lack of emphasis on the in-service professional development of teachers. This lack of emphasis can be seen in the Educational Reform Act of 1988 which focused on the implementation of a national curriculum and assessment as the main influences on improving quality in education. Market forces are encouraged through the publication of league tables and a privatized inspectorate. The support structures for the professional development of the existing teaching force were largely ignored in these policies except for the principle that the market would provide.

Severe reservations about these policies have been delivered at the American Educational Research Association meeting by, Gipps (1993) and Simons (1993). This brings me to another concern with much 'policy'-driven research. The conceptual forms of analysis offered by such educational researchers in their critiques, do not directly address the implications for their own educational development, of their workplace experiences of the policies they are critiquing. Consequently they do not help others to understand what a creative response to the experience of these policies might look like. I have in mind the kind of creative response which shows how the researcher is using the implications of his or her own critique to keep alive the values of education and educational research in her or his workplace.

The second possibility is that researchers on the political left, such as some in the Policy Studies Institute, are using methodologies and epistemologies which are derived from social science, rather than grounded in education as the basis for their research into the formation of educational policy (Lomax, 1994b). Unless such policies are grounded in the experience, improvement and representation of educative relationships and educational development, is there not a danger that they will serve to sustain purely conceptual forms of educational policy? I am arguing that these are now as dysfunctional to policies on improving in-service teacher education as it would be to apply the discredited 'disciplines' approach to educational theory. Whilst space does not permit me to develop the argument I think this point also extends to policy on initial teacher education.

I agree with Gaby Weiner's (1993) point that:

> . . . the Right nevertheless has maintained its hegemonic position over moral values. Thus, its ethical posturing on issues such as law and order, discipline and standards, family values, the justice of the market and so on, has not only prospered but has seemed to relegate the Left to defend value positions often perceived as outdated and moribund. . . .
>
> I therefore propose that a new values position and praxis be constructed around greater emphasis on and exploration of the following: social justice/

equality concerns at micro- as well as macro-political levels; the importance of changing practice as well as structures; the complexities of human experience which render relations of dominance/subordination as more problematic than in the past: and the necessity of greater openness and the need to be responsive to changing circumstances and demands.

However, I recognize that the logic of her proposal is the same logic as that in the conceptual structures of policies and analyses informed by social-science research. I think a transformation in this kind of thinking is necessary to develop educational policies which are grounded in the experiences, improvements and representations of educative relationships which embody the values which Weiner wishes to see lived in the world. I think Morwenna Griffiths (1995) offers a way of achieving this transformation when she grounds her abstract thinking in the realities of trying to do educational research. The essential feature of her analysis is the conversation between the researcher and the theory.

The conversation that educational researchers have with feminism and post-modernism must be a continuing one, a conversation that informs ongoing research rather than produces yet another method or methodology to choose or reject. (p. 233)

I want to extend the idea of a conversation into the dialogical and dialectical form of answers to practical questions of the kind, 'How do I improve my practice?' and 'How do I live my values more fully in my practice?' and to locate these enquiries in the lives of academics as they tell truth to power (Said, 1993; Foucault, 1977; Whitehead, 1993).

As the research selectivity exercise in universities is followed by evaluations of teaching quality, the role of academics, as teachers as well as researchers, will be emphasized. In thinking about policy on in-service teacher education. I am thus including the professional development of academics as teachers. Both Said and Foucault have stressed the importance of the relationship between truth and power in the context of the academic's workplace. I accept Foucault's belief that the individual academic, by supporting the power of truth against the truth of power in the workplace, can contribute to transforming the particular regime of truth which structures society.

My reconceptualization of policy on in-service teacher education is grounded in the lives of teacher researchers as they explore the implications of asking practical questions of the kind, 'How do I improve my practice?', whilst expressing values which include academic freedom, autonomy and integrity, and social justice and democracy. Such explorations include telling truth to power in the sense of producing autobiography, for legitimation within the academy, in which the teacher-researcher describes and explains his or her own educational development in the context of supporting the power of truth against the truth of power in her workplace and society. I am assuming that the power of truth is served by the values distinguished by Tasker and Packham (1993) in their analysis of the differences between the values of academia and the values of the market place. Values such as freedom, justice, integrity and democracy are embraced by academic communities. Values of competition and profit are embraced by markets. Academics may find themselves under pressure from market forces to support the truth of power. I have suggested that one response to this pressure, which could support the power of truth, would be to produce an autobiographical account of an enquiry such as, 'How do I live my values more fully in my practice?'

I attach particular significance to the role of academics as teacher-researchers because of their influence in legitimating what counts as educational knowledge. Some academics are in positions to legitimate the educational knowledge of claims by school-based teacher researchers, to know their own educational development. However, the widespread transformation in what counts as educational knowledge, could depend on university-based teacher-researchers reconstituting educational knowledge through case studies of their own educational development in the academy. There has been a recent upsurge of interest in the use of biography in research. There is an excellent special issue of the Journal of Management Education and Development (Mann and Pedler, 1992) devoted to the use of biography. The papers by Judi Marshall (1992) on *Researching Women in Management as a Way of Life* and by Kath Aspinwall (1992) on *Biographical Research: The Search for Meaning*, illustrate the emphasis on biography. I am suggesting a further move into autobiography for case studies by university-based teacher-researchers. I believe that the explication of the epistemology of their claims to know their own in-service educational develop-ment will reconstitute educational knowledge in the way I have outlined above.

At the present time very few professors of education have offered accounts of their educational development as they ask, 'How do I help my students to improve the quality of their learning?' Tom Russell (1993) is a notable exception. The contributions of most professors of education to educational research are still derived from their training in the methodologies and epistemologies of philosophy, psycho-logy, sociology, natural science, history and management. Their contributions are not grounded in their experiences, meanings and representations of their educative relationships, educational development and educational theories in the workplace.

The above reconceptualization of policy on in-service teacher education has been based on a living form of educational theory. I claim that this theory is being constituted by the descriptions and explanations which individual learners are producing for their own educational development. The policy has not been developed through the imposition of a conceptual structure, but in the living relationships of teachers and academics as they ask questions of the kind, 'How do I improve my practice?' The living policy is being developed from the experiences of individuals as they work at overcoming the tension of feeling that their values are not being lived fully in their practice.

I have pointed to an example from Kevin Eames (1993a, b, 1994) of how such a policy on in-service teacher education has already been realized in practice in a partnership between a school and a university action research group. In this part-nership, teachers and academics have produced case studies on their enquiries of the form, 'How do I improve my practice?' These have been included in an Action Research and Educational Theory Case Study Collection (Reason, 1993).

I am thinking of those educational researchers who live a principled life in the service of education. I am suggesting that those teachers and academics who are working in this way should produce autobiographies, as part of their educational development, in which the principles are the values they use to give a particular form to their lives in education. In following Weiner's call for a new values position I am suggesting a transformation in the way teachers and other educational researchers think about the values which constitute education. Rather than presenting policies as conceptual structures in which values exist as linguistic abstractions, I am suggesting that policies on in-service teacher education should now be seen, as Eames suggests, in terms of ways of supporting teachers who are asking questions of the kind, 'How do I improve my practice?' I am thinking of the kinds of in-service support which will enable teachers to produce autobiographies of their educational development in which their values are shown to be embodied in their educative relationships with their pupils, and whose meanings are clarified in the course of their emergence in practice. As I have said above, and I think it bears repeating, such a transformation in epistemology and methodology in educational research will require academics' thinking to *ascend* from the abstract to the concrete in legitimating such claims to educational knowledge. This in turn may depend upon the recognition that whilst philosophers interpret the world the point is to improve it.

To Conclude

In this chapter I have proposed a reconceptualization of policy on in-service teacher education. This was based on the idea that educational theory is being constituted in the autobiographies of practitioner researchers as they explore the implications of answering questions of the kind, 'How do I improve my practice?' If what counts as educational research is defined in terms of both what educational researchers do and a view of educational theory, then this new view of educational theory has implications for those educational researchers who wish to constitute and test theory. If it becomes the dominant view of theory then a transformation will have occurred in the way educational researchers think about their subject. The implication of this chapter is that the thinking of teachers, educational researchers and other policy makers should be so transformed.

I intend to continue with my own in-service professional development in the educational enquiry, 'How do I improve my practice?', in the context of supporting the power of truth, I am anxious to focus my questioning on those experiences which are likely to be most fruitful for making original and scholarly contributions to knowledge of my subject, education. What would you advise me to focus on in the immediate, medium-and long-term, given my finishing date is 2009? One idea I am thinking of continuing to explore is focused on my in-service educational development in my educative relationships with the truth of power and the power of truth in the university. I am thinking of studying my educational development in relation to the market forces which are increasingly a source of pressure in my life as an academic. I thought that I would link my experiences of appraisal interviews in which judgments on my performance are made, and encounters with the promotion structures which link performance to pay. What I hope to clarify in this research are the educational values which are forming my life as an academic and to enhance our understanding of how an attempt to live a principled life in the service of education can show the contribution of a living educational theory to the creation of a good social order.

Another idea I am working on is the possibility of constructing an integrated programme of teacher education through a collaborative enquiry with teachers at Wootton Bassett School. With the recent moves towards school-based initial teacher education. I will be tutoring PGCE students for the educational and professional development components of their course. Ten of these students will be based at

Wootton Bassett School, where I will also be tutoring a group of teachers for their action-research programmes of professional development. Over the past three years Moira Laidlaw, a colleague in the Action Research Group, has tutored groups of PGCE students as they carried out action enquiries on their teaching practices and produced case studies of their educational development as they worked at improving the quality of their pupils' learning. These studies form part of the Action Research and Educational Theory Case Study Collection. Her tutoring has been based on the above view of a living educational theory and this gives me hope that it should be possible to develop an integrated programme which embraces both initial and in-service teacher education.

What advice could you offer which might help to improve the quality of my research into in-service professional development in teacher education? Responses would be welcomed before my retirement in 2009!

References

ASPINWALL, K. (1992) 'Biographical research: The search for meaning', *Journal of Management Education and Development*, **23**, 3, pp. 248–57.

BUDD, P. (1992) 'How can I support change in a way which fits my beliefs in equality of opportunity', Advanced Certificate in Professional Development, University of Bath.

CLANDININ, J. and CONNELLY, F.M. (1993) (Eds) *The Professional Knowledge Landscape*, New York, Teachers College Press.

CRAIG, C. (1993) 'Tim: Coming to know sacred stories in the field of education', in CLANDININ, D.J. and CONNELLY, F.M. (Eds) *The Professional Knowledge Landscape*, New York, Teachers College Press.

DE CET, D. (1991) 'How Can I Develop My Teaching of Poetry to My GCSE Classes?', Advanced Diploma in Professional Development, University of Bath.

EAMES, K. (1985) 'Teaching Argument Essays', Paper to the Annual Conference of the British Educational Research Association, University of Sheffield, 30/8/85.

EAMES, K. (1987) 'The Growth of a Teacher-Researcher's Attempt to Understand, Writing, Redrafting, Learning and Autonomy in the Examination Years', MPHIL, University of Bath.

EAMES, K. (1988) 'Evaluating a teacher researcher's choice of action research', *Assessment and Evaluation in Higher Education*, **13**, 3, pp. 212–18.

EAMES, K. (1993a) 'Action research in schools: Into practice', *British Journal of Curriculum and Assessment*, **3**, 3, pp. 29–33.

EAMES, K. (1993b) 'A dialectical from of action research-based educational knowledge: A teacher-researcher's view', in GHAYE, T. and WAKEFIELD, P. (1993) (Ed) *C.A.R.N. Critical Conversations A Trilogy: Book One, The Role of Self In Action Research*, Hyde Publications.

EAMES, K. (Ed) (1994) *Journal of The Education Council*, **1**, 1.

EISNER, E. (1993) 'Presidential Address to the American Educational Research Association', Atlanta, Georgia, Educational Researcher, Forthcoming.

FOUCAULT, M. (1977) *Discipline and Punish: The Birth of a Prison* (translated from French by Sheridan, A.) London, Allen Lane.

FOUCAULT, M. (1980) in GORDON, C. (Ed) *Power Knowledge*, Harvester, London.

GHAYE, T. and WAKEFIELD, P. (Ed) (1993) *C.A.R.N. Critical Conversations A Trilogy: Book One The Role of Self in Action Research*, Hyde Publications.

GIPPS, C. (1993) 'The Role of Educational Research in Policy Making in England', Paper to a Symposium of the British Educational Research Association at the American Educational Research Association, Atlanta, 12–16 July.

HARPER, D. (1992) 'Developing a method of assessment which aids the pupil learning process', Advanced Certificate in Professional Development, University of Bath.

HAYWARD, P. (1993) 'How do I improve my pupils' learning in Design and Technology?', MEd dissertation, University of Bath.

HIRST, P.H. (Ed) (1983) *Educational Theory and its Foundation Disciplines*, London, Routledge.

HIRST, P.H. and PETERS, R.S. (1970) *The Logic of Education*, Routledge, Keegan, Paul.

HOLLEY, E. (1991) 'I can speak for myself', in WHITEHEAD, J. (Ed) (1991) *A Tutorial Guide for Action Research*, Action Research Group, University of Bath.

HOLLEY, E. (1992) *Accountability: Rendering an Account*, Action Research Group, University of Bath.

HOLLEY, E. (1993) *Accounting for Myself*, Action Research Group, University of Bath.

LAIDLAW, M. (1992) *Action Research: A guide for use on initial teacher education programmes*, Bath Action Research Group, University of Bath.

LARTER, A. (1985) 'What ought I to have done? An examination of events surrounding a racist poem', Paper to the symposium, Action Research, Educational Theory and the Politics of Educational Knowledge, BERA.

LARTER, A. (1987) 'An Action Research Approach to Classroom discussion in the Examination Years', MPHIL, University of Bath.

LOMAX, P. (1986) 'Action researcher's action research: A symposium', *British Journal of In-Service Education*, **13**, 1, University of Sheffield, 30 August, pp. 42–50.

LOMAX, P. (1989) 'The Management of change', *Multilingual Matters*, Clevedon, England.

LOMAX, P. (1990) 'Managing Staff Development in Schools: An action research approach', *BERA Dialogues*, **3**, Multilingual Matters, Clevedon, England.

LOMAX, P. (1991) 'Managing better schools and colleges: The action research way', *BERA Dialogues*, **5**, Multilingual Matters, Clevedon, England.

LOMAX, P. (1994a) 'Standards, criteria and the problematic of action research within an award bearing course', *Educational Action Research*, **2**, 1, pp. 113–26.

LOMAX, P. (1994b) 'Inaugural professorial address', *University of Kingston*, Surrey, UK, February.

MANN, S. and PEDLER, M. (1992) 'Editorial', *Journal of Management Education and Development*, **23**, 3, pp. 181–83.

MARSHALL, J. (1992) 'Researching women in management', *Journal of Management Education and Development*, **23**, 3, pp. 281–89.

McNIFF, J. (1993) *Teachers as Learners: An Action Research Approach*, London, Routledge.

MUNBY, H. and RUSSELL, T. (1994) 'Teaching the Authority of Experience: Moving Beyond Systemics in Pre-service Teacher Education', Paper to AERA Conference 1994, New Orleans.

REASON, P. (1993) *Collaborative Inquiry*, **10**.

RICHERT, A. (1992) 'Voice and power in teaching and learning to teach', In VALLI, L. (Ed) *Reflective teacher education: Cases and critiques*, Albany, State University of New York Press, pp. 187–97.

RUSSELL, T. (1993) 'Recognizing the authority of experience: Returning to the physics classroom to re-think how one learns to teach physics', Paper to the Canadian Society for the Study of Education, Ottawa, June.

SAID, E. (1993) 'The Reith Lectures', *Independent Newspaper*, 22 July.

SIEBERT, P. (1992) 'How can I develop and improve reading strategies within the national curriculum for my secondary school pupils?', Advanced Certificate in Professional Development, University of Bath.

SIMONS, H. (1993) 'Ethics and Politics in Educational Research', Paper to a Symposium of the British Educational Research Association at the American Educational Research Association, 12–16 April, Atlanta.

TASKER, M. and PACKHAM, D. (1993) 'Industry and higher education; A question of values', *Studies in Higher Education*, **18**, 2, pp. 127–36.

WHITEHEAD, J. (1977) 'Improving Learning in Schools — An In-service Problem', *British Journal of In-service Education*, **3**, 2.

Jack Whitehead

WHITEHEAD, J. (1980a) 'The Observation of a Living Contradiction', Paper to the Annual Conference of the British Educational Research Association.

WHITEHEAD, J. (1980b) 'In-service education: The knowledge base of education', *British Journal of In-service Education*, **6**, 2.

WHITEHEAD, J. (1983) 'The use of personal educational theories in in-service education', *British Journal of In-Service Education*. **9**, 3.

WHITEHEAD, J. (1993) *The Growth of Educational Knowledge: Creating your own Living Educational Theories*, Hyde Publications.

14 Why is Action Research a Valid Basis for Professional Development?

Christine O'Hanlon

Introduction

There are increasing numbers of tutors in higher education unwilling to passively accept traditional approaches to the professional development of teachers and other professionals. These tutors sustain their educational ideals regardless of situational and institutional difficulties, if necessary suspending them until such time as they have developed the competence or created the right environment to implement them. In looking at what is essential for the further professional development of teachers and other professionals who have already completed their initial training and are practising qualified practitioners, it is necessary to ask if it is the reproduction of existing skills or the improvement of practice that is the educational aim of continued professional development? Professional skills are no longer seen purely as performance skills but include the cognitive attributes of professionals of which reflective teaching is a basic principle.

In order to develop a reflective practice in higher education, institutions have to make adjustments in practice to allow for it. To develop improved professional practice as a result of in-service or professional development courses requires more than the simple transmission of expertise. It requires the fostering of facilitative forms of professionalism based upon reflective practice and a research-based process of deliberate and active change. Professional courses require a long-term aim of providing the means to understand and improve the quality of professional practice. It is an endeavour with possible lifelong use. Reflective practice and enquiry is both a way of understanding how teaching relates to learning, and an approach to improving teaching for learning.

The reflective practicum demands intensity and duration far beyond the normal requirements of a course (Schon, 1987). Educational professional development which focuses on reflective practice makes demands on the 'student' beyond normal taught courses based on the transmission of knowledge through lectures and literature. The demands made on the teachers can be severe in the continuous modification and reconstruction of their practices. 'Educating the reflective practitioner' is the role of an increasing number of tutors in higher education who are charged with teacher education. Now, professional educators point to practitioner-based enquiry and its related forms — action research, practical investigation, teacher as researcher, collaborative action research, classroom research, reconceptualist enquiry and the enquiring practitioner — as effective and emergent approaches which are making an impact on schools in the UK (Elliott, 1991).

Forms of Teacher Enquiry

Action research, practical investigation, and the enquiring practitioner are all terms used to describe related forms of enquiry in the educational process which are designed to develop innovation in the curriculum and in teaching methods. The teacher as researcher, and classroom research emphasize the close relationship between teaching and learning and focus on the role of enquiry in the teaching process. Collaborative action research reminds the enquirer that action research must be undertaken in a collaborative framework because education is a collaborative activity.

Reconceptualist enquiry takes place when curriculum developers use research methods from a broad range of disciplines to interpret hidden or personal influences which affect the curriculum. All of the terms refer to forms of naturalistic enquiry into the effectiveness of teaching processes, which use a similar conceptual framework based upon grounded enquiry. All of the approaches may be included under the broad term of practitioner enquiry.

Practitioner-based enquiry emphasizes the direct study of a particular issue in the immediate context where pupils are learning or where children's needs are being considered. Such enquiry is helpful insofar as it provides insights into pupils' lives and the particular environment within which the teaching takes place. It provides the opportunity to understand and improve contextual practice through reflection on it and using the information gained to directly benefit the pupils. It helps staff in schools to evaluate the best pedagogies by providing information on such matters as pupils learning needs and styles, teaching methods and materials in their own classrooms and institutions. The insights gained can affect the nature and quality of the pedagogy, the teaching materials, the assessment and the total learning environment for pupils. A conceptual framework for practitioner-based enquiry emerges from the articulation of the nature of teaching.

Within the different methodologies for professional education being perpetuated at the present are evaluative approaches, social constructivism and scholarship (Alverno College, 1993). Action research may combine and emphasize key aspects of the methodologies in varying degrees in different academic contexts. In an evaluative methodology there are implicit judgments made about values and assumptions in teacher pedagogy, which raise questions about the value of particular teaching and learning activities. Practitioner questions that ask about the pupils' experiences of teaching are consistent with the concerns of illuminative evaluation (Parlett and Hamilton, 1976) where the findings become the basis of both improving educational practice and systematically evaluating its impact. When the judgments of value are made explicit, then the overall process, from conceptualization to the evidence for inferring judgments is open to critique.

The social constructivist perspective (Bruner, 1986) draws out the motives and hidden assumptions in what teachers do in their everyday practice. Through the narrative of action in the explication of the meaning behind practice, speculation about the reality of classrooms becomes open to criticism and leads to a sharing of the culture. From the perspective of scholarship, there is the investigative purpose of compiling a scientific knowledge base to influence policy, combined with the literary forum where the purpose is to critically read, speak and write about research texts. The combination of methodologies within a practitioner enquiry approach yields practical improvement and also articulates and makes public teachers' knowledge, ideas and values.

Teachers' education, in the context of empirical enquiry, deliberate curriculum investigation and reconceptualist enquiry which uses a broad range of research methods such as ethnography and hermeneutics to interpret hidden or personal meanings identified with the curriculum, is a process of curriculum evaluation. Reflective practice and enquiry requires making decisions about what values in teachers' work need to be acted upon. The reconstruction of pedagogical practices must follow a procedure that allows professionals' values to be appraised in the light of new knowledge. This process I recognize as action research.

Action Research

Action research is a process of investigation, reflection and action which deliberately aims to improve, or make an impact on, the quality of the real situation which forms the focus of the investigation. It is a form of enquiry which involves self-evaluation, critical awareness and contributes to the existing knowledge of the educational community.

There are three basic reasons why action research is good for teachers' professional development:

- It is enquiry based and allows teachers to investigate their own worlds;
- It is aimed at the improvement of teaching and learning in schools; and
- It leads to deliberate and planned action to improve conditions for teaching and learning.

Action research is a process which enables participants to realize their pedagogical aims by:

- focusing on changing the pedagogy to bring it into line with their aims and ideals;
- collecting evidence about the extent to which the practice is consistent with their aims;
- identifying and explaining inconsistencies between the aims and the practice thus reframing and problematizing the theories which guide the practice;
- generating and testing new forms of action and reconstructing practical theories; and
- reflexively guiding the pedagogical enquiry which integrates research and practice into one process.

The process incorporates the following practices:

- research and investigation;
- analysis of practice;
- applying theory through action;

- evaluating practice/curriculum;
- involvement of colleagues and others concerned;
- reflection, discussion and sharing of meanings;
- validation of professional change;
- continual professional reframing and transformation; and
- constant curriculum renewal.

Most higher education courses currently aimed at professional development, consist of instruction which is focused on specific subjects and these are taught through a model of direct transfer of knowledge and skills. It is normally because of the expertise in the particular subject that the tutor is chosen to teach (or lecture) on the course. Qualified professionals are often not given the opportunity to participate in an active way. The transmission approach does not allow for a constructivist orientation where new experiences are interpreted in connection with existing internalized theories and models of practice. The active learning stance of the professional is required to enable individual decisions to be made about proposed changes for better quality practice which are planned as a result of new perceptions. Without the active decisions of the professionals about the practice there is no sense of ownership over the changes. The sense of ownership is important for the relationship the professional makes to the enquiry and his or her responsibility for its successful implementation.

Action research is an educational procedure because it uses investigation and enquiry as a basis for the collection and analysis of data with the aim of improving the quality of action in the situation or case under investigation. It is a process of enquiry beginning with the professional's educational concerns on a topic which may begin at either the micro or macro level. It may originate in a small–classroom issue like the updating of children's reading materials and may lead to the consideration of influencing national policy related to reading materials in schools. The wider and greater action which may emerge from the micro issue depends upon the professionals' sphere of influence, timescale and attitude to the implementation of new procedures. Action research is not simply the investigation of issues and concerns at the classroom level but a deliberate attempt to develop greater understanding to influence and change the situation at the school, local authority, or national level. The investigation aims to deepen the professional's understanding of the situation, and what kind of response for better quality education is appropriate. The research methods include the interpretation of events through the eyes of the participants i.e., the pupils, teachers, parents, or others brought within the scope of the topic under enquiry. The action-research methods allow for the exposure of personal bias and prejudice and it supports case study in a narrative process illuminated by concrete description.

There are four fundamental aspects to the process of action research, namely, investigation; planning; action; and reflection.

1 Investigation

To begin the process of action research the professional selects a research question or educational concern which needs further investigation. For the teacher it may be a question like — Which reading methods best suit the age and background of my pupils? or it may be an issue or concern about pupils not making greater progress in reading in a particular class or school. The decision, for example, to focus on pupils' reading progress necessitates the investigation of the question or issue identified and the collection of data at the outset of the research to confirm that the focus is a valid one and necessitates further study. The initial investigation and observation will then support or disconfirm the research focus as originally conceived. At this stage the focus may be redefined or reframed. After which the investigation proceeds to monitor planned action aimed to improve the practical situation. The first step in action research therefore begins with reflection on an issue or research question which defines the focus of the subsequent investigation.

Investigation is the corroboration of the research question or issue in the practical situation and begins with the initial collection of data to endorse (or not) the original conception of the research question or issue. Investigation through the observation of the situation may confirm the need to continue to look more deeply into the focus of the enquiry. For example, for the teacher the issues may relate to how reading progress is measured, why the progress is considered as slow, what methods are currently being employed, why, and does the particular background and age of the pupils demand special consideration? If the data confirms that the research question or issue originally identified does deserve deeper investigation then the professional can continue to analyse the original evidence from the initial observation and to redefine the question or issue more specifically in light of the new data. If however the initial data collection does not support the need to continue the investigation focused on the original issue, then the professional has the opportunity to reframe the research question or refocus the enquiry e.g., to the investigation of teaching methods related to the pupils of a particular minority or gender group.

2   Planning

Planning is constructed action and by definition it must be forward looking and based on the evidence already collected. It must be flexible in relation to unforeseen circumstances and constraints. It should be chosen to allow the professional to act in a more educationally effective way, over a greater range of circumstances and with more understanding and wisdom. Intended outcomes should be identified as the rationale for the changes. As part of the planning, the discussion of possible courses of action with others is essential, as too is reflection on the earlier observational data collected.

3   Action

Action refers to deliberate and controlled changes in the activities in practice. The professionals thoughtfully and constructively put their ideas into action in the real situation and monitor their effects in order to judge their success. Action must be intentional rather than definitive because of the nature of the changing circumstances in dynamic educational situations. Exercising practical judgment in the implementation of the plan may require skilful negotiation and an element of risk-taking.

4   Reflection

Reflection is a reconsideration and reframing of the activities recorded in the initial investigation and the subsequent monitoring and observation of planned action. It has an evaluative aim to judge whether practice confirms the planned direction for further action and monitoring, or indicates a need for new ideas and redirection.

Reflection may take place on three levels: on the technical level where the professional considers the best way to reach an accepted but unexamined goal; on the practical level where the professional examines the means of achieving the goals as well as the goal itself and its implications, by asking questions about what should be happening in the best interests of the pupils; and, on the critical level where the moral and ethical issues concerned with social justice, equality, power and control are considered along with the methods and the intentions of the research plan.

In the process of reflection each professional reviews, reconstructs, and critically analyses their own practices through grounding their explanations in their evidence. The aim in reflective teaching is to produce professionals who are able to apply educational principles and techniques within a framework of their own experience, contextual factors, and social and philosophical values. The critical reflective practitioner addresses the 'why' of the situation before the 'how', and makes decisions about practice on a sound pedagogical basis validated in the enquiry process. Reflection on practice in an action-research paradigm leads to a willingness to examine and re-examine teaching from a variety of perspectives and theoretical viewpoints. It challenges accepted orthodoxies which are unexamined and repeated in contexts that are differentiated and complex. The action-research process requires professionals to differentiate their methods and activities in contextually appropriate ways.

A diary is an important means of record keeping and reflection for teachers engaged in action research. In fact the keeping of a diary is essential to qualitative professional development. There is no one designated method of keeping a diary, all that is required is the ability to make a record of significant events, ideas, and understanding of the professional issues which concern individual teachers. However, because of the complex and varied nature of active classroom research the teachers must be allowed the freedom to write and express themselves in their own individual and idiosyncratic manner. A diary is primarily a vehicle for the retrospective recording of professional and personal experiences. It can be used to record facts, impressions, feeling and interpretations. It may, in time, develop into a journal of interpretative and analytical notes which describe the teachers' development through the research process. The diary is a means of acknowledging the writer's value position in the face of contradictory evidence. By making personal values explicit in the diary values are being made explicit in the process of reflective practice. Participating in reflection with colleagues in schools and with the focus group members (in higher education), allows values and assumptions in the practical reality to be challenged and compared.

Professional development in reflective practice is an important resource for professional reconstruction and reflection. The teacher sees himself or herself as a professional who is deliberately attempting to improve his or her school practice. There is an essential dialogue which needs to focus primarily on the teacher as an agent of change, who identifies and reconstructs the significant aspects of professional experiences he or she considers relevant to that purpose. These experiences are predominantly school-centred. Occasionally more personal experiences may impinge however, when writing the diary becomes more reflective. As the diary becomes more reflective, the teachers become more reflexive and aware of what is actually happening to them and the inferences of their professional intervention. Writing taps the teachers' tacit knowledge and brings into awareness that which is sensed but could not be explained (Holly, 1984).

Practitioner research and reflective writing are parallel activities. The diary is an unstructured, free-flowing, individuated blend of concrete and interpreted reality. It is unassessed in most formal course contexts, yet it is an essential supplement to the teachers main case study which is their account of their educational improvement.

A Democratic and Personal Educational Process

In the enterprise of educating professionals to become more proficient and sensitive in their role of improving and developing teaching and learning, there is a need to consider each professional as an individual. As individuals they are capable of making their own autonomous decisions, judgments and plans about what they consider to be the best action in specific individual contexts. The educational endeavour with respect to the improvement of professional practice which takes place in higher educational institutions aims to be democratic through its attempts to treat all professionals in an equal and respectful manner. The respect is demonstrated in the recognition of each professional's prior experience and practical wisdom gained as a result of their work over time. It is also based in the belief that they are capable of progressing their learning in a situation that is facilitative and non-threatening.

The actual methods employed in the development of action research in higher education are based on different views of the aims of education. Action research is carried out in many forms in different institutions depending on context-specific values in practice. However, the methods that I favour as a facilitator of action research are based on the following principles of democratic education which enable professionals to become persons who:

- are able to take self-initiated action and to be responsible for those actions;
- are capable of intelligent choice and self-direction;
- are critical learners, able to evaluate the contributions made by others;
- have acquired knowledge relevant to the solutions of problems and the creation of better quality teaching and learning;
- are able to adapt flexibly and intelligently to new and changing situations;
- have internalized a means of coping with complex situations by utilizing all pertinent experience freely and creatively;
- are able to collaborate effectively with others in these activities;
- work, not for the approval of others, but in terms of their own values and ideals.

The principles are based on the views of Carl Rogers about the ways that people learn. The principles offer an innovative basis for learning which involves autonomous action and judgment. It provides an alternative to traditional instruction and the transmission model of knowledge. Rogers also contends that:

We cannot teach another person directly. We can only facilitate his/her learning;
A person learns significantly only those things which s/he perceives as being related to her/his self. (Rogers, 1962)

Moreover, the educational situation which most effectively provides significant learning is one in which:

— threat to the self of the learner is reduced to a minimum;
— differentiated perception of the field of experience is facilitated. (Rogers, ibid.)

Therefore, professionals as learners in action-research courses may be guided through the process with the added dimension of facilitated learning and self-relational foci, in a situation that is unthreatening and offers differentiated perspectives. A learning situation that is truly educational is one which ultimately involves professional growth through change in the person, which inevitably, in time, must bring about situational change. Developing discussion and questioning in a critically supportive mode is one crucial way that the Rogerian principles are extended through action research and the reflective enquiry process.

A Theory of Professional Growth

I will now proceed to develop a theory of professional growth which is influenced by these guiding principles. The process I outline consists of three basic phases:

- the phase of direction and self-awareness;
- the phase of monitoring practice; and
- the phase of deepening reflection and transformation.

Professional/teacher education is a process involving other people both 'inside' and 'outside' the specific professional community where each person works. In schools the 'inside' people are pupils, parents, colleagues etc. with whom the teacher comes into contact in the everyday activity of education. The 'outside' people are the new friends and acquaintances drawn into the educational world through the sharing of discourse in the process of reflection, investigation and action planning. The critical enquirer emerges from a discursive process with both 'insiders' and 'outsiders' in education. The process of developing teacher education through critical enquiry is made up of three phases which combine both the professional and personal development into one (see Figure 14.1).

Phase One

In phase One of the process, the teacher/professional finds himself or herself in the college or course in higher education which is directed towards his or her professional concerns. One becomes more aware of one's professional role, because the focus of the research is centred around one's ideas, and issues related to one's concerns. This focus exposes one's educational values because one is being asked to 'publicly' express one's educational concerns which are visibly value-laden. One is talking and being listened to in a group context with a transformative purpose. Other professionals enrolled on the same course all play a role in the discussion of their mutual educational concerns and their intellectual development in action. The 'peer' group for professionals in an action research process is central to professional and situational transformation, because talking to the professional in an educational process implies that the speaker is prepared to act upon the ideas expressed, otherwise the discussion is just 'talk' and not discourse with a purpose. The talking and listening process involving colleagues, implies a shared responsibility in extending and acting on the

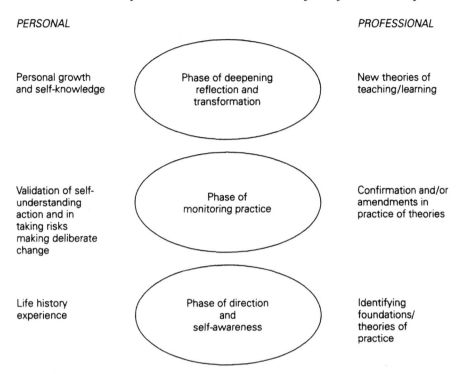

PERSONAL   PROFESSIONAL

Personal growth   Phase of deepening   New theories of
and self-knowledge   reflection and   teaching/learning
                         transformation

Validation of self-   Phase of   Confirmation and/or
understanding   monitoring practice   amendments in
action and in   practice of theories
taking risks
making deliberate
change

Life history   Phase of direction   Identifying
experience   and   foundations/
                         self-awareness   theories of
                                                          practice

Figure 14.1:   Process of developing teacher education through critical enquiry

ideas expressed in the group, through discourse in a collaborative process. The support of listening and responsive colleagues provides confidence to the speaker, because it provides reassurance and validates his or her articulated concerns over time. The expression of professional concerns and intentions, allows the professionals' voices to be heard in a mutually supportive, yet appreciative and evaluative environment which is 'critical' because it provides constructive critique of the ideas and evidence presented in the group context. The action-research process often refers to 'critical friends' who provide perceptive and constructive feedback to the enquirer on different aspects of the research from, defining an enquiry focus, to investigatory methods and proposals for action within the action-research process.

A professional development group or 'focus' group, carrying out action research provides critical and evaluative support for colleagues in the same group. Some direction from the facilitator or group tutor is necessary to keep the discourse focused and to ensure equal access to time for talking and listening. The facilitator's role is to support and direct the process of active listening to enable productive feedback and constructive questioning. Members of the focus group form an identity together through practising the role of the 'critical friend' under the course tutor's direction. However, feedback from 'critical friends' is also encouraged, from insiders in the school, or from key participants in the broader educational situation.

In phase one, professionals review their beliefs and ideas about the aspect of professional practice that they wish to investigate. This involves the consideration of the basis for their views from a 'theoretical' as well as a practical perspective. In reviewing their understanding about what they believe is influential in the specific enquiry focus, professionals often explore principles derived from educational 'theory'. For teachers/professionals who have been recent students, their theories may be recalled from professionally recognized writers like Vygotsky, Bruner etc. For others their understanding may be based in the 'theories' they have formed from their own experience and practice or the practice they have experienced as children in school. The reflection and awareness-raising of the current professional's beliefs and values, necessarily form a foundation for validating the focus and direction of the enquiry. But it is not only the professional experience that mature adults bring with them to courses in higher education contexts.

Professionals have personal lives, histories and experiences which they bring with them and integrate into their professional lives. How far the persons' life experiences are acknowledged in professional courses is debatable, but most training is put down on top of life experiences as an extra layer, like a veneer on the rest. Little consideration is given to personal experience and attributes, because they are not considered relevant or important. Yet the person's position in time, in life and in self-knowledge, all have an influence upon his or her successful engagement with the enquiry process. The attitudes, beliefs and values surrounding the research question or issue are individualized and contextualized for each professional and need to be openly unpacked, reorganized and recognized before the reconstruction process is successful.

Phase Two

In phase Two, which is the phase of monitoring practice, the professional confirms that his or her earlier held theories are a valid basis for continued practice or, alternatively, amendments and readjustments are made to theories in the light of the investigation of practice. The issue under investigation is developed through observation and the collection of research evidence which is subsequently analysed to reveal whether deliberate and planned action has brought about the desired outcomes. A process of self-validation is brought about by the proactive stance of the professional in making a confident and competent bid to influence the situation. Action is implemented on a basis of the need to make changes identified in phase One. The professional tries out actions designed to improve educational practice and carefully monitors the results. The individual professional finds the limits and possibilities for the proposed change within the constraints of the social situation and the person's own disposition for taking risks. Phase two is the most intense phase for action and reflection and therefore for interaction and feedback from others involved in the 'school', and also from colleagues and peers in the focus group in the higher education course. In this period, professionals discover the limits of their influence and power and there is a validation of individual judgment in the realization of their plans.

Phase Three

Phase Three is the phase of deepening reflection and transformation. The person, as a result of a period of detailed investigation of an issue or topic, e.g., reading practice, has developed a new awareness and has evaluated the research issues or question identified in phase One. Perhaps the earlier views or theories have been confirmed, thus validating previously held values and beliefs. Perhaps they have been disconfirmed and replaced by a more relevant, context-situated and specific set of hypotheses and ideas which could be referred to as a 'new' educational theory which has been reframed by the professional to replace an early untested theory. At phase Three the person has now completed a process of practical investigation which has formed the basis of new self-knowledge and personal growth. The new self-knowledge and personal growth is created as a result of:

- appropriate on-the-job training and professional induction;
- the valuing of intellectual honesty, curiosity and personal experience;
- the encouragement of scepticism and a self-evaluative attitude to their work;
- the use of literature in the 'subject' area;
- the creative development of educational ideas;
- the care for their pupils which is implicit in the educational improvement plans;
- the communication of the ongoing results of their work to their peers, colleagues and others;
- the concern and ethical considerations about the effects of the action plans and the investigation on others involved;
- the responsiveness to the needs of their pupils, other colleagues and parents; and
- the recognition by peers of their commitment and intentions for better quality in education.

Individuals construct and reconstruct themselves in interaction with the social environment throughout their lives. They do this through a sense of identity which is personal to each individual and through the response of others to their personal behaviour and presence in their living environments. The self-knowledge possessed by persons is culturally influenced to produce a personal representation of social practices and cultural knowledge. We construct ourselves and our worlds in a framework of cultural shared symbols like language, which is a reason for the inclusion of professionals in focus groups during an action-research course. As an indication of the paradigmatic shift of thinking from the objective to the subjective reality in education Bruner (1986) has moved towards an interpretative stance of the world as he stresses more the cultural influence in our representational systems through the function of symbols like language. He acknowledges the construction of our own representations of the world, in our interaction with it, which implies a changing construction of reality as that reality appears in different ways to us. This lends a legitimation to subjective views of the social world in educational contexts, perpetuated by discourse in group situations.

The research context in education is one such context. It is a field of study which had previously been characterized by psychologists such as Bruner an objective reality which may be observed and assessed through different scientific strategies and devices. The 'minds' of the pupils were categorized according to a separate intellectual measurement like Piaget's stage theory or Bruner's levels of representation. We cannot fully invalidate these theories as presented, but we must critique them on the grounds that they are the subjective theories of two thinkers who have a unique view of human learning and who present their ideas to the world in a structured and powerful way. Each individual researcher has the potential to do the same. Professionals who engage in action research have the potential to create dynamic educational theories and to change the world through the power of their investigation and renewed understanding. It is possible in educational reconstruction to become empowered through one's reframed knowledge and to reconstruct action both in the individual and in the community context, which includes both the personal and the professional world of the actor.

In the ten factors involved in the process of professional growth is the implicit recognition and acceptance of the influences of life experience on the values underpinning professional practice — the strength of personal bias and prejudice — the limits of personality and self-knowledge — personal attitudes to the taking of professional risks and taking action for deliberate change. Therefore personal values must form a constant source of reflection throughout the action-research process. The personal attributes and experiences affecting the professional in the active pursuit of continued development must be considered in relationship to the practice throughout the enquiry. The personal identity within the professional, needs to be revealed for the deeper awareness of unreflective practice and to enable changes to be made in the professional's personal behaviour as well as in the situational context.

Conclusion

Too many courses for teacher development aim to change the environment for learning by focusing on pupils' activities, without consideration of the teacher's intentions and motives. Simply 'acting out' plans for better practice may lead to an unsuccessful long-term professional strategy if there is not reflective understanding of the individual's impact on the situation under investigation, and their relationship to the process. Questions like the following, support developing reflexivity.

- Is the issue/s under investigation freely chosen?
- Why do I behave in a particular manner during the investigation?
- Why do I react in a particular way to the feedback situation (triangulation)?
- Why do I resist the openness of the focus group?

The questions asked will encourage the professionals to examine their own motives and behaviour and be honest about the way that they carry out professional practice and their feelings in specific situations that occur in everyday practice. Unreflective practice that is unexamined will be perpetuated if it is not identified and challenged in a professionally unthreatening, supportive but challenging context away from the locus of action as for example in a professionally focused course in higher education. Intentional actions planned with goodwill, may backfire without reflexivity and self-understanding.

Professional development that is devoid of a means to advance increased self-knowledge is mere technical development. It is only a technical means of improving the quality of practice without long-term and lasting educational results, because changing the person and facilitating self-understanding will invariably bring about situational change. In professional contexts, changing the person in a reflective and personal process will ensure greater awareness of personal agency in the continuation of professional practice. The action-research process outlined above aims to provide a means for lifelong reflective professional practice.

References

ALVERNO COLLEGE RESEARCH AND EVALUATION COMMITTEE (1993) 'Reflecting on Our Practice: Practitioner-Based Inquiry to Understand and Improve Teaching and Learning Across the Curriculum', Paper delivered at AERA 1993.

BRUNER, J. (1986) *Actual Lives: Possible Worlds*, Cambridge MA, Harvard University Press.

ELLIOTT, J. (1991) *Action Research for Educational Change*, Milton Keynes, Open University Press.

HOLLY, M.L. (1984) *Keeping a Personal-Professional Journal*, Deakin University Press.

PARLETT, M. and HAMILTON, D. (1976) 'Evaluation as illumination: A new approach to the study of innovatory programs', In GLASS, G. (Ed) *Evaluation Studies Review Annual*, 1, pp. 140–57, Beverley Hills, CA, Sage.

ROGERS, C. (1962) *On Knowing*, Cambridge, MA, Belknap Press.

SCHON, D. (1987) *Educating the Reflective Practitioner*, London, Jossey Bass.

15 Professional Learning and School Development in Action: A Personal Development Planning Project

Christopher Day

Abstract

The project described here provides an example of the use of materials as a means of stimulating and supporting teachers' involvement in systematically reflecting upon practice alongside others, in their school contexts. It was founded on the belief that the challenge of enhancing teacher development is significantly a local matter and that, therefore, local communities of teachers are the means of enhancing professionalism. It is thus based upon an epistemology of practice which recognizes that effective development is both a private and public affair. This is characterized by Donald Schon as a relationship between 'knowing-in-action' and 'reflection-in action' (Schon, 1987). The former locates theory and practice in a teacher's normal practice (knowledge is in the act); and the latter indicates that the action as well as the knowledge which is implicit in the action is reflected on outside the act. In short, whilst teachers do not always consciously consider the theories which dictate and guide their values, thinking and actions because of psychological, social and practical constraints, nevertheless, the theories exist as part of what is referred to — sometimes disparagingly — as practical knowledge. (Connelly and Clandinin, 1984).

The history of research concerning teacher development is that teachers have not generally taken an active part in the production of knowledge about their own teaching — indeed there has been a tension between so called 'scientific' knowledge (theory) and professional or practical knowledge (practice). In a sense teachers have been disenfranchised. They are perceived as basing their practice on their professional, practical knowledge and experience.

> Teachers are cut off, then, both from the possibility of reflecting and building on their own know-how and from the confusions that could serve them as springboards to new ways of seeing things. (Schon, 1992, p. 119)

Important issues therefore, are how practice can become reflective, and by what means the teacher may be supported in developing reflective teaching practice at different levels (Day, 1993). It is equally important to recognize that, to date, much learning through reflection has been private. Conditions of service and the organizational cultures in many schools do not allow for regular professional dialogue about teaching which goes much beyond anecdotal exchange and the trading of techniques. Conscious reflection in the classroom is limited for most teachers who develop repertoires and routines to an implicit level (Clark and Yinger, 1977). Furthermore, opportunities and motivation for professional discourse about teaching with colleagues will be limited according to both the culture of the school (Little, 1990; Schein, 1985) and the rhetoric–reality roles played by teacher as educationist and teacher as practitioner (Keddie, 1971). These and the privacy norms which, even now are characteristic of the professional serve to undermine or diminish the capacity for teacher learning and sustained professional development (Rosenholtz, 1989; McLaughlin and Marsh, 1979). These problems of educational discourse make it difficult for teachers to understand and review their own knowledge base without support. Experience itself, then, is limited as a source of development, as is support for teacher development contributed by research and researchers.

The importance of personal, practical knowledge and its potential contribution to teacher growth has been emphasized in a growing number of studies worldwide over a number of years. Many of these have been reported in publications related to the work of researchers on teacher thinking (Day, Pope and Denicolo, 1990; Day, Calderhead and Denicolo, 1993); and in those related to research on teacher careers, life history and biography (Sikes, Measor and Woods, 1985; Ball and Goodson, 1985, Goodson, 1990). Many of these studies involve teachers' voices actively in the production and elaboration of knowledge about teaching, teachers, schooling and the conditions which contribute to these. Implicitly and explicitly, the researchers themselves provide 'value-added' support to teacher learning (which is natural, often intuitive and largely *ad hoc*), and the effects of the researchers' interventions are to cause teacher development (which is planned, conscious, and systematic). In doing so, they demonstrate a concept of educational research which builds upon notions of collaborative action research, research as educative, teacher as researcher, and the teacher as extended professional. The work of those who link personal, practical knowledge research directly with the improvement of practice without taking account of the broader aspects of teachers' lives has been criticized for being too selective, seeking only parts of the teachers' story and thus failing to engage sufficiently with teacher development (Goodson, 1991, pp. 141–2). There are signs, however, that this is changing. There is no doubt that teachers' stories and narratives, for example, do embody the spirit of the principles and philosophy informing their own teaching (Elbaz, 1990; Nelson, 1993); and that 'educative research' which significantly affects roles and relationships between the 'researcher' and the 'subject' which takes account of biography, context, life history, thinking and practice, does make a difference (Day, 1991; Gitlin *et al.*, 1992).

Despite all of this work, criticisms remain about its usefulness to, and utilization by, a broader range of teachers than those relative few who are directly involved in the research projects. Writing about the contribution of teachers' thinking to professional development, Calderhead asks 'How might research help to illuminate, guide or justify teacher education practices?', quoting Shulman (1986) and McNamara's (1990) criticisms of its narrow focus and lack of generation of findings which may be easily applied to efforts to improve teaching (Calderhead, 1993, p. 12). He argues that there is (still) a need to develop much closer links between research, which should be more widely defined (beyond the single specific positivistic, phenomenological and critical paradigms) and practices in education, and to abandon 'fairly insular conceptions of both research and practice and a tendency to view research purely as a means of supporting and informing practice rather than in terms of a reciprocal questioning and exploration' (Calderhead, 1993, p. 17).

Huberman develops this notion of reciprocity in a different context. In a study of the dissemination of research and its effects on practice and theory he found that research teams engaging in 'sustained interactivity' with practitioners, 'produced changes in practitioners' ideas, understandings and practices', and that this finding held 'even in settings where practitioners were initially sceptical or hostile to social science theory' (Huberman, 1993, p. 4); and this confirmed the findings of a number of 'case-study' teacher educators in England, Canada and America (Day, 1985; Oberg and Field, 1987; Kagan and Tippins, 1991).

The personal-development planning project and associated materials described in this chapter provide one example of a structured attempt by a team of teachers and researcher-teacher educators to utilize existing research knowledge about teacher learning and professional development so that teachers in a variety of schools would be encouraged to examine their thinking and practice systematically with critical friends or key colleagues in relation to personal histories and the organizational contexts in which they worked, for the purpose of constructing a lifelong process for monitoring and enhancing their development. Two models of 'sustained interactivity' were used. In the initial (six months) phase of the project a team of nine teachers, two researchers from higher education and an external consultant designed a set of personal-development planning materials. In the second phase over the following eighteen months these materials were trialled in schools across eight local educational authorities (school districts) by volunteers. The materials were then revised in the light of the evaluation conducted through questionnaire and interview. Because each school in which the materials were trialled had a coordinator, and because coordinators met with the project team individually and collectively through regular networking meetings this might at first glance appear to represent a 'social-interaction' model of innovation. However, this would not be an accurate description of the innovation. The materials themselves were designed to be used according to principles of reflection, autonomy (teachers chose where to start and what to emphasize according to individually identified need) and collaboration (feedback and disclosure) in order to enhance teachers' personal and practical knowledge. Additionally, they focused not upon curriculum development but upon *personal* development. Thus for each individual, the use of the materials had a personal significance. This was crucial to the transfer of ownership necessary for the successful sustained utilization of the materials.

In reality, then, the materials and their dissemination were rooted in principles of teacher ownership and autonomy. In order to participate, teachers had not only to investigate aspects of their own thinking and practice and the biographical and social contexts from which these came and in which they existed, but they also had to share these with significant others. Whilst the organization was 'top–down', the application was 'bottom–up'. Traditional social influences of identification and compliance were avoided by adopting the principle of 'voluntarism', thus encouraging internalization. Finally, the research and development team itself was made up predominantly of teacher practitioners. Research itself then was collaborative and never regarded as the province of one or more 'high status' distant from practice theoreticians.

The Personal Development Planning Project

More than 200 teachers from twenty schools representing all phases of compulsory school across eight local education authorities (school districts) participated in the piloting of materials which were designed by the central research, development and support team. The team represented primary, middle and secondary phases of education. It met on twelve occasions during the one-year implementation phase of the project. The work in schools was 'managed' by school-based coordinators who regularly networked (informally and formally) with each other and the design team during the life of the project.

The materials were designed to encourage action and interaction rather than 'readerly' assimilation. They were intended as stimulus and support but not a substitute for personal review and development planning, a tangible focus for the work of personal and whole-school review. They consist of a mixture of description, teachers' comments, questions and activities, aiming to provide an interface between knowledge generated about teachers and schools by teacher-researchers from higher education and teachers' personal practical knowledge. They are organized in nine parts.

Materials designed to assist teachers in curriculum development have a history of failure, partly because they often address the concerns of the designers or policy makers and not teachers' own professional or personal-growth concerns, or the conditions in which they work. They do not take account of problems of transferability, ownership and utilization. Nor do they address explicitly what is known about teachers' thinking and development processes. Recognizing that distance-learning materials will always have limited value, the project team nevertheless attempted to maximize opportunities for teachers to interact with the materials by, for example:

- ensuring a sense of 'practicality' through the inclusion of personal and organizational review and forward planning tasks;
- differentiating between the needs of teachers and schools who might be at different phases of development by providing information about different phases and inviting teachers to use those parts of the materials which were most relevant to their perceived needs;
- allowing teachers to engage in different levels of reflection by the inclusion of writing about these;
- ensuring through different but related sections that teachers could begin by either addressing their own individual needs or those of the organizational leadership and culture;
- building 'critical friendship' processes into the use of the materials;
- deliberately naming the materials *personal*-development planning in order to emphasize the value placed on their holistic development; and
- building in local and regional networking functions through school-based coordination and continuing support of a member of the project team. Communication links between 'producers' and 'users' are critical to the adoption of a particular innovation (House, 1974).

Built into the project design were the intentions to promote the teacher as reflective practitioner within an actively supportive community on the assumptions that:

Extract 1

Part 1 Using the Materials
This presents the purposes of the materials and summarizes the contents of the folder. It also provides alternative routes through the materials.

Part 2 Recognizing the Importance of Personal Development Planning
This sets out the ways in which personal-development planning can support professional learning and development. It also indicates the benefits to the school, the governing body and the LAD.

Part 3 Planning for Personal Development
This deals with the processes involved in personal-development planning and considers the vital importance of 'reflective practice' — submitting experience to systematic review in order to make informed choices about future activity.

Part 4 Critical Friendships
This outlines the process involved in working on these materials with a colleague. Sometimes called 'critical friendship' this process is designed to provide a helpful and supportive structure to the self-development planning process.

Part 5 Building on Experience and Achievement: Your Personal Development Profile
This presents a structure for the profile and guidance on how a start may be made in planning for the profile within a developing portfolio of selected experience and achievement. It contains some practical activities to try out. These may be photocopied and used regularly to build up a comprehensive portfolio of management development.

Part 6 Developing Organizational Collaboration
This focuses on collaborative school management. It offers a framework for developing a collaborative-management culture and provides a series of activities designed to facilitate whole-school management review and development.

Part 7 Accrediting Experiential Learning and Prior Achievement
This contains information about how you can use your work on these materials and previous management experience to gain credits towards a further professional qualification.

Part 8 Making it Work: a Guide for School Coordinators
The pilot project which tested these materials in a wide range of schools found that both individual teachers and the school as a whole benefited from the work of a school coordinator. This section contains practical guidance for those taking on such a role in school.

Part 9 Addressing Appraisal, Equal Opportunities and Governor Involvement
The links between personal-development planning and appraisal are discussed and the issues of equal opportunities and governor involvement are considered. The materials are designed to be of benefit to all teachers whatever their position in the school and their length of experience.

Whilst the materials can be used in conjunction with management initiatives, such as appraisal, primarily they provide a means through which teachers and other colleagues may be encouraged to identify and value their achievements and to have these more publicly recognized where appropriate. Essentially, the materials in this pack represent a unique attempt to assist teachers in developing lifelong career and professional-development profiles within a portfolio of self-generated selected evidence of learning and achievement.

PURPOSES

1 Working as an Individual
The materials in this folder have been designed to help you to:

- identify, document and analyse systematically your personal and professional needs;
- enhance your professional self-esteem;
- recognize the range of contributions you make to your own school and the wider education service;
- provide a framework through which your own management development may be recognized, valued, supported, challenged, documented and related to your school's development plan.

2 The Whole-school Approach
When used as part of a whole-school approach these materials will help to:

- provide a framework for reviewing whole-school management development;
- develop systematic approaches to management development and planning;
- encourage consideration of the value of collaborative structures and processes in effective management.

- teachers are the school's greatest asset;
- all teachers are managers;
- personal and professional development are central to continuing effective management of classrooms; and
- given the right conditions, all professionals are capable of learning from their experience of the job.

The project team believed that schools are likely to be more effective if

- leaders actively promote processes of interaction between individual and whole-school review and development planning (the prime function of school leadership is to support teachers); and
- teachers' personal professional development needs are recognized, supported and based upon self-managed personal-development planning.

Since effectiveness is about relating achievement (outputs and outcomes) to some set of intentions or expectations a necessary first stage in personal and school-development planning is that of review, and this will inevitably involve reflection.

Personal and Institutional Development: Two Complementary Strands

Two key issues were addressed through the project. The first relates to our understanding and use of reflection — an essential part of teachers' learning and growth processes; and the second to the need for partnerships and coalitions (e.g., critical friendships) within collaborative organizational cultures which are necessary to support opportunities for the different kinds of reflection so necessary to learning, and thus contribute to the development of individual professional learning cultures in the 1990s. In short, the project sought to provide a structure to support teachers in their career-long personal and professional aspirations.

Extract 3

Planning for personal development will:

- assist teachers in preparing for discussion of development needs;
- contribute to the achievement through negotiation of a synthesis of organizational and individual development;
- gather evidence of personal development which does not directly relate to teacher practitioner and institutional needs but which impinges on these (see Figure 15.1)
- provide opportunities for individual teachers to take stock of their job learning and career stages; and
- provide opportunities for teachers to engage in long-term professional and career-development planning.

This part contains material on:

- job and career development;
- kinds and benefits of planned learning opportunities;
- benefits of systematic reflection; and
- effective management of time.

The project itself had two principal complementary strands. One focused upon the establishment and monitoring of whole-school management-development strategies which would be effective in supporting personal-development planning by teachers. Its aims were to provide support and further development of whole-school management cultures which would support the development of personal-development planning. The other strand focused upon the implementation and accreditation of a personal development-planning framework across schools in the consortium of nine local-education authorities. Its aims were to provide initial induction support and network coordination to teachers in the pilot schools in order to assist them in the development of personal-management development planning. By the end of the project it was intended that participating schools would have:

- used the materials to evaluate their management cultures;
- modified the materials and where appropriate, developed further their management support; and
- designed strategies to support and monitor the development of teacher profiling in cooperation with teachers.

That teachers would have:

- developed and documented their own personal development plans;
- considered the use of personal-development plans in whole-school management and individual review procedures; and
- where appropriate participated with higher education establishments in establishing criteria for accreditation of management learning, experience and achievement.

Central to both strands were the valuing and recognition of experience, learning and achievement (Parts 5 and 7).

Attention to product — however temporary — as well as process was crucial, for it enabled participants to apply skills of analysis, interpretation and selection in order to build a portfolio which was of personal developmental significance. As

classroom manager, as a member of a school community), it is essential that all of these professional learning opportunities should be available within a school-management support portfolio.

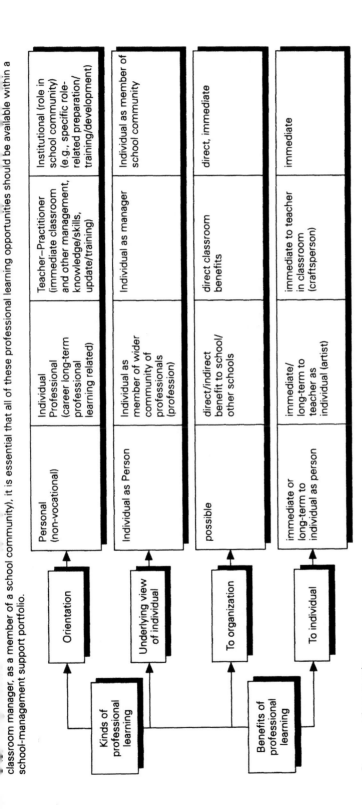

	Personal (non-vocational)	Individual Professional (career long-term professional learning related)	Teacher–Practitioner (immediate classroom and other management, knowledge/skills, update/training)	Institutional (role in school community) (e.g., specific role-related preparation/training/development)
Orientation				
Underlying view of individual	Individual as Person	Individual as member of wider community of professionals (profession)	Individual as manager	Individual as member of school community
To organization	possible	direct/indirect benefit to school/other schools	direct classroom benefits	direct, immediate
To individual	immediate or long-term to individual as person	immediate/long-term to teacher as individual (artist)	immediate to teacher in classroom (craftsperson)	immediate

Kinds of professional learning

Benefits of professional learning

Some questions to ask:
- What is the balance of professional learning opportunities in your school?
- How do you achieve this?
- What proportion of your resources (including in-school time) is devoted to: —
  - Personal learning opportunities
  - Individual professional learning opportunites
  - Professional practitioner learning opportunities
  - Institutional learning opportunities

Figure 15.1: Kinds and benefits of planned learning opportunities

Munby (1990) reports in relation to records of achievement schemes for school students, they

1   help to enhance pupils' self-esteem and confidence by recognizing their achievements;
2   provide detailed feedback to learners so that they are clearly aware of their progress;
3   indicate the criteria for assessing their work;
4   give them short-term achievable targets;
5   the process helps pupils to evaluate their own learning and to develop strategies to improve it.
(Munby, 1990)

The same could be said for the development of profiles or portfolios for teachers. However, these must be portable and subject to the owner's' choice, have the potential to be used in several ways:

- as evidence for use in appraisal;
- as career review and development-planning documents;
- as records of prior learning and achievement which may be used also for 'advanced study' or 'remission' from part of a course of study in higher education.

If its uses were to include: appraisal, personal review and career development, in-service planning, and functional role preparation and development, the portfolio had to be an accurate reflection of an analysis of the teachers' values, beliefs, thinking, practices and aspirations and not merely a simple accumulation of data, as in a curriculum vitae. It therefore contains four sections which are linked with levels of reflection, analysis and purpose.

From the outset, the development team recognized the need to produce materials which could encourage teachers and schools to build upon current practice. They were not, therefore, designed to be used prescriptively or sequentially. Additionally, the language was to be clear and the presentation in ring binder format so that teachers and schools could re-order, re-write, reproduce, supplement and remove.

The Evaluation of the Project

Whilst it is not possible to provide detailed information for each section of the project materials, the evaluation of their use is presented in order to include references to and apt illustrations of these. The project was evaluated by means of the collection and analysis of information by the teacher participants themselves (through the keeping of logs/diaries); from the teachers and school co-coordinators (through completion of centrally designed and administered questionnaires); and through in-depth interviewing of participants from six schools at different stages of the project. (All extended quotations in this chapter are from this evaluation). Whilst individual schools' detailed responses varied according to their own developmental contexts, most reactions and outcomes were common to all the schools and teachers involved in the project.

Over half of the participating teachers returned completed questionnaires. The replies are summarized under three headings: 'Enhancing Personal and Professional

Extract 4

Section 1: What I Have Done (a summary record)
This is a curriculum vitae of the kind many teachers compile prior to job application, a summary list of achievements set out in a quantifiable way, a 'professional record'. It is descriptive, in note form and date order. It records *what* has been achieved, e.g., it might well include keeping a running record of the activities you are involved in on the theme you have set. This will include experiences and activities in school (relevant whole-school events, team meetings, development time with other staff, meetings with colleagues who visit the school).

Section 2: Self-evaluation/Review of Critical Incidents (including role competences where appropriate)
This involves the process of *selecting* and listing key examples of particular on or off site, 'landmark' incidents, situations, events, roles, activities, competences which you believe are of particular relevance to your learning, achievement, growth, contributions to the school. Many of these may relate to items listed in Section 1. It will be a form of qualitative and quantitative, interpretative, self-reflection and evaluation, also recorded in note form. It *may* require the informal assistance of a 'critical friend' or 'key colleague', and will involve participants in theorizing about the action.

Section 3: Application to Thinking and Practice
This involves reflection on *how* your thinking and/or practice has changed as a result of the 'critical incidents' selected in Section 2, the recording of what knowledge, skills or concepts have been gained, and what attitudes and thinking have changed, and *examples of these gains in practice*. The situations themselves should be described briefly, placed in their social and institutional contexts, and comments from yourself (and others if appropriate) on *the learning/achievement gained* should be recorded. The section will illustrate the application of gains made and recorded in Sections 1 and/or 2. Wherever possible, *third* party *verification* should be sought as a check on self-perception. This implies the active and formal use of a mentor/critical friend/'key colleague'. Additionally, it implies self or other *confrontation* as well as reflection, and the ability to be evaluative (qualitatively).

Section 4: Decision-making (Key Targeting)
This involves action planning based upon the synthesis of experiences recorded in Sections 1–3. It will be a form of development planning for personal individual professional teacher-practitioner and organization role growth.

Development Thinking'; 'Recognizing Whole-school Development Needs'; and 'Leadership, Learning Support and School Cultures: Recognizing the Need for Sustained Interactivity'.

Enhancing Personal and Professional Development Thinking

Of 110 replies to the question 'What have you learnt from reading the materials?', ninety-eight were positive. The project had offered a structure for identifying and focusing upon their own needs, valuing their own achievements 'reawakening' the link between their personal and professional lives. Participants were asked whether the project had affected their development. Of the 132 responses to this question, ninety-eight were positive. Many (twenty-four) stated that the project had given them 'clearer ideas' of their development. They were, 'more aware of the need to sit and plan', to, 'think through the development experiences' to 'focus' on their use of time. Others claimed that involvement in the project had made them, 'more aware of strengths and weaknesses', 'present and future aims', 'my own role in relation to the school', and they were, now, 'more aware of the experiences I need'.

Extract 5

Role Review	Date:

---

1 The parts of my job I feel I do really well are . . .
2 The main challenge in my present role is . . .
3 I should like to develop my current role by . . .
4 An important initiative I have recently led was . . .
5 I could contribute more to whole-school development if . . .
6 The skills and qualities which are not currently well used in my role are . . .
7 The sorts of support that would enable me to make more of my role are . . .
8 The skills and qualities I should develop are . . .
9 The particular contribution I feel I have made to the school in this role is . . .
10 Over the next few years I should like to . . .

In response to the question, 'Has it changed anything in the balance between your personal and professional commitments and how you feel about them?', seventy-nine said that the balance had not changed, while for fifty-five participants the project had caused them to recognize that, 'there's more to the job than professional development'.

Of 122 replies to the question, 'Have you learnt anything new from doing the tasks?', 101 were positive. These wrote of their increased confidence and self-esteem — 'I have more to offer than I thought' — and a greater awareness of the need for planning career development. 'It gave me the opportunity to analyse target needs, plan', '. . . more confidence in seeing a career move . . .', '. . . time to reflect on my own strengths, classroom practice, weaknesses, areas in need of development . . .', and '. . . provided much needed structure to our personal and professional development planning'. A newly qualified teacher found 'the energy to discipline herself' to complete the tasks, although there were problems with time. She learnt to 'value the school environment', became aware of 'gaps in myself', and 'development needs'. It had made her think: 'We so often accept things without question. I think about health and happiness. I am looking for the priorities and learning sometimes to say "*no*" '.

The project had also helped teachers in thinking of their career development. Many had become, more involved with management with a view to a career move (thirteen); been made more aware of the experiences they needed (eleven), and their role in relation to the school (four). Others wrote of their increased confidence in the context of renewed resolve to develop their careers.

> The coordinator has applied for the headship. The teacher with seventeen years' experience is applying for promotion, and accreditation of her work in the project.

The project had also helped a teacher 'to see what I am doing now is a stage in my development, and that I needn't feel guilty about not being where other people are!' Thirty-two responses concerned this kind of awareness-raising, and the value of this form of 'self-assessment'. 'I have an idea of needs of professional development which I had not considered before . . .' Respondents were '. . . beginning to think about professional development in a more structured way . . .' becoming 'clearer about the precise nature of long- and short-term targets'.

Recognizing Whole-school Development Needs

Extract 6

Management Review			Date
	For the individual	For teams and groups	For the school as a whole
What sort of management culture do we want to develop for the school?			
How will personal-development planning be of benefit in building this culture?			
What specific goals do we want to pursue?			

In the context of school management, the project had also provided teachers with 'a greater awareness' of their individual contributions to the department and school, a greater understanding of management structures and school cultures, and a greater sense of the importance of collaborative work. An experienced teacher talked of her growing awareness of the idea of 'management' and began realizing that she already had and put to good use these skills. In this school there was the opportunity to take a meaningful role in the management of the school as a member of a team. This message appeared to have taken a higher profile in the minds of head, deputy and members of staff in the school. 'The level of trust, already healthy, increased as did the respect for each other . . .' One teacher talked about considering one's development in 'a wider context — individual development first and aims of the school, second — how to fit the needs and aspirations of both, together.'

Participation in the project tasks had clearly demonstrated the need for more detailed whole-school planning in order to realize and support the development needs of staff so that both individuals and schools could benefit. There was evidence that some schools had grown to recognize the need to use the potential of staff to contribute to whole-school development planning more fully. By the time one design team member visited a school six months into the project, a personal professional-development policy, based upon the folder contents, was in place and being implemented. The coordinator had produced a model, built from the common experience and contribution of colleagues. The staff had also been supportive as he tackled plans for future management procedures. In another school, staff were:

> . . . considering a more democratic approach to whole-school management as a result of the project. Individuals were beginning to see management as part of the whole.

The project had been particularly useful in the understanding and introduction of appraisal for professional and school-development purposes. In several schools, elements were being used 'as a framework for personal development (target setting), and whole-school planning and appraisal' . . . Many teachers (thirty-six) referred to the project as having 'great value when it comes to being appraised' 'supporting staff development programmes' (twenty-nine), and 'allowing the review process to become part of the planning strategy . . . running parallel to, and independent of, the appraisal system'. In a community college, the evaluator wrote:

> Within the group the pilot has now had a significant effect upon the staff attitude to appraisal and the personal/professional materials and activities are widely used and appreciated.

Participation in the project had helped to identify a complementarity of individual and school needs. In particular for many, it had served to highlight and promote interaction between personal and institutional development issues, often being used as a basis for school-management plans (ten).

Leadership, Learning Support and School Culture: Recognizing the Need for Sustained Interactivity

Participation in the project and use of the materials had provided a heightened awareness of the importance of collaborative work in the process of personal planning in the school context. The project tasks called for concerns to be shared, and support by the school for development needs identified by individual teachers. The evaluation identified an existing supportive culture in one school:

> the level of success, in terms of depth of understanding and interpretation, firstly depends upon the amount of personal concern and respect for others, which already exists there.

In another, however, the leadership culture was less supportive. Here was the problem of the remote head and a senior-management team unbalanced in terms of gender — one woman and four men. Differences in the philosophy upon which the project was conceived and documented between head and coordinator caused delay in the launch of the project. The coordinator was quite justifiably unable to proceed until the general philosophy of the design team was accepted for the way forward. These problems undermined confidence, and 'union problems' within the school at the same time, made the initiation even more difficult, as these were principally concerned with time commitments. 'Morale was precarious'. Many staff were in a position of 'retreat', and not ready to talk about 'feelings', or 'development'! The coordinator allowed time to lapse and then arranged for the group of participants to leave the premises for some hours, together. This was designed to enable them to take ownership of the development of the pilot.

The evaluator later wrote of the same institution:

> There is however the danger that lack of awareness and interest from 'the top' will stifle any real whole-school movement and progress, and destroy the energy and confidence of, key staff.

One hundred of the 118 responses to the question concerning the effectiveness of the roles taken by the school coordinator were positive. Many of the responses to questions concerned the leadership and coordination of the project at school

Extract 7

Developing Organizational Collaboration

Although a great deal of importance seems to be attached to the nature of the human environment in which change takes place it has not traditionally been the subject for much deliberate attention. This part is divided into two sections. The first considers the nature of school-management cultures, and their possible impact upon opportunities for personal development planning. The second contains a sequence of activities designed to enable a review of your school's management culture and the way in which you would like it to develop.

Section 1:   Leadership and Culture

A number of writers have used the notion of culture in relation to the work of schools. Fullan and Hargreaves describe it as:

> ... the guiding beliefs and expectations evident in the way a school operates, particularly in reference to how people relate (or fail to relate) to each other. In simple terms culture is 'the way we do things and relate to each other around here'. (Fullan and Hargreaves, 1992)

Nias, Southworth and Yeomans (1989) use the term to describe the multiple social realities that people construct for themselves. Westoby (1988) refers to organizational culture as 'social habitat', including the informal, ephemeral and covert as well as the visible and official. Essentially then, culture is about people in the organizational setting and is characterized by behaviour — what people say and do; relationships — how they work with and through each other: attitudes and values — how assumptions, beliefs and prejudices affect the formal and informal workings of the organization.

One of the keys to successful whole-school development is a sensitive attention to what affects culture. Essentially this means trying to make sense of why people behave as they do; the extent to which their behaviour is culturally determined and the ways in which culture can be deliberately built and developed in ways that optimize the organizational purposes.

> the only thing of real importance that leaders do is create and manage culture, . . . the unique talent of leaders is their ability to work with culture. (Schein, 1985)

Some cultures struggle to maintain the status quo in the face of demand and expectation — for change. Others are anxious to avoid any sense for sameness or complacency. Most organizations live a life somewhere between these two extremes.

The quality of leadership of adults in school and college is as important as the quality of leadership by teachers in classrooms, so attitudes of leaders are important in enabling the full potential of staff to be recognized and enhanced. But what does 'culture' look like in practice? Are there different kinds, and are some more effective than others?

---

level. Eighty-nine respondents cited the high quality, 'sensitive', 'low-key' clear introductions given by the school coordinators to the project materials. They clearly played a key catalytic and supportive role, 'making people feel at ease at the beginning of the scheme', 'keeping the momentum going' and providing time, 'to meet with individual staff and as a team'. In each of the six schools visited, the importance of the coordinator's role in relation to personal and whole-school aspirations was highlighted and the qualities needed by a coordinator working in circumstances in which differences of philosophy with the head existed identified.

In a nursery school, qualities of 'commitment' and 'dedication' minimized the 'inadequacies' of resource provision; and in an upper-secondary school the coordinator was 'full of enthusiasm and extremely sensitive to the needs of the staff and the pressures upon them. He appeared to have the complete support and confidence of his head and immediate colleagues.'

Extract 8

It is important to become a *friend* before becoming a *critic*. Essentially the role of a critical friend (or 'key colleague') is to provide *support* and *challenge*.

What is the nature of the relationship between critical friends?

Critical friendships embody the notion of *partnerships* in which:

> Colleagues talk to one another about teaching, often at a level of detail that makes their exchange both theoretically rich and practically meaningful . . . It illuminates underlying principles and ideas in a way that allows teachers to understand and accommodate one another, to assist one another and sometimes to challenge one another. (Little, 1990)

What roles may a critical friend play?

You will find that at different times you will be an enabler, a coach, a counsellor, a challenger (of ideas, opinion) a catalyst, or just someone to talk with!

How do I begin?

You may decide to begin just by talking things through.

How does it work in practice?

Essentially, every critical friendship that works is one in which both colleagues help each other within a relationship which is both person and task centred.

The relationship may be informal or formal, but always there should be an expectation that both colleagues will gain from the friendship both professionally (conversations will be designed to enhance reflection upon practice) and personally (conversations will be designed to encourage the growth of self-esteem).

Do we need to agree ground rules in advance?

Sometimes, it can be helpful to consider forming an agreement or contract: the helping process needs to be 'owned' by both critical friends and there needs to be some basic understanding as to the major goals to be pursued and procedures to be used in the helping process so that there is both a sense and a reality of mutual gain.

An explicit contract, between critical friends, whether verbal or written, can help achieve agreed goals. It need not be too detailed or too rigid. It should clarify mutual expectations, goals and methods and provide a structure for the relationship and the work to be done without being frightening or overwhelming. Inflexibility and irrevocable commitment to initial goals should be avoided.

In summary:

- The agreement should be negotiated not imposed, by the parties involved.
- The agreement should be clear to all involved parties. They should know what 'helping' is about.
- Some kind of oral or written commitment to the agreement should be obtained.
- The agreement should be reviewed as the parties progress and revised if necessary.
  (Based on Egan, 1982)

Coordinators themselves referred to a wide range of skills used and developed during the period of coordination.

- managerial skills — planning leadership, reviewing, organizing and advising;
- interpersonal skills — counselling, negotiating, persuading, supporting and delegating;
- listening — the single most frequently highlighted skill; and
- the importance of tact and patience.

A key strand in the innovation strategy for the piloting of the materials was to encourage participants to consider the benefits of learning not only through independent self-review and the development of reflection but also through sharing this experience and its outcomes with key colleagues through 'Critical Friendships' which were defined as:

> practical partnerships entered into voluntarily, based on a relationship between equals and rooted in a common task or shared concern, . . . critical friendships can serve to decrease isolation and increase the possibilities of moving through stages of reflection to confrontation of thinking and practice . . . (Day, Whitaker and Johnston, 1990)

In a special school the first aspect of the project to be introduced was 'critical friendships':

> These were organized in twilight sessions and based upon previously completed self-evaluation documents. This would further aid movement into appraisal. There was evidence that people became less negatively critical towards colleagues and more gentle, friendly and understanding.

It had run a successful training day, 'when all the staff had engaged in critical friendship activities producing useful documentation'.

An upper-secondary school group had met after school on five occasions during the project. The evaluator noted

> . . . . a greater level of common concern . . . towards the end of the project.
> . . . People ask more and seek others out. Documentation has been and continues to be reviewed and improved . . .

There was a recognition, however, that even critical friendships may provide only limited opportunities for challenge and support, given problems of discourse and lack of support external to the inevitably limited and limiting cultural and temporal contexts which provide the opportunities for conversation.

Discussion: What Did the Project Teach about Professional Learning?

Research on the effectiveness of in-service education (Steadman *et al.*, 1992) suggests that schools need to be able to plan INSET which meets local needs, the processes of which are based upon knowledge of how teachers learn; and which demonstrate through support mechanisms an understanding of the longer-term processes of change.

The effects of participation in the personal development-planning project had been to provide a supported, structured framework which had created conditions for a powerful form of teacher development. Teachers and schools had claimed that, as a result of participating in the project, they had:

- grown in self-confidence and self-esteem;
- raised their awareness of the complexities of management;

- recognized the importance of their contributions to whole-school development;
- identified and targeted more clearly professional and career-development needs;
- participated actively in the growth and development of collaborative-management cultures so increasing their involvement in, and commitment to, the visions and goals of the school; and
- developed critical professional friendships with key colleagues in extending forms of self-review and reflective practice.

They affirmed that effective self-review and planning is central to the development of appraisal schemes, and that the project had contributed to a greater sustained interaction between whole-school and individual review and development planning.

Key variables which affected the achievement of these benefits had been:

- the provision of time to reflect and interact;
- the involvement of a 'significant other';
- the quality of leadership and culture of the school; and
- the balance of professional development opportunities available.

Learning through Reflection

In the early 1970s Argyris and Schon (1976) developed the notion of single loop and double loop learning and stressed the need from time to time to move from the former in which planning, teaching and testing remains at the private often tacit level, thus disempowering growth, to the latter. In which thinking, practice and discrepancies within and between the two are raised to an explicit publicly accessible level. Yet the conditions necessary to enable and support this in schools continue to remain elusive. Furthermore, whilst there has been an increasing popular use of the term 'reflection' as a process of learning through which teachers may seek to review and improve their practice relatively little attention has been given to either its different components or levels or its link with the private-public dimensions of learning.

Reflection in teacher education, as characterized by Grimmett and Erickson (1988), may involve thoughtfulness about action: deliberation and choice among competing forms of good practice; or reconstructing experience, the end of which is the identification of a new possibility for action. This is similar to Mezirow's (1990) concept of reflection which differentiates between thoughtful action where one draws upon past experience, and reflective action which is based upon critical assessment of assumptions and presuppositions. Killion and Todnem (1991, p. 15) suggest also that it is possible to distinguish between, on the one hand reflection in and on practice (Schon, 1983) which are essentially reactive in nature, and 'reflection-for-practice' which is proactive 'the desired outcome of both previous types of reflection' and guides future action.

Much has been written in Australia, Europe and North America over a number of years about the nature and practice of reflection, particularly by those researcher-practitioners involved in the action-research movement. All of this work is essentially

Extract 9

ESTABLISHING CRITICAL FRIENDSHIPS
Getting a new perspective through self-reflection

Experience in the pilot project confirmed that:

> Immersion in the world of routine practice can tend over time to reduce the capacity of the practitioner both to contemplate alternative courses of action and to continue to gain insight into everyday events. As insight goes, so some of the intellectual excitement of teaching goes too. A new perspective is needed that can bring back freshness of vision. (Rudduck, 1987)

What is Reflective practice?

One way of gaining new perspectives is to engage in explicit and systematic reflection on practice.

Writing recently about the difficulties of engaging in reflective practice Griffiths and Tann (1991) observed that, reflection relies on the ability to uncover one's own personal theories and make them explicit.

They identified a 'five level' model of reflective practice:

1 rapid reaction (instinctive, immediate);
2 repair (habitual, pause for thought, fast, on the spot);
3 review (time out to re-assess, over hours or days);
4 research (systematic, sharply focused, over weeks or months); and
5 re-theorize and re-formulate (abstract, rigorous, clearly formulated, over months or years)

and claimed that:

> reflective teaching requires that public theories are translated into personal ones and vice versa unless teachers are going to allow themselves to be turned into low-level operatives, content with carrying out their tasks more and more efficiently, while remaining blind to larger issues of the underlying purposes and results of schooling. (Griffiths and Tann, 1991, p. 100)

Levels 1 and 2 are part of our day-to-day survival and maintenance strategies but we do need to move further than this from time to time if we are to engage in personal development planning. We need to reflect on teaching and other roles we play systematically.

---

concerned with the deconstruction and reconstruction of meaning; and its proponents recognize either implicitly or explicitly the existence of a 'reflective spectrum' through which personal theories may be examined and made public.

Reflection, like experience, is often initially understood at the level of personal impressions. If it is to serve developmental purposes it must contain other components. In a synthesis of research on teachers' reflective thinking, Sparks-Langer and Colton (1991) identified three elements which play significant roles in encouraging reflection and reflective practice among teachers: *cognitive* — knowledge that teachers need in order to make good decisions in and about the classroom; *critical*, 'moral and ethical aspects of social compassion and justice'; *narrative* — teachers' own accounts which contextualize their classroom experience.

Smyth argues, with Day (1985) that in order to develop and sustain a critical form of teaching, teachers need to be concerned with four processes:

1 describing... (What do I do?);
2 informing... (What does this description mean?);

3 confronting . . . (How did I come to be like this?); and
4 reconstructing . . . (How might I do things differently?)

(Smyth, 1991, p. 106)

Conditions in schools which do not engage in sustained interactivity will almost certainly ensure that the third of these processes will rarely be addressed. Teaching is, in some respects, subject to routinization, and teachers all too often come to see only what they expect to see, transcribing the surface realities of classroom interactions and constantly reconstructing the familiar past in its own image (Rudduck, 1991). In order to move through levels and processes of confrontation and ethical justification, reflection will need to be analytic and involve dialogue with others. The project sought to encourage and provide structures for this to occur. Structures themselves must be focused on helping teachers, 'to see things afresh that habit has made ordinary'.

However, whilst reflection is necessary it is not always a sufficient condition for professional development (Day, 1993). There is still comparatively little empirical research on ways of making private theory explicit and public. Certainly, teachers will need active, planned support from key colleagues if they are to move, for example, beyond processes of reviewing (deconstructing) in a descriptive way what they do through a consideration of how and why this is so within personal and organizational contexts (i.e., to confront their practice and the reasons for this at social and ethical levels) to planning (reconstructing) how they might do things differently. Even this cannot be assumed to be a linear, rational movement, for the kind and quality of the data and thus the authenticity of information upon which confrontation will be based will be dependent on how the teachers' abilities and skills are affected by their biographical, psychological, social and work contexts and the available support from significant others. Reflective and non-reflective practitioners, then, are not two fundamentally irreconcilable groups. Rather, teachers reflect in different ways at different times according to personal and environmental histories and present experience. Much more research needs to be undertaken explicating the links between career and life-cycle development, school culture and in-service teacher development.

Acceleration through Intervention

The project was built upon the notion of planned intervention to enhance teachers' natural learning which is embedded in, and arises from, their experiences of individual and institutional environments. Intervention in support of teacher development must, therefore take account of

- development of professional expertise;
- cognitive development;
- developmental stages of concern/career development;
- the life-cycle; and
- teacher socialisation. (Leithwood, 1990; Veenman 1984; Nias, 1989)

The emphasis in each of these is on development which is conceived as natural, gradual, evolutionary. Those involved in supporting and challenging teacher development may, however, be characterized as *intervening* in teachers' natural professional development lives in order to provide opportunities for what Rita Nolder (1992) called 'accelerated' professional development. She suggests that, 'cycles of accelerated development whether prompted by internal or external factors, are likely to occur at any point in an individual's professional life'.

Nolder's research with secondary-school teachers revealed that there were certain conditions which provide for development 'spurts'. These have been variously described as 'critical incidents', 'key events in an individual's life' around which pivotal decisions revolve. They provoke the individual into selecting particular kinds of actions, which lead in particular directions' (Sikes *et al.*, 1985, p. 57). These critical incidents are often associated with a critical phase in a teacher's professional biography and represent, 'the culmination of a decision-making process, crystallising the individual's thinking, rather than being responsible of itself for that decision' (Sikes *et al.*, 1985, p. 58). In proposing a model of accelerated professional development, Nolder was not suggesting that teacher development was discontinuous but rather that within continuing professional development it is important to be able to identify key stages at which in the interests of the individual teacher and school, support for development is crucial. Watts (1981), for example, noted that an individual might be in, 'a state of transition or stuck at one level in some areas while more advanced in others'.

Personal and Institutional Complementarity: School Culture and Leadership

Whilst many of the outputs of education are intangible and cannot be quantitatively measured (Dror, 1973, p. 26), school-effectiveness studies (e.g., Rutter *et al.*, 1979, Mortimore *et al.*, 1988) consistently reveal the important contribution of school climate, ethos or culture. It seems that differences between schools are, 'systematically related to their characteristics as social institutions'. Following a review of non-educational research into the function of organizations, Rutter *et al.* (1979) concluded that there is value in:

> considering patterns of social organisation in institutions; patterns which reflect styles of management and control, quality of relationships, participation and involvement, responsibilities and decision-making, and the overall emotional climate as well as the details of how individuals interact with one another. (Rutter *et al.*, 1979, p. 20)

A significant feature of management literature is the identification of the positively correlated relationship between homogeneous culture and a successful organization. Martin and Meyerson (1988) characterize this as the 'integrationist' perspective on organizational culture. Examples of this are to be found in the work of Nias *et al.* (1989) and Deal (1985). They reveal the pivotal role played by the headteacher/ principal in creating and *managing* school culture:

> It all goes back to me, really, in the sense that I think that the school should — I didn't mean everybody's got to do the same thing — but I think they've got to all follow the same pattern. I think that's got to be the underlying philosophy. (Nias *et al.*, 1989, p. 99)

In a recent research project which studied whole-school curriculum management conducted by NFER, Weston *et al.* (1992) concluded that:

> schools' capacity to develop a whole school curriculum vision and a strategy for implementing it . . . depends very heavily on the ability of the senior management to mobilise the skills and energies of the staff themselves. (Weston *et al.*, 1992)

Not all the participating schools were at the same stage in their organizational development. Management and leadership cultures were different. It was clear from the responses of teachers that the quality of support from line management was crucial to the success of the work. The project design had set out deliberately to minimize the 'support' role of the central team, and thus the potential dependency of participants on externally provided support. However, it was also apparent that school-based support would be necessary both indirectly from the headteacher or senior management and directly from the school coordinator and 'critical friend' if work of this kind is to influence the professional development culture of the department or school.

Carlgren and Lindblad (1991) in discussing the 'inner' and 'outer' logic of teachers' work, highlight the 'complex interplay between internal and external determinants on teaching in specific cases', and David Hargreaves argues for a synthesis of professional and institutional development similar to Fessler's (1985) notion of 'personal environment' and 'institutional environment'. He proposes that the two are interdependent.

> To improve schools, one must be prepared to invest in professional development; to improve teachers, their professional development must be set within the context of institutional development. This synthetic approach to professional and institutional development is one which, the current wisdom seems to say, you must take or you risk wasting much time, energy and money . . . (Hargreaves, 1992)

However, the evidence from this project is that whilst this may be the case, an orientation of professional-development work which begins with individual teachers' interests is likely to pay better dividends.

The essential messages are that the responsibility for professional development must extend beyond the individual but not exclude him or her; that essential complementary of 'personal' and 'professional' development must be recognized so that professional development extends beyond classroom practice; that support for the personal and long-term professional thinking and practice needs of the teacher are legitimated; and that personal practical knowledge is extended beyond 'learning from experience'. Without this, the tendency by governments over the last decade to regard development as 'training' which may be achieved in short, sharp bursts and which must be directly related to policy implementation will be exacerbated (Gilroy and Day, 1993). The consequences will be the downgrading of teachers as autonomous, responsible and accountable 'thinking' professionals to teachers as operatives who follow orders.

Teacher Professionalism

The concept of teacher professionalism is complex. It involves notions of professional accountability:

1 a moral commitment to serve the interests of students by reflecting on their well-being and their progress and deciding how best it can be fostered or promoted;
2 a professional obligation to review periodically the nature and effectiveness of one's practice in order to improve the quality of one's management, pedagogy and decision-making; and
3 a professional obligation to continue to develop one's practical knowledge both by personal reflection and through interaction with others.
(Eraut, 1992)

The 'personal-development planning' project described in this chapter was designed to support teachers directly in the second and third of these notions.

The new 'self-managed' system of devolved staff-development funding in England continues to have strings attached in the form of 'national priority areas' on which most of the funds must be targeted. Schools and colleges may well, in a climate of externally imposed innovation through national curriculum, staff appraisal, testing, be tempted to swim with the tide and ensure that immediate problems provide the principle focus for supported staff-development activities. Indeed, some studies indicate that both teachers and administrators may favour an emphasis on technical rationality in professional-development programmes which leads to a reinforcement of teacher as technician (Sachs and Logan, 1990; O'Donohue *et al.*, 1993). John Elliott warns against the twin dangers of oversimplifying the nature and practice of support for reflective learning and the parochial pursuit of instrumentalism:

If practical reflection is solely construed as a form of technical or instrumental reasoning, then there is little room not only for philosophical self-reflection about values, but also for the ethical dimension of social practices. (Elliott, 1991, p. 52)

Successful models of professional development for the 1990s and beyond must assert connections between thinking, learning, planning and practice through *self-generated* reflective work, at a number of levels, which is perceived as relevant by each individual teacher, which is appropriate to each teacher's lifelong developmental needs as well as those of the organization, and which is shared and enhanced through appropriate intervention which challenges and supports. Researcher-developers from higher education have a key role to play in this, as do collaborative school cultures which build and develop strategies for challenge and support within the notion of teacher autonomy. Both recognize the need for teachers to retain a high degree of control over the direction of their work and the confidentiality surrounding their contributions, whilst at the same time having access to appropriate critical support.

Essentially, successful professional development in the future will need to be based upon close knowledge of the factors which constitute 'need' and on intervention support which contextualizes need in short- and long-term contexts. Traditional notions of teacher professionalism and educational research will themselves be redefined through a breaking down of traditional individualistic bifurcated cultures. Government and school policy may thus, through continuing dialogue between stakeholders, become at times, although not always, at one with individually defined needs and supportive of teacher autonomy. In this way the move towards treating the teacher as technician will be prevented. Personal development planning provides one means by which teachers, the schools' greatest asset, may be, alone and with others, actively involved in their own growth and that of their schools.

Note

The materials are available from The Resource Centre, School of Education, University of Nottingham, University Park, Nottingham NG7 2RD, England.

References

ARGYRIS, C. and SCHON, D.A. (1976) *Theory in Practice: Increasing Professional Effectiveness*, San Francisco, Jossey-Bass.

BALL, S.J. and GOODSON, I.F. (1985) *Teachers' Lives and Careers*, London, Falmer Press.

BOLAM, R. (1990) 'Recent developments in England and Wales', in JOYCE, B. (Ed) *Changing School Culture Through Staff Development*, The 1990 ASCD Yearbook, ASCD, 1250N Pitt Street, Alexandria, Virginia 22314, USA, pp. 147–67.

CALDERHEAD, J. (1993) *The Contribution of Research on Teachers' Thinking to the Professional Development of Teachers*, in DAY, C., CALDERHEAD, J. and DENICOLO, P. (Eds) *Research on Teacher Thinking: Understanding Professional Development*, London, Falmer Press.

CARLGREN, I. and LINDBLAD, S. (1991) 'On Teachers' Practical Reasoning and Professional Knowledge: Considering Conceptions of Context In Teachers' Thinking', Paper presentation to A.E.R.A, Conference, 1991, Chicago, USA.

CASE, C.W. and REAGAN, T.G. (1994) *Becoming a Reflective Practitioner: How to Build a Culture of Inquiry in the Schools*, California, Corwin Press.

CLARK, C.M. and YINGER, R.J. (1977) *Research on Teacher Thinking: Curriculum Inquiry*, **7**, 4.

CONNELLY, F.M. and CLANDININ, D.J. (1984) 'Teachers' personal practical knowledge', in HALKES, R. and OLSON, J. (Eds) *Teaching Thinking: A New Perspective on Persisting Problems in Education*, Heirewig, Holland, Swets.

DAY, C. (1985) 'Professional learning and researcher intervention', *British Educational Research Journal*, **11**, 2.

DAY, C. (1991) 'Roles and relationships in qualitative research on teachers' thinking: A reconsideration', *Teaching and Teacher Education: An International Journal of Research and Studies*, **7**, 5/6, pp. 537–47.

DAY, C. (1993) 'Reflection: A necessary but not sufficient condition for professional development', *British Educational Research Journal*, **19**, 1.

DAY, C., CALDERHEAD, J. and DENICOLO, P. (Eds) (1993) *Research on Teacher Thinking: Understanding Professional Development*, London, Falmer Press.

DAY, C., POPE, M. and DENICOLO, P. (Eds) (1990) *Insights into Teachers' Thinking and Practice*, London, Falmer Press.

DAY, C., WHITAKER, P. and JOHNSTON, D. (1990) *Managing Primary Schools in the 1990s: A Professional Development Approach*, London, Paul Chapman, p. 194.

DEAL, T. (1985) 'Healing our Schools', in LIEBERMAN, A. (Ed) (1990) *Schools as Collaborative Cultures*, London, Falmer Press.

DROR, Y. (1973) *Public Policy Making Reconsidered*, Aylesbury, Leonard Hill.

EGAN, G. (1982) *The Skilled Helper*, Monterey, California, Brooks/Cole.

ELBAZ, F. (1990) 'Knowledge and discourse: The evolution of research on teacher thinking', in DAY, C., POPE, M. and DENICOLO, P. *Insights into Teachers' Thinking and Practice*, London, Falmer Press.

ELLIOTT, J. (1991) *Action Research for Educational Change*, Buckingham, Open University Press.

ERAUT, M.E. (1991) 'Indicators and Accountability at School and Classroom Level', Paper for General Assembly on International Education Indicators, OECD/CERI.

ERAUT, M.E. (1992) 'Developing Professional Knowledge within a Client-Centred Orientation', Unpublished paper, Institute for Continuing and Professional Education, Falmer, University of Sussex.

FAY, B. (1977) 'How people change themselves: The relationship between critical theory and its audience', in BALL, T. (Ed) *Political Theory and Praxis: New Perspectives*, Minneapolis, University of Minneapolis Press, p. 207.

FESSLER, R. (1985) 'A model for teacher professional growth and development', in BURKE, P. and HEIDEMAN, R. (Eds) *Career Long Teacher Education*, Springfield, Illinois, Charles C. Thomas.

FULLAN, M. and HARGREAVES, A. (1992) *What's Worth Fighting For in Your School*, Buckingham, Open University Press.

GILROY, P. and DAY, C. (1993) 'The Erosion of INSET in England and Wales: Analysis and proposals for a redefinition', *Journal of Education for Teaching*, 19 February.

GITLIN, A., BRINGHURST, K., BURNS, M., COOLEY, V., MYERS, B., PRICE, K., RUSSELL, R. and TIESS, P. (1992) *Teachers' Voices for School Change: An Introduction to Educative Research*, London, Routledge.

GOODSON, I.F. (1990) *Studying Teachers' Lives*, London, Routledge.

GOODSON, I.F. (1991) 'Teachers' lives and educational research', in GOODSON, I.F. and WALKER, R. (Eds) *Biography, Identity and Schooling: Episodes in Educational Research*, London, Falmer Press.

GRIFFITHS, M. and TANN, S. (1991) 'Ripples in the reflection', in LOMAX, P. (Ed) *BERA Dialogues*, 5, Clevedon, Multilingual Matters Ltd.

GRIMMETT, P.P. and ERICKSON, G.L. (Eds) (1988) *Reflection in Teacher Education*, New York, Teachers' College Press.

HARGREAVES, D. (1992) 'The New Professionalism: The Synthesis of Professional and Institutional Development', Keynote Presentation to the Fourth International Conference on Teacher Development and School Improvement, University of New England, NSW Australia, July.

HOUSE, E. (1974) *The Politics of Educational Innovation*, Berkeley, CA, McCutcheon.

HUBERMAN, M. (1989) 'The professional life cycle of teachers', *Teachers' College Record*, **91**, 1, Fall.

HUBERMAN, M. (1993) *Changing Minds: The Dissemination of Research and its Effects on Practice and Theory*, in DAY, C., CALDERHEAD, J. and DENICOLO, P. (Eds) *Insights into Teachers' Thinking and Practice*, London, Falmer Press.

KAGAN, D.M. and TIPPINS, D.J. (1991) 'How teachers' classroom cases express their pedagogical beliefs', *Journal of Teacher Education*, **42**, 4, pp. 281–91.

KEDDIE, N. (1971) 'Classroom knowledge', in YOUNG, M.F.D. (Ed) *Knowledge and Control*, London, Collier-Macmillan.

KILLION, J. and TODNEM, G. (1991) 'A process for personal theory building', *Educational Leadership*, **48**, 6, pp. 14–16.

KREMER-HAYON, L. and FESSLER, R. (1991) 'The Inner World of School Principals: Reflections on Career Life Stages', Paper Presentation, 'Educational Development: The Contribution of Research on Teachers' Thinking', 23–27 September, University of Surrey.

LEITHWOOD, K. (1990) 'The principal's role in teacher development', in JOYCE, B. (Ed) *Changing School Culture through Staff Development*, The 1990 ASCD Yearbook, ASCD, 1250N Pitt Street, Alexandria, Virginia 22314, USA.

LITTLE, J.W. (1990) 'Teachers as colleagues', in LIEBERMAN, A. (Ed) *Schools as Collaborative Cultures*, London, Falmer Press.

MARTIN, J. and MAYERSON, D. (1988) 'Organisational culture and the denial, channelling and acknowledgment of ambiguity', in PONDY, L.R., BOLAND, R.J. and THOMAS, H. (Eds) *Managing Ambiguity and Change*, New York, John Wiley.

MCLAUGHLIN, M.W. and MARSH, D.D. (1979) 'Staff development and school change', in LIEBERMAN, A. and MILLER, L. (Eds) *Staff Development: New Demands, New Realities, New Perspectives*, New York, Teachers College Press.

MCNAMARA, D. (1990) 'Research on teachers' thinking: Its contribution to educating student teachers to think critically', *Journal of Education for Teaching*, **16**, 2, pp. 147–60.

MCNAMARA, D. and DESFORGES, C. (1979) 'Professional studies as a source of theory', in ALEXANDER, R.J. and WORMALD, E. (Eds) *Professional Studies for Teaching*, Society for Research in Higher Education, Guildford.

MEZIROW, J. AND ASSOCIATES (1990) *Fostering Critical Thinking in Adulthood*, San Francisco, Jossey Bass.

MORTIMORE, P., SAMMONS, P., ECOB, R., STOLL, L. and LEWIS, D. (1988) *School Matters: The Junior Years*, Salisbury, Open Books.

MUNBY, S. (1990) 'Assessing, recording and reporting achievement — after the Education Reform Act', in EVERTON, T., MAYNE, P. and WHITE, S. (Eds) *Effective Learning: Into a New ERA*, London, Jessica Kingsley.

NELSON, M.L. (1993) *Teacher Stories: Teaching Archetypes Revealed by Analysis*, Ann Arbor, Prakken Publications.

NIAS, J. (1989) *Primary Teachers Talking: A Study of Teaching as Work*, London, Routledge.

NIAS, J. (1989) 'Teaching and the self', in HOLLY, M.L. and MCLOUGHLIN, C.S. (Eds), *Perspectives on Teacher Professional Development*, pp. 156–72.

NIAS, J., SOUTHWORTH, G. and YEOMANS, R. (1989) *Staff Relationships in the Primary School*, London, Cassell.

NOLDER, R. (1992) 'Towards a model of accelerated professional development', *British Journal of In-Service Education*, **18**, 1, pp. 35–41.

OBERG, A. and FIELD, R. (1987) 'Teacher development through reflection on practice', *Australian Administrator*, **8**, 1 and 2.

OECD (1989) 'The condition of teaching: General report', Restricted Draft, Paris, Quoted in SIKES, P.J. (1992) 'Imposed change and the experienced teacher', in FULLAN, M. and HARGREAVES, A. (Eds) (1991) *Teacher Development and Educational Change*, London, Falmer Press.

O'DONOHUE, T.A., BROOKER, R. and ASPLAND, T. (1993) 'Harnessing teachers' dilemmas for professional development: A Queensland initiative', *British Journal of In-Service Education*, **19**, 2, Summer.

ROSENHOLTZ, S. (1989) *Teachers' Workplace*, New York, Longman.

RUDDUCK, J. (1987) 'Partnership supervision as a basis for the professional development of new and experienced teachers', in WIDEEN, M. and ANDREWS, I. (Eds) *Staff Development for School Improvement*, Lewes, Falmer Press.

RUDDUCK, J. (1991) 'Universities in partnership with schools and school systems: Les liaisons dangereuses?', in FULLAN, M. and HARGREAVES, A. (Eds) *Teacher Development and Educational Change*, London, Falmer Press.

RUTTER, M., MAUGHAN, B., MORTIMORE, P. and OUSTON, J. (1979) *Fifteen Thousand Hours: Secondary Schools and Their Effects on Children*, Wells, Open Books.

SACHS, J. and LOGAN, L. (1990) 'Control or development? A study of in-service education', *Journal of Curriculum Studies*, **22**, 5, pp. 473–81.

SCHEIN, E. (1985) *Organisational Culture and Leadership: A Dynamic View*, San Francisco, Jossey-Bass.

SCHON, D.A. (1983) *The Reflective Practitioner: How Professionals Think in Action*, New York, Basic Books.

SCHON, D.A. (1987) *Educating the Reflective Practitioner*, San Francisco, Jossey-Bass.

SCHON, D.A. (1992) 'The theory of inquiry: Dewey's legacy to education', *Curriculum Inquiry*, **22**, 2, Summer, pp. 119–39.

SHULMAN, L.S. (1986) 'Paradigms and research programs in the study of teaching: A contemporary perspective', in WITTROCK, M.C. (Ed) *Handbook of Research on Teaching*, 3rd ed., New York, MacMillan.

SIKES, P.J., MEASOR, L. and WOODS, P. (1985) *Teacher Careers: Crises and Continuities*, London, Falmer Press.

SMYTH, J. (1991) *Teachers as Collaborative Learners*, Buckingham, Open University Press.

SOCKETT, H. (1989) 'Research, practice and professional aspiration within teaching', *Journal of Curriculum Studies*, **21**, 2, pp. 97–112.

SPARKS-LANGER, G. and COLTON, A. (1991) 'Synthesis of research on teachers' reflective thinking', *Educational Leadership*, **48**, 6, pp. 37–44.

STEADMAN, S., ERAUT, M., FIELDING, M. and HORTON, A. (1992) 'Inset Effectiveness', Report to the Department for Education.

VEENMAN, S. (1984) 'Perceived Problems of Beginning Teachers', *Review of Educational Research*, **54**, 2, pp. 143–78.

WATTS, H. (1981) 'Can you feed a frog on tadpole food?', *Insight: Journal of the National Conference of Teachers' Centre Leaders*, **4**, 2, pp. 32–40.

WESTOBY, A. (Ed) (1988) *Culture and Power in Educational Organizations*, Milton Keynes, Open University Press, **54**, 2, pp. 143–78.

WESTON, P., BARRATT, E. and JAMISON, J. (1992) *The Quest for Coherence*, Slough, NFER/Routledge.

16 Integrating Enquiry into Teachers' Professional Lives

David Frost

With Circular 9/92 the DFE made a deliberate and forceful thrust towards school-based initial teacher education. By comparison the Government's strategy regarding INSET has always been more indirect if nonetheless determined. The establishment of development days in the late 1980s encouraged schools to plan INSET related to their school's development priorities. The introduction of local management of schools and grant-maintained status put control of the funding for staff development directly in the hands of headteachers and, in so doing, gave considerable impetus to the growth of school-based in-service teacher-education schemes.

Kent has more than its fair share of opted-out schools and so it is perhaps not surprising that there have been some interesting innovations here in response to these changes. This chapter arises from my own action-research connected with the development of a school-based, award-bearing in-service scheme now operating in a large number of secondary schools across the county. The scheme in question began with a close collaboration between Southlands Community Comprehensive School and Canterbury Christ Church College — a higher education institution linked to the University of Kent — having the express purpose of delivering tangible results in terms of the school's development priorities and higher professional qualifications for the participating teachers.

The motivation to establish this scheme grew out of the school's dissatisfaction with the INSET provision experienced over many years. It may be helpful therefore to briefly examine some of the background to the links between INSET and curriculum development.

Curriculum Development and Professional Development

There is now a fairly well-established tradition in educational discourse which is concerned with the essential connection between professional development and curriculum development. It is easily traced back to the 1970s.

The James Report (DES, 1972) proposed that INSET should be more supportive of curriculum development and the view there was a fairly instrumental one which saw INSET as a form of training to support the innovations funded by the schools council. The idea that such INSET should be at least school focused if not actually school-based was put forward and it is significant that one of the main issues addressed by James was the question of the links between higher education and the school context.

Lawrence Stenhouse and his colleagues at the Centre for Applied Research in Education (CARE) were actively engaged in wrestling with these dilemmas at that time but the experience with the Humanities Curriculum Project (HCP) suggested the need for something which went beyond instruction in new methods and the dissemination of new materials. The Ford Teaching Project followed on the heels of HCP as a means of tackling the problem at the level of the consciousness of the teachers involved in the innovation. The idea of the teacher-as-researcher suggested that successful curriculum innovation depended on the possibility of developing teachers' pedagogical understanding through research.

Stenhouse encapsulated the idea neatly in the mid-1970s when he argued that there can be no curriculum development without teacher development (Stenhouse, 1975). Although it must have been clear to him that it would be difficult to establish classroom research as a routine activity for the profession as a whole. Reflecting on the work of the Ford Teaching Project he said:

> But it remains an enterprise for enthusiasts, people who tinker in their classrooms as motor cycle enthusiasts tinker in their backyards: prepared to give a lot of time to increasing performance. (Stenhouse, 1980a, p. 251)

Development Planning

The idea of teachers collaborating to take the curriculum forward through some sort of collaborative enquiry-based process became more systematized in the form of GRIDS (Guidelines for Review and Internal Development in Schools). It is interesting that the emphasis here was on the idea of the whole school being involved in a rational and managed developmental process (Abbott, R. *et al.*, 1988). Being a system for whole-school review and development, GRIDS did address the question of the curriculum in its institutional setting as a direct focus for enquiry. The system provided a means by which a school could evaluate its curriculum provision and set targets for development. One crucial variable in this approach is the use of the outsider in the role of 'critical friend'. The review process itself can be facilitated by outside agencies or consultants but the quality of the enquiry and development work which arises depends on the evaluation criteria the school sets itself. GRIDS was promoted and supported by the now-defunct Schools Council but the lessons learned through GRIDS have been taken up and given direct (if rather tacit) backing by the Government through the advice it has disseminated on whole-school development planning. The concept of the curriculum audit is now enshrined in documentation which carries the DES stamp of approval (Hargreaves and Hopkins, 1991).

The concept of the 'audit' has been with us for some time as a term used by the managing classes to refer to the data-gathering activity which is required when managers wish to 'take stock' as a prelude to decision-making about curriculum provision. It is a term which may have seemed to some people more legitimate than the term 'action research'. 'Action research' is a term which smacks of the emancipatory rhetoric which Stenhouse espoused while 'audit', being part of the language of accountancy, tends to put us in mind of the cost effectiveness/account-ability culture of the 1980s.

INSET and Curriculum Development

In spite of this stimulus for school-based enquiry it seems to be the case, in Kent at least, that reflective practice and research-based teaching have struggled to keep a foothold. There will, of course, be individual schools who will claim that they are ahead of the crowd in this respect but, in my experience, inquiry-led development is still in its infancy. It may well be true that schools have been able to undertake the rational, whole-school review which has identified targets for development and so on but the difficulty is that once these targets have been set, individual teachers have then to undertake the necessary professional development and this has tended to be limited to 'INSET'. This term is generally used as a label for a commodity consisting largely of off-the-shelf, content-based, instructional programmes delivered at a college of higher education, a teachers' centre or in the school itself. Since TVEI (Technical and Vocational Educational Initiative) of course it has been common place to use a hotel.

The key question is whether such INSET programmes lead to or are supportive of any meaningful professional action on the part of those who have attended. Course providers have for a long time struggled with this problem. One way of dealing with it has been to follow the advice set out in the James Report and include some instruction about the management of the implementation process. So the story of the 'myth of the hero-innovator' is invariably trotted out to demonstrate the need for the organizational development which must accompany or even precede curriculum innovation (Georgiades and Phillimore, 1975). However, understanding the problem does not necessarily lead to successful implementation. INSET course providers have also tried strategies which are based on the notion that if the individual has the will and the management skills to go with it they will be able to prevail over an inert institution or reluctant colleagues. This leads to end-of-course workshops which enable participants to set targets, short-, medium- and long-term; workshops which enable course participants to engage in self-assessment exercises to sharpen up their leadership skills and so on. Some courses providers have even adopted amusing strategies such as asking the participants to write down personal statements of intention which are then posted to them some months after the end of the course in the hope that this reminder will shame them into more strenuous action. Despite all these attempts on the part of INSET providers, school-staff development co-ordinators still report that they find it difficult to ensure that their school reaps the benefit in return for the money spent on sending individual members of staff on such INSET programmes.

Action Research and Curriculum Development

Whatever the case it is probably true to say that research or inquiry activities conducted by teachers are most likely to flourish or at least be made public in the form of case studies when linked to some kind of long-term, award-bearing programme validated by an institution of higher education. This particular form of support can distort the nature of the activity of course (Elliot, 1991) but I shall be discussing that problem later in this chapter.

There is, of course, a strong tradition of action research in the context of award-bearing programmes and this is an achievement which is to be celebrated. It would seem to be the case that teachers have successfully colonized the world of higher education and have helped to shape masters and diploma programmes in such a way that they tend now to be more purposeful and directly supportive of curriculum development. This is manifest in a variety of forms: accounts of action research in dissertations, short papers based on critical narratives about episodes of curriculum development for example. Latterly the idea of the curriculum-development portfolio has emerged as a key device for the accreditation of institution-based enquiry and development.

The difficulty with all these developments however is that they tend to be individualistic and so the problem of the match between the needs of the individual and the needs of the institution remains. On the one hand the individual teacher has professional and academic concerns which are determined in part by the individual's biography; their vested interests; their values and conception of good professional practice. These concerns are also embraced by the individual's need for self-actualization; the need to express and develop their point of view. On the other hand there are the policy imperatives of the institution; the vested interests of various groups and individuals within the power structure of the school; the priorities determined by whatever may be the apparatus for corporate planning within the institution.

The School's Priorities and the Interests of Individual Teachers

What was common ground between myself and my collaborators at Southlands School was the belief that it is vital to support teacher research with all that implies about the development of a genuine criticality but in a way which enables the school to secure the maximum benefit in terms of their curriculum-development priorities. In addition, the shift in funding arrangements for INSET has brought the problem into sharper focus for those of us working in teacher education.

We turned our attention then to ways in which we might be able to offer more systematic encouragement to colleagues who were prepared to engage in such research. We decided to develop a partnership between the school and college which would enable us to set up within the school itself an award-bearing, programme of support for action research. We — myself as the college tutor and Jim Nixon, the newly promoted staff-development coordinator — would be co-tutors on a bespoke diploma programme and staff would be invited to apply to the headteacher for a free place. The introduction of the project was supported by a brochure the central message of which hinged on four key words:

- recognition;
- support;
- enhancement; and
- accreditation.

It was put to colleagues that they were the unsung heroes of curriculum development most of whom engaged in hard work which generated results which in other contexts would be dignified by terms such as 'study' and 'research'. It was time that this valuable work was made visible and due credit given. It was also put to colleagues that innovation and development were often thankless tasks which resulted in feelings of isolation and frustration. Our diploma project offered the possibility of support through membership of a curriculum research and development-support group. Within this group, protected as it would be by rules of confidentiality, individuals could share their problems and derive much needed succour. The third principle was concerned with the idea of enhancing the development work normally undertaken by providing a structured framework and criteria against which to judge the outcomes. We had in mind a process model in which we would offer the challenge and critique which would make the research and development work more rigorous. Finally we put forward the notion that we were offering a means by which colleagues could put forward evidence of their research and development work in order to claim credit towards a diploma and subsequently an MA in curriculum development.

In practical terms this meant a series of monthly 'twilight' sessions held at the school and jointly led by the college tutor and the in-school tutor. Reports of enquiry-based curriculum-development work would be assembled in the form of a curriculum-development portfolio. The portfolio idea was a key element and one which underwent radical development within the first year of the project.

The headteacher of Southlands was prepared to support the project on the understanding that the school would benefit in the ways indicated earlier. It was our view, however, that the project was recognized by the head as having benefits which go far beyond support for curriculum development and subsequent interviews supported this view. The head said that:

> I believe that teachers are professionals and should be self-reflective practitioners. The more we can do to encourage them to step back, look at their role, and analyse it the better. It leads to better teaching and, in the end, the kids benefit.

We also assumed that the school was prepared to back the project because of the obvious implications for the culture of the school as an organization. The rationale for the project together with its aims were included in the portfolio guidance document provided for the participants and these are reproduced below:

Rationale for the Project

The Southlands/Christ Church Professional Development Project is based on a process model. That is to say that it rests on the following assumptions:

(a) that the school is accountable for the allocation of funds for professional development;

(b) that the school has a responsibility to allocate such funds in ways which will increase the quality of the curriculum as experienced by students in the classrooms;

(c) that the curriculum can best be improved through the enhanced professionalism of teachers;

(d) that the practices of teachers are improved when they take responsibility for their own professional learning by engaging in action-research and reflecting systematically on practice;

(e) that the school has a responsibility to ensure that the teachers' curriculum and professional development work is fully recognised.

It is central to the project that individual teacher's professional concerns are matched with the priorities identified through the process of whole-school development planning. It is axiomatic therefore that the focuses of action-research are the subject of negotiation. In this way it is hoped that the project will make a major contribution, not only to the curriculum but perhaps more importantly to the development culture of the school as a whole.

Aims of the Project

The project seeks to support curriculum and professional development which will enhance the quality of learning experienced by students at Southlands School. Specifically the project will:

- provide a framework for colleague's professional action plans;
- support and encourage collaborative action research;
- enable colleagues to develop their capacity for reflective practice;
- provide opportunities for debate and discussion about the curriculum; and
- enhance colleagues' career development through the recognition of professional learning and development work.

Aiming for Empowerment

In fact our aims might be best understood in terms of the empowerment of teachers and the promotion of a range of values related to reflective practice, professional collegiality, and the development of critical pedagogy.

Through our dialogue about professional development and school improvement we had been able to articulate for ourselves a set of values which, if fully realized in practice would lead to a range of outcomes which are centrally concerned with the empowerment of teachers to:

- develop their capacity for curriculum debate;
- develop their self-awareness and sense of professional growth;
- increase their ability and motivation to engage in curriculum decision-making;
- increase their capacity for honest self-evaluation;
- develop a critique of educational policies at both local and national levels; and
- increase their ability to build and test theories about teaching and learning.

To some observers this aim of empowering colleagues in the school may seem to represent a contradiction. It is assumed by many that he who pays the piper calls the tune. Holly, for example, has argued that action research and schools have 'dichotomous, polar tendencies'. His cautionary comments suggested that:

Action research fosters collegiality, informality, openness and collaboration across boundaries, etc. while institutions veer towards the hierarchical, bureaucratic and formal. (Holly, 1984, p. 100)

When the project was first floated it was suggested by one of the university members of the board of examiners (all college courses were validated by the University of Kent) that the location of the project within the single school might be an inhibiting factor — that, for example, the role of tutor as exercised by the school staff-development coordinator might prove to be a tool of senior-management manipulation. We were also aware of the benefits that can be derived from offsite residential courses in terms of honest reflection and a dynamic sharing of ideas and viewpoints.

Nevertheless we were optimistic that the project could be made to work in such a way that the interests of the parties involved — the school, the teachers, the college — could be served. I would argue that we consciously set about the building in of safeguards which would promote academic freedom and offset the power advantage that the school had through its control of funding. Firstly there were initiatives which were concerned with the ethical framework of the project and secondly there was the research perspective adopted by the project leaders.

The Ethical Framework for Action Research

At the outset of the project the participants expressed concerns about the extent of their freedom in respect of data gathering and the confidentiality of our group discussions. As tutors we had demanded that our discussions should be regarded as confidential amongst ourselves but what about the school's right to know? The participants themselves were quite anxious about this. One member of the group said that her head of department had already demanded that any data-gathering exercise should be approved by him in advance and that he should have the right to have first sight of any data collected. Another senior manager had demanded the right to see any papers the participants wrote in the context of the project. After discussion with the group we drew up a list of ethical principles (listed below) which we asked the senior management to agree to. These principles have now been incorporated into the portfolio guidance booklet for the scheme as a whole.

Ethical Guidelines for an Action Research Group

1　Discussions and tutorials which take place in the group and in tutorials must be regarded as absolutely confidential.
2　It would be unethical for any individual to make use of disclosures within the group in other decision-making contexts.
3　Each individual's portfolio should be regarded as their own property and should be used entirely at their own discretion.
4　Whilst group members are asked to produce appropriate papers for professional audiences at regular intervals they should not be obliged to present all their papers to audiences within the school.
5　In the writing of evaluative material, group members should avoid identifying individual colleagues or students who may feature in the data.
6　Where individuals can be identified because of the context, the writer should always seek the agreement of those identified, firstly as to the validity of the data and secondly as to whether the material may be published.

7　Group members should have the right to develop a critical analysis of current practices and policies without fear of damage to their standing in the school.

The agreement to these principles provided all of us in the project with a clear framework for action and, as a result, participants felt considerably safer. We also believed that colleagues outside the project would be reassured about the gathering and use of data.

An essential part of this ethical dimension was the question of the roles of the tutors and those of the managers who had oversight of the work of the project. Jim Nixon and myself acted as co-tutors with complementary areas of experience and expertise. We had deliberately cast others in the role of 'line manager'. The process at the core of the project demanded that participants consult with their line manager about the focus of their development work. The intention was to stimulate a dialogue between teachers in the school. It was clearly important for Jim to try to remain detached from the policy questions embedded in the participant's proposals. The tutor's role in this situation was to become a 'critical friend' who could advise and challenge colleagues in terms of their enquiry strategies, their analysis and the presentation of their ideas. It was for the participants' line managers who were not directly involved in the project to agree on the validity of the focus of the participant's work. It was significant I think that Jim was not then a member of the senior-management team and it raises the question of whether senior managers could ever adopt a plausible critical friend role within their own schools.

In the second year of the project the whole question of accountability and audience was re-examined and a new policy was agreed. This is dealt with more fully later on in this chapter.

Adopting a Research Perspective

The second dimension of what I have referred to above as 'safeguards' is concerned with our commitment as project leaders to research as a means of self-monitoring and as a way of opening up the project to public scrutiny. It must also be borne in mind that we had to demonstrate a commitment to action research as part of our presentation to teachers in the school. We felt obliged to practice what we preached and therefore both of us engaged visibly in classroom self-evaluation in the school and shared accounts of this with the group. More importantly perhaps, was our commitment to treating the project itself as problematic and open to ongoing evaluation.

The portfolio-guidance booklet issued to all participants at the start of the programme included the following statement:

The scheme is also framed as research and will therefore be the subject of monitoring and evaluation which will enable the school and the college to develop:

(a)　new understandings about the possibilities for school-based professional development; and

(b)　more effective strategies for the management of professional development in schools.

It was important for us to reflect on the development of the project and to encourage the group as a whole to engage in such reflection. As in-service tutors we have found Stenhouse's simple statement that research is 'systematic enquiry made public' most useful in the context of the promotion of action research within the school and, in relation to our own action research we have taken steps to make our work visible and to generate discussion about the project (Stenhouse, 1980b).

From the outset we established a number of procedures for the gathering of evidence and set up a panel of disinterested scrutineers to help us consider the issues emerging in the early stages. This early evaluation enabled us to make immediate changes, the most significant of which are described below.

Developing the Portfolio Structure

Before the project began the potential participants were consulted over the structure of the portfolios. We were keen to address the need to make the 'practices of everyday life' visible and credit worthy within an award-bearing programme but had not really thought beyond the traditional case-study approach. It was decided that each participant would undertake three separate tasks: the first would be a paper which provided an account of an episode of classroom-based self-evaluation; the second would be a paper which analysed a curriculum area of particular concern (e.g., careers education) and the third was a paper which examined the management of change implications of the writer's curriculum development work. These papers would be put together and made coherent by the inclusion of a reflective commentary which put the material in context; highlighted the writer's professional concerns and accounted for the development which had arisen from the research. There were some difficulties with this approach however: although the project aimed to accredit the curriculum-development work teachers were undertaking as part of their professional commitment the structures we put in place to support reflection and enquiry were getting in the way. We seemed to be guilty of engaging in what Elliott has termed 'academic imperialism'. These accounts of self-evaluation and curriculum development were not that far removed from the sort of traditional essays written by students on the college-based diploma. This is not to say that these papers were not perceived to be useful as the following extract from one of the participants' commentary illustrates:

> There is no question in my mind that the work in this portfolio has guided my thinking on a number of important issues both theoretical and practical. During a period of considerable change in education and particularly within this school, the need for research, evaluation and reflection upon the issues and problems which are very real to us has been invaluable.

The papers clearly did provide a framework within which participants could conduct systematic enquiry and reflect on the professional issues which confronted them but unfortunately they were also perceived to be *extra* tasks which for some proved to be an intolerable burden. Our aim had been to enhance professional practices rather than to add on new demands; in this respect we felt that we were failing. Elliott's point is that higher education institutions have tended to transform the way professionals reflect on their work so that it fits into the traditional academic arrangements. He asks the question:

> Are the academics transforming the methodology of teacher-based educational inquiry into a form which enables them to manipulate and control teachers' thinking in order to reproduce the central assumptions which have underpinned a contemplative academic culture detached from the practices of everyday life? (Elliott, 1991, p. 14)

As project leaders we were obliged to find a way to narrow the gap between the academic requirements of the programme and the professional obligations of the participants.

The Concept of Reflective Action Planning

As a response to this problem we devised an approach to portfolio development which we refer to as 'reflective action planning'. Essentially this involves a piecemeal approach to the collection of evidence of systematic, enquiry-based, curriculum development and reflection. It entails a requirement for participants to produce action plans which are the subject of consultation with both the line manager in the school and a college tutor. The line manager ensures that the development work matches the priorities identified through the school's development planning arrangements and the tutor challenges the enquiry strategies specified in the plans.

Our new portfolio structure was based on the distinction between items of evidence which were intended for professional audiences and ones which were intended only for academic audiences. Some items would serve both purposes of course. So participants would be asked to write an 'initial development plan' which would be a short statement describing the main focus for curriculum development work envisaged over the forthcoming twelve-month period and some indication of priorities. This document would be used by the participant as a basis for consultation with the line manager and quite often would be used as a starting point for discussion about roles, responsibilities and incentive allowances. The development plan would be followed by a series of action plans in which the participant would be asked to specify the particular focus for development over the forthcoming few weeks, the intentions regarding implementation, inquiry and possible outcomes. This plan would again facilitate consultations with both the line manager and the project tutor about the wisdom of the course of action to be pursued. The plan would specify any inquiry to be carried out whether it be some kind of curriculum audit or an evaluation of a unit of teaching. A most crucial aspect of the action plan is concerned with reporting and I think that it is worth dwelling on this because of its relevance for accountability.

Reporting and Accountability within the School

The action-planning format provided in the portfolio guidance booklet asks the participants to identify their intentions regarding the reporting of their development work. It is for the participant to decide what kind of reports are professionally appropriate and to agree this with the line manager. This issue emerged as quite a contentious one in the development of the project. In the first year of the project the participants were asked to produce a series of papers the focus of which had to be agreed by both the line manager and the college tutor and, while the participants were encouraged to present their papers to colleagues in the school, in practice they tended not to. During the interviews conducted in the third term the headteacher pointed out that he knew very little about the outcomes of all this inquiry and development work. He wanted to know a great deal more about what he was getting for his money and thought that 'tangible outcomes' should be widely available within the school. A simple solution offered by one of the senior managers in the school was that all participants completed portfolios should be handed in to the deputy head responsible for the project. This was resisted by the project tutors on the grounds that we would have to renege on the ethical principles agreed at the outset of the project. We did not believe that participants would feel sufficiently free to reflect fully on the issues or on their own performance if they knew that all of their work would be seen by the senior-management team. Nevertheless we agreed with senior managers that the school had a right to expect some tangible outcomes which went beyond the more general aims of supporting reflective practice. After some discussion we arrived at the idea that in their action plans every participant should specify the professional audience they would report to, on what date and in what form. We also agreed that the school had a right to expect a report of some kind at least once per term. These documents might take the form of, for example, a short audit report presented to colleagues within the participant's department or to a middle-management team. The important thing is that the audience, the format and the timescale were to be agreed with the appropriate line manager.

Evidence of Reflection and the Academic Audience

So the portfolio would contain a development plan, a series of continuously updated action plans and whatever professional reports were agreed to be useful but this would not be sufficient for a portfolio submitted as a module within the college's diploma and MEd structure. There also needed to be evidence of reflection which went beyond what might have been deemed to be professionally useful. Participants were encouraged to keep journals, to record aspects of their participation in the project and to draw upon this data together with the professional-inquiry tasks they had undertaken in order to write a 'critical narrative' at the end of each term. The critical narrative would provide an overview of the development work and would highlight and explore the issues which arise from that work. Some of this analysis might be of the sort which the participants could not comfortably share with colleagues in the school. Micropolitical issues for example might have to be glossed over if all papers were to be presented to the deputy head. So the critical narrative provided an opportunity for the participants to address issues which went beyond the day-to-day professional discourse within the organization of the school. On this basis we sustained the agreement that the portfolios as such would not have to be presented to the senior management unless a particular participant chose to do so. Additionally, to ensure that the portfolio would make sense to an outside audience such as the external examiner it was important that participants should also include a thread of reflective commentary which put the evidence in context and provided some basic signposts.

The Portfolio Guidance Booklet

This rather more sophisticated approach to portfolio development required a more complex set of guidance materials. I devised a portfolio guidance booklet which was intended as a reliable source of information and guidance on the matter of evidence for the portfolio. The current edition of the booklet runs to about sixty pages and contains pages of information such as 'Assessment Criteria'; it also contains pages of explanation such as 'The Reflective Action Planning Process'. But the most crucial part of the document is perhaps the guidance on evidence for the portfolio. Each type of document is introduced with some brief guidelines and then in each case a format consisting of a series of annotated headings is set out. Participants report that the guidance booklet is a reliable tool which allows a flexibility of response.

Continuing the Research through Parallel Case Studies

As indicated earlier the original project was developed at Southlands School where it is now in its third year. As I write, the scheme is operating in a similar form in thirteen schools but it is clear from my own experience and that of my colleagues that there are significant variables in terms of the dilemmas and issues from school to school. For example, in one school the line-management system is well advanced but in another it is unheard of. In one school tutorials for participants are facilitated by the school providing release during the school day but in another school the project can only operate after 5.00 pm. The essential research questions emerging are concerned with the interface between teachers' action research and the school cultures within which they operate so it is imperative to examine the development of such groups in more than one school. It seems sensible therefore to try to set up parallel case studies in which the same themes are explored through a common data-gathering approach in three or more schools. Such an approach would also have the advantage of extending the dimension of collaboration as far as this research is concerned.

So far my research endeavours have only involved, in a direct sense, myself and my co-tutor at Southlands. But, as the scheme continues to develop it is important to extend the research activity to include a wider circle of collaborators and external sceptics. I needed therefore to draw my colleagues into a collaborative research process in the much expanded tutor team. However, I am concerned that, in spite of a contractual obligation to engage in 'scholastic activity' it may be seen as unreasonable to expect colleagues to engage in extensive data gathering and analysis which is very time consuming. It is therefore incumbent on me as a facilitator of this action research to devise a research method which can be built-in to the day-to-day professional undertakings of tutors on the scheme rather than one which belongs to the disembodied world of 'research'. I have to avoid the trap encapsulated in this comment:

> All too often research is viewed as something teachers do *on* their practice. They step out of their pedagogical role. Teaching and research become posited as separate activities, whereas from the standpoint of the practitioner reflection and action are simply two aspects of a single process. (Elliott, 1991, p. 14)

The case studies will rest therefore on evidence gathered according to an agreed system which is fully integrated into the tutor's work with the school-based groups. The system will be based on similar principles to those governing the portfolio-guidance material.

A small research grant enables me to support a collaborative process in which we meet to consider the evidence presented in the case record and clarify the issues and dilemmas arising within each theme. The grant also makes it possible to gather additional data through interviews conducted by an outsider. As a team we will then consider and develop a set of principles of procedure which are based on my experience with the Southlands Project. Throughout the next academic year the themes already established will be explored using the evidence coming forward from several school-based action-research groups in the scheme and the composite case record will be used as an evidential base for a fresh thematic analysis and the testing of our principles of procedure before a variety of disinterested and sceptical audiences.

The Case Record

Our experience of the last three years has been gathered together to establish what Stenhouse called a 'case record' (Stenhouse, 1978). The purpose of the case record is to make the evidence accessible to others and open to critical interpretation. Essentially the case record consists of:

- summaries of tape-recorded conversations between myself and my co-tutor recorded immediately after each group session;
- summaries of field notes and journal entries;
- summaries of evaluation sheets;
- extracts from participants' portfolios;
- a selection of documents such as minutes of meetings, discussion papers etc.;
- a selection of teaching materials such as facsimiles and case studies; and
- summaries and quotations from semi-structured interviews.

The items of evidence are assembled with a commentary which puts them into a time frame and explains the context in which they were created. So this case record constitutes the evidential base which has enabled me to conduct a thematic analysis and establish the focus for further investigation.

Thematic Analysis from the Case Record

So, the experience of the Southlands Project has made possible the identification of the major issues and dilemmas which can now be explored more systematically through the parallel case studies. These issues and dilemmas are best dealt with under thematic headings which enable me to do two things: firstly, the identification of themes enables us to tap into the experience of others by providing a number of focal points for study of the available literature and, secondly, it has provided a framework for the design of the procedures for gathering further evidence.

Dilemmas and Issues Emerging

So what are the issues and dilemmas which form the core of the next stage in this enquiry?

1 The nature of collaborative relationships

The project is a collaboration between schools and the college; between in-school tutors and college tutors; between the participants and their line managers; and between the participants themselves. The word collaboration has a comforting ring to it but we cannot afford to take for granted the nature of this collaboration. We need to explore the dynamic of the collaboration in these various relationships; the degree to which aims are shared; the extent of the commonality and difference between co-tutors' roles; the questions of authority, power and vested interest which may arise in the relationship between participants and their colleagues in the school.

2 The management of development priorities

It is an essential characteristic of the project that the schools' managers have influence over the participants' research and development work. The portfolio guidance material asks participants to consult their line manager about their personal-development plan and action plans for the curriculum-development work they have agreed to undertake. Participants are also required to report to appropriate professional audiences in the school. Here we need to explore the nature of the role of the line manager and the participants' expectations of it; the nature of the consultation process; the kind of discourse that takes place during these consultations and the impact of them on the direction and content of the participants enquiries.

3 The nature of the tutor's role

This project has taken the college tutors out of their traditional setting and presented them with particular challenges. The project relies on tutors being able to facilitate and support systematic curriculum-development work based on sound principles of enquiry but this takes place in the 'real world' context of the school where the tutor has relatively little control. Tutors are expected to sustain some kind of leadership role in the group and this relies on a measure of trust and acceptance on the part of the participants. The tutor also has to develop mentoring and counselling skills to be able to support individuals' action planning and reflection. In more traditional settings tutors have been able to draw upon expert knowledge in particular specialist areas but in this scenario, tutors find themselves leading seminars about topics which are relatively unfamiliar territory. These facets of the tutor's role are challenging and can lead to problems of role clarity. We need therefore to examine more systematically these dimensions of the tutor's role and to consider in particular the nature of the pedagogy which is developing in this sort of context. The impact of the work on tutors' self-image and professional development is also a crucial question.

4 The effectiveness of the support group

The project is supported by a programme of monthly workshops which provides support for the reflective action-planning process and enables the tutors to conduct seminars on themes chosen by the group. The group provides a forum for debate and for the sharing of ideas but, more than this perhaps, it helps individuals to overcome the isolation which many participants have identified as a characteristic of their working lives. So, we need to explore the strategies used by tutors to facilitate critical debate in such a closed, micro-political environment; the strategies and skills employed in supporting individual action planning; the processes involved in maintaining a balance between the everyday reality of the school and the introduction of ideas and experience from outside; and the dynamic of the group sessions.

5 The benefits to the institution

From the outset it was intended that the project should lead to enhanced curriculum and professional development but, towards the end of the first year doubts arose about the lack of 'tangible outcomes'. The project was then adapted in order to express more clearly the requirement that participants report to professional audiences within the school but this does raise the question of what counts as 'tangible outcomes' and how such outcomes can be recognized and evaluated. Interviews with senior managers in the school indicate something of a contradiction in that outcomes are seen by turns as the development of participants' professionalism and then in terms of more concrete action. It is critical then that we explore the notion of 'tangible outcomes' to try to clarify how a school can benefit from such a project, what counts as 'benefits' and how these benefits can be recognized and acknowledged.

6 The benefits to the individual participants

Clearly if the development of the participants' professionalism is seen as a benefit to the school it begs the question of what kinds of benefits there could be for the individual participants and what tensions there are between the institutional and individual benefits. The foundation of the project assumes the possibility of mutuality here. In other words we proceed with some faith that the enhancement of individuals' skills, knowledge, competence, understanding, personal qualities and qualifications in terms of both professional and personal development will be seen as beneficial to the school and will be recognized in terms of promotion and career advancement. It is immediately clear then that we need to focus on the question: what kinds of enhancement does the project lead to and what is the impact of this on the institution? We also need to explore the costs to the individual participants. This kind of exploration needs to take full account of individuals' personal lives as well as the professional roles they play.

7 The nature of evidence and the process of accreditation

Perhaps the most innovative aspect of the project is the development of the structure of the portfolio and the design of the guidance materials which supports the process (see Frost, 1993). This system enables participants to accumulate and present evidence of their systematic curriculum development work and of their critical reflection on that work in a format which is more in keeping with actual professional work rather than in a way which is seen as a bolt-on academic exercise. The move away from the traditional essay or report writing tends to be perceived initially as an easy option but the nature of the portfolio presents unexpected challenges. Many of the participants take time to adapt to a system where they are called upon to generate authentic evidence of professional work. Others find difficulty in distinguishing between documents which are produced for professional audiences in the school and those written for purely reflective purposes. There are also difficulties with the presentation and labelling of documents and these may be purely practical ones but they may also indicate some underlying conceptual problems. This is therefore a clear focus for further investigation and one which should lead to further improvements in the design of the portfolio structure.

8   The organizational environment of the project

It has already been made clear that the project is a collaborative one funded and managed by the school. The project depends on the notion of participants having line managers with whom they can negotiate their development priorities and to whom they can report progress. So far we have experienced difficulties with this in that some individuals have reported that their line manager does not have time to talk to them or that there is lack of clarity about who occupies this role. The project makes demands on the management of the school in that participants need support in establishing their priorities and in maintaining momentum. To some degree, action planning arising from the project has been linked to appraisal and this tends to provide clarity and support for the individual. In other cases individuals find it difficult to engage with their own institutions and to be clear about how their professional work fits into the school's development plan. The project has also presented challenges to the organization when participants' analysis of particular curricular problems conflict with the assumptions of their line managers. Here we are beginning to test the limits of the development of criticality within the single institution. More positively, the project has seemed to contribute to the development culture of the school by enabling participants to explore more systematically issues concerned with the management of change. Whatever the case, there is a clear need to examine more closely the interface between the project and the school as an organization.

This initial thematic analysis enables us to generate some provisional 'principles of procedure' which will provide a guiding framework for action and a focus for continued evaluation.

Principles of Procedure

The project was born out of certain beliefs and value positions shared between myself and my co-tutor at Southlands School (see Nixon, 1992). We developed and rehearsed these shared values and beliefs about our work through an ongoing dialogue and they formed the criteria for judgment as we developed and evaluated the scheme. However, in extending the collaboration I am conscious of the need for a more coherent and detailed expression of principles which can be shared and developed in collaboration with my fellow tutor-researchers. The term 'principles of procedure' is one which Stenhouse took from R.S. Peters and used to mean those criteria which determine validity in an educative process (Stenhouse, 1975). There is always a danger in any systems-based approach that the technology involved — in this case, it is mostly embodied in the portfolio guidance booklet — can become a stultifying straitjacket which undermines tutors' and participants' sense of ownership. Our scheme can only move forward as a team effort which necessarily entails the development of shared values and practices (see Rudduck, 1991). Statements about principles of procedure do not dictate particular strategies nor particular learning outcomes. Instead they provide a set of process criteria which can be debated and used to evaluate particular strategies. Set out below is the first draft of a proposed set of principles of procedure:

A school-based, award bearing, in-service, curriculum-development support project is likely to be successful if it:

- is tutored collaboratively by a member of the school staff and a tutor from an HEI;
- is conducted in a fully equipped seminar room on the school premises or other convenient site;
- provides support and sanction for open-ended enquiry;
- provides a framework of guidance for individuals' professional action planning;
- facilitates the matching of individuals' action planning to the school's development priorities;
- is supported by the management arrangements of the school;
- provides a confidential forum for critical analysis of curricular issues;
- challenges participants' assumptions about educational issues;
- demands rigour in participants' professional enquiries;
- facilitates the recognition of individuals' professional achievement;
- supports the use of enquiry strategies which make a good fit with teachers' professional work;
- values and accepts piecemeal evidence of systematic curriculum development work;
- provides guidance and clarification about the nature of evidence of action planning, development work, enquiry and critical reflection;
- engages teachers in critical dialogue with their line managers about curricular and professional issues;
- facilitates career development through the award of further professional qualifications;
- encourages teachers to take responsibility for their own professional learning;
- provides an ethical framework for the development of critiques of educational policies at both local and national levels; and
- empowers teachers to benefit from, and contribute to, wider educational discourse.

This list of principles of procedure is merely a first attempt and will be developed through the collaborative process and through discussion with critical friends and disinterested scrutineers. What I hope will emerge from our collaborative research is a more complete and definitive set of principles which can be used to guide such schemes in the future.

In addition our research should yield more effective strategies for enabling teachers to integrate systematic enquiry into their everyday professional work. Our case studies should serve to make our work visible so that other schools and HEIs may be able to learn from our experience but what is perhaps more important is that, through our case studies and the principles which are emerging, we will be able to contribute to the debate about the value and the limits of school-based, action-research approaches to continuing teacher education.

David Bridges has argued that the assumptions underpinning reflective practice, derived as they are from pragmatist philosophies, may lead to an impoverishment of teacher education in a school-based setting. He has expressed the view that both new and experienced teachers need to be challenged by:

> the abrasion of viewpoint against viewpoint, and the expansion and challenge to one's own assumptions which comes from being confronted actively and critically by the ideas, principles, moral commitment and professional theories (in the widest sense of the word) of others. (Bridges, D., Ch. 18 in this volume)

Although this research began from a position of optimism about the promotion of authentic and genuinely critical forms of enquiry it would be naive to deny the possibility that we may also discover the limits of such endeavours within a relatively closed institutional setting. However we are fully committed to ensuring that participants draw fully on the traditions of action research and on the experience of others through reading and critical debate and our experience so far suggests that our initial optimism is not entirely unfounded.

References

ABBOTT, R. (1988) *GRIDS School Handbooks*, York, Longmans.

BRIDGES, D. (1995) 'Teacher Education: The poverty of pragmatism' (see chapter 18 in this volume).

DES (1972) *Teacher Education and Training — The James Report*, HMSO.

DFE (1992) Circular 9/92.

ELLIOTT, J. (1991) *Action Research For Educational Change*, Milton Keynes, Open University Press.

ELLIOTT, J. (1993) *Reconstructing Teacher Education*, London, Falmer Press.

FROST, D. (1993) *Portfolio Guidance Booklet — A Guide to Reflective Action Planning*, Canterbury Christ Church College.

GEORGIADES, N.J. and PHILLIMORE, L. (1975) 'The myth of the hero-innovator and alternative strategies for change', in KEIRNAN, C.C. and WOODFORD, F.P. (Eds) *Behaviour Modification with the Severely Retarded*, Netherlands, Elseveir Excerpta Medica, North Holland.

HARGREAVES, D. and HOPKINS, D. (1991) *The Empowered School*, London, Cassell.

HOLLY, P. (1984) 'Action Research: A Cautionary Note', *CARN Bulletin No 6*, Cambridge Institute of Education.

NIXON, J. (1992) 'The Accreditation of Curriculum Development: Enhancing the Process of Reflection through Accreditation — A New Partnership Between Schools and Higher Education', Unpublished MA Dissertation, Canterbury Christ Church College.

RUDDUCK, J. (1991) *Innovation and Change*, Milton Keynes, Open University Press.

STENHOUSE, L. (1975) *An Introduction to Curriculum Research and Development*, London, Heinemann Educational Books.

STENHOUSE, L. (1978) 'Case study and case records: Towards a contemporary history of education', *British Educational Research Journal*, **4**, 2.

STENHOUSE, L. (Ed) (1980a) *Curriculum Research and Development in Action*, London, Heinemann Educational Books.

STENHOUSE, L. (1980b) 'The study of samples and the study of cases', *British Educational Research Journal*, **6**, 1, pp. 1–6.

17 The Hunter-gatherer Academic in the Higher Educational Jungle: A View from a University School of Education

Rob McBride

Introduction

This is a personal narrative. I argue that this type of presentation is particularly effective at a time of great change. It is during such periods that it is difficult to accurately represent oneself or one's feelings and sometimes the temptation is to cry out. I suspect many people engaged in education have felt like this in recent years. There is a sense of betrayal (see MacLure, 1989; McBride, 1994). This piece, then describes my situation as *I* see it. Plainly I cannot make a strong claim that I am representing a group or that my situation is replicated around the country yet I would be surprised if my situation was that unique. I make a 'soft' claim that what I describe here is replicated elsewhere but the most important reason for writing is not to linger on such claims but to describe my situation. It is immediate and unclear but it seems to be happening. I leave the power of generalization to the reader.

All of this volume deals with the learning and treatment of teachers, as they undertake either initial or in-service education. This is the age of concern for teachers. In the educational literature teachers are seen as being badly treated in their work and without control over their central task — creating the curriculum with their pupils. This chapter deals with myself as an academic, still a teacher but employed in a university.

In 1987, I decided that after some years of trying I could no longer be part of what I considered to be the educational establishment. I had moved from being a teacher to being an LEA adviser, I had worked in a large research and development project funded by the Department of Education and Science and had subsequently returned to the classroom. The last of these experiences had helped me to recapture some of my love for schools and teaching but there was still a vacuum to be filled. With the support of my family I moved to the School of Education at the University of East Anglia as a PhD student and shortly after my arrival I was employed there, albeit in a part time and lowly capacity. This is an essential part of my story for while I have always been committed to research and academic endeavour, I also needed to contribute my share to the income of my family with its three young children. I have had to be prepared to hustle for my living. I would not do anything I considered wrong, bad or very dull but I have had to survive. In the circumstances I have become, partly to my surprise, what can be called a hunter-gatherer.

The Context

At the time of my arrival in September 1987, the School of Education at UEA was beginning to undergo a major reconceptualization of itself. The school had received a double knock to its income in the mid-1980s. In 1985–6 it found that its large BA programme would no longer satisfy new regulations from the Council for the Accreditation of Teacher Education [CATE] and decided to close down the degree and transfer its student numbers to its Post Graduate Certificate of Education. The transfer never completely occurred and the school lost both students and the associated funding. During the same year, across the board financial cuts from central government meant that in total the school's income was cut by some 27 per cent in one year.

In 1986 the Local Education Authority Training Grant Scheme [LEATGS] or GRIST (Grant Related In-service Training Scheme) as it was popularly known, was introduced (McBride, 1989). One effect of this scheme was to remove almost at a stroke, all full-time in-service training of teachers and, of course, the fee income it brought in.

Further funding problems were initiated in 1990–1 when UEA, along with many other universities introduced a new resource allocation model following changes in centralized funding. In this model resources allocated to each school reflected income from all sources including funding council grant and tuition fee income. The funding council of the time considered that every part-time student was worth half of a full-time student and assumed that universities were charging on a similar basis. But like many schools of education, UEA was not charging half of full fees to part-timers. In the commercial speak of the time the School of Education was perceived as being a 'debtor' school which could not pay its way. It was faced with the choice of either cutting the costs of courses or raising the fees. The latter was chosen. Between 1991–2 and 1993–4 the cost of a normal modular masters degree increased by 66 per cent and while we cannot draw a tight correlation between price and demand, the general feeling in the school is that it became much more difficult to recruit teachers to the MA at the higher price.

The net effect of all these changes was that the school had to see itself as an operator in the educational market place if it was to prosper. The wind of commercialization had clearly begun to blow through the school's corridors and its reconstructive activities were influenced by the school's perception of the work of its own semi-autonomous research centre, CARE (Centre for Applied Research in Education). CARE had traditionally sought part of its income by attracting evaluation and other research contracts. Its expertise in programme evaluation had often brought it into areas of education other than schooling. In particular in 1984, CARE secured a contract to review police probationer training and was then engaged in developing and implementing changes to such training until 1989. Subsequently in both CARE and in the rest of the School, other contracts have been secured in the National Health Service, the social services and elsewhere. These activities suggested avenues for the school as a whole to develop in the 'educational market'.

Responses

It was in this context that my hunter-gathering activity began. I had no work unless I could bring in money. My stay at UEA had been blessed by the support of a colleague who had a permanent post in that his salary, unlike mine, was not dependent upon generating new income. He had always supported my employment at UEA and we decided very clearly that we would try and ensure that, amidst all of the changes we were experiencing, we would continually seek to define situations for the benefit of ourselves and of education. Much of the progress we have made has been through working with friends and personal contacts and our first 'break' came about through discussion with one of his PhD students.

The student was an advisory headteacher in a neighbouring authority who believed he could 'sell' an inexpensive award bearing course in the teaching of children with Special Educational Needs (SEN) in his Local Education Authority (LEA). It was decided to provide a course in the form of an MA module which required relatively little input from already overstretched staff but which could be supported by LEA advisers. It was, in essence, a distance-learning course, though considerable tutorial support was provided. A book of readings was put together using the work of advisers, and other staff at UEA and in the LEA. My colleague constructed a study guide which explained the course and its assessment and the course was soon up and running. To everyone's surprise the course recruited in excess of fifty students when many similar courses on our modular masters degree struggled to reach the minimum cut-off level of ten students. This new money provided a reasonable part of my income and I became involved developing the course and in leading the tutorial groups that met at UEA. Other local meetings for teachers were led by LEA SEN advisers. We had very few problems at this stage with students, nearly all passed and some used the credit they received towards an MA, joining the 'normal' taught courses provided by the school.

In the following year another neighbouring LEA provided funding for a similar and overlapping course and the school used what appeared to be a rich source of funding as a basis for an approach to the university for developmental funding for a small unit which we subsequently called the Enquiry Learning Unit or ELU. In October 1992, the UEA authorities responded with sufficient funding for myself and a part-time secretary for one year in which we were to encourage the expansion of distance-learning courses to cover a greater number of subjects and to be available beyond the existing LEAs. It was anticipated that ELU would be self-supporting in future years from the 'sale' of masters level and other courses.

There were few constraints upon my activities. I had to essentially find 'markets' for our courses and sell them in order to pay my salary. With the research selectivity exercise in mind, the school could see the additional possibility of publication of the books of readings. While I was given my head, there were some demands made of the courses I was to sell. They were not constraints to me because the demands merely supported my own inclinations but the courses were to have certain features.

The Courses

Our dean, and indeed other members of our management team, were insistent that our courses should have a research or enquiry element. We came to describe this qualitative research element as consisting of action research or evaluation and considered either of these to be fundamental educational processes within the courses. In all of the books of readings that we have so far produced, the first section is an introduction to qualitative research and the rest of the reader consists of papers rooted in the content of the subject matter.

Teachers are expected to take one of these processes and research their own practice supported by readings on the subject matter and a series of small group meetings where their progress and difficulties are discussed. It has been our view that our 'generic materials', i.e., the research papers, can be coupled to any subject matter, and, indeed, more recently we have done so. The papers are currently about to be used as part of a TEFL course in the Czech Republic and, with relatively small changes, for a course for managers in industry. Similarly the study guides for each of the courses have much in common.

The Funding

If ELU and indeed, my own employment, was to survive I had to sell courses. I was given conflicting advice or at least there were a range of different scenarios. In some LEAs I was told that all Inset money had been committed in the previous April and it was now October. In other cases it seemed that there were pockets of money still unspent. By this stage LEAs had been forced to devolve large percentages of their Inset money to schools, particularly secondary schools, who were now able to 'buy' Inset. My search for money included these schools as much as it did LEAs.

At this stage our priority was to find an individual, a group or an institution that held a sum of money on behalf of students or who could recruit students on our behalf. Our funding was so shaky that we could not invest in creating courses when we were unsure they could be sold. We felt that had we simply created courses and advertised in the national press, we would find it almost impossible to support an individual student in Cornwall and another in the Hebrides.

We investigated the following possible sources of money:

- Schools: Many large secondary schools seemed to be having difficulty spending their devolved Inset allocation. Of course this was not true of all but some headteachers were struggling to find what they considered to be a good Inset package. Many small schools, in Norfolk and Suffolk for example, did not have sufficient funding to pay for a single person to do a part-time award-bearing course.

     We arranged meetings with interested parties in our home county of Norfolk and found considerable interest in non award-bearing courses, especially very short courses which it was difficult for us to provide. Many staff also had reservations about providing lectures on a one-off basis which did not engage teachers in a practical way or expect teachers to research and reflect upon their own practice.

     We approached the rather large number of grant maintained schools in Norfolk as we were aware that many of them had far greater Inset budgets than LEA schools. The headteachers of the schools managed to fit us into a very busy meeting but we felt that our approach made little impact. In my view these schools seemed to want what amounted almost to instruction in subject-based matter which we felt we did not want to provide. A later meeting with Inset coordinators in the same schools left us feeling much more hopeful but no 'orders' resulted.

- LEAs, despite losing most of their funding, still controlled sizeable lumps of money. In some cases they administered fairly large sums on behalf of the Department for Education, GEST 11 being one such area. GEST 11 courses have to be registered with the DFE and a list of registered courses is sent to LEAs, who can then choose where to spend their allocated money. Despite having the only distance-learning courses in some categories we failed to recruit students.

  We remained very fortunate, however, in that SEN budgets held by the LEAs we had been providing courses for retained control of sizeable budgets to continue these courses. After fairly intensive negotiations we expanded our offer to these two LEAs. They agreed to provide a common course, and instead of us providing random SEN courses we agreed to construct a number of common courses which together made up an MA. We recruited record numbers of students onto these courses and these alone assured that ELU will survive.

- A third source of potential income for us was business. We were well aware that the sums of money that can be secured in industry are far larger than those we in education are used to. We explored and continue to explore the potential for high-tech electronics to facilitate the delivery of tailor-made courses to students who live and work at a distance from UEA. We are still in the early stages of such developments.

  We have endeavoured to meet as many business people as possible. Our general overview of training for managers is that it is not impressive. We were approached by a past Ph.D student who ran an agency which provided courses for large training bodies and associations and we now offer a masters degree in management learning for managers in industry but this took some time to set up.

- The final focus of our fund-raising efforts was what we can call the overseas market. There are all sorts of stories about the 'growth areas' of the future. With hindsight it has been our experience that the Pacific-rim countries are inundated with all sorts of universities and others who are seeking to cash in. We appear to have been more successful in less 'glamorous' countries where we have created strong working relationships. The gestation period of such courses can be very long.

What Happened Next

As we approached the end of the academic year 1992–3 my stay at UEA began to look, once again, very tenuous. My hopes rested upon three initiatives which, even by July, looked desperately unhopeful. The first was the hope that our two local LEAs would register sufficient teachers on our masters degree in teaching children with special educational needs. Even if we broke all records and registered a hundred teachers my full salary, with oncosts, would not quite have been covered. Second, we had placed a small bid into our internal university fund for research promotion. This was to fund a small piece of research into distance learning the results of which might be used to inform other schools in the university and possibly other bodies. This small sum would, with sufficient funding from the masters degree pay my full salary for the coming year. Finally, in late June we had received a letter from the Egyptian Education Bureau in London which was seeking places in an English university for some two hundred graduate teachers each year for the next five years.

To my knowledge we had never had a contract as large as the Egyptian one nor a contract which provided so many teachers for the school. The programme was non award-bearing but very interesting because of its major importance in Egypt. Additionally, Egypt was a country about which very little had been written in the various research journals. Our first response was that this programme would be too large for us to handle and far too complex with its inevitable cultural misunderstandings, language difficulties and school placements. We had previously had a contract for Turkish teachers which had failed to excite staff academically and which had foundered on language and other difficulties. Moreover, it was not a research contract. On the positive side it would provide much needed jobs, especially for me, and would provide interesting possibilities for development and writing with perhaps research coming later. After some debate we eventually submitted a proposal to carry out the work. We were concerned, however, that the programme would be very difficult to deliver.

By the end of July my life had changed drastically. I find that academics in similar positions to my own always overbid to cover themselves in the knowledge that only a small percentage of programmes they try to secure actually get off the ground. In the event all three of these bids were successful. In the space of three days we received the information that the MA SEN had recruited approximately one hundred teachers, that the small research project had been approved, and most shocking of all, that we had been short-listed for the Egyptian project. It was soon confirmed that we had, indeed, been awarded the Egyptian contract. These were exciting times, and as someone who had major concerns about his job, I was now in the position where I had too much work. In the short-term there was nothing I could do to jettison work in that I had nearly finished the written materials for the distance-learning courses. The research could take place later in the year so that was not a major problem. I took two weeks holiday I had previously planned and on my return I was informed that the first group of seventy Egyptian teachers were to arrive the same day.

Let me just take stock. Here I was, feeling I was at the bottom of the academic pile and very insecure about my employment and position in the School of Education, suddenly finding myself with far too much work and the holder of the largest single project that the entire university had ever had. The Egyptian work, while not a research project was a developmental one with some responsibility for the development of the educational system of a whole country. Possibly research would follow (and it has). In the first year of this scenario I worked harder than I have ever done in my life and at one time became ill. I was working seven days a week until the school was eventually able to find someone to take over my distance-learning work. The Egyptian project became a very complex one to manage in that there was infinite scope for cultural misunderstandings in both the School of Education and in the rural schools of Norfolk where Egyptian teachers spent seven of their fourteen-week programme. Most of the difficulties were pastoral as opposed to academic but the project continued for one year and we have since secured further contracts. Our relationship with the Egyptian Education Bureau in London remains excellent and while it is always complex, the Egyptian programme has continued to develop.

It is now Autumn 1994. I am full-time director of the Egyptian programme but still dependent upon bringing in money. I am often introduced to visitors in the School of Education as an 'entrepreneur'. I have been advised that my future is one which will include an element of management, a director of something or other. But when I look back this is what I was trying to avoid. Having said all of that I would not want the reader to conclude that I am actively unhappy. I love the work I do and I am grateful to work with academics I respect, as academics, in the School of Education. Yet there are vacuums, both professional and personal.

Conclusion

The important question here is what arises from the above that has ramifications for teacher education? The first point I wish to make is that there is plainly a great deal of effort in this School of Education now going into areas other than English schools. This is a mixed blessing in that we are enriched by the lessons we learn from overseas teachers, policemen and women, and others. Yet there seems to be an imbalance in that there is limited scope for transference back into schools. We are spending less of our time, as an institution, with English teachers and I feel we are both losing. This is especially pertinent when a group of headteachers explain to me, as they did recently, that their central interest is not in long-term Inset but in 'tooling up' for the next round of national curriculum changes.

In my experience there are many schools who are spending their Inset budgets on visiting speakers who drift in and drift out with little effect on the life of the school. Many do not have sufficient funding, anyway, to pay for the professional development of their staff. Yet I believe that large numbers of teachers would like to take part in professional development and, of course, we would like to help. Professional development requires a long-term commitment (see McBride, 1992) from both institutions of higher education and from schools and teachers. Of course there are teachers who are able to find the time, though many complain that there is little spare time for study.

An additional issue is that of funding. The 'spread thin' problem (McBride, 1992) means that many schools cannot commit sufficient money to assist teachers who wish to complete a long-term award-bearing course, which I would argue is necessary (though not sufficient) for professional development to take place. Money for Inset is available for courses such as those funded by GEST 11 but not all teachers want to take part in courses which are over concerned with national curriculum issues at the expense of personal issues.

As worrying for me is the maintenance of the quality of our courses and there are two concerns here. As a hunter-gatherer I am always anxious to explain to potential purchasers that we can provide 'bespoke' courses. We do endeavour to provide what teachers and others want but as a university we have a responsibility to provide courses which we as academics feel we can defend to other academics in the field of teacher development. At this stage we have not yet had major difficulties in reconciling our values with purchasers but there have been occasions when we have had to 'press on', paying greater attention to our version of quality rather than that of, say, an LEA or school manager. I would defend these actions but one wonders whether hunter-gatherers in other universities are providing programmes that could be defended in the same way. We have, for example, come across government ministries in middle eastern countries who will not recognize distance-learning courses following their experience of poor-quality courses offered by some North American colleges.

A second quality concern arises out of the sheer pressure placed upon myself as a hunter-gatherer. When one includes the oncosts that a university has to cover in order to employ an academic it is not easy to cover a salary. A hunter-gatherer in 1994 has to bring in approximately £33 000 to cover an average salary. Moreover, as some negotiations have to be conducted with fairly sophisticated people who are seeking good value for money, hunter-gatherers need to be experienced people who tend to earn at least an average salary. The point is that hunter-gathering is a very intensive and stressful trade. It is not clear that I am always able to find sufficient time to engage in the reflection, debate, reading and research that my academic activities require.

The situation is made worse when, as in my case, I bring in enough money and have sufficient work to employ other people. To keep others employed I feel responsible to bring in multiples of £33 000 and, plainly, this is all the more wearing. As my own activity has expanded there are now additional numbers of people who are employed in a temporary capacity. I am not sure that the casualization of staff benefits either the staff involved or the School of Education. Academic work requires a long-term commitment to research, reflection and debate. If we have too many casual staff there is a risk that the entire academic venture will be diminished. There have been changes to the ethos in this School of Education. To survive in the market place we are carrying out work that we would not have done in the past. The Egyptian programme is one such example and as I have pointed out we do benefit from it. But the perpetual pursuit of money and contracts has resulted in what I would describe as a change in our horizons. In general, we have a stronger eye on the short-term than on the long-term.

As a hunter-gatherer of people for courses I have concluded that we should all move closer to the distance-learning courses I have helped to pioneer. Too many postgraduate courses for teachers are overtaught. Distance learning gives teachers 'space' to pursue their own interests to a greater extent than taught courses. Teachers are able to work at their own pace and in their own time and as long as there are opportunities for discussion with academic staff and other teachers, the courses are popular. It is a prerequisite, especially for the courses we produce, that teachers have to be given the resources and equipment to research their own practice. Our distance-learning courses are inexpensive compared to many taught courses. A large part of the costs are for creating written materials and for marking. Given that written materials can be reproduced for subsequent courses, they are not expensive.

Despite our intentions we have still not put our distance-learning courses on the 'open market' as it were. This is partly due to pressure of work and my preoccupation with the Egyptian programme. We have a lingering concern about being able to support solitary teachers in distant places and it would be of enormous help to have a single or small number of fund holders to deal with. In this respect we regret the demise of LEAs and the introduction of devolved funding. Currently, sources of future work look likely to be overseas authorities who hold money or commerce and industry who likewise control large budgets.

My feelings about my own situation as a hunter-gatherer are mixed. Essentially I want to be, in simple terms, a university academic who lectures, researches and writes. I do benefit from negotiating contracts and this negotiation often leads to better courses. But from time to time I feel that the balance between being with students and negotiating contracts leans too far towards the latter. Above all I still do not have a job if I do not bring in money, though the university may well help me for a short while if I lose all income. Many other university staff no longer have tenure but my position is less firm. In addition, I am not able to take part in some parts of university life. At present I am not able to attend the final examination board for some of the courses I teach. I find this offensive. Shortly after my contract is renewed each year I find I am turned away from the university library which has not yet been told that I remain a university employee. When one considers the large sums of money I bring into the greater university and therefore the library I find this offensive too. I cannot apply for promotion. This does not necessarily affect my salary but does affect my formal status within the school. I cannot apply for study leave along with other colleagues who are able to use this time to catch up with their writing. As I am dependent upon contracts I cannot choose which one to take. The Egyptian contract is a developmental one with a research element but I feel that there has been too little research within this programme, at least in the past. I have a reputation as being a hunter-gatherer, and more recently as a manager, rather than as an academic who writes and researches. I do not want to be button-holed into hunter-gathering simply because I have met with success. I want to keep finding time for research and writing so that before too long I may be able to seek employment as an academic rather than as a manager. In the meantime I am happy to just have a job.

References

MacLure, M. (1989) 'Anyone for Inset? Needs identification and personal/professional development', in McBride, R. (1989) *The In-service Training of Teachers*, Lewes, Falmer Press.

McBride, R. (1994) 'Helping headteachers to search for their values: A preliminary study', *Cambridge Journal of Education*, **24**, 3, Cambridge.

McBride, R. (1992) 'INSET, professional development and the local management of schools', in Wallace, G. *BERA Dialogues Number 6. Local Management of Schools: Research and Experience*, Clevedon, Multilingual Matters.

McBride, R. (Ed) (1989) *The In-service Training of Teachers*, Lewes, Falmer Press.

Part 4

Broader Considerations and Summary

18   Teacher Education: The Poverty of Pragmatism

David Bridges

Introduction

Philosophical theories have a disconcerting way of lodging themselves in public and political consciousness so that they continue to shape and inform public policy in a form long discredited in even the lowliest philosophical circles. In ethics every undergraduate sharpens his or her critical tools pulling apart Bentham's and Mill's essays on Utilitarianism, which however continue to inform and indeed dominate the development and defence of public policy.

In theory of knowledge, in the Anglo-Saxon world at least, a popularized form of pragmatism dominates the popular world view even more than scientific or quasi-scientific empiricism. Pragmatism is the banner of common sense.[1] To take a pragmatic approach is in ordinary language to eschew lofty theory, ideology and even rarefied scientific claims which, however researched, conflict with common-sense understanding. To take a pragmatic approach is to try out a course of action against our own ordinary experience and to see if it 'works'. If it does then we will accept it; if it does not, then we shall look for an alternative. What could be more sensible?

I believe that this popular and appealing theory of knowledge has come to dominate, too, a good deal of policy in relation to teacher education, in which reference to the need to learn from experience, to test out approaches in the classroom and hence the need to ground both initial and in-service education in the practical settings of the school and classroom predominate. It is not just recent government initiatives which have moved thinking and practice in this direction. The classroom action-research movement reflects too, theories of knowledge rooted in a similar tradition as do the influential advocates and admirers of experiential learning as synthesized popularly by, for example, David Kolb (Kolb, 1984; Jamieson, forthcoming).

In this chapter I want to recall the character of the philosophical pragmatism, which underlies (and is not so far removed from) the popular version indicated here, and then to elaborate some classic and personal criticisms of this theory. I then want to suggest that these criticisms constitute also some fairly serious reservations to developments in teacher education (or indeed higher education more widely) which rest increasingly narrowly on the conviction that professional development can rest more or less exclusively on the tries and tests of experience.

Pragmatic Theory of Knowledge and Learning

The Chicago Pragmatists (notably Dewey, Peirce, James, Mead and Kilpatrick for my purposes) were a loose-knit group with overlapping concerns and points of view, rather than a single programme or set of commitments, so what follows is a generalization based on a number of sources (Dewey, 1938; Rucker, 1969; Morris, 1970; Scheffler, 1974).

For the pragmatists, learning and the development of knowledge and understanding had its roots in an interest, purpose, task or project which an individual was engaged with or pursuing, with some kind of frustration to its pursuit (engendered by false belief or expectation, error or ignorance) and thence some kind of frustration, uncertainty, doubt or perplexity. Thus Murphey, summarizing Peirce and Dewey, explains: 'A problem situation exists whenever we find our established habits of conduct inadequate to attain a desired end — and the effect of a problem situation upon us is the production of doubt' (Murphey, 1961, pp. 160–1). This perplexity arises because the knowledge, understanding or skills which we have, do not seem to be sufficient, because our existing repertoire of responses or solutions do not 'work'.

Faced with this perplexity or frustration, we have to modify or expand the cognitive apparatus which has proved inadequate: we have to develop an alternative hypothesis, strategy, interpretation, understanding or belief and see if with this revision we can proceed more successfully (see if it works). If it does not, then we are thrown once again into doubt and perplexity and we have to repeat the revisionary process. If our modified belief, expectation etc. 'works' however, then that becomes part of the revised cognitive apparatus (knowledge and understanding) which we carry with us to the pursuit of future purposes until such time as in its own turn it proves inadequate. This process can be described diagramatically in a form which is not far removed from Kolb's more recent learning cycle.

Part of the attractiveness of this kind of account (not least to educators) is that it offers simultaneously: a theory of learning or of the conditions under which learning take place; a theory of knowledge and a theory of truth. As a theory of learning, it places the learner and the learner's own interests at the centre of the picture — and has provided an important source for and legitimation of 'child-centred' and more recently 'learner-centred' education. As a theory of knowledge, it has demonstrated the roots of knowledge in subjectivity; the constraints imposed upon that subjectivity by an external world; and the provisionality, but yet utility, of what passes for both individual and social knowledge — a temptingly eclectic picture. It offers a picture of knowledge which is provisional, functional and conveniently 'self reparative'. 'Thus' says James, 'do philosophy and reality, theory and action, work in the same circle indefinitely.' (Burkhardt, 1977, p. 149).

As a theory of truth, it is perhaps at its weakest, for essentially its claim is that the test for the truth of a belief is that it 'works', that it serves to enable us to pursue our interests, to act upon the world (physical or social) in a way which does not lead to frustration and perplexity. 'If and only if a belief is true will it yield sensibly satisfactory results in experience when thus acted upon.' (See Scheffler, 1974; though Scheffler observes some differences between Pierce and James on truth.) But attractive as pragmatism may be both in its more philosophical form and its ready translation into more commonsensical terms, there are some rather fundamental problems attached to it which bear upon both — and it is to these that we should now turn.

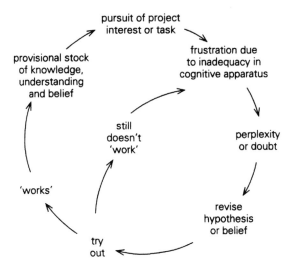

Figure 18.1: Diagramatic summary of pragmatic theory of knowledge and learning

The Limits of Pragmatism

Pragmatism is at its most convincing within the realm of technology (technology even more than science) and indeed it probably suffers from having taken the technological domain as paradigmatic of all knowledge. Technology comes into play in very much the way that the pragmatists describe, when people want to do something or get somewhere, when they try out a solution. If that works and allows them to do what they want, then that is enough. The solution joins the current stock (personal or social) of technological knowledge. This applies in principle whether one is operating within a material domain (e.g., applying technology to lifting weights or bridging spans) or in the social domain (e.g., persuading people or perhaps teaching them). Even in this field, however, pragmatism appears to be a necessary but not sufficient test for the adequacy of a solution, or alternatively the test of whether a solution 'works' or not is a great deal more complicated than might at first be supposed.

First, we have become very much more aware in recent years that technological solutions to tasks in engineering, agriculture and health, for example, commonly fail to define the technical problem sufficiently widely. For example faced with the problem of disease afflicting wheat, an agricultural chemist may devise a spray which satisfactorily eliminates the disease. But someone else may respond that the problem was too narrowly perceived or defined, that it should have included technical dimensions to do with safeguarding wildlife, avoiding any health hazard to people, a concern not to allow any chemical trace elements to enter the wheat produce itself. In other words the fault of the agricultural chemist was in his or her failure to conceive of, or define, the technical problem adequately — a failure rooted in the conceptual apparatus brought to the conceptualization of the problem, rather than an inadequacy of the solution to the problem as perceived, which in its own terms 'worked' entirely successfully.

An extension of this problem raises even greater difficulties for pragmatism. In popular parlance 'pragmatic' solutions to problems stand in contrast with those which rest on some kind of moral or social principle, and pragmatic solutions are typically ones that either ignore or beg questions to do with the morality of what is proposed. This is not surprising, because philosophical pragmatism is at its weakest in trying to apply itself to this area and pragmatists wriggle and squirm somewhat to accommodate morality within the theories of knowledge and truth outlined above.

But one of the distinguishing features of moral discourse — and this is why it is so difficult to accommodate to pragmatism — is that it is about what is right categorically rather than what is right technically or conditionally ('hypothetically' as Kant would put it) for the achievement of some further end. To act honestly 'because honesty is the best policy' is not to act morally but to act prudentially or for the technical purpose of achieving some other end (see Kant, 1958 ed. 82ff). From this stand-point the pragmatic test of whether a particular piece of knowledge or understanding enables us to pursue our project or interest is neither here nor there in strictly moral terms. Rather, moral beliefs derived in some other way have to be brought to bear in evaluating the projects or interests we are pursuing (i.e., we have to ask about the rightness or goodness of our ends) and they have to enter as an independent set of principles in considering the rightness or goodness of the means we discover for pursuing those ends. We have to ask not merely, for example, whether a particular solution to our perplexity will 'work' technically, but whether it is acceptable morally.

The reality is that pragmatism cannot offer an adequate theory of morality (no more than it can offer an adequate theory of religion, but that is a separate issue). Hence, pragmatists tend to ignore or disguise issues of moral or social principle both in their definition of problems to be solved and in their solutions to those problems. This observation leads to a third problem with pragmatism which is of particular educational significance. The problem is that pragmatism — and a lot of the educational practice that goes with it — potentially leaves too much unchallenged. It suggests that the learner has almost physically to bump into problems before perplexity is engendered — and that the task then is to resolve that perplexity as simply and directly as possible. The pragmatic person does not look for 'unnecessary' problems. This is not just a contingent feature of pragmatic theory. Peirce in particular was seeking a psychological foundation for the denial of Cartesian doubt — and he had found this in the writing of the nineteenth-century philosopher/psychologist Alexander Bain:

> To escape doubt and reach belief is . . . inherent in man; indeed, belief is our natural state, for we have an initial trust or belief in the continuation of the present state and the continued efficacy of our mode of behaviour. But experience disappoints us and so generates doubt, which must continue until a new pattern is established which does yield the desired result. (Bain, 'The emotions and the will', quoted in Fisch, 1954, pp. 419–20.)

The consequence of this predisposition in favour of settled opinion is that, in both its popular and its philosophical form and practice, pragmatism begs or eschews many fundamental questions. Now this probably sounds perfectly right if you are an engineer staring at a crack in a bridge, but from a more critical stand-point, philosophers and teachers want to extend learners' perplexity, to disturb their satisfaction with solutions, to make problematic what they took for granted, to raise wider moral, social and political issues about their apparently straightforward, pragmatically satisfactory solutions.

School-based Training and the Limits of Experience

This discussion ought to serve to caution us against overreliance on experience-based learning and classroom practice, both of which pragmatism might appear to endorse, and to give an indication of what in addition the proper development of applied knowledge and understanding requires.

First, we need to pay attention to the conceptual structures which student teachers are able to bring to their definition of their task; their capacity to recognize 'problems' in the classroom and their definition of such problems; and their observation of what is going on in classrooms. All of these are really part and parcel of the same problem which is rooted in the principle that 'all seeing is seeing as' and that our capacity for seeing and experiencing is a function of the conceptual apparatus and affective dispositions (Bagehot's 'experiencing nature') which we bring to observation and experience. We are familiar with the blindness which constrains any of us in an observational setting and the way in which, as possibilities are pointed out to us, categories are identified and labels provided, distinctions are drawn and connections are made, we come to see things which were previously invisible not because they were physically unavailable to our eyes or ears but because conceptually they were not discernible to our intelligence.

In the context of teacher education Calderhead (1988) has pointed to the unhelpfulness of the observation of classroom practice in the early stages of teacher training when students simply cannot make sense of all the noise and movement around them, do not understand the significance of the teacher's actions and are unclear what they are even looking for. Copeland (1981) describes such trainees' experience as 'a bewildering kaleidoscope of people, behaviours, events and interactions only dimly understood' (p. 11). Students need changed cognition (Berliner, 1987), new concepts, schemas and scripts in order to make relevant pedagogic sense of their observations, and 'the fact that new trainees have not yet had the experience to form these concepts is associated with the problem of not being able to "see" ' (Maynard and Furlong, 1993).

However these limitations affect whole groups as well as individuals — so that an entire community becomes conceptually blind to alternative constructions of their experience, to the selectivity and distortion of consciousness and hence in some instances to forms of oppression and discrimination latent in the situation which they are observing or 'experiencing'. To offer an elementary example, many of us taught or observed in classrooms for years without in fact observing the enormous variety of ways in which teachers operated to discriminate between boys and girls. Once alerted to this and its social significance it becomes difficult to observe any classroom without noticing this dimension of practice.

Freire observed this kind of limitation on perception some years ago and argued for an educative process of action and reflection through which participants 'simultaneously reflecting on themselves and on the world, increase the scope of their perception . . . (and) . . . *begin to direct their observations towards previously inconspicuous phenomena*' (Freire, 1972, p. 55 my emphases). But individual reflecters/observers, individual student teachers let us assume, whatever the dynamism of their reflective processes, are still trapped to some extent in the self-reinforcing and self-limiting world of their own conceptual framework. Isn't this a problem in the context of, in particular, a pattern of school-based experience, observation and practice? To some extent this is clearly addressed in school-based training schemes, because the teacher/tutor or school mentor has responsibility for, among other things, supporting and extending the conceptual apparatus which students bring to their observation and experience. 'Mentors', write Maynard and Furlong, 'are in a unique position to be able to support trainees as they begin to form concepts about their practical work. They are also uniquely placed to expose trainee's developing concepts and help them to see the implications of various ways of working' (1993, p. 9). But a number of recent critics have questioned the extent to which practising teachers in a particular context can extend the critical and questioning understanding of their trainees. Elbaz, for example, asks 'how does one work from and with the reality of teachers without becoming bogged down in conventional views of schooling?' (Elbaz, 1988, p. 174) and Handal has suggested that even teachers who engage in the research and reflective processes of school-based action research spend most of their time 'constructing practice' at a technical level and little time 'deconstructing practice' at an ideological level (Handal, 1991). Maynard and Furlong's conclusion nicely reflects the prevalence of pragmatism — and its limitations — among school-based teacher trainers 'Studies of practice have found that too often trainees' and co-operating teachers' reflections centre superficially on issues such as whether a particular strategy "worked", on the children's apparent enjoyment of an activity or whether specified objectives had been met . . . in essence focusing on the "safe" and not the challenging; on the "existing" and not on the possible' (Maynard and Furlong, 1993, p. 10. Calderhead, 1987; Ben Peretz and Rumney, 1991).

By contrast, Easen, in a distinctly unpragmatic vein, argues that among the central conditions for the development of classroom practice is 'the problematization of those aspects of classroom life that are taken for granted by the teacher but whose development is crucial to the creation of new norms of practice in the classroom. In particular, this includes the typifications used for making sense of what happens and the accompanying routines. This suggests that practice development may involve ideological development through the process of perspective transformation . . .' (Easen, 1992, p. 63). It is interesting in the context of claims such as this to ask what kinds of learning have contributed most towards educational change in, say, the last thirty years. Is it the steady accumulation of professional wisdom grounded in the pragmatic processes of trial and error and hard experience? I suggest not. In fact we seem to contribute surprisingly little to educational change in this way. Rather, the transforming influences in educational practice (for good or ill — I am concerned here with their potency rather than their beneficence) seem to have been rooted in conceptual shifts and counter currents: the notions of child-centred education; of comprehensive schools; of curriculum as an entitlement; of education as a partnership between parents and schools; of the application of market principles to education; of flexible and open-learning systems; of competence-based assessment; of gender as a source of inequality in education; of the profiling of achievement; of education for a multi-racial society — to make a somewhat arbitrary selection.

Of course these notions, radical and challenging in their day, become part of the taken-for-granted world of the profession or part of its ongoing debate with itself and with the wider community, but new entrants still need both to make them their own, and all teachers need to be part of the process which is constantly re-examining these and drawing on fresh imaginative and intellectual sources for the transformative thinking which will shape the future development of education. What all this seems to call for is something stronger, more challenging and more public than is conventionally conveyed in notions of reflection or reflective practice. Reflection is undoubtedly part of what is demanded, but an individual's capacity to reflect has the same kind of limitations as his or her capacity to experience. These are partly dispositional limitations (to do with the inquisitiveness, contrariness, engagedness and other features of the individual's personality) but, more importantly in this argument, they are limitations to do with the conceptual apparatus which supports his or her reflection, enquiry, experiencing or imagination and which governs the practitioner's capacity both to perceive or pose problems and to generate and evaluate responses to them.

Schon's (1983) distinction between 'problem-solving' and 'problem-setting' is helpful here. The pragmatist focuses on problem-solving and tends to beg the question of what is the problem which really ought to be posed. But we neglect problem *setting* at our peril, for it is this which shapes all that follows.

> When we set the problem, we select what we will treat as the 'things' of the situation, we set the boundaries of our attention to it, and we impose upon it a coherence which allows us to say what is wrong and in what directions the situation needs to be changed. Problem setting is a process in which, interactively, we name the things to which we will attend and frame the context in which we will attend to them. (Schon, 1983, p. 40)

Schon illustrates in clearly pragmatic terms the kind of circumstances which destabilize the stock of commonly unstatable and tacit knowledge which for a time at least serves our purposes in action. These are, for example, 'situations of uncertainty, instability, uniqueness and value conflict' (Schon, 1983, p. 50). It is these which (see Figure 18.1) create the puzzlement or perplexity to which we have to respond with changed assumptions, understanding or beliefs. Schon also observes the variety of human conditions which lead us to avoid such perplexity: boredom, 'over-learning', burn-out, selective inattention to phenomena that do not fit our preconceptions, an inability to recognize or explore puzzling events (ibid., p. 61). But though such references give some hints of the dispositions which 'reflections-in-action' requires (an openness to, and tolerance of, perplexity? an active curiosity? an inventive imagination?) they provide little insight into the kind of cognition knowledge and understanding and even 'meta-cognition' (see Bridges, 1994), which professional practitioners need to bring with them to reflection-in-action. In particular we need an account of the kind of conceptual apparatus which makes possible the questioning of the taken-for-granted assumptions not just of the individual practitioner but of the professional — in this context the school staff — community in which he or she is located. MacKinnon (1987) emphasizes the way in which we draw upon 'a repertoire of past experience and *ways of apprehending experience*' (p. 8 my emphasis) to reframe problems 'but neither he nor Schon says much about these "ways of apprehending experience" their sources and evolution or the qualitative difference which there may be between some such ways and others. Munby and Russell argue that '(Schon's) work is not sufficiently analytical and articulated to enable us to follow the connections that must be made between elements of experience and elements of cognition so that we may see how reflection-in-action might be understood to occur.' (Munby and Russell, 1989, p. 74). It is however not just Schon who stands accused of this neglect. In a fairly sweeping critique of advocates of reflective practice and classroom action research Clarke concluded:

> there is a quite systematic failure to realise that reflection, being a distinctive operation of scrutiny, must be performed *with* as well as upon something, and that professional teachers need to be equipped with sophisticated competence in whatever it is that reflection is with. (Clarke, 1994, p. 69)

Where is the Antidote to Pragmatism to be Found?

The implication of these arguments is that new teachers need to extend, and experienced teachers need to continue to extend, the conceptual apparatus which they bring *to* experience, which, of course, then interacts with experience and not merely to expect to derive that apparatus from experience. This requires among other things the abrasion of viewpoint against viewpoint and the expansion and challenge to one's own assumption which comes from being confronted actively and critically by the ideas, principles, moral commitments and professional theories (in the widest sense of this word) of others.

Reading permits a measure of this in a psychologically protective environment. It also gives the curious and receptive student access to an enormous range of the experience and thought of others gathered over historical time in a remarkably available form, to be skipped, scanned or slowly savoured according to its relevance and interest. There is no possibility that personal observation and experience could provide for any one individual the range, diversity or elaboration of thought available in literature — life is simply too short. And yet reading seems to be a form of learning which has been rendered almost obsolete in the education of teachers.

But it is critical discussion and argument among people with different perspectives but with a shared interest in illuminating what is before them which can provide one of the most salutary antidotes to conceptual and perceptual myopia — precisely because it is the nature of such discussion to extend the range of ways of looking at a situation or piece of evidence available to one individual through interaction with another (Bridges, 1988). Griffiths (1993) argues that 'change in experience comes about from changes in language' and that 'this is most easily done by changing the composition of communicating groups' (p. 20). 'Knowledge can only be gained using a method which allows for reflection on experience, using theory, in a number different group/political perspectives, which will bring that experience into question, and may require changes in language.' (p. 22). But even such interaction requires the dynamism of people who can offer diverse, enriched and extended perceptions of experience, a depth and breadth of perspective, and people whose process function in the group is to challenge the taken-for-granted and to raise, for example, the uncomfortable moral issues which are otherwise conveniently neglected — in other words people who through the conceptual apparatus which they bring to discourse and the examination of experience and through their critical disposition are able to offer an antidote to pragmatism.

This function *may* of course be fulfilled in a school setting or in a university;

it *may* be carried out by school teachers or university lecturers (and I consciously prefer the plural form here). It is certainly not obvious that students' training in the context of a small university school of education will necessarily be confronted with the mind-extending exchange of a range of viewpoints on (in particular) the teaching of their subject which this chapter argues for. The condition which needs to be met in whatever context is that new teachers are brought into contact with people 'fluent in the evaluation of educational ends as well as means' (McLaughlin, 1994) who can themselves bring a breadth and variety of perspective to the interaction; who can together represent, communicate and engage students in thought and reflection and the extension of their understanding; and who can stimulate their curiosity and questioning nature.

Such people may in principle be found in schools or universities (and it is, perhaps, an implication of Griffith's argument that we should in any case be seeking the perspectives of both). What is important is that we create or maintain conditions in both in which the sort of engagement with ideas which I have described actually takes place. Though the university has traditionally been regarded as the place above all others where such engagement is sanctified and celebrated, recent developments in higher education (the massive increase in student-to-staff ratios, financial constraints, the commodification of research and teaching, the growth of the higher education bureaucracy and the triumph of the higher education entrepreneurs) seem to me to have put at risk the universities' single-minded commitment to such values and processes and their capacity to sustain them. School staffrooms, however, look hardly more promising. There are notable exceptions (I think), but ironically there are few institutions more proudly anti-intellectual than an English school staffroom. Perhaps, and I know that this is the aspiration of some headteachers and teaching staff, the addition of a training/mentoring role to the school and the presence in it of student teachers hoping for an initiation into a dignified profession will itself contribute to a change in the culture of the staffroom. I hope so. For, if it does not, then pragmatism with all its intellectual and moral poverty will have won the day in yet another setting, and both the teaching profession and the children in its trust will be the poorer for it.

Note

1   Some of the material in the critical discussion of pragmatism is drawn from a paper by the author previously published in *The Curriculum Journal*.

References

BEN-PERETZ, M. and RUMNEY, S. (1991) 'Professional thinking in guided practice', *Teaching and Teacher Education*, **7**, 5–6.

BERLINER, D.C. (1987) 'Ways of thinking about students and classrooms by more and less experienced teachers', in CALDERHEAD, J. (Ed) *Exploring Teacher's Thinking*, Cassell.

BRIDGES, D. (1988) *Education Democracy and Discussion*, Lanham, University Press of America.

BRIDGES, D. (1991) 'From teaching to learning', in *The Curriculum Journal*, **2**, 2, pp. 137–51.

BRIDGES, D. (1994) 'Transferable skills in higher education: A philosophical perspective', in BRIDGES, D. (Ed) *Transferable Skills in Higher Education*, Norwich, University of East Anglia/ERTEC.

BURKHARDT, F.H. (1977) (Ed) *A Pluralistic Universe: The Works of William James*, Cambridge, Massachusetts, Harvard University Press.

CALDERHEAD, J. (1987) 'The quality of reflection in student teachers' professional learning', *European Journal of Teacher Education*, **10**, 3.

CALDERHEAD, J. (1988) 'Learning from introductory schools experience', *Journal of Education for Teaching*, **14**, 1.

CLARKE, C. (1994) 'Some reflections on reflecting practitioners', in Papers of the Philosophy of Education Society of Great Britain, Mimeo.

COPELAND, W.D. (1981) 'Clinical experiences in the education of teachers', *Journal of Education for Teaching*, **7**, 1.

DEWEY, J. (1938) *Logic: The Theory of Inquiry*, London, Holt, Reinhart and Winston.

EASEN, P. (1992) 'Practice Development in the Primary School: Collaboration and Conflict', PhD Thesis, University of Newcastle-upon-Tyne.

ELBAZ, F. (1988) 'Critical reflection on teaching: Insights from Freire', *Journal of Education for Teaching*, **14**, 2, pp. 171–87.

FISCH, M.H. (1954) 'Alexander Bain and the genealogy of pragmatism', *Journal of the History of Ideas*, **15**, June.

FREIRE, P. (1972) *Pedagogy of the Oppressed*, Harmondsworth, Penguin.

GRIFFITHS, M. (1993) 'Auto/biography and epistemology', paper presented to CARE Research Seminar (mimeo).

HANDAL, G. (1991) 'Collective time — collective practice', *The Curriculum Journal*, **2**, 3, pp. 317–34.

JAMIESON, I.M. (forthcoming) 'Experiential learning in the context of teacher education', in HARVARD, G. and HODKINSON, P. (Eds) *Action and Reflection in Teacher Education*, New Jersey, Ablex Publishing Co.

KANT, I. (1958) (Ed) *Groundwork of the Metaphysic of Morals*, PATON, H.J. (Trans), New York, Harper and Row.

KOLB, D.A. (1984) *Experiential Learning: Experience as a Source of Learning and Development*, New Jersey, Prentice Hall.

MACKINNON, A.M. (1987) 'Toward a Conceptualisation of a Reflective Practice in Science Teaching', Paper presented at the Second International Seminar, Misconceptions in Science and Mathematics, Cornell University (Department of Math and Science Education, University of British Columbia, Vancouver, BC).

MAYNARD, T. and FURLONG, J. (1993) 'Learning to Teach and Models of Mentoring', Paper presented to Bedford/ERTEC conference on mentoring (mimeo).

MCLAUGHLIN, T.H. (1994) 'Mentoring and the demands of reflection', in WILKIN, M. (Ed) and SANKEY, D. *Initial Teacher Education: Collaboration and Transition*, London, Kogan Page.

MORRIS, C. (1970) *The Pragmatic Movement in American Philosophy*, New York, George Braziller.

MUNBY, H. and RUSSELL, T. (1989) 'Educating the reflective teacher: An essay review of two books by Donald Schön', in *Journal of Curriculum Studies*, **21**, 1, pp. 71–80.

MURPHEY, M.G. (1961) *The Development of Peirce's Philosophy*, Cambridge, Massachusetts Harvard University Press.

RUCKER, D. (1969) *The Chicago Pragmatists*, Minneapolis, University of Minnesota Press.

SCHEFFLER, I. (1974) *Four Pragmatists*, London, Routledge and Kegan Paul.

SCHON, D.A. (1983) *The Reflective Practitioner: How Professionals Think in Action*, New York, Basic Books.

SCHON, D.A. (1987) *Educating the Reflective Practitioner: Toward a New Design for Teaching and Learning in the Professions*, San Francisco, Jossey-Bass.

19   Teacher Education: Notes towards a Radical View

John F. Schostak

Teacher education cannot begin to find its way until it finds first a way of reconceptualizing the purpose, the vision, the nature of education. If there were a world where knowledge progressed unfailingly in an upward curve towards perfect understanding, where the rational ego was sufficient to itself and truth was the self-evident basis for social and personal action then for example, the training of teachers for children would consist in delivering acquired knowledge in the most cost-efficient manner and children would rationally calculate that it was to their advantage to acquire the knowledge required for their benefit and as quickly as possible.

As it is, teacher education for the teaching of children is in a political trap. It was a trap formed at its very inception, a trap not unlike an oedipal crisis. Education lives, works and acts within that very nexus of parental authority appropriated for political and economic reasons by states, and its subversive 'other' the desire and yearning for a free, spontaneous, future. To take on the mantle of the 'father' (and it still usually is male/fatherly/paternalistic authority that dictates, authorizes) is to deny the very emancipation from the closure and conservativism of tradition that is the liberatory promise of education. In its place is schooling disguised as an 'education system'. To take on the freedoms of thought, expression, and action that education can draw from the imagination is to depose the father and thus to incur the wrath of powerful vested interests.

Has the West lost the sense of the radicality of education? Salman Rushdie, I suppose, gave not a moment's thought to the danger of writing the *Satanic Verses*. Yet all such challenges to a world view, like it or not, are deeply educational in the sense of making a challenge, or making an imaginative leap that generate a sense of there being an alternative view, another interpretation, another way of knowing, believing, living. Perhaps, like Galileo, Salman Rushdie should have had more common sense.

In this chapter I want to explore teacher education in its widest sense and as applicable in the largest number of possible contexts: not just the context of teaching children, but also those of teachers of the many professions, arts, crafts and sciences that today contribute to the knowledge and cultural bases of society in ways which uncover, examine, explore and contest the 'common senses' of everyday life. The exploration begins with discourses of schooling which position subjects for purposes of social order and control. It ends with education as the process through which order is suspended to create space for creative dialogue and action.

John F. Schostak

Teacher Education for Schooling

Upon reading many newspapers and listening to politicians whether right or left, one can begin to conclude that teacher education is about training teachers to deliver a curriculum in schools in a way which results in a disciplined 'subject' willing and able to take up what ever employments are on offer 'schooled to think of themselves as subjects not citizens; as people with freedoms granted by government, not with rights guaranteed against government interference' (Broder, 1989).

Turn now to the make up of schools of education. They tend to comprise subject specialists who then specialize in teaching others how to teach those specialist subjects. Then there are the specialist psychologists, sociologists and philosophers of education who provide a 'wider perspective', who inform prospective teachers about the nature of human development, learning theory, schools as agents of social control and the nature of 'knowledge'. From the varieties of discourses about education — both popular and professional — and from the ways in which teacher education is organized, it is difficult to escape the conclusion that education itself is not a self-contained distinct 'discipline' nor 'perspective' but is rather a collage of 'disciplines' and 'perspectives', each competing to tell teachers how to deliver the curriculum (whether the hidden curriculum or the discipline-based curriculum of discrete subjects as conceived in the National Curriculum). By and large, a delivery model of education dominates and curriculum discourse has been debased. Within the contemporary debased curricular and pedagogical discourses the teacher is trained to provide a kind of postal service, carrying curricular messages from a variety of 'senders' (politicians, religious bodies, social pressure groups, 'knowledge producers', 'guardians of culture', industrialists and so on) to specified addressees. If the message does not arrive then one can blame the postal service, or the individual carrier, or the addressee (didn't pick it up, threw it away, incapable of decoding it, and so on).

Within the 'delivery model' approach to defining the field of education a politically important split occurs. It is the split between the 'real' world and the world of 'theory'; a split between the world of 'action' and the world of 'thought'. Upon each side of this split there is a range of subject positions available for individuals. There is not a great deal of choice as to the kinds of subject positions that individuals may adopt. For example, for the child the general subject position is that of 'pupil' in school and out of school child splits into 'son' or 'daughter' of . . . Further subject splits appear as the child can be socio-economically located as being of a 'good' or 'bad' family background and so on. Similarly, within school various subject positions split into the usual and well documented binary categories (high–low ability, conformist–deviant and so on). For each subject position stories can be told, stories that set into relationship the subject positions of schooling and the 'real' world. The adoption of such subject positions is neither entirely through choice nor entirely through compulsion (Davies and Haré, 1990; Schostak, 1991, 1993). It is not an either-or logic but rather a fuzzy logic of multiple possibilities (Kosko, 1994). The process of choice involves a progressive drive towards the extreme: either be this or that but not both. This drive towards the extreme is the function of schooling. Schooling cannot countenance a fuzzy world, a world of multivalent possibilities, of multiple interpretations, of multifaiths, and multiple worlds. All its strategies strive for the production of binary choices as between categories that are clear and hierarchically valued. For schooling to exist there must be a text (or set of texts) that are authorized by society. The function of schooling is to bring about the internalization of these texts within populations. These authorized texts then act as reference codes by which to interpret and order experience as the basis for action within the community. Schooling is thus a structure for the transmission of authorized texts. Transmission is judged successful when addressees have internalized authorized texts in such a way that their decision-making employs the internalized texts as master codes.

A useful comparison with Lotman's (1990) analyses of the transmission of text can be made:

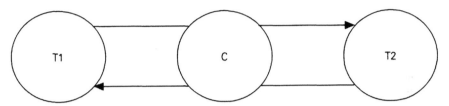

Figure 19.1:   Transmission of text

In this situation a text (T1) is transmitted to an addressee who receives and decodes that message employing code C to produce a second text (T2). If the addressee employs a code that is the same code used by the sender to produce T1 then T2 will be identical to T1. Transmission will then be achieved.

Think of T1 as the National Curriculum. The task of the teacher is to transmit (dictate) the prescribed text to pupils. The task of the pupils is to interpret the T1 in such a way that the teacher assesses it to be 'correct'. In short, the task for the teacher is to internalize in students the appropriate code so that T2 is always a reproductive of T1 at least for assessment purposes. In this way the pupil is placed into a passive subject position as receptor and reproducer. The teacher is no less passive being merely the transmitter. The master code in effect manoeuvres the individual into the subject position of 'teacher of the code'. This is analogous to Lacan's conception of the ego of the individual being constructed through the master signifiers that the individual identifies with. The implication then, for teacher trainers would be to bring about a situation in which student teachers identify with the master signifiers and master codes of the profession in order to facilitate the internalization of code C in pupils to accomplish not only the reproduction of T1 for assessment purposes but also the appropriate subject positions (encoded in C) demanded by society. While the model is to some extent crude it is nevertheless reasonably recognizable as a key feature of the intentions of government to influence the processes of learning and socialization in school.

In practice while T1 may still represent the National Curriculum, T1 should be read as a complex of texts some explicit, some implicit, many vague which together comprise the reality of the National Curriculum. Again, there is no single code C which is fully consensual, rather C may be seen as a complex of codes which overlap to some degree. Further, it is useful to define text more broadly than in its commonsensical use to refer to the printed page. Its wider application is recognized when people talk about being able to 'read a situation'. In walking down the street in a strange area one needs to be streetwise, to be able to read the signs, to be able to tell when a situation is becoming dangerous. In this way the 'street' is a text. Fashion can be read as a text: clothes, makeup, hair style (Barthes, 1985). In order to make sense of the world some synthesis of visual, aural, oral, kinetic texts is required. This process of 'making sense' through some kind of synthesis is different from 'transmission'.

In general, except in specialized contexts in the use of artificial languages and machines, living-language communication is not employed solely for transmission purposes where T2 is a simple reproduction of T1. When translating a novel or a poem from English into French a particular text (T2) is produced. However, a translation back from T2 into English would not necessarily produce a text identical to the original. Indeed, it would be most unlikely. In this, and other situations and contexts T1 and T2 are not exact translations of each other. No language exactly corresponds with another. Furthermore, two translators working on T1 will produce different translations (T2 and T′2) which will not be identical to each other. Returning to the example of the National Curriculum, there will be a multiplicity of possible codes which may be employed to translate T1, some of which may be considered by government ministers as 'legitimate' and others as 'too radical', 'liberal', 'subversive'. Generally speaking, of any text, there is an indefinite number of translations. Of course, one or more may become accepted as 'definitive' or 'authorized' but how this arises is less to do with 'truth' and 'exactness' and more to do with the social and cultural structures of power and authority. Diagrammatically, the effect of different codes in the production of translations of T1 is schematized by Lotman (1990) as follows:

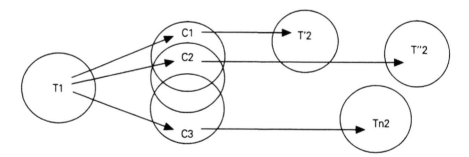

Figure 19.2: Effects of different codes

Schooling is not creative but reductive and reproductive. Success is judged to be when T2 is a faithful rendering of T1. If C1 is the master code, then the role of schooling is to repress C2 and C3 or to place them into a hierarchy of value such that C1 is preferred over C2 which in turn is preferred over C3. If the master text may be seen as deriving its power from what Lacan calls the *Nom du Père* — the Name of the Father — then teacher stands in the place of (or the subject position of, and with the voice of,) the Father, speaking the text of the Father. As the principle of power, authority, legitimacy, it is in the 'Name of the Father' that the conservative, traditionalist processes, elements and structures of culture and society find their force to preserve vested interests. In the National Curriculum, its voice can be heard in the demands for history as a narrative of kings, wars and scientific triumphs, the demands for the teaching of English to be subjected to the 'laws' of spelling, grammar and 'Literature' (Shakespere, Dickens and so on), the censoring of sex education, education about AIDS/HIV and drugs, the demands for (Christian) religious education and the act of daily worship, the criticism of schools which have emphasized multiculturalism, anti-discrimination and environmental awareness (Schostak, 1991, 1993). The whole apparatus of testing, inspection, league tables and marketization has provided the mechanisms which reward conformity/traditionalism and punish difference/progression, albeit under the political guise of radical reform. It is a radical narrowing and splintering of vision.

If the role of education, as argued here, is as a creative exploration of possible texts, then its function includes the suspension of the 'authority' of the master code and the suspension of any hierarchy of value as between possible alternative codes; that is, no one code is judged 'better than' another. It is the very process of playing with alternative text-codes (C1, C2, C3 . . .) to produce alternative readings (T′2, T″2, ... , Tn2) that leads to the creative production of meanings that is in the essence of educational processes. But this is only part of what is at issue in attempting to provide a radical view of education. Education always takes place in the 'Place of the Father', that is, within a system, or context of laws, traditions, censorings, exhortations that together comprise an authorized heritage, and a set of cultural identities, practices and a vision of the world. Where schooling transmits this vision, education plays with it, destabilizes its certitudes, makes the tacit explicit, and creates alternatives. It is the very condition for change, growth, difference.

In the Place of the Father

In the Place of the Father it is a battle ground. As a delegate for the Father what the teacher says is critical. However, as an 'intellectual' the teacher has access to a variety of codes many of which are subversive of accepted master codes. The teacher's voice is thus subject to considerable social, legal, moral, political surveillance. Against the power of rulers, intellectuals have long tried to make deals with the powerful. The Enlightenment was born out of such deals. When Kant sought to negotiate a stand off with Frederick the Great 'committing himself to applauding the sovereign's suppression of politically subversive acts in exchange for his own intellectual liberty' (Harpham, 1994) he made manifest the paradox. In short, the deal is to be allowed to think what you want while doing as you're told. There is a double code here. It is essentially unstable, like Booth's (1974) unstable irony which sets up a message which continually eats into itself, incapable of producing a stable end point (e.g., I am a liar — the 'truth' of the statement is undermined by the statement). The code is essentially 'act this way, think otherwise'. It assumes no necessary relationship between thought and action. However, thought, particularly thought revealed to the world through the written text, is itself a form of action. In Baskhar's (1994) and Sayer's (1992) terms while there may be no necessary causal relationship between thought and events in the world, there is at least a causative, or mutually conditioning relationship between them. It is a pact that the powerful cannot afford. In the Place of the Father, the Law of the Father is unconditional.

The paradox can be seen in another form with Mill as Simon (1960) describes:

> Mill argues strongly against those who hold 'that the human race ought to consist of two classes — one that of the oppressors, another that of the oppressed'. On the contrary, the question whether the people 'should have more or less of intelligence, is merely the question, whether they should have more or less of misery, when happiness might be given in its stead'.

Theoretically, therefore, all classes should have an equal degree of intelli-gence'. But there is a 'preventing cause' which is this, that 'a large propor-tion of mankind' is required for labour, and therefore has not the necessary time for the acquisition of 'intelligence'. 'There are degrees of command over knowledge too which the whole period of human life is not more than sufficient'; it follows that 'there are degrees ... of intelligence, which must be reserved for those who are not obliged to labour. (Simon, 1960, pp. 146–7)

Here the question is not so much about being able to think as one pleases but in having access to 'intelligence' or knowledge. This access is socially distributed according to the degree of 'obligation to labour'. It is again a double code forged from a liberal deal with the powerful who have vested interests in the existing conditions of econ-omic production in society. One side of the double deal can never quite be made explicit. Schooling has the function of silencing, of making invisible this other side.

These two 'double-codes', combined with a split between objective and sub-jective provides the basis for the entrapment, exploitation and subjugation of people whilst deploying a democratic 'liberal' rhetoric. The code that assumes the rhetoric of 'objectivity' implies that it has the inside track to some sort of certain (or at least, well 'researched') basis for action; whereas the subjective implies bias, whim, illusion. When Mill argues all should have 'an equal degree of intelligence' he sides with all those who see an alliance between the morality of equality and the logic of reason. However, he links reason with the economics of vested interest which becomes a 'preventing cause'. There is then a bridge that is created which allows the liberal mind to walk across from the side of rational equality to the other side that allows economic inequality.

In contemporary politics the objective–subjective split reveals itself in the apparently reasonable demand for 'balance' while at the same time creating bridges for the gentle walk across to intolerance and censorship. This demand has variously been made of teachers and of television reportage. The 1980s saw a sustained governmental attack on what can be taught and how information can be presented in the media in terms largely of sexuality, gender, politics, multiculturalism and history (Schostak, 1993). In its soft liberal form, it is found in the reduction of the status of 'knowledge' to 'opinion'. Once accepted a variety of possible moves may be made. For example, in confronting political opposition to nuclear power stations the Government may cite conflicting findings concerning the occurrence of cancers in people living near or working in power stations. Since a link has not been absolutely proved, then there is no reason to stop building power stations. Similarly, with the link between smoking and lung cancer, it took many decades of accumu-lating evidence for any governmental acknowledgment to be made of the link. Until overwhelming proof is admitted, reasonable concern has to be 'balanced' by the other side which stands upon the assertion that as yet overwhelming proof has not be found. This 'other side' is typically sustained by powerful vested interests. Mean-while many millions die.

As Rorty (1982, p. 192) has argued objective knowledge is founded upon the view that the language of science is successful because it corresponds to 'Nature's Own Language'. Hence, the method of science has involved not only 'ordering one's thoughts, but *filtering* them in order to eliminate "subjective" or "non-cognitive" or "confused" elements, leaving only the thoughts which are Nature's Own.' This offers a powerful policy strategy for politicians allowing policy to be sorted into two kinds of category: that which requires proof before decision/action; that which requires value assessment before decision/action. Since the former requires proof and proof is rarely immediately available and the latter is subject to political discourses then decisions can largely be made in the interests of the governing political group. In the framework of Figure 19.1, if Nature's Own Language is T1, then the scientists task is to identify the right code (C) to produce T2 in the image of T1. However, in the political realm this framework is imported into Figure 19.2 and T1 is subjected to alternative codes. In the absence of proof that any version of T2 is 'true', then a politically authorized code will take its place. Rorty:

> suppose we picture the 'value-free' social scientist walking up to the divide between 'fact' and 'value' and handing his predictions to the policy-makers who live on the other side. They will not be of much use unless they contain some of the terms which the policy-makers use among themselves. What the policy makers would like, presumably, are rich juicy predictions like 'If basic industry is socialised, the standard of living will (or won't) decline,' 'If literacy is more widespread, more (or fewer) honest people will be elected to office,' and so on. They would like hypothetical sentences whose consequents are phrased in terms which might occur in morally urgent recommendations. When they get predictions phrased in the sterile jargon of 'quantified' social sciences ('maximizes satisfaction', 'increases conflict', etc.), they either tune out, or, more dangerously, begin to use the jargon in moral deliberation.

In practice, a professional will be faced with a multiplicity of texts each claiming some degree of legitimacy — e.g., the texts derived from 'research', those of professional bodies (like the National Union of Teachers), those deriving from the cultures of occupational practice (that is, 'in this department we do things this way'), those from politicians, the media or even from friends and family. The professional will also have access to a multiplicity of codes (as in Figure 19.2). How does the professional begin to discriminate? In the 'Place of the Father', the professional is not free to discriminate, to deconstruct, to re-assess.

Is it a matter of think what you want but do what you're told? In order to act in the Place of the Father the professional must internalize the authorized code (C) of Figure 19.1 so that in justifying any action taken, the text of that justification (T2) is judged as an acceptable interpretation of the text (T1) which is able to authorize actions. In this circumstance the professional may think one thing but not be able to justify it in terms of the key authorized text. People often say, 'oh yes it's alright in theory but not in practice'. In this way theory may become separated from practice, if practice is the source of authorized texts. And practice itself may be dominated by the discourses of laws, accountability, auditing, performance assessment, appraisal. In practice then, the only law that matters is 'Think what you want but in action cover your back'.

The Challenge of Education

In the Name of the Father the child is brought up, made legitimate, schooled into 'wisdom' and ways of seeing, knowing and believing, given rights and takes on an identity, like father like son. It is a sad story. But stories can be contested by other stories — her — stories as some have been called, in the Name of the Mother. The challenge by the alternative story is an educational challenge, drawing out not only the potential for giving voice to difference but also for transforming the world. An eventuality that from the dominant view is judged as a threat to the life of all that 'we' have known and loved. The vanquishing of a once dominant view is not always a victory for education, but a victory for another way of schooling people into restrictive visions that are merely different, speaking to new vested interests.

Lotman (1990, p. 29) sees two forms of communication and these may serve as a way of thinking about the process of education itself. To summarize:

> In the first instance we are dealing with already given information which is transmitted from one person to another with a code which remains constant for the duration of the act of communication. In the second instance we are dealing with an increase in information, its transformation, reformulation and with the introduction not of new messages but of new codes, and in this case the addresser and addressee are contained in the same person. In the process of this autocommunication the actual person is reformed and this process is connected with a very wide range of cultural functions, ranging from the sense of individual existence which in some types of culture is essential, to self-discovery and auto-psychotherapy. (Lotman, 1990)

At its most general, education is the creative articulation of experience as selves and worlds. To this end, education faces many challenges. Since education is essentially a process which passes through transformations and is itself transformative of prior and current frameworks, those challenges occur at every level of human existence and action.

To think through the kinds of transformations that educational processes bring about, it will be useful to consider the following schema alongside the textual discussions so far.[1]

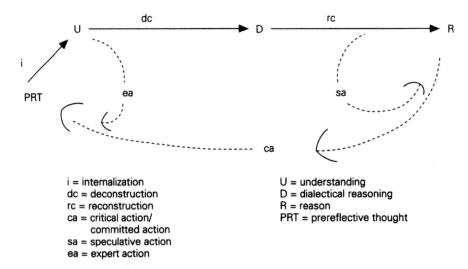

i = internalization
dc = deconstruction
rc = reconstruction
ca = critical action/
    committed action
sa = speculative action
ea = expert action

U = understanding
D = dialectical reasoning
R = reason
PRT = prereflective thought

Figure 19.3: Transformations through educational processes

The starting point for Figure 19.3 is at PRT which refers to prereflective thought which among other possibilities for interpretation can refer to the commonsense, everyday practical thinking which in the words of phenomenologists is 'taken for granted until further notice' (Schutz, 1976).[2] Everyday life in this sense has formed a rich field of study for symbolic interactionists, phenomenologists and ethnomethodologists. Imagine any individual acting in everyday life. Action would be impossible without the shared understandings that 'this is the way the world is', and without the traditions, the everyday forms of politeness, and the 'knowledge' of how men and women are supposed to be, how they are supposed to act and what they are supposed to believe in. Within this frame of mind, to act differently is to risk acting out of character. In a sense the individual is subjected to his or her biography shared with friends, family and community. One becomes positioned by the shared narratives of 'who I am', and 'people like us' who are different from 'them'. The stock of stories that I can tell about myself and others and how the world is, defines my 'reality', what I consider to be the natural order of things.

This 'sense of reality' can be transformed or challenged by schooling or expert forms of knowledge as PRT forms of knowing come to be replaced by expert forms of understanding (U). Imagine a child about to enter the processes of schooling or equally a young graduate about to enter teacher training or some other profession. The task to be accomplished by schooling is to internalize in the child the categories of thought, belief and forms of action authorized by expert systems. Essentially, there is a transformation from PRT forms towards various degrees of expertise in the socially valued disciplines of study either as defined by a national curriculum, exam boards, a university or professional body. Common-sense taken-for-granted forms of knowledge are replaced by the authorized or accepted forms of discipline-based or professional knowledge which correspond to the stage of understanding 'U' in the schema. Kuhn (1970) has described such a process through which scientists are schooled into the paradigms of normal science. These paradigms constitute the master texts in Lotman's terms. Again, this process has been a rich source of study for sociologists interested in the social construction of professional/expert action, identities and discourse. On the one hand, the transformations involved from PRT to U typically represent challenges to the beliefs and accepted practices of everyday life; on the other, they reposition the individual within the framework of available subject positions, and hence transform subjectivity from 'uninitiated' to 'initiate', from ignorant/inexpert to expert, from member of the masses to member of the élite, from powerless to powerful and so on. The process brings about an internalization of the schooled ways of thinking and being that transform the subjectivity of the individual. Depending upon the power and mastery that accrues to the individual from the process of internalization and self-transformation into an 'expert self' as distinct from the naive self of the PRT stage, the individual increases his or her vested interest in the continuance of the system. At this point, the expert judgment of the expert self feeds back into everyday practice in terms of expert action (*ea*) which derives its power and authority from a perceived mastery of events and situations that those who are not initiated have little insight into controlling or dealing with. There are similarities here with what Lacan (1977) calls the 'Imaginary' which develops from the 'mirror stage'. The 'Imaginary' has to do with the perception of unity, of synthesis which provides a greater sense of mastery of self and world. For the young child it occurs when catching sight of himself or herself in a real mirror (or in the social/linguistic mirror provided by parental talk) or makes the leap of understanding that the unity of the mother's body is an analogue for his or her own unity. Although inwardly all may seem fragmentary even chaotic to the child, and although the child's mastery of the body is not yet up to adult standard, the 'Imaginary' grasp provides the basis for perceptions of unity, synthesis and the promise of mastery. Similarly, with the advent of understanding (U) a greater mastery of the world about is promised, assumed and internalized.

As an example, the trainee teacher coming to grips with the complexity and seeming chaos of handling a class may envy the skill and apparent mastery of the experienced teacher. The experienced teacher may then become a role model — i.e., being a picture/image of mastery — for the novice who tries to shape his or her self in the image of the experienced teacher. Alternatively, a teacher newly acquainted with the latest fashions on behaviour management (e.g., Rogers, 1990) may well want to engage in some action research in order to 'improve the quality of social action' (Elliott, 1991) in his or her classroom. The attraction of such a book is that it provides the promise of replacing 'behaviour problems in the classroom' with 'mastery over behaviour in the classroom'. As such the appeal of the book operates at the level of the imaginary where the sense of improvement is essentially a form of mastery. Rogers provides a number of categories for labelling behaviours, and offers a number of procedures for handling behaviours. As such this book can be used as the master text which supplies the interpretative codes for analysing behaviour and formulating action. All the better if the categories employed are reinforced by other master codes — the National Curriculum documentation, OFSTED reports, the professional discourses of colleagues and so on which construct the image of the teacher as a master, as one in control. Referring back then to Figure 19.2, if T1 is read as the behaviour exhibited by a particular pupil, the alternative codes (C2, Cn) which may be supplied during interviews with pupils, parents or others rather than challenge the dominant code, may by interpreted in the light of the dominant code (C1) to produce an 'expert' interpretation of behaviour (T'2). This clearly constitutes a reflective cycle in itself which follows an apparent research process involving the triangulation of perspectives. In this case, the process has involved the views of the pupil which have been 'triangulated' with those of the parent and with those of teachers and the triangulation has been carried out within the framework of interpretation provided by the expert code.

Reflective practice as a term has, of course, been adopted throughout the professions. Everywhere there seem to be professionals aspiring to be reflective practitioners. Through reflective practice, theory and practice are in some way integrated and thus the dreaded theory–practice gap overcome. This could be thought of as an example of applied research or action research that is carried out within a given paradigm which leads to 'expert action' within the context of professional practice. Such expert action never moves beyond a kind of fine tuning of techniques to produce behaviour desired by the master codes of society unless some powerful break in the smooth surface of the master mirrors occurs casting doubt upon the master codes.

Such eruptions may occur as a result of disputes between particular 'schools of thought' and anomalies, contradictions or mysteries in any complex body of knowledge or theory. The recognition of these can lead to a fundamental questioning of the dominant paradigm(s) or master codes through which people have come to understand or make sense of the world. The basic category systems that have previously been used may be deconstructed or reframed in ways which reveal contradictions where all had seemed clear and distinct. For example, in the previous example on behaviour-modification approaches to the question of how to handle the behaviour of others range from authoritarian control to democratic procedures. Upon examining his or her own values and practice a professional may perceive a contradiction between the practical employment of authoritarian techniques and a personal belief in democratic forms of organization. Or, a group of professionals, in reflecting aloud on their beliefs and practices may find contrary standpoints being expressed about how the school should respond to issues of behaviour. When reflecting upon the ways in which school is organized and the curriculum constructed a professional may begin to perceive grave contradictions between those forms of organization and his or her basic beliefs concerning the nature of education and humanity. Still more disconcertingly, a professional may inquire into his or her basic beliefs and theories concerning the nature of education and find internal contradictions; or even, that there is no coherent view regarding the processes of education, its nature, its purpose and its role in personal and social life. Perhaps the process of deconstruction may also be regarded as a process of disconcerting, an experience akin to that when one 'looks awry' at something and sees something that lurks in the shadows (Zizek, 1991). It is a sideways glance that turns shadows into the feeling that something is there, looking, waiting. It is the experience of 'other-ness', the 'other' that resides outside of the text, that cannot be captured or explained by the text.

Recognizing that there is a lack of theory, or an anomaly or a confusion, or an other-ness, in itself does not necessarily reveal a way forward, an alternative way of thinking about and perceiving the world. However, it may be the precondition of creativity:

> A rhetorical effect occurs when one text is juxtaposed with another that is semiotically nonhomogeneous with it. Meaning is formed as much by the interaction between semiotically heterogeneous, mutually untranslatable layers of text as by the complex conflicts of meaning between the text and its context. (Zizek, 1991)

Other-ness may be experienced in two ways: first, as the radical untranslatability between texts; second, as the irreducibility of the 'real' to a text of any kind. In each case, expert action (*ea*) is suspended or unworkable until some kind of new synthesis emerges. A process of speculative reasoning is required through which some resolution to what had seemed alien, contradictory or anomalous can be made. Take for example the anomaly that democratic values places individuals on a level of equality, while traditional forms and conceptions of teaching place the teacher on a higher level (whether of authority or of expertise) than that of the pupil. The term 'democratic teaching' would then seem anomalous. However, it is only anomalous if the basic code underlying the process of teaching is that of 'transmission'. In this code, the role of the teacher is as the expert transmitter of master texts/codes whose task is to shape the pupil (as receiver and as novice code user) into being a reliable and consistent user of the master code. If the transmission code is replaced by say a 'play code', then both teacher and pupil roles fade to be replaced by the roles of 'co-players' in the mutual enterprise of creative interpretation (that is, two new subject positions emerge which act upon subjectivity itself). Rather than the imposition of one code upon all others, the process involves a play of codes. For some new synthesis to emerge there must be a play of imagination and reasoning through which a reconstruction can take place to produce a new point of understanding, a new synthesis — R in the schema. The move from transmission-code to play-code is critical. Its implementation in practice will require critical action (*ca*) which is quite distinct from expert action (*ea*) since critical action will not only challenge common sense, but will also challenge expert action. Critical action would have to be brought to bear upon the prevailing social practices, resource allocations and social structures to transform them for new purposes, challenging vested interests in the process. In this sense critical action is revolutionary in a way that expert action is not. Where, continuing the example, expert action fine-tunes the processes of transmission, critical action will challenge and subvert the transmission-code through the play-code. Critical action is only critical in the sense that it seeks to transform practice and subjectivity and to reorder, reconceptualize and reallocate resources in the real, material world as a material support to the new ideas, practices and subject positions that emerge.

Through critical action of this kind, adopting a 'play' standpoint cannot be regarded as an echo of what has been called 'wet liberal' rhetoric that never results in committed action. However, the process of play may stand for the strategy of exploring possible alternatives, of experimentation, of speculation at a point before full commitment to a particular alternative occurs. Play is action, and at this point in the cycle of reflection such play results in speculative action (sa in the schema) that does not require commitment but can lay the conditions for commitment to occur. It is only after reflection upon the results of the speculative action that a decision to engage in committed action (ca) may arise.

The challenge of education is not at the point of speculative action (sa) to 'take sides' in the 'transmission' versus 'play' debate but rather to explore fields of action and expression that are opened up and closed down in the whole cycle of reflection and transformation that has been discussed so far. If after the exploration of speculative action individuals wish to take sides, to make cases, to provide intricate and illuminative maps to guide human thought, feeling and action, then they may claim that their committed action is as a result of an educational process. However, ca is not educational action. Educational action is the whole cycle that proceeds without end. Education has as its field of studies the processes involved and the implications for persons, groups, societies, cultures of such forms of expression and action that result at every stage of the cycle.

The Question of Power

Since education, action and the challenge to all prevailing forms are woven inextricably, the question of the power cannot be ignored. Education, in the place of the Father cannot expect to make deals. Its only authentic strategy is to make explicit the implicit and to deconstruct the so-called 'absolutes' by means of which vested interests are preserved and reproduced. But this by itself is not sufficient for education. Education addresses the relationship between knowledge and power in ways which augment freedom (from prevailing forms of thinking, and for speculative action) and the transformation of self and world. However, the Enlightenment paradox cannot merely be swept aside in the search for alternatives. Rather some understanding of the ways in which power and thought/knowledge interact must be sought. Politics in the Place of the Father is the first object of an educational critique.

In contemporary debates, many postmodernist writers have seemed to erode the question of what to do in the face of power. There is in the wake of this a nostalgia for the apparent great labour movements that seemed to promise an end to inequality, exploitation and fascism. Nevertheless, these great 'master narratives' (Lyotard, 1984) of rational and socialist progress seem to have been torn down with the Berlin Wall and scattered across the internet, left at the mercy of virtual financial markets, and seduced by satellite mediated images of consumer/pop culture (Baudrillard, 1990). Where many still seek nostalgically for some rational community to arise through debate which will someday encompass the world (Habermas, 1984), others play in the cyber-babble of globalized virtual-space creating new information-based worlds which have no need for, nor desire to create some dialectical rational unity (Benedikt, 1991). In this information age, what is the scope for political action?

Every stage in the cycle described in Figure 19.3 is political. Following the cycle around R might stand for the kind of synthesis that Enlightenment Age rationalists, reformist and socialist revolutionaries promoted, a master narrative/text that explained all, that promised incremental progress until total mastery was achieved. Postmodernism with its scepticism toward all master narratives has seemed to erode the possibility of political action to relieve inequalities and injustices. Rather than class solidarity and action, there seems to be a splintering into 'taste or faith communities', a valuation of difference and a suspension of value hierarchies so that no valuation of one taste community can be set above another. A taste community can refer to anything from people who follow a particular kind of pop culture to a reconstruction of the 'little Italy' in some American city. A faith community can refer to anything from the moonies, a belief in rationalism, to a Christian denomination or other religious faith. At its most extreme, fascism could be regarded in a postmodern view as just another taste/faith community amongst others with an equal value and right to expression. In Figure 19.3, rather than R being created as the great new synthesis encompassing the universe of experience, a multiplicity of speculative actions may through increasingly committed action create not R as a global synthesis but 'r' as a local synthesis. Rather than a unity, there is a plurality; not one world, but multiple worlds. The potential both for creative freedom to explore alternative lifestyles and for an increasing xenophobia and intolerance of other taste communities can be realized in practice in such a postmodern arena. What then is the role of education, and in particular, teacher education?

Education: Global and Local Futures

Defining itself in its own image and not the image of others is the major radical task facing education. This is not to deny the immense debt owed to the political thinkers, sociologists, philosophers and others who have so enriched educational practice and understanding. But gifts and inheritances are not enough. The old name has to be forsaken to see the world (or worlds) anew.

This is not an abandonment. The look ahead presupposes the path travelled. But in looking back, the path may no longer look quite as it seemed. In joining contemporary debates about issues education does so from a different perspective.

No longer positioned by the vested interests of other points of view, education forms its own vantage point to take a perspective on the world(s) around. Long positioned as an agent of social control or as a tool for social transformation — in each case doing the bidding of political masters — educationists are at liberty to counterpose their own account of the educational field(s) of endeavour.

This field has already been hinted at above. It is at the point of the clash between powerfully held world views that a glimmer of the work, the arena of action comes into view. *Education has generally left the big questions to others,* preferring instead to focus on the role of the 'education system' in reproducing social order and social divisions watched over by the social and political theorists. Positioned as an element of something else, something greater, education has always known its place in the academic, social and political order and done its duty according to its chosen master.

But education comes alive as its own centre and field of activity at the very point where all is in contest, all is in question, and uncertainty, provisionality and possibility rule. Kuhn has painted a picture of science as proceeding by revolutions not by incremental progression. In this picture, it seems to me, education comes into being at the point where perception is given a jolt, where the duck that used to be seen takes the form of a rabbit and the question of identity is raised and not necessarily resolved. This question of identity that always remains questionable, perhaps even illusory, is the scene of play for the educational eye. But this is not a liberal 'I' open to all but committed to none.

Identity raises both a local and a global question. The tension implicit in this question provides the context within which a radical view of teacher education takes shape, not as a settled body of doctrine or as a discipline of practice and of knowledge but as a process of continually shifting perspectives. There is always an alternative, always another way of seeing things and always a dialogue to encourage and action to explore.

As merely a functionary in a system of National Curriculum delivery the role of the teacher is reduced to fitting individuals for the purposes of increasingly globalized systems. As the facilitator of alternatives the role of the teacher becomes that of a facilitator of challenge, of critique on the one hand; and on the other as a support for creativity, the cultural expression of individuals and communities and social action. In this latter view the focus for teacher education shifts from 'learning' and the conditions that produce predefined learning outcomes, to the support structures, the principles and the procedures that underpin creative production in all its forms in personal, social, economic, cultural, political life. In this latter view, 'learning' does not evaporate, rather it is integrated within the processes of reflection through which judgment is educated in all its rational, practical, aesthetic and ethical forms over all the fields of personal, social, economic, political and cultural action. This is not a curriculum of 'knowledge packages' but a curriculum of action through which individuals make themselves present in a world the structures of which at *once predates their own existence but also through cultural work is ever open to* possibility.

Though education alternatives proliferate both as challenges to the globalizing structures of modern societies and as a means of renewal — not reproduction — of ways of life for individuals, their communities and their wider social/global structures. Education conceived of only as a delivery system for the National Curriculum and for the needs of employers and 'citizenship' does not meet these requirements. The question of how to develop the structures, principles and procedures for the alternative sketched here remains open and relatively unexplored. Teacher education at present does not meet the challenge. In order for it to do so, it must consider such matters as:

- how to challenge and support challenges to authorities (whether social, cultural, political, religious);
- how to facilitate dialogue between different, even opposing world views and value sets;
- how to handle individual/group/community action within the context of the needs and interests of others;
- how to critique and bring change in social conditions;
- how to support the development of a multiplicity of forms of expression in the development of self and community identities and practices;
- how to facilitate an imaginative play of cultural possibilities as individuals attempt to make sense of themselves, their neighbours, their communities, the global structures within which they live, their cultural legacies and their histories;
- how to formulate futures; and
- how to give expression to present experiences and conditions.

The list is not exhaustive, not placed in order and many of the issues overlap. It is meant to provoke both dialogue and action. Of any text, local or global, questions can be asked of its key subject and object positions that individuals may take and of the key relationships between these. It is the subject who speaks and the object which has no voice and discounted as simply an object to be used for the purposes of the subject.

The Education of Voice

If teacher education is to salvage some intellectual independence, its role can be seen in the education of voice. Voice connotes being a presence, having something to say, having an agenda of needs, interests and hopes, having to be taken into account in all decision-making and action. If this is so, then no voice can be raised above another in such a way that the other is silenced. If this is so, then teacher education is another name for a continuing process of mutual education — a mutual education of voice.

It can be asked in this mutual process, who is speaking, how is this speaking voice constructed by the master texts of the taste/faith community, in whose interests is it speaking? How are individuals manoeuvred into a given subject position? What are the range of subject positions? Which of these are authorized and which are forbidden? Which are of high and which of low value? How are individuals manoeuvred into object where their voice is suppressed, where their bodies are ventriloquist's dummies for the master voice? How is it possible to create the dialogue where individuals find their own voice and speak in their own interests? How finally, is it possible to speak of political action?

It is not enough, it may even be a betrayal, to speak for another, in their best interest (Chow, 1993). This is the position of a collective subjectivity — a 'We' that knows best — whether it is a benevolent paternalism or a maleficent totalitarianism. The education of voice marks a transition from collectivities of this sort to a recognition of mutuality. Mutuality does not presuppose either an homogeneity of interests nor heterogeneity. The work of mutuality is to bring to presence the needs, interests — in short, the life agendas of each. Finding one's voice submerged in the Place of the Father may be difficult, but not impossible (e.g., Haug, 1987; Freire, 1970). How similarities, differences and disputes are handled is a matter of education; to maintain an educative principle of voice the strategies of voice are drawn out: strategies of interpretational play (Figure 19.2), leading to an educative cycle of reflective practice/action (Figure 19.3) where personal, local or global syntheses are sought through negotiation, cooperation, mutual support, or agreement to differ, that is tolerance. The result is an education of personal, social, cultural experience in all the fields of social action (Schostak, 1993). Education is not a final solution. It is a process. The responsibility for what happens remains a matter of voice.

From Conclusion to Non-clusion

Education, in whatever guise it takes, in whatever age, is political. Its politics is, however, without a final closure. It plays with the possible, the radical alternative and forms the quest for action in whatever field of social endeavour exists. Not so teacher education in the western world. Teacher education as a service industry meeting the needs of the global market and the national interest is in political thrall. The 1980s and the early 1990s has seen it teetering on the edge of extinction as a viable liberatory and critically independent intellectual arena of debate and cultural production. This is not so much due to a lack of intellectual activity or lack of creative and cultural production as to a resource squeeze and a political restructuring of the system through which the activities of educationists are 'constrained', 'managed', 'controlled'. Yet this does not fully explain why education as a discipline has been so politically easy to pick off.

While educationists may have recognized the radical nature of their profession, in general, they have not fully grasped and implemented it. Their eyes have largely been glued to the arena of the traditional classroom in the school, the college or the university. They have traditionally done their job as deliverers of more teachers on the one hand, and on the other, as educational researchers they have criticized the system of delivery employing not an educational perspective but a range of sociological, psychological and political frameworks for critique. If an educational perspective is claimed at all, it is only as a particular focus within a wider field of social, political, economic and psychological activity. What they have rarely accomplished is to develop a genuine 'education' capable of generating its own framework of critique capable of positioning other fields of human study and activity within its own framework, a framework that is sufficiently robust and visionary to do the job of critiquing the sociologies and psychologies that have imposed their visions and methods on education as well as critiquing the social and cultural forms and processes which provide the social and material frameworks for educational activities. In short, educationists have been content with intellectual hand-me-downs from their big brothers and sisters in the disciplines of philosophy, sociology, psychology, politics and so on. It is time education grew up and challenged these 'Fathers'.

Notes

1 This has developed through a reflection upon Bhaskar's (1993) schema for Hegelian dialectics.
2 PRT may be questioned since it can be argued that reflection takes place all the time. However, it is being used here to mark the point of a particular kind of transformation: the stage before individuals are introduced to some process of authorized systematic theorization which they had not previously encountered and hence leads to a new sense of understanding or mastery.

References

BARTHES, R. (1985) *The Fashion System*, London, Cape.
BHASKAR, R. (1994) *Dialectic: The Pulse of Freedom*, London, New York, Verso.
BAUDRILLARD, J. (1990) *Seduction*, Montréal, New World Perspectives.
BENEDIKT, M. (Ed) (1991) *Cyberspace: First Steps*, Cambridge, Massachusetts, London, MIT Press.
BOOTH, W.C. (1974) *A Rhetoric of Irony*, Chicago and London, University of Chicago Press.
BRODER, D.S. (1989) 'Mrs. Thatcher and the erosion of British liberty', *Manchester Guardian Weekly*, **141**, 5, p. 7.
CHOW, R. (1993) *Writing Diaspora: Tactics of Intervention in Contemporary Cultural Studies*, Bloomington, Indianapolis, Indiana University Press.
DAVIES, B. and HARRÉ, R. (1990) 'Positioning: The discursive production of selves', *Journal for the Theory of Social Behaviour*, **20**, 1, pp. 43–63.
ELLIOTT, J. (1991) *Action Research for Educational Change*, Milton Keynes, Open University Press.
FREIRE, P. (1970) *Cultural Action for Freedom*, Harmondsworth, Penguin (published by Penguin 1972).
HABERMAS, J. (1984) *Theory of Communicative Action*, **1**, London, Heinemann.
HARPHAM, G.G. (1994) 'So . . . What *Is* Enlightenment? An Inquisition into Modernity', *Critical Inquiry*, **20**, pp. 525–56.
HAUG, F. (Ed) (1987) *Female Sexualization: A Collective Work of Memory*, CARTER, E. (Trans.), London, Verso.
KOSKO, B. (1994) *Fuzzy Thinking: The New Science of Fuzzy Logic*, London, Harper Collins.
KUHN, T. (1970) *The Structure of Scientific Revolutions (2nd edition), Vols. I and II. Foundations of the Unity of Science*, Chicago, University of Chicago Press.
LACAN, J. (1977) *Écrits: A Selection*, London, Tavistock/Routledge.
LYOTARD, J.F. (1984) *The Postmodern Condition: A Report on Knowledge*, BENNINGTON, G. and MASSUMI, B. (Trans.) *Theory and History of Literature*, **10**, Manchester, Manchester University Press.
LOTMAN, Y.M. (1990) *Universe of the Mind: A Semiotic Theory of Culture*, London, New York, Tauris.
ROGERS, B. (1990) *'You Know the Fair Rule'*, *Strategies for Making the Hard Job of Discipline in School Easier*, London, Longman.
RORTY, R. (1982) *Consequences of Pragmatism*, Minneapolis, University of Minnesota Press.
SAYER, A. (1992) *Method in Social Science: A Realist Approach* (2nd Edition), London, Routledge.
SCHOSTAK, J.F. (Ed) (1991) *Youth in Trouble: Educational Responses*, London, Kogan Page, Norwich, CARE, University of East Anglia.
SCHOSTAK, J.F. (1993) *Dirty Marks: The Education of Self, Media and Popular Culture*, London, Boulder, Pluto.
SCHUTZ, A. (1976) *The Phenomenology of the Social World*, WALSH, G. and LEHNERT, F. (Trans.) London, Heineman.

John F. Schostak

SIMON, B. (1976) *The Two Nations and the Educational Structure 1780–1870*, London, Lawrence and Wishart.
ZIZEK, S. (1991) *Looking Awry: An Introduction to Jacques Lacan Through Popular Culture*, Cambridge, Massachusetts, London, England, MIT Press.

20 Drawing the Threads Together: A Summary

Rob McBride

Introduction

This summary rests upon the evidence collected from the previous chapters in this volume.[1] Its outcome will be a set of ideas which will suggest a new way forward from the existing policies on teacher education. I will begin by discussing the approach to be taken.

There are two central issues. First is the relationship between policy and practice. It is all too easy to write as if teachers and schools obeyed policy word for word. They do not. The Tory government has since 1979 put great efforts into trying to ensure that its education policies are followed carefully. To that end the National Curriculum is enshrined in law; In-service training policy is governed by categorical funding (see McBride, 1989) which steers money to certain types of activity and so on. If we take the latter it is clear that neither schools nor HE providers obey the rules completely. For example, I recently visited a school which was ostensibly having a maths in-service training day used the money in the maths Inset budget for a drama day because that was what the staff wanted. There are numerous HE courses which existed prior to the days of categorical funding which are unchanged but renamed as 'The Management of . . .' because there is Inset money for management training.

When writing about policy there is a balance to be struck between the policy and its implementation and researchers need to take both the policy and the practice into account. To explain this further there is an interesting debate between Hatcher and Troyna (1994), on the one hand, and Ball (1994) on the other, about how policy should be investigated and characterized. The former accuse the latter of placing too great a focus on practice, ignoring the influence of policy upon practice, while Ball defends himself. The question is to what extent teachers and schools are able to continue to exercise their professional judgment. To what extent are they free and policy irrelevant on a day-to-day basis. Plainly policy tends to influence practice but teachers also make decisions themselves and most of the chapters in this volume have tried to take both policy and practice into account in the individual cases they describe.

This leads me to the second consideration; the nature of theoretical analysis. How do we theorize? One possibility is to present grand or meta-narratives as characterizations of a situation. For example, one might argue that the root of the problem is the 'swing to a centralized system'; or that a major factor is the 'increasing globalization of information'. The difficulty with arguments of this genre is that they become stock explanations and gradually all issues become reduced to one, or a small handful, of simple general characterizations. Such meta-narratives are too sweeping. They become reified and therefore disempowering of people (see Harvey, 1989 as well as Schwab's seminal paper of 1971).

In this brief summary I will try and avoid the use of meta-narratives. The view represented here is that there are strands of activity but no clear and general picture. The realities of schools and teachers are complex and varied. By limiting myself to the use of research evidence from the chapters in this collection I will suggest that the most significant steps that the Government (*any* British government) should take involve simply loosening its hold and encouraging (and paying where necessary) practitioners to take responsibility for their own education. I propose policy changes that are not prescriptive but allow teacher education to be dynamic in the way that David Clemson has described in Chapter 8. There should be a range of institutions producing teachers with a variety of values. I will argue that there is no single best method of training teachers. Moreover, I will suggest that institutions of HE are critical to teacher education at every stage and to any regeneration of it.

A reader might retort that all of the chapters in this volume are written by HE staff and that therefore there is a bias in favour of HE. There is plainly some truth in this suggestion but part of the responsibility that academics bear is to make their work and their views public so that at least they can be commented upon. Who else, it might be asked, is in a position to comment as authoritatively? Who else researches this area and provides evidence? Many different groups have a justifiable interest in teacher education and this summary reflects the arguments that can be justified by research-based evidence and experience.

I will take it too that teacher education does not consist of discreet parts. The structure of the book identifies three periods of teacher education but as it was explained in Chapter 1 this was adopted to assist analysis. There are not seamless moves between each period and each needs to dovetail, to some extent, with what happens before and/or after.

I will argue that teacher education needs to be professional education. I have elaborated my views on the nature of professionalism elsewhere (see McBride, 1992 and 1993). I take it that most people would accept that a professional teacher operates in largely non-routine situations, especially when children's learning is taken into account, and therefore teachers have to have some freedom to make judgments. We cannot educate teachers by giving them lists of simple rules.

A professional teacher has to give pre-eminence to the interests of children. The values implicit in such action are not written down. I argue that we have to create a code of ethics to guide teachers and that this task is best carried out by teachers in the public domain in consultation with other groups such as parents, school governors, political parties and the like. This discussion and the ensuing documentation would support the third element of professional teaching and that is the requirement that professional teachers have to be socialized into the values of the professional community. There is a culture or community of teachers which is diverse and fragmented at present. It cannot be touched or seen but those who work with teachers are aware of it.

Finally, an organized profession of teachers should have some influence in the shaping of national education policy, over the operation of professional responsibilities, and some autonomy in relation to the State. These, or similar, notions of professionalism are assumed by most of the contributors of previous chapters.

In Chapter 9 Sidgwick suggests that LEAs were a useful 'third force' which policed induction in schools. In the scheme outlined here I see no place for LEAs. LEAs have not been concerned in a major way with the conception and delivery of long-term award bearing teacher-education programmes and as such programmes are central to my conclusions I cannot see a role for LEAs. Indeed, I am not concerned with policing teacher education. Policing cannot be central to any educational scheme as it does not help bring about learning and if it needs to take place at all, is the responsibility of politicians.

The current force of policy is to support detailed and imposed curricula in the form of technical rules and regulations. These deprofessionalize teachers rather than enrich them and their practice. Frankly government has to decide whether to trust in people or in processes and while it is easy to dismiss these sentiments at this time, I argue in favour of the former (see also Hargreaves, 1994).

Having outlined the approach and the source of data I will now describe teacher-education policy and practice as they are according to the evidence here, and as they might be.

Initial Teacher Education

The Existing Arrangements

The early impressions of the newly designed programme are not particularly favourable. Chris Husbands (Chapter 2) has noted positive reaction to the changed circumstances but other writers are not as enthusiastic. Of course it is early days and one would not expect trouble-free innovation. Yet the MOTE project supplies evidence which suggests that at this stage there has been little change in school practice with respect to ITE. Teachers, by and large, are still not involved in students' written assignments or in assessing them.

The core change in ITE of giving schools more responsibility, and indeed more money, was imposed by central government with no particular enthusiasm from anybody. Edwards and Collison (Chapter 5) make a telling comment:

> the UK experience of one year funded initiatives and the imposition of unfeasible practices have confirmed the majority of teachers in their suspicion that externally imposed initiatives are likely to be transitory and of value only if they provide funds to enable schools to meet their own priorities.

It is not surprising that there is some evidence of integration but little of 'partnership'. That is to say there is evidence that HE and schools are organizing together but that the work of educating trainee teachers is carried out by two organizations treading somewhat separate paths. It could be argued that it is too early in the new scheme to expect partnership but I suspect that the future holds little prospect of improvement in this respect. The central task of schools is to teach children and as Sally Brown (Chapter 4) reveals Scottish teachers prefer HE to retain control of ITE. I doubt that English teachers hold a different view.

Partnership could be conceived of as swopping staff between institutions; certainly the basis of partnership must rest upon staff interaction. It is not easy to see the advantage, for some HE institutes at least, in having their own academic staff with part-time appointments in schools or having temporary lectureships filled by teachers. If university staff are working in schools they are not researching or writing. With respect to teachers as lecturers, universities, by and large, seek academics who are publishing and researching. Part-time and temporary appointees are unlikely to pull their weight in this respect. If we are seeing a split between 'teaching' and 'research' universities, such appointments might be worthwhile in 'teaching universities' but this says very little for the status of ITE. One of the great problems of ITE in recent years is that it has been delivered by too many university staff whose publication record in educational journals and books has been poor. They have been 'teachers' who have not conducted sufficient educational research. This is not surprising in view of their heavy teaching loads. The messiness and the demands of research are not easily compatible with a heavy teaching load. Giving ITE to 'teaching universities' or seeing it as primarily a 'teaching' task creates a set of problems about quality.

There might be some advantage for teachers seeking an academic career but I doubt whether headteachers will willingly part with their best teachers. Equally, will schools want part-time or temporary lecturers in schools? Who controls the appointment of an existing lecturer in a school, the school or the HE institute? How many lecturers can return to teaching in school after years of absence? And what advantage will there be for academic staff in such an arrangement which cuts back research and writing time? Another means of fostering partnership might be through mentoring schemes. This will be discussed, and advocated, in the following sections.

A fundamental problem, referred to in several chapters, is the length of the current Post Graduate Certificate in Education [PGCE]. Bennett (Chapter 7) argues that there is too much to cover in one year. It can be argued too, that it is not just a question of having insufficient time to cover content but insufficient time for trainees to embed enough educational wisdom into their thinking. These shortfalls might be made up in either or both of two ways. The PGCE might be extended over a longer period, and/or the induction period might redress any deficiency which arises from the lightweight PGCE. I will argue in favour of both in the next section.

A New ITE Policy

National policy should enable HE institutions to take greater control of ITE. While 'teaching universities' could continue taking some of this work, I think the hand of opportunity should be extended to research universities. At least ITE should be seen as a research and development activity and partnership should be forged on the basis of research carried out at all levels. Tutors in HE should be offered the opportunity to carry out research of their own practice, and of the practice of schools.

Mentors in schools should be a crucial link between HE and the schools they work in. Mentors should be offered the opportunity to complete masters level courses which give them an award and which would also act as a form of training. They could research their own work, that of their protégés in schools and also the courses they attend. Trainees, as Chris Husbands has outlined, would be able to research their courses, their mentors, their tutors, and their own practice. In this way I believe research activity could act as the cement which binds all of the groups together into a partnership. Schools should be paid for their mentoring activities and HE mentoring courses should be subsidized. Mentoring would provide personal and professional development for existing staff.

What would be the other advantages for such a scheme? ITE areas in HE and schools could be centres of lively and academic debate about educational issues. Visits to schools by academic staff would not be superficial observations, as they tend to be now, but opportunities to discuss research and development of trainees and of the school at large. ITE and Inset would be faces of the same coin. Chris Husbands and I, have indicated that ITE has been very limited in outlook for too long with far too many HE staff settling in to rather stale and weary teaching careers, doing minimal research. This state of affairs was indefensible in the face of government attacks in recent years. The variation which David Clemson seeks could be allowed to develop if we embraced the policies I have described and the education service as a whole would benefit.

HE tutors would be given the space to research and write in re-invigorated institutions which would no longer be peopled so heavily by entrepreneurial hunter-gatherers concerned about job security, stability and short-term success in raising money. Instead they would be able to make a longer-term commitment to ITE, to the schools they work in and to good quality academic work.

Trainee teachers would gain from seeing and carrying out research with more experienced practitioners. It is important to consider too, that ITE should not be a final year tacked on to the end of a first degree. Rather I favour a course which would be spread out over two or three years to allow trainees to understand research and to allow their understanding of educational processes to embed themselves into their personas. We could find the Department for Education [DFE] offering part funding for joint degrees such as maths or biology or English and education. Students might spend part of each of the four years such a degree would take, no longer than present but better apportioned, to study schools and schooling. An alternative might be something along the lines of a BEd.

I do not accept that the shortfalls of short PGCE programmes might be rectified by an enhanced induction programme alone. Teachers have to be ready to teach when they begin. A period of less than good teaching, while they wait for the induction process to bite, is not acceptable. I would add that the oft heard criticism that the university element of the PGCE is too 'theoretical' may well be a reaction from trainees who are so short of understanding about the business of education that they cannot relate theory to what amounts to too little practice. I suspect that if trainees had three years to assimilate an understanding about the practice of education they would be better prepared to theorize about their own practice rather than merely hope to 'survive' when they first enter the classroom. Student teachers would feel that they were based in, say, a university where they could read and develop theories, in association with colleagues, as they gradually come to terms with the practice complexity of schools and teaching. Having trainees based and dispersed in schools does not support a notion of education which includes meetings, discussion and learning by comparison.

None of these plans would prevent inspection of ITE training by the Teacher Training Agency or its future equivalent. I would hope that inspection teams included people who were sufficiently knowledgeable about research but this is not to preclude other people who might be part of such a process. I cannot see any advantage in hiding ITE practice from anybody who is able to understand it and judge its value. I would hope that positive inspection reports would actually strengthen the basis of research-based ITE courses.

John Elliott has described a similar set of ideas (see Elliott, 1993). The means of bringing it about are not complex. I am not suggesting that the Secretary of State for Education legislates for this type of programme, rather that he is prepared to approve such programmes if institutions of HE are prepared to run them. The decision to allow such programmes is simple, let us not mystify the decision process, and I have no doubt that those institutions which wish to take this track would require only a few months to prepare. One argument against freeing up the existing regulations is a concern for cost. I will discuss this matter in the final section of this chapter but I do not consider it a major obstacle.

To conclude this section, the scheme I have outlined would place responsibility on HE institutions for creating and sustaining partnerships. I doubt whether government can do any more than pressurize us towards superficial integration, as seems to be the case at present. I believe too, that this arrangement allows both HE and schools to concentrate on what it does best. If there are colleges and universities wishing to continue with the existing scheme let them. Let students, schools and other 'consumers' judge what is best. In addition let us hope that government allows HE/school alliances to grow and develop so that like Sally Brown's reference to Scotland (Chapter 4) the English and Welsh can claim they are delivering ITE within a 'consensual approach based on historically viable institutions. We can hope that both schools and HE can, if they wish, retake control of their institutional missions and their visions of ITE which will then not be limited by the language and frameworks of government' (see the claim of Edwards and Collison, Chapter 5).

Induction

It is apparent that the first year, and possibly the next three or four, are important years in the socialization of teachers (see Tickle, 1987). It is these years that influence their practice and those in which good quality induction programmes need to foster their potential as professional practitioners. In a more modest but no less important way Sidgwick (Chapter 9) reports that HMI have argued that 40 per cent of schools have excessive expectations of NQTs. It will be argued here that just as HE should be given responsibility for ITE they should also orchestrate and conduct induction.

The Existing Arrangements

There is little doubt that induction is the Cinderella area of teacher education to which little thought and few resources are directed. Sidgwick has suggested that schools operating in market environments tend to cut corners by giving insufficient support to NQTs. In Chapter 11 Tickle observes that NQTs can easily be satisfied with 'what works' and primarily concerned with predictability and security. The reflective practice which Tickle describes is limited to procedural matters and will not raise the quality of teaching.

The notion of a probationary year for NQTs has been dropped and we see evidence of lack of commitment by schools to the needs of NQTs. Sidgwick, as I have noted above, argues for a 'third force' to somehow 'police' induction. I will argue, instead, that good-quality mentoring schemes under the aegis of HE will re-invigorate, and provide a basis for, good quality induction.

A New Policy for the Induction of NQTs

In keeping with this general approach to teacher-education policy the steps I suggest would be required are few and simple. There are three elements;

- all NQTs should be given a clear written statement of legal entitlement. They should teach for no more than 75 per cent of a full school timetable; they should be eligible for support for a part-time education course which lasts for three years; and they should be able to expect the in-school support of a mentor;
- if funding is made available to NQTs for long-term award bearing courses, HE institutions should be able to attract NQTs on courses. To run such courses HE institutions should be eligible to apply for start up funding and should feel relatively confident that once such courses began that they could continue to fund them. A three-year safety net should be available from an appropriate government funding body;
- schools should be able to apply for some funding to pay for a mentor who would be expected to complete an HE course in mentoring, who would support up to, say, three NQTs, and who would work with an HE institution to provide mentoring support for an NQT. Mentors, like NQTs, would be able to apply for funding to undertake an award-bearing course in mentoring NQTs in an institution of HE. Likewise, HE institutions should be eligible to apply for funding to run such courses for a minimum of three years.

Vonk provides an enormous amount of advice and guidance for any institution wishing to engage in an induction scheme. Of course, many other types of courses could be developed and I have little doubt that good quality arrangements would provide beneficial personal and career development for mentors. Vonk argues that mentoring should be the responsibility of the whole school and not just a mentor. Imaginative schools would undoubtedly benefit as a whole.

This raises the question of what would happen to unimaginative schools. In recent years education policy has revealed little trust in teachers. Rather politicians have sought to impose structures, such as the National Curriculum. The sort of policy I am advocating needs to be based on trust. I have no major concern about inspection. Let OFSTED or the Teacher Training Agency or their future replacements inspect such schemes and comment upon them as it wishes. I have some confidence that many would be successful. If not let market forces take the hindmost; those schools which do not attract NQTs or which attract criticism of their efforts may find that they are no longer able to engage in induction.

There are three further points which need to be made. The first is that I resist placing the practice of mentoring into some kind of notion of a structured teaching career, which the Dreyfus model, for example, as described by Elliott (1993) might be used to justify (Elliott, by the way, does not use the model to justify a fixed structure). I would argue that there are all sorts of people who might be best placed to be mentors. They might be enthusiastic young 'rising stars' who would respond positively and develop their own understanding of teaching by working with NQTs. Alternatively I could imagine a teacher in the later years of a career who could provide shelter conditions and experienced guidance for a young teacher.

Second, the NQT mentor is a crucial person who relates theory to practice. The mentor is in the school on a daily basis but should also enable the NQT to understand and make sense of the school and its work through theory. He or she would not be the same person who was responsible for mentoring trainee teachers who were part of the ITE scheme. There are two different jobs to be done. Nevertheless, the two mentors could support each other and discuss their research activities. Third, we need some kind of guidance or regulation of induction schemes. It has been suggested by Sidgwick that we need a professional body to guide instruction. I will comment on this issue below. Changes to national policies that give HE the opportunity to take up these challenges would surely be grasped readily. As with all teacher education, induction needs to be seen as part of a longer-term commitment by the education service and should dovetail with wider Inset arrangements. I turn to consider these next.

Inset

The Existing Arrangements

It is interesting that most writers have paid little attention to the broad policy situation, rather they concentrate on the processes that good courses require. Possibly this is explained by the complexity and technical crudity of policy documents — they are hardly interesting to write about. My own chapter (17), while clearly making no general claims, nevertheless paints a picture which is all too real in HE around the country. There are fewer teachers participating in long-term award-bearing courses; there is a new assemblage of 'consultants' who provide inexpensive 'kiss-me-quick' Inset as opposed to professional development; HE staff are increasingly casualized; many schools cannot afford long-term Inset and even if they could they have problems identifying their own needs and then satisfying them — schools are not strong in providing their own Inset without support; finally, as I have demonstrated elsewhere (see McBride, 1989) the national policy for Inset ensures that only certain types of Inset are funded. Schools and HE do subvert the system to some extent but schools are limited in the ways they can spend their 'own' money.

A New Inset Policy

As with ITE and induction the key to policy should be to set HE free. Within this volume there is very close agreement about the nature of good-quality courses. They should concentrate on helping teachers improve their practice; teachers should be helped to research their classrooms and schools; professional development goes hand in hand with personal, school and curriculum development. Each writer has a slightly different approach. Each should be allowed to flourish and indeed this is the nub of each of these sections on teacher-education policy. Policy should allow the enormous vigour and experience that resides below the surface in HE to provide impetus for these schemes. They could be inspected and evaluated; I am confident that many courses would stand up to scrutiny. More importantly, each institution should be responsible for evaluating itself beyond anything organized by the State.

HE must be helped by the provision of more stable funding. The current market forces arrangement leaves HE at the end of the line in that they are forced to respond to all that has gone on before. HE has to wait for policy, schools and sometimes LEAs to decide on their priorities and then they have to seek to provide support. I have already alluded to some of the problems which arise. The greatest of these is a debilitating short termism which puts enormous pressure on individual staff, on planning and on quality. Policy quite simply needs to cushion HE from these and to do this Inset programmes should be supported for three years at a time. As long as HE can demonstrate that they have sought students, provided imaginative programmes and brought in some funding they should feel that they can continue to provide and develop their Inset programmes.

Broader Issues

In this section I will refer to the two chapters which precede this one as well as the issues of funding and the need for a professional body. First I will refer to Chapter 18 in which David Bridges has written about the limitations of pragmatism. 'Common sense' cannot provide a basis for teacher education because it accepts without questioning and, as David rightly points out, can even steer us away from identifying the appropriate issue. Yet he has gone further to criticize the notion of action research. In this respect he is in conflict with the following chapter by John Schostak who argues that educational approaches need to move away from global approaches to more localized ones. The point is that approaches such as action research place a high value on the wisdom of practitioners, as indeed do the chapters in Part 3.

Action research is rooted in the pragmatism of John Dewey (see Adelman, 1993) but has developed a great deal from these early beginnings to recognize the interests of both individual teachers and the wider community of teachers. The problem with papers which criticize action research as merely pragmatic is that they ignore the importance of the notion of a practice (see MacIntyre, 1981 and McBride, 1992). There is a risk here that we will become entangled with abstruse grand narratives but MacIntyre has traced the notion of a practice to Greek times. He writes:

> By a practice I am going to mean any coherent and complex form of socially established co-operative human activity through which goods internal to that form of activity are realised in the course of trying to achieve those standards of excellence which are appropriate to, and partially definitive of, that form of activity with the result that human powers to achieve excellence and human conceptions of the ends and goods involved, are systematically extended. (MacIntyre, 1981, p. 175)

I do not want to make strong claims about the existence of a teaching practice but I do believe that there is a culture of teaching which is passed down, which is serviced by a literature and which transcends schools. The culture develops on its own (see Elliott's account of the growth of action research in Elliott, 1991) and has a broad awareness of many of its own values. Bridge's account of pragmatism does not mention a developing practice and is in this sense limited. When we take the practice into account I find it difficult to believe that teachers can continually manage with 'what works' without colleagues, line managers and the educational literature (in the case of widespread adherence) being aware and commenting. The action-research literature is fairly active and perceptive and while all literatures have their limitations, this one does not seem worse than others.

Of course, teaching should always be open to widespread debate and criticism but if we underestimate the role of teachers in the improvement of teaching we run the risk of improving nothing. Teachers need to be major players (see Sarason, 1990, for example) and I feel certain that David Bridges would not wish to deny that. Possibly the argument about the poverty of pragmatism and his comments about action research might be seen as leaving him open to the criticism that he undervalues the role of teachers in educational improvement. I do agree with David, following my comments in Chapter 17, that universities are being undermined in their activities as enablers of change in schools.

Throughout I have argued for the funding of both teachers and HE. Where does the money come from? This seems to me to be extremely simple. The setting up and development of the National Curriculum has cost in the region of £500m according to figures bandied about in the popular press. The nation has found money at very short notice in recent years to pay for the Falklands war in 1981, policing of the miners strike in 1984, the National Curriculum in 1988, the Gulf War in 1991 and to support the pound on Black Wednesday in 1993. What has been outlined for teacher education here will come to a small fraction of any of these and could be funded by reductions in spending on the National Curriculum and its associated Inset.

In Chapter 17 I described courses which were delivered by distance learning. Many universities are now cutting down contact time by providing written materials and beginning to make use of electronic communication to deliver courses and support students. Good quality distance-learning courses require personal contact between HE tutors and teachers but, in general, distance-learning methods do help keep down costs. I would argue, in addition, that in my experience a distance-learning element can improve courses in that many courses are overtaught. Teachers need the time to investigate for themselves and by reducing contact time between tutors and teachers there is a tendency for academic imperialism to be undermined. Government could enrich teacher education at all levels by investing, through HE, in the preparation and delivery of distance-learning courses.

Before concluding I will comment briefly on the issue of a professional body. In the early 1990s we seemed to come close to having a General Teaching Council. It seemed to be a reasonable idea yet the view from a distance was that a group of people had run with the idea and almost elected themselves to run the organization. If this was the case an organization that needs to be reasonably democratic would have led off in the wrong direction. I have reservations about a professional organization that has a national remit. If HE is to be at the heart of the various forms of teacher education there needs to be opportunities for local teachers and their representatives to discuss their work; to generate and publish papers about their values and activities; and to reveal the results of their research. The possibilities are enormous. Of course there would be difficulties, disagreements and problems but I would expect such arrangements to be vastly more invigorating than the current burdens of the National Curriculum and controlled Inset. Broader regional conferences might occur where groups could deliver papers and ideas which have emerged from more local groups.

These plans are not fanciful. There are groups around the country that have existed and which continue to exist. One example which did but no longer exists was the Kettering Alternative Approach. This consisted of a group of six schools which decided not to compete but to keep its intakes constant and to form a Curriculum Development Unit using their own seconded staff (see Bartlett, 1989). The KAA as it was known could have provided the basis for a very exciting national scheme of teacher education which operated at the local level.

More recently, groups of headteachers have been forming around the country to take some control over their own Inset. Headteachers are currently very powerful figures who often control substantial budgets. In Cambridgeshire, for example, the Cambridgeshire Secondary Education Trust has held several conferences and books and journal articles are beginning to emerge from it (see West, 1993 and McBride, 1994). Small groups of headteachers are beginning to sprout up around the country and to prosper. They could provide an interesting basis for further development.

Conclusion

Despite more than a decade of changes in the various elements of teacher education there remains a sense of great waste. If only given the chance the educational community, and higher education in particular, could regenerate the system. There is little evidence in this volume that current teacher-education policies are encouraging good practice. I have argued that it would cost comparatively little; there is no need for a tome of rules and regulations, merely a loosening of the grip that government has placed around education. Some activities and some institutions would not change but there is a group of very energetic researchers and educators, who are represented in this volume, who would seize the opportunities with enormous enthusiasm.

One key is the encouragement of research by teachers with the support and help of HE. With teacher trainees, NQTs, mentors of both, other teachers, managers and HE tutors all engaged in research we could see the emergence of partnerships at all levels and development focused on children's learning. Indeed, we might place learning, rather than training, at the heart of school activity. Government would have to place trust in education, in a new professional body and provide stable funding for teacher education.

Trust in people is the second key to change. It is easy to dismiss a simple notion like trust when recent policies have concentrated on LMS, a national curriculum, examination results and other more tangible factors. As Hargreaves (op. cit.) has indicated government seems to have greater confidence in processes than in people. It is odd that education continues to be the subject of increasing technical regulation by a government that played a leading part in the destruction of communism and the Berlin wall in the name of freedom. After all the changes there is no consensus between educationalists and the Government about the present or the future of education and as Lawton (1992) has contended, sooner or later we will have to come together. It could be simply done.

Note

1 I would like to thank my colleague Barbara Ridley for her support in editing this chapter.

References

ADELMAN, C. (1993) 'Kurt Lewin and the origins of action research', *Educational Action Research*, **1**, 1.

BALL, S. (1994) 'Some Reflections of policy theory: A brief response to Hatcher and Troyna', in *Journal of Education Policy*, **9**, 2, pp. 155–70.

BARTLETT, T. (1989) 'Within the LEA — A collaborative model for inset', in McBRIDE, R. (Ed) *The In-service of Training of Teachers*, Lewes, Falmer Press.

ELLIOTT, J. (1991) *Action Research for Educational Change*, Milton Keynes, Open University Press.

ELLIOTT, J. (Ed) (1993) *Reconstructing Teacher Education* (chapter 6), London, Falmer Press.

HARGREAVES, A. (1994) 'Restructuring restructuring: Postmodernity and the prospects for educational change', in *Journal of Education Policy*, **9**, 1, pp. 47–65.

HARVEY, D. (1989) *The Condition of Postmodernity*, Oxford, Polity Press.

HATCHER, R. and TROYNA, B. (1994) 'The "Policy Cycle": A ball by ball account', in *Journal of Education Policy*, **9**, 2, pp. 171–82.

LAWTON, D. (1992) *Education and Politics in the 1990s: Conflict or Consensus*, London, Falmer Press.

MACINTYRE, A. (1981) *After Virtue*, Duckworth, London.

McBRIDE, R. (Ed) (1989) *The In-service Training of Teachers*, Lewes, Falmer Press.

McBRIDE, R. (1992) 'Inset, professional development and the local management of schools', in WALLACE, GWEN (Ed) *Local Management of Schools: Research and Experience*, BERA Dialogue No. 6, Clevedon, Multilingual Matters.

McBRIDE, R. (1993) 'Towards a Theory of Centralised Inset, 1986–90', Unpublished Ph.D. Thesis, University of East Anglia.

McBRIDE, R. (1994) 'Helping headteachers to search for their values: A preliminary study', in *Cambridge Journal of Education*, **24**, 3.

SARASON, S. (1990) *The Predictable Failure of Educational Reform*, San Francisco, Jossey-Bass.

SCHWAB, J.J. (1971) 'The practical: A language for curriculum', in LEVIT, M. (Ed) *Curriculum: Readings in the Philosophy of Education*, Chicago, University of Illinois Press.

TICKLE, L. (1987) *Learning Teaching, Teaching Teaching: A study of partnership in teacher education*, Lewes, Falmer Press.

WEST, S. (1993) *Educational Values for School Leadership*, London, Kogan Page.

Notes on Contributors

Neville Bennett is professor of primary education, and director of the Centre for Research on Teaching and Learning, in the School of Education, University of Exeter. His research interests include teaching — learning processes in classrooms, classroom management, cooperative learning and teacher education. Current projects include mentoring processes in school-based teacher education, teachers' conceptions of play, and personal transferable skills in higher education.

Colin Biott is reader in education at the University of Northumbria. He is currently researching professional learning, practice development and staff membership in schools and hospitals, and he has a particular interest in practitioner research in education and health care. Recent publications include *Working and Learning Together for Change* (with J. Nias) and *Collaborative Learning in Classrooms and Staffrooms* (with P. Easen).

David Bridges is professor of education at the University of East Anglia and director of the Eastern Region Teacher Education Consortium (ERTEC) having previously been deputy principal of Homerton College, Cambridge. He has long experience in initial and in-service teacher education. He directed an early (1979–81) project on School Centred In-service Education and a series of evaluations of in-service programmes in Suffolk, Norfolk and Cambridgeshire. His most recent publication in the field of teacher education was *Developing Teachers Professionally*, which he edited with Trevor Kerry.

Sally Brown is professor of education at the University of Stirling and was formerly director of the Scottish Council for Research in Education. She has been involved in educational research for more than twenty years and her current interests and publications include teacher education, teachers' thinking and the relationships among policy, practice and research. Her experience of teacher education is within the Scottish system which is distinctive in several ways from that of the rest of the United Kingdom and operates in a political context where the Party which controls national policy has had little support from the electorate over the last decade and a half.

David Clemson taught for thirteen years then undertook research at Plymouth Polytechnic before joining the Schools Council as a Research Officer. He moved into teacher education in higher education in 1983 and is now head of programme development in the School of Education and Community Studies at Liverpool John Moores University and reader in primary education.

Jill Collison is post-doctoral researcher at the University College of St Martin, Lancaster. She is a former primary school teacher with a research background in agricultural sciences. For the past three years she has been tracking student experience of school-based training on a pilot primary-school partnership programme.

Christopher Day is professor of education, Chair of School of Education and Head of Advanced Studies, University of Nottingham. Prior to this he worked as a teacher, lecturer and local-education authority adviser. His particular concerns centre upon the professional development of teachers, teachers' thinking, leadership and school cultures. Recent publications include *Insights into Teachers' Thinking and Action* (co-edited with Pope, M. and Denicolo, P.) (1990) Falmer Press, *Research on Teacher Thinking: Towards Understanding Professional Development* (co-edited with Calderhead, J. and Denicolo, P.) (1993) Falmer Press, and a series for Open University Press entitled 'Developing Teachers and Teaching'.

Anne Edwards has a chair in educational research and is director of the Unit for Applied Research at the University College of St Martin, Lancaster. Her research over the past twenty years has been in the fields of adolescence and early education. For the last three years, with a group of tutors and researchers at St Martin's, she has been examining the impact of school-based training on schools and students.

Eileen Francis, MPhil, DipCSLT has worked as a speech therapist and as a lecturer in higher education. She is a member of the Scottish Institute of Human Relations and a past president of the Scottish Educational Research Association. As senior lecturer: Enterprise at Moray House Institute of Education, Edinburgh, she initiated the development of the Centre for Specific Learning Difficulties. She has coordinated research studies on discussion, enterprise and values in education. In 1991 she established the Francis Group to provide research, consultancy and training services to a range of public and private-sector organizations. She currently coordinates VECTOR, a project on values education supported by the Grodon Cook Foundation.

David Frost is a principal lecturer in education at Canterbury Christ Church College. The college is one of the largest centres for award-bearing INSET in the country and, as director of secondary INSET, David is currently responsible for the management of over forty school-based INSET projects. He has tutored on the PGCE course for the last eight years and also directs the college's MA in curriculum studies and the diploma in curriculum development. He has published on the subject of mentoring within school-based teacher education and has recently established a collaborative action-research project to examine the effectiveness of the school-based, award-bearing INSET scheme operated by Christ Church.

John Furlong is professor and head of the Department of Education at the University of Wales, Swansea; **Geoff Whitty** is the Karl Mannheim professor and chair of the Department of Policy Studies at the Institute of Education, University of London; **Len Barton** is professor and head of the Division of Education at the University of Sheffield; **Elizabeth Barrett** is a post-doctoral research associate in the Division of Education at the University of Sheffield; and **Sheila Miles** is senior lecturer in education at Homerton College, Cambridge. Together they form the Modes of Teacher Education (MOTE) research team. MOTE is a collaborative research project, funded by the ESRC which is monitoring changes to teacher education in England and Wales over a five-year period (1992–6).

Chris Husbands is senior lecturer in education at the University of East Anglia, Norwich and director of the UEA Secondary Partnership PGCE. Before entering teacher education he taught in secondary comprehensive schools in London, Norwich and Hertfordshire. He has written widely on the nature and management of school-based teacher education.

Dr Rob McBride researches, lectures on and writes about teacher education in Britain and other countries, particularly those in the Middle East. He is currently researching the activities of secondary headteachers in Britain. A particular interest is personal and professional development.

Christine O'Hanlon is senior lecturer in education at the University of Birmingham, formerly senior lecturer at the University of Ulster. (She is presently engaged in research in the EU and with European partners investigating the integration of pupils with SEN into mainstream and the early acquisition of English for bilingual pupils.) She uses action research as a means of professional development with teachers and other professionals and has written on the subject in different UK and European journals. She was Action Research with teachers and other professionals researching at higher degree level and Co-ordinates research programmes for students in the School of Education.

John Schostak is professor of education at the University of East Anglia. His current research and publication interests include evaluations of nursing and midwifery education, police education, the development of multimedia distance learning and educational critiques of popular culture and the media. In the past he has researched and published in the areas of youth culture, the impact of information technology on schooling, deviance and classroom-based research.

Susan Sidgwick is a lecturer in the Department of Educational Studies at Goldsmiths College where she teaches on the secondary PGCE programme and manages the department's courses for newly qualified teachers. She is coordinator of the steering group overseeing development of the PGCE in partnership with secondary schools, and is researching and writing in the area of policy in relation to teacher education.

John Spindler is principal lecturer responsible for post-qualifying teacher education at the University of Northumbria. He is also course leader of the MEd programme. His current research interests include teachers' professional learning and practitioner enquiry.

Les Tickle has completed thirty years in the service of education, as teacher, manager, teacher educator and researcher. He is a senior lecturer in education at the University of East Anglia, where his research and teaching have focused on both Initial Teacher Education and Continuing Professional Development. In recent years he has worked on the development of provisions for new qualified teachers. His book *Teacher Induction: reflective professional practice* was published by Cassell in 1994.

J.H.C. Vonk is associate professor of the Teacher Education Department of the Free University of Amsterdam. He graduated in maths and science, studied thereafter educational psychology and sociology of education, and obtained a doctorate in social sciences. For eight years he was a teacher in maths at a lyceum. Since 1982 he has been leading a research programme on professional development of teachers in secondary education. His own research concerns the study of teachers' professional development during the first five years of service, in the context of which he has written a number of books and articles concerning the induction of teachers. He is past president of the ATEE (Association for Teacher Education in Europe) and has published a number of articles on developments in teacher education in Europe.

Jack Whitehead was born in 1944 and has a tenured post at the University of Bath until 2009. He is the convenor of the action research in Educational Theory Research Group and has worked for the past twenty years on initial and continuing teacher-education programmes. He continues to criticize the market focus of government education policy from a value base which emphasizes the importance of living educational theory for the revitalization of culture. He is a member of the Centre for School Improvement of the School of Education at Bath where he promotes the view that teacher researchers can enhance professionalism in education by focusing their enquiries on questions of the kind, 'How do I help my pupils to improve the quality of their learning?' He is also a member of the Centre for Action Research in Professional Practice and tutors practitioner researchers with colleagues in the School of Management.

Author Index

Subject Index